Table of Contents

In the modern context, standard policies of deception result in consequences much more far-reaching and deadly than the expected government playground bullying behaviors and corruption that they predictably cultivate.

Weapons research (including nuclear, technological, and biowarfare) and the subterfuge deemed necessary for their functioning are hidden under an archaic 25 to 100-year classification blanket of secrecy. This is not a viable or safe practice in modern times.

We now have the volatile mix of advanced weapons research and technology, combined with a persistent corruption of government and being steered by our enemies that we have not yet learned how to effectively manage and wrangle under control.

Due to this highly problematic combination, there is a very significant concern regarding the implementation of strategies and weapons technology that can maim or eradicate a majority of the world population before the public has permission to know and reasonably respond accordingly for self-preservation.

Forget the sanctity of classification. What is going on behind it is thinning us out, and will only get worse.

To honor, protect, and fund something that is actively harming us is insanity. Before the rule of government comes the rule of life. If no one lives, there won't be a government to protect.

♘ Stage 1: Recruitment

Silencing yourself and living in the dark
leaves you exposed to the type of people
who wander the dark looking for
victims who won't scream.

I didn't have a mother for long enough for her to gently tie society's blindfold over my eyes and keep it there. I've seen everything coming, unblinking, and in the room with it. It's not a pleasant experience, but someone had to live it.

I entered the world shortly after my pregnant mother jumped (or much more likely - was pushed) off a balcony in Argentina in an attempt to escape officers from a military dictatorship.

We dropped from that height and hit the concrete below in the midst of heavily U.S.-sponsored state terrorism in South America under Operation Condor, a written and signed multinational Intelligence agency agreement that had some of its strongest taloned roots in Paraguay and Argentina. The written intention was to root out and eradicate any potential opposition to willing-puppet dictators in the region.

SECRETO

00186F 1573

Copia Nº 2/3
EMG-FF.AA. J-2
ASUNCION-PARAGUAY
Setiembre 12, 1972

ASUNTO: Acuerdo Bilateral de Inteligencia FF.AA.PARAGUAY/Ejerci-
to ARGENTINO.

1. Las FF.AA. de la Nación y el Ejercito ARGENTINO, a fines de
coordinar acciones en la lucha contra la subversión y los grupos de insurrección que desde la clandestinidad fomentan la insurrección y/o agitación ideológica tendiendo reducir el poder
militar, político, económico y/o sicológico de ambos paises,vi-
sando además oponer la opinión pública y a la población contra
sus gobiernos, han acordado:

A. Aunar esfuerzos para la reunión e intercambio de informa-
ciones attravés de sus Agendias de Inteligencia sobre estas acti-
vidades, en especial sobre grupos y/u organizaciones que tengan
conexiones en ambos paises.

B. Colaboración mútua en la lucha contra la subversión, me-
diante medidas oportunas que visen desalentar a los elementos que
desde uno de los paises esten comprometidos o alienten a grupos

Image Source: The National Security Archive

Translated text: "The Armed Forces of the Nation (Paraguay) and the Argentine Army, in order to coordinate actions in the **fight against subversion** and insurrection groups that from clandestinity promote insurrection and/or ideological agitation **tending to reduce military**, political, economic and /or psychological of both countries, also aiming to oppose **public opinion** and the population against their governments..."

Text Source: The National Security Archive[1]

In addition to funding, the U.S. gave them the blueprint. The Central Intelligence Agency was already surveilling their own citizens and using much of the same terminology that Operation Condor would come to use, just in a different language.

---

[1] The National Security Archive, Asunto: Acuerdo Bilateral de Inteligencia FF.AA. PARAGUAY/Ejército ARGENTINO, September 12, 1972, https://nsarchive2.gwu.edu/NSAEBB/NSAEBB514/docs/Doc%2001%20-%20r186f1573%20-%201580.pdf

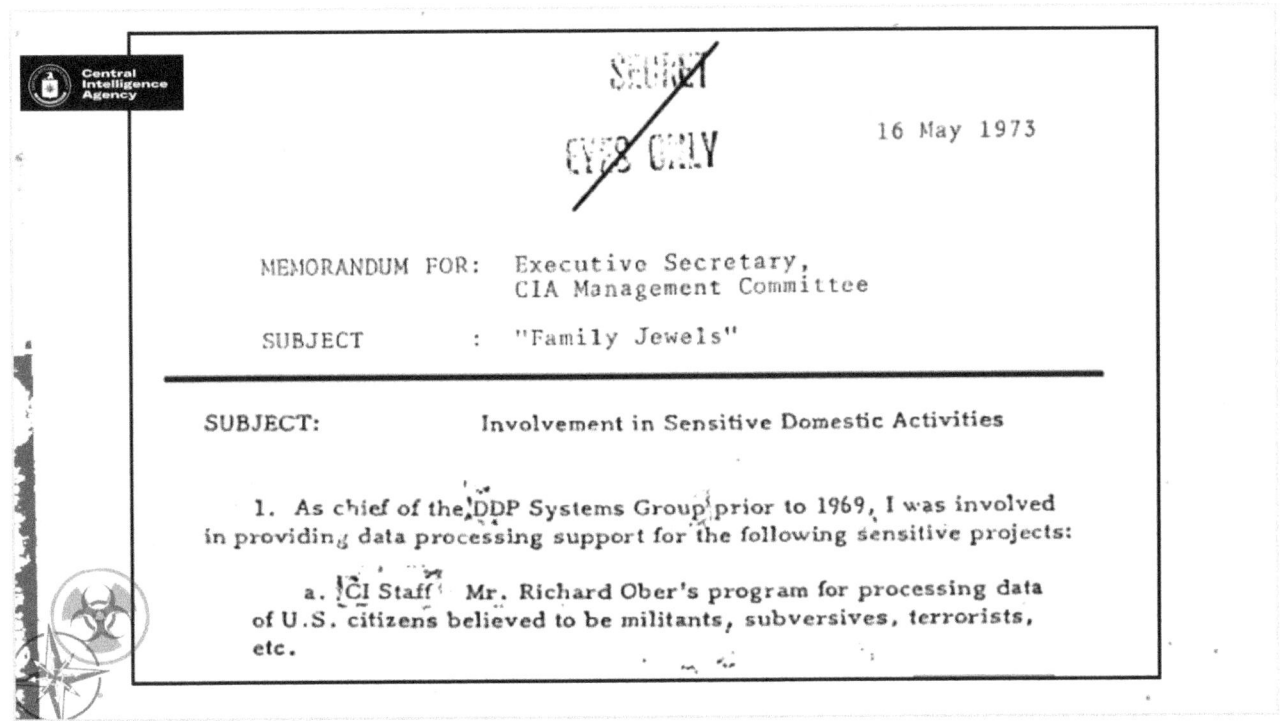

"Prior to 1969...program for processing data of U.S. citizens believed to be militants, subversives, terrorists, etc."

The struggle has always been (Military) Intelligence against the citizens it claims to protect. It is a government's self-preserving and brutal response against attempts by the citizens to get a corrupted government back under control and functioning as a stable and balanced mechanism of promoting and maintaining a healthy, sane, noncoercive, non-exploitative, and nonviolent stability of infrastructure within a nation's borders, in support and protection of its citizens, as all but the most rabid of us prefer governments to be.

---

[2] Central Intelligence Agency, Memorandum for: Executive Secretary, CIA Management Committee, Subject: Family Jewels, https://www.cia.gov/readingroom/docs/DOC_0001451843.pdf

This becomes most poignant and clear when it's finally our personal day for them to knock down our door, enslave our children, and kill our parents for a thinly veiled lie of it being "for the greater good" that no one in our family, community, and country will collect the benefit of. The only "greater good" in the vocabulary of liars and country-level thieves is in the draining of a nation's resources directly into the pockets of corrupt politicians in support of arms, human trafficking, hardcore drug trade, and the exploitation and overburdening of its people, and often while government mouthpieces insincerely, underhandedly, and disrespectfully claim to be doing the exact opposite.

The biggest insult is when they claim they are protecting us - from their own crimes.

These types of actions, and they continue through today, have always been to protect the financial and political interests of unhealthy governments from the people they use as an infinite resource to exploit. They are desperate and continuing moves to stay in power when there is no longer effective governance and it is no longer in the best interests of the countries being exploited.

It has nothing to do with our survival as a people of a nation. Ask yourself, would you need to be coerced, manipulated by public policies, and lied to in order to join the military in fighting a just war to protect your own borders and families? No, you would not. There is no realistic reason to manipulate the people "for our best interests." We are quite capable of making the right choices for our survival when it comes down to it, even if that survival requires increasing the number of bodies within the military. The pervasive mass manipulation we all endure is unnecessary. All it does is make a nation weaker and provide an army of dispirited henchmen for private interests and corrupt politicians - against our own people and survival.

These damaging and manipulative maneuvers are often allowed because people mistakenly see Intelligence as a part of their country. But when something is working that hard in opposition to your basic need to exist and to speak when you are being crushed by the mechanisms of an overburdening government, it is not a part of your country. It has been usurped. Frequently in the case of Intelligence and the corrupt, by agreement and consequences it has become part of a multinational entity and is no longer yours.

Government policies are most often created with mechanisms deceptively written in to allow control and power to be easily usurped. In the early stages of a nation or a party's control, they are often overlooked because they are seen in a positive light - a taking control of a nation for the people. But when you create a method of control, eventually it won't be you at the helm, even if the new captain is wearing your flag or your party's insignia for convenience. Just because we have always known something to function in a particular way does not mean it is the best way. We have been living with snakes for a very long time, and seemingly without creating basic methods to ensure that we can live peaceably with them, without being bitten and then consumed.

Back in Argentina when I was still a small child, unlike what the news would play on television screens, the results of the crisis manufactured by Operation Condor would not stay confined to South America. There's no way they could have - it was an international operation that would grow to touch multiple continents.

However, the University of Buenos Aires and surrounding areas had become the primary at-gunpoint forced recruitment area exploited by the U.S. military and Intelligence during the turmoil of state terrorism. That was ground zero.

With the welcome invitation of Argentina's military dictatorship, U.S. and foreign forces walked right in via Operation Condor. They selected the best people from the academic and scientific communities in Argentina and then framed them as the political opposition in order to force them into what was very much a coerced "come work for us or die here" scenario. Quite a few countries were in a post-World War II phase and wanted as many people as they could get to create bigger and better weapons and strategies for the next wars. In the West, the U.S. was taking the lead. How no one ever realized that they always targeted universities is beyond my comprehension.

Operation Condor opened up one of the largest government-sponsored international human trafficking funnels of that time, and it was emptying right into government pockets, offices, and military research labs across more than two continents.

The reality is that it was a resource grab, as all wars are, and was blanketed in divisive excuses, as wars tend to be. It was the military reaping machine against a field of people, and they never even saw it for what it was, thanks to the distraction and haze of well-rehearsed media and political rhetoric.

The U.S. was also doing the same thing domestically, with more subtlety and less obvious bloodshed. They would entrap their own university-educated citizens, make them political prisoners, and then coerce them while they were being held in indefinite detention. The methodology was nearly identical to what the U.S. still does to imprisoned drug addicts to turn them into informants, but with a heavier hand for the military and Intelligence.

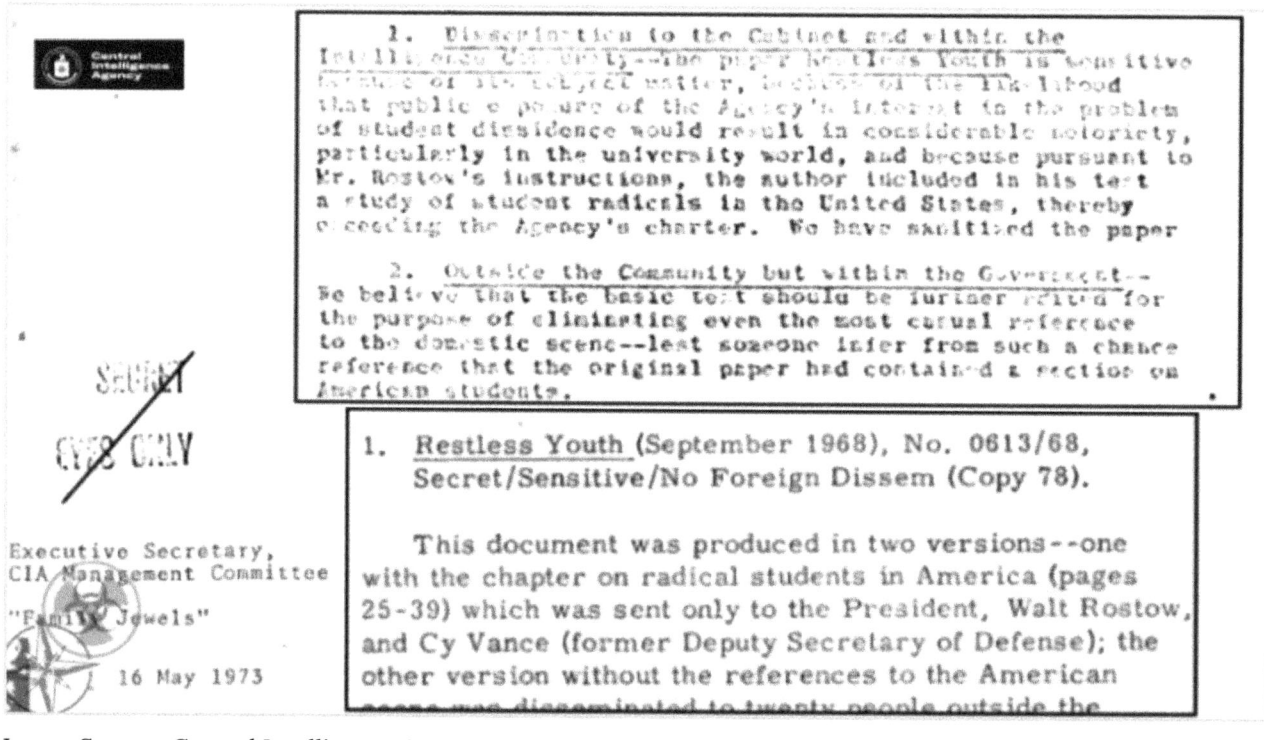

Image Source: Central Intelligence Agency

"...because of the likelihood that public exposure of the Agency's intent in the problem of student dissidence would result in considerable notoriety...We believe that the basic text should be edited for the purpose of eliminating even the most casual reference to the domestic scene - lest someone infer from such a chance reference that the original paper had contained a section on American students..."

This document was produced in two versions – one with the chapter on radical students in America... was sent to the President, Walt Rostow, and Cy Vance (former Secretary of Defense)."

Text Source: <u>Central Intelligence Agency</u>[3]

In Argentina, they had full reign to forcibly recruit however they wanted, so they didn't hide it. They did it in the open and with a combat boot.

Every person on this planet is living in the aftermath of what would go down over the next several decades as a result of those manipulative recruitment practices. The television newscasters simply haven't been honest about it yet. It's doubtful that they ever will be.

There's at least a decade left on the classified documents from my early years before they can drag it out into the public view and do their customary song and dance of, "See, we made inhumane mistakes, but we were less ethical back then. Thankfully, we're more modern, evolved, and saintlike now," all while hiding their current atrocities under yet another 50+ year blanket of secrecy. Rinse and repeat until someone in the endgame labs finally gets it right, and we all have more than the unshakeable sniffles, as if that wasn't already enough of a nuisance.

On a personal level, if there was anything worse than being jolted into this world by military thugs, it was in having my records sealed by those same military thugs, so I would be forced to spend a lifetime feeling as if I were standing alone to contend with a public, a multitude of people, kept intentionally blind to where I have been or what I would go through, thus hindering any real chance of unentangling myself and finding safety.

[3] Central Intelligence Agency, Memorandum for: Executive Secretary, CIA Management Committee, Subject: Family Jewels, https://www.cia.gov/readingroom/docs/DOC_0001451843.pdf

In 1980s Argentina both details were more than suspect. The country was slowly returning to democracy after the "dirty war" waged by the military dictatorship under Jorge Videla, known as the "Hitler of the Pampa". After the 1976 coup, Argentina's military set about crushing any potential opposition and eventually 30,000 people were killed or disappeared, almost all of them civilians. Pregnant prisoners were kept alive until they gave birth and then murdered. At least 500 newborns were taken from their parents while in captivity and given to military couples to raise as their own.

Image Source: <u>The Guardian</u>

"Argentina's military set about crushing any potential opposition and eventually 30,000 people were killed or disappeared, almost all of them civilians. Pregnant prisoners were kept alive until they gave birth and then murdered. At least 500 newborns were taken from their parents while in captivity and given to military couples to raise as their own."

Text Source: <u>The Guardian</u>[4]

If there was something worse than that, it was in being forced to stand next to more of those military thugs, holding their instruments for them, as they methodically worked on killing both my people and theirs - all under yet another layer of sealed documents, a seal that for some reason everyone's more terrified of than the actual looming threat of death hiding beneath it.

[4] The Guardian, Adopted by Their Parents' Enemies: Tracing the Stolen Children of Argentina's 'Dirty War', https://www.theguardian.com/global-development/2023/jan/16/tracing-stolen-children-of-argentina-dirty-war

And the one thing worse than that? When many of those I tried to warn preferred to blindly trust in and prostrate themselves to an authority with money, secrecy, and war as priorities; rather than believe the gravity of the words of a child witness whose sole need was a civilization safe enough to grow up in.

So, they abandoned us children, living evidence of a war against the people, and forced us to grow up within the cold hands of foreign enemies, in pain; to watch in horror the slow grinding carnage of the preparation for the demise of the people of multiple nations, including the nations that abandoned us and the ones into which we were illicitly adopted after being moved by military caravans, some of which were manned by people from our own nations.

That eats at a person.

The recruitment during state terrorism in Argentina wasn't the first time the U.S. had used coercive wartime methods to forcibly hire weapons research specialists, scientists, scholars, and war strategists overseas. It has been documented that they were doing it in other locations only one decade prior (right before the 50-year classification secrecy cover comes down on us all). But I'll get to those prior recruitments in a bit, with references.

The door for foreign involvement was opened wide by the military needs of Argentina, a country where most of the carnage would occur. Some of the country's soldiers found that rounding up and killing their own people was unsettling, especially when their victims were primarily in the same age group they were. This was made obvious by their bizarre methodologies of murder, such as drugging students and then shoving them out of planes without a parachute. To the uninitiated, that type of behavior seems incredibly sadistic and evil.

Ironically, the reality is behavior like that is often a sign that no one had the stomach to shoot their own people at point-blank range. They had to devise a way to do it that was

13

more removed. Don't believe me? Ask anyone with a soul who has ever had to kill a chicken how that first kill went for them. Nine times out of ten, it's not quick and clean. They'll have a story about awkward attempts, feathers flying everywhere, and the bird escaping at least twice. There's a hurdle in the human mind that needs to be overcome first. Now, imagine it's their neighbor's son and not a chicken.

To manage the mass incarceration, murder, and trafficking of their own citizens in exchange for a war bounty, Argentina's government needed help from foreign military and Intelligence on the ground. The nations and authorities behind Operation Condor were ready to respond to the expected request. They killed the Argentine citizens they saw no monetary value in and trafficked the ones, like my injured mother, who they thought they might be able to use elsewhere. While I know my mother's fate, I honestly don't know what happened to my father after the dictatorship dragged him away.

Before my heavily pregnant mother jumped from that balcony, my parents weren't grungy hand-rolled-cigarette smoking guerrillas in dingy back rooms reading CIA-made communist propaganda and crafting makeshift bombs, as the dictatorship's foreign-Intelligence-run media arm would bizarrely claim all their victims were. According to the limited public records that exist, my dad was in medical school. My mother was a history major who volunteered at a local children's hospital.

While their vocations and socio-economic status are not the important parts here, the fact the government and media lied about it, and absolutely everything else, is.

We were comfortable enough and Argentina still had a thriving economy at that time. We weren't clawing from the bottom, fighting some neo-political socio-economic war between the haves and the have-nots.

And yet, the strategists behind Operation Condor smashed me to the bottom and said I'd always been there. Then they put on their false crown of a rescuing savior of the poor and indigent, and would claim me for themselves, never to let go again.

As for my mother, they would keep her for nineteen excruciating years in total, squeezing every bit of value they could from her before finally taking her life.

They took those university students and graduates because they had monetary and military value. It was never about rhetoric, philosophies, or political bickering. It has always been about resources and for the war machine.

And to help dispel the myth of the United States as the wealthy white knight, here are the "low-income degenerate communist mud huts they liberated us from." This was the neighborhood of Buenos Aires my parents called home:

Image: La Plata, Buenos Aires

Source: Turismo[5]

Sometimes, I wonder if where my parents grew up is why I always seek a city near the sea: to be a little closer to the family I lost. I've often situated their photo frames in my home with the water seen behind them, so I can still share it with them.

---

[5] Turismo, Ciudad Soñada, https://turismo.laplata.gob.ar/sobre-la-plata/

As for why they were taken from me:

My mother's crimes: knowing history and my father.

My father's crime: not wanting to coerce, corral, or experiment on and kill his own people for the military.

My crime: being their child and thus "the next wave of the enemy."

I would become a child political prisoner in one of the most dangerous prisons on the planet (most dangerous according to a Guardian journalist). I grew to call it home.

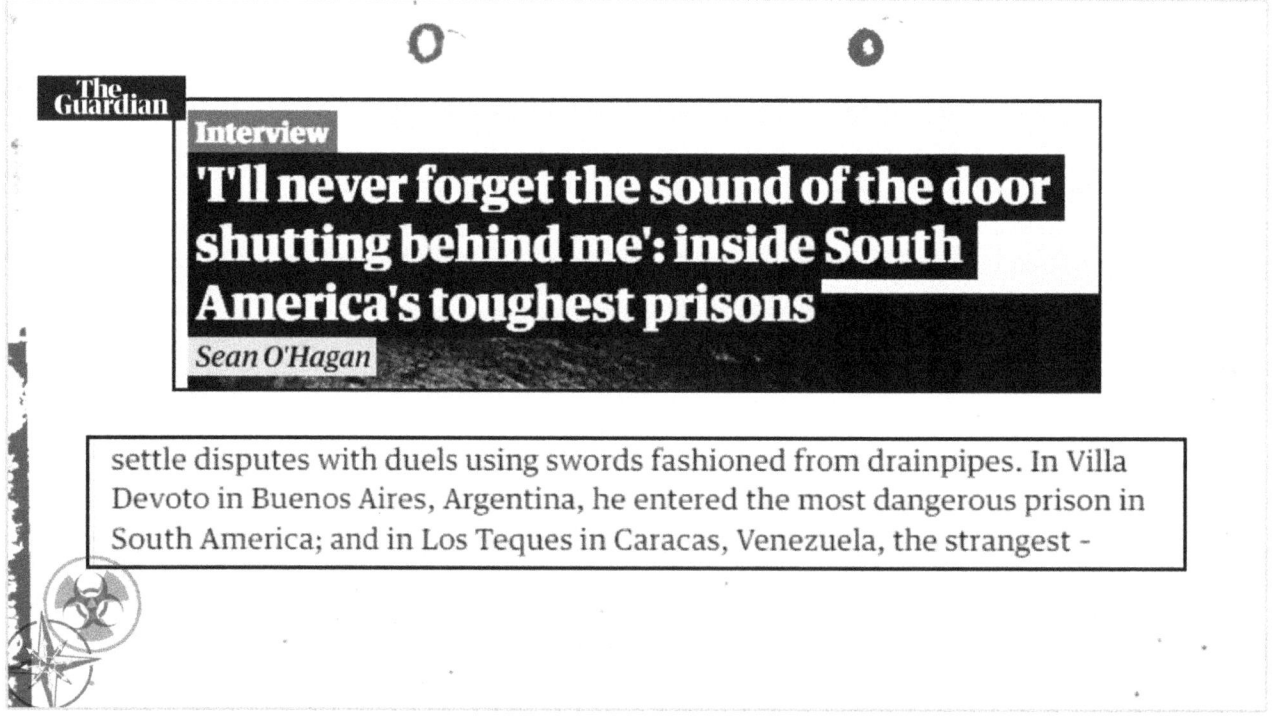

Image Source: The Guardian

"In Villa Devoto in Buenos Aires....the most dangerous prison in South America."

Image Text: The Guardian[6]

---

[6] The Guardian, Interview: I'll Never Forget the Sound of the Door Shutting Behind Me: Inside South America's Toughest Prisons, https://www.theguardian.com/artanddesign/2015/jun/14/inside-south-america-toughest-prisons-valerio-bispuri-interview

In internal disputes, when politicians dehumanize their political enemies enough and paint them as unrealistically grotesque and grungy caricatures, they convince the public to think that's a good place to keep their manufactured enemy's women, infants, and children. They exsanguinate the mothers and roll the infants in prison yard dirt while praying it sticks so those babies can appear to match the stories told about them.

And why? Because the media arm of government and military promises that those grotesque caricatures of neighbors want to take away the diminishing rights that government still allows. And on a different television channel, the opposing political party has told their own followers the same exact thing about them. We're all the enemy of the government. They've simply delegated the effort of anger and dehumanizing. They delegated the tasks to the masses after conveniently separating them into opposing teams. The fact that so many people so easily go along and sacrifice their own neighbors and family makes me question if there is anything within human nature to salvage.

Internal politics can destroy a nation's humanity until it begins to consume itself. But you might be figuring that out by now.

That playbook was written long before any of us. It genuinely does not matter which country or party uses it. The results are the same - some of us lose our humanity and some of us lose our lives. The modern complexity of the age-old problem is that we're now getting to a stage at which we may all become the latter.

I know, you're thinking, "But you were one kid in Argentina who obviously went through some trauma. What does it have to do with me or the current state of where I am?" Patience. I didn't remain a child and this isn't a "Dear Diary."

However, you need to become aware of the human element and how it affects the larger picture, and I will walk you through that experience while pointing out the government and military maneuvers and catastrophes along the way. Think of me as your endgame warfare and secrecy backstage tour guide, the one you never knew you needed but absolutely did.

Tip of the Spike

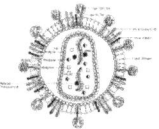

You're being killed
without knowing how
or what direction it's coming from.
As if blindfolded and helpless,
standing still in an open field,
and waiting for the firing squad.

In this case, the year of one of humanity's many attempts at suicide by enemy, as well as my birth, was 1977.

The location, as noted: Argentina.

In Argentina, parental custody of child political prisoners defaulted to the same state that imprisoned us and killed our parents. That alone should have been enough of a red flag for the sane in this world to put a stop to the madness. It wasn't. I don't think crimes against children ever really have been enough to move the world away from its madness. We are expected to endure and spend a lifetime, from cradle to grave, carrying the weight of the sins of the wars we are born into so that those who create and support the wars have no weight to carry themselves. It is on the shoulders of infants that the carnage of war thrives.

After spending my earliest years in prison, I was unadoptable, still in that same prison, and the military was stuck with me whether I was useful to them or not. I was in one of the last and oldest batches of kids still remaining in the prisons by 1980 when the active portion of Argentina's state terrorism was starting to wind down.

I can't claim to remember the earliest details of my life, but the information I've managed to glean aligns with the evidence and what I remember from later on. My first memories would emerge around the time I was turning three years old and was still residing in the Buenos

Aires prison that my mother and I had been carted off to at some point. As for the effects of that fall, MRI scans of my neck have always looked like those of a victim of a car wreck. The first image below is of the vertebrae in my neck. The second image is of an unnamed patient's uninjured neck, using the same MRI scanning angle and technique, for comparison.

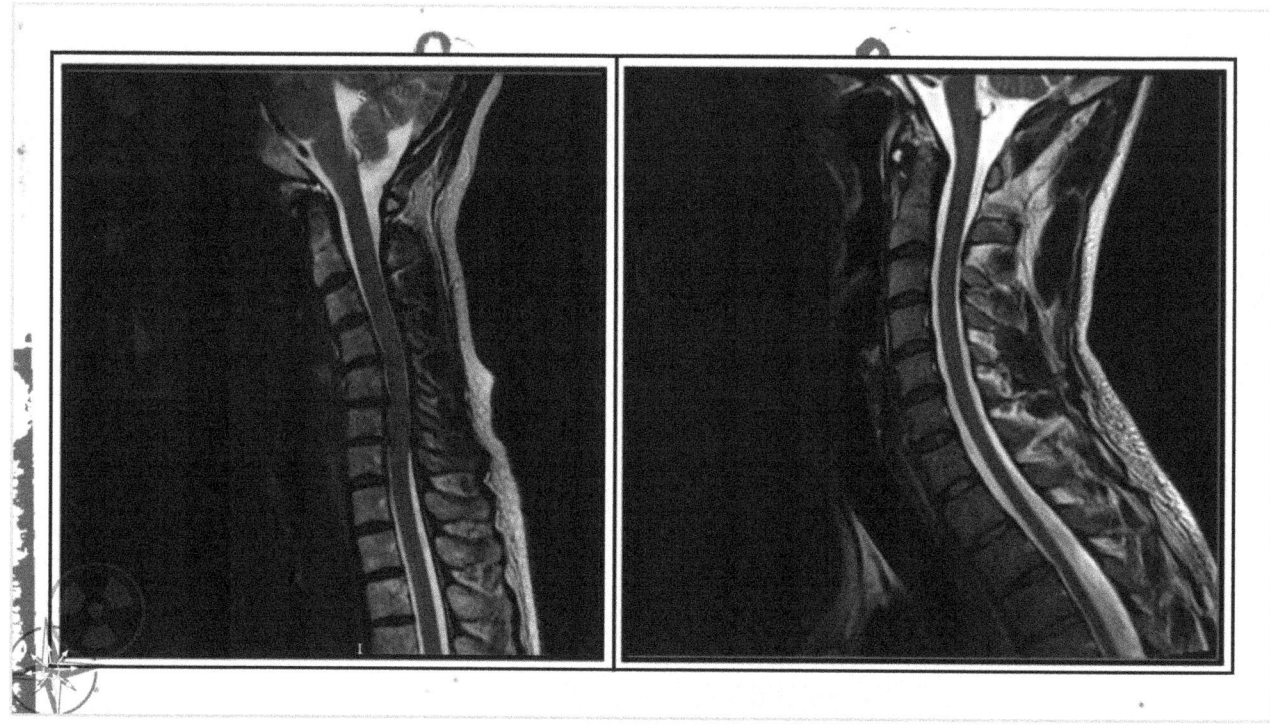

First Image Source: Author's Personal Medical File, Cervical Spine MRI 2018, Age 41[7]

Second Image Source: Example of a Healthy Cervical Spine MRI, Radiopaedia[8]

And the damage to my mother? In all my memories, I never actually saw her walk. I think she may have been crippled by the fall.

Spending my early years in the prison, a sprawling mass of buildings taking up a city block and known back then simply as Cárcel de Devoto, left me with other scars that I have worn

---

[7] Author's Personal Medical File, Cervical Spine MRI 2018, Age 41

[8] Radiopaedia, Normal Cervical Spine, https://radiopaedia.org/cases/normal-cervical-spine-mri-1

throughout life. How so many chose not to see them was beyond my comprehension back then.

In retrospect, a significant factor had been the public adoption of hiding group and government-caused harm. They do so for the sake of group cohesion and the outward appearance of behaving as just and law-abiding for their temporary self-preservation and protection. Rooted in the small villages and tribes of our ancestors, the behavior was likely more beneficial than not for centuries. However, in our larger groups and societies, it has slowly caused the development of a significant level of pervasive knee-jerk-reaction blind callousness that reaches nearly every aspect of civilization that I have seen and has seeped into every facet of modern life at the expense of our long-term survival.

What was originally created to protect us now feeds the predators among us and scatters our children to the wind.

One of the first scars I gained, during the process of Argentina's government turning on its own citizens, was likely caused by inhaling smoke at such a young age. About a year after my arrival, there was the "masacre en el pabellón séptimo." Mattresses were ignited on the men's side of the prison.

Inmates died when the guards still refused to let anyone exit the building. The (1)prisoners made no real effort to overpower the guards to attain an exit (instead, many escaped to the roof, the opposite of survival when fire moves upwards), the (2)guards did nothing, and (3)no one on the outside effectively advocated for the prisoners and reasoned with or removed the guards.

This was despite there being enclosed outdoor areas and other prison buildings within the sprawling prison complex. The soon-to-be-dead could have been corralled to those alternative areas via established gates and prisoner walkways if their imprisonment (mostly for suspected thought crimes, according to government mouthpieces) was still a high priority. To have one or two of these non-survival-reaction elements occur together is unfortunate. To have all three occur is a sign of societal collapse.

Neither (1)prisoner, (2)prison guard, nor (3)witness intervened to prevent unnecessary deaths.

Image: Aftermath of the 1978 Cárcel de Devoto Fire

Source: Infobae[9]

As a baby locked into the next building over, the smoke left a portion of my lungs scarred. To this day, I can feel those scars tug on my left side when I breathe. I may not be able to remember the event, but my body carries the reminder, and I feel it with every inhalation.

Some of the scars are more visible, such as the ones above my elbows that resulted from being forced against a metal surface in the hot sun. Others aren't physical at all. They reside deep in my psyche, my heart, and my struggle against an ever-darkening perception of humanity. They were only born in the prison and were intermingled with good, with childhood innocence, with memories of my mother, and with hope despite those concrete walls.

---

[9] Infobae, "Quémense de a Poco": El Horror de la "Masacre de los Colchones" en Villa Devoto,
https://www.infobae.com/sociedad/policiales/2018/03/14/quemense-de-a-poco-el-horror-de-la-masacre-de-los-colchones-en-villa-devoto/

In the end, it wouldn't be the prison that truly darkened my perception of humanity. It would be what I witnessed and experienced when I entered the wider world that had kept us there.

War's Broken Social Contract

Infinite cycles. Infinite path.
How do I explain to you that war does not end?
It never ends.
It simply goes through cycles
of open activity and concealed preparation.
That silence you hear.
That silence you may have lived your life in.
It isn't peace.
It's preparation.

Our mothers gave us the best advice that they could in the situation. I had a friend living down the hall in another cell with a mother who told her the stark reality of everything, including that she would be adopted out to the enemy. Trading in infants and small children was a common practice by the dictatorship that would have long-lived consequences politically for Argentina, as well as for the children who were traded in exchange for foreign military support).

Instead of speaking about adoption, my own mother chose to give me tools for surviving the situation. She gave me things to read, she educated me, and she taught me how to be a good hostage. That last lesson both cost and saved me in the end, because I kept it with me throughout life and far beyond those prison walls. The method of deception necessary to be a good hostage would gain me acceptance by the enemy. It would also keep me entrenched within them, sacrificing any attempt at fulfilling a child's need for true human connection and protected vulnerability.

My mother had explained that I always needed to tell people what they wanted to hear, even when what they wanted to hear wasn't real or realistic. She taught me how to read people's expectations, not necessarily by the words they spoke, but by indicators of what they believed they would hear when I spoke. I would watch their eyes, the levels of tautness and

movement of the muscles beneath the skin of their face, the manner in which they leaned in or away, and I'd listen to their breath to see which of my words it caught on, so I would know where to pivot my speech to match what they expected to hear from me based on what they perceived me and the situation to be.

She had shown me the easiest and yet most destructive path, the path that no one ever questions – one of accommodating and matching the unique biases of each individual person whom I spoke with. I became a mirror of their expectations and views of the world. I reflected back at them the world they anticipated they would see. And in that, I became a comfortable and expected part of the scenery - a near-perfect background actor for every scene.

It would get me into some small (and large) issues over the years. When I was brought along on jobs to play a child's role (a parent and child have more access to underground and grassroots groups than any single male ever will, but not everyone wants to bring their own children to infiltrate what they deem to be dangerous or opposing groups, hence the use of stolen children and disposable war orphans), people would look at me and assume I had certain traits and knowledge or affiliations with any of a wide variety of random groups, schools, or cultures that I knew nothing about and thus struggled to mimic or discuss. In those moments, I would use distraction or play dumb. There are quite a few people out there in the world who may think I'm legitimately mentally challenged. It was preferable to them discovering that I wasn't who or what they assumed I was, and neither was the situation.

And it made me a perfect hostage. It was easy to end up wrapped up within a group or pigeonholed by them, often by my own doing. It took decades to begin to escape those self-inflicted shackles. I'm still working on breaking the last links in their chains as I write this. The weight of misguided public expectations will always be a heavy one and difficult to entirely set aside. This writing has been an exercise in providing the honesty I would prefer to see.

If that last thought on public expectations made zero sense, let me clarify:

A lie does not exist simply because one person states it. There needs to be someone on the other end to bend enough to accept it. Every lie requires two active participants: the giver and the receiver. In most cases, once they engage, both become just as invested in keeping the lie afloat. The public is constantly asking to have lies confirmed, and it's often easiest and seemingly polite to go along with that. But by doing so, if we continue to do so, we adopt the lies ourselves and then feel obligated to continue to prop them up as valid. It takes concentrated effort to avoid that entire situation.

There's a reason that it's a million times easier to get someone to accept a lie than it is to get them to acknowledge that they were lied to. It requires unentangling them and removing the hook that silently slid in when they first accepted their part in giving life to the lie.

While subterfuge for self-protection is a necessity in many cases, the trouble is in balancing that with and separating it from the danger of the results of exploitative subterfuge. Brutal honesty and active discernment are required to get close to attaining that balance and separation, and even more would be necessary to consistently maintain them at a useful level in perpetuity. Maintaining honesty in communication is an exhausting but often-important series of battles.

Back to the prison for now...

Our days were uneventful for the most part, despite the war that brought us there. Our routine was usually predictable, dictated by a military regime and prison that needed the facade of precision control and authority in order to maintain their positions in governance. The days were so predictable and the prisoners were so kind to me, most likely because they could finally see how important life was in those moments when it promised to end. Memories from my time in that prison are the stable and humanity-filled moments that I cling to. They are what I remember fondly when I look back on my life.

War isn't all shock and awe for the television viewers. It is predictable. It lulls you into a sense of false security as each day washes over you, as you learn to adapt and you come to understand how little you can actually live with and still survive. It becomes a daily life that chips away all that is unnecessary and leaves only the human core. It brings out the best in

people, not just the worst. It's when we become closest to ourselves, our humanity, and we can see and feel it so clearly that it becomes tangible.

To me, it felt like home.

Over the decades when I would fight to get back to my mother, that was the feeling I was searching for. I thought if I could get home, I would find it again. Back then, I didn't understand that pure humanity is not a place. It's a condition brought about as a reaction to being about to be extinguished, that final flare of life before it goes dark. That's the condition under which we finally truly come to life - the moment we are face to face with death. Unfortunately, by then, there are usually no lessons to be learned or remembered because most die in that moment. They cannot return from death to show you the light. And even when they can, even when they manage to pull back from that brink and share it with you, you aren't able to see it yet. Some things really do need to be experienced firsthand.

Each morning, we were separated from our mothers to spend our afternoons with the other children, generally within the administrative buildings of the prison. There, we watched babies leave through the front door, adopted, and never to be seen in our small world again. As we stood in the street-facing adoption room with a row of cribs, my friend once expressed wonder about why her own adoption was taking so long and on which day it would occur. I never had a similar thought.

I never wanted to leave my mother.

Even now, the wound of being ripped from her has never healed. How could it? It's still hidden beneath the purposely created fog of limited public perception, even with the active part of that particular deception-heavy war long over.

No one has ever gone back through the newspaper articles and annotated them with evidence of what truly went on. It's easier to manipulate the public by keeping them perpetually in a state of mind that allows them to permit the results of war to persist, and for their own citizens to be systematically and indefinitely imprisoned, tortured, kidnapped, and killed. When in that state of mind, people will bury their own neighbors and family. That makes much less work for an infiltrating enemy. It also left me an orphan for life, separated from where I came from and only acknowledged as a "child criminal" deserving of my fate.

There's an almost admirable simplicity in the use of influence, dehumanization, and deceit. You rarely have to get your hands dirty. You only need to trigger someone else with rage and then point them in your desired direction to have them make your crusade their own. Those with the vocation of war managed to figure that one out before the rest of us.

Image Source: The Guardian

"Adopted by their parents' enemies: tracing the stolen children of Argentina's 'dirty war'... After the 1976 coup, the military brutally crushed its opponents. At least 500 babies were taken from their captured parents and given to military couples to raise. Many still live unaware of their true identity."

Text Source: The Guardian[10]

---

[10] The Guardian, Adopted by Their Parents' Enemies: Tracing the Stolen Children of Argentina's 'Dirty War', https://www.theguardian.com/global-development/2023/jan/16/tracing-stolen-children-of-argentina-dirty-war

On one of the days that has always left me wondering about the long-term survival of humanity, of its ability to fight off even the weakest chains, the group of children I belonged to were walked through the main bureaucratic part of the prison, as we were at the end of most days. On the bureaucratic/nonprisoner side, the door we went through to get to the hall our cells were on had an old fashioned (maybe modern at the time) metal number-lock on the door, with a vertical line of metal buttons that was used to enter a short numeric code to unlock the door.

By then, we had been through the door enough that I had memorized the combination. As the guard entered the numbers, I carelessly said them out loud. She looked at me and told me to never use them or to repeat them again. I complied. But it makes me wonder. If a three-year-old can memorize a short code to open one door, how can an entire prison of adults who vastly outnumber the guards, and who are being threatened with death (every one of the political prisoners was), not find a way to break through those doors?

If you are going to die anyway, wouldn't you want to die trying to gain freedom?

Even when faced with death, people tend to act overly compliant and trusting. It's a part of human nature that leaves me entirely perplexed. There is nothing wrong with courtesy and mutual respect. In fact, it is possible to show respect for the safety of others while also respecting yourself by making certain that you remain protected from them. When they do the same, it's called mutual respect. When they don't do the same, you were very right to protect yourself.

Absolute trust in any situation should be avoided, especially when in the hands of an enemy. And demands for absolute trust? Down here in reality, those are simply insane.

Domestic Breaches and International Infiltration

To understand how our current policies of secrecy
sew things together in ways that will always result
in the implementation of endgame
weapons and strategies,
it's easiest to start where motivation and preparation
for the next war are sparked
- in the fires of the previous war.

There were a few other significant events that happened within those prison walls that would end up having an impact on my life, some sooner rather than later. The results of one would shake my world the most and cast a shadow on an otherwise exciting landmark moment in my life.

At roughly the age of three, we were finally allowed to play outside. Prior to that, many of my brief moments outdoors had been briskly walking between administrative buildings while hurried along by cruel chaperones who promised us, small children who had done nothing wrong other than being born into the circumstances, that "this didn't count as being outside." That level of bullying from the adults would be reflected in the behavior of the children as they became older. There were quite a few children who were simply too abusive and angry to deal with, and I went out of my way to avoid any interactions with them. Avoiding any unnecessary interactions with the adults was a given.

When one of the adoption workers told me the news that I was finally allowed to play with the older children, I checked twice to make sure I hadn't misunderstood or misheard. I was very aware of the danger of breaking the rules. After all, they had callously threatened us with the removal of our mothers multiple times for the slightest of infractions. That threat left me in a constant state of anxiety more than anything else. I was always acutely aware of every microscopic part of my behavior and how it might result in losing my mother. Often, the result was me being frozen, silent, and afraid to do anything at all, even when I needed

something simple, like access to a restroom after three hours of desperately needing to use it.

Once I had confirmed what the adult had said was real, I went bounding through the doors and down the stairs, finally allowed to experience playing with the older children.

I went through one room and then entered another. Or at least I thought the second one was a room. Having mostly believed the lies that our prior moments outside "didn't count as outside," and due to the fact that the area they now sent us into was blocked off on most sides by the surrounding buildings, I naturally assumed that it was simply a large room decorated to appear like it was outside. After all, in my mind, while I knew the outdoors existed, I did not think that they were actually reachable.

My excitement became apprehension, being suddenly surrounded by older children in a setting unfamiliar to me. I stood against a wall not far from the door and watched the game, listening to the bouncing of the ball and the shouts of the children echoing loudly between the buildings. The level of noise was painful to my ears, something that was often the case during my time in the prison, especially with the noise level of the combined screams of the women in the larger prison area at the end of the hall my cell was on. My ears always ached.

I waited patiently, with my head resting against the wall, until an older boy invited me to join the game. I would not have entered the game without the invite. My shyness in that moment had been overwhelming.

Later, I would hear about that day from a different perspective, from an adult observer from the United States whom I had not noticed in the moment. The foreigner, brought in to assist with Operation Condor, explained that she saw a child who stood silently on the side, observing and learning the rules of the game before entering it. She spoke positively about the trait and saw it as useful.

She – not the prison, not the state terrorism and senseless deaths – but she would become the darkest shadow that would hang over the rest of my life. That first moment of truly breathing in and acknowledging the outside air was both my first and my last moment of freedom.

That was the moment she chose me as her own.

If you're still among the "that doesn't happen" crowd, I'd like to introduce you to two concepts:

One: Once a military policy is established, it is written into procedures manuals and continues, regardless of the particular war, state terrorism, or catastrophe.

Two: Operation Baby Lift had recently set a policy precedent and established a roadmap for largescale confiscation of children over international borders during the later stages of wars and during the post-war cleanup stage, permanently removing healthy adoption-age infants and children, very frequently without their parents' consent and/or knowledge.

Image: Operation Babylift Infants
Source: The Australian Women's Weekly via PressReader[11]

---

[11] The Australian Women's Weekly via PressReader, Children of War, https://www.pressreader.com/australia/the-australian-womens-weekly/20170601/281590945491471

Image: Operation Babylift Newborn Infants

Source: SelfCare for Healthcare[12]

The pictures above were taken only five years prior to U.S. military involvement in my removal from Argentina. Even if the fallacy of militaries becoming "more evolved and more humane" during the time it takes to declassify something were true, no one had time to evolve and learn from their mistakes in five years. If they had evolved, they would have returned those Vietnamese babies to their parents. If they had evolved, they wouldn't still be writing it into their policies nine years after they took me (dated document below). Even now, in the 2020s as I write this, they still haven't evolved to embrace humane practices or to return the stolen children.

Operation Babylift was the large-scale removal of infants and small children from Vietnam to countries including the United States, France, Austria, and West Germany towards the end of the Vietnam War. In April of 1975, approximately 3,300 children were transported out of Vietnam.

---

12 SelfCare for Healthcare, Hear LeAnn's Operation Babylift Story, https://www.selfcareforhealthcare.com/operation-babylift/

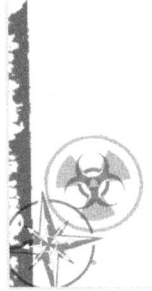

> The evacuation of orphans and refugees was a unique episode in the annals of USAF history. As no precedent for this type of operation had been previously established, numerous and novel problem areas were encountered from the embryonic stage through conclusion. . . . The knowledge acquired as "lessons learned" at Clark was passed on in the form of TDY assistance in establishing Operation Newlife at Guam.
>
> Major General Leroy J. Manor, Commander, 13th AF.[1]

November 1989

Military Airlift Command
Scott Air Force Base, Illinois

MAC and Operation BABYLIFT:

> diplomatic climate deprived MAC of control of the BABYLIFT. Then, despite MAC's best efforts things beyond the command's control—a plane crash, civilian adoption agencies, non-contract airlines—interrupted the air flow. Yet, even with these hurdles, the operation succeeded. Operation BABYLIFT illustrated the parts of a noncombatant evacuation operation planners can control and the parts over which they have little or no control. There have been few substantive changes in noncombatant evacuation operations since 1975, therefore the lessons of BABYLIFT are still relevant to today's planners.

Image Source: U.S. Department of Defense

"Military Airlift Command...November 1989:

The evacuation of orphans... was a unique episode in the annals of USAF history. As no precedent for this type of operation had been previously established... The knowledge acquired as 'lessons learned' at Clark was passed on in the form of TDY assistance in establishing Operation Newlife at Guam.

Major General Leroy J. Manor, Commander, 13th AF.

...There have been few substantive changes in noncombatant evacuation operations since 1975, therefore *the lessons of BABYLIFT are still relevant to today's planners.*"

Text Source: U.S. Department of Defense[13]

---

[13] U.S. Department of Defense, MAC and Operation Babylift, https://media.defense.gov/2012/Aug/31/2001330018/-1/-1/0/AFD-120831-032.pdf

If you think the government baby snatching policies has changed since 1989, the odds are extremely high that your perspective, as well as the lives of tens of thousands of children, may be a victim of a different government policy: one of using secrecy to hide potential embarrassment and tarnishing of a country's reputation, rather than simply behaving in a way that would not cause embarrassment to begin with.

For public consumption back in Argentina, they would paint the killing of mothers and stealing of their infants with the authoritative and caring undertones of adoption by upstanding and stable military members who would take on the role of parents and guide the infants to live a proper and useful life within society, a type of training that the original sinful parents could not provide.

Obviously, back here in reality and away from their insincere and delirious thoughts of grandeur, when military members use the convenience of war to abduct an enemy's baby from her family, it is rarely due to compassion or a need to improve the life of the child. And yet, even that gets repainted by self-deception, group authority, and an almost religious sense of infallibility and righteousness on the side of the kidnapping party.

But when I looked into that baby-snatching U.S. military woman's eyes, when she stepped into my world, I was face to face with the glaring truth of being a child in the theater of war. There were no media banalities or distance to insulate me from it. The small dark eyes looking at me were those of a predator seeking someone unprotected and too little to fight back, to utilize as human bait and lure within war and the preparation for war. She wasn't looking for a child to join her family (and in fact, I would always live separate from her family). She was looking for an untraceable multiuse tool - a living and breathing pocket knife without a paper trail. In other words, a female war baby who was no longer in diapers.

What I experienced and would live through was not an adoption, despite the deceptive paint they thickly layered on it for the public so they could pat themselves on the back and sleep at night, feeling as if the vulnerable orphans created by their political needs were in the care of, at best, heroes, and at worst, stable disciplinarians.

The type of people who kill a dog and take its newborn puppies are not the type of people who care for or have compassion for the puppies. They are almost invariably the ones we later discover have kept those puppies locked in a dark closet in an attempt to mold them into attack dogs. That lingering callous and exploitative psychology of predators is worse when they kill a human mother and take her infant, because the memory of murdering a mother in cold blood to steal her helpless baby remains long after the memory of killing a dog would fade.

They see the reflection of the dead mother in that child's face, and they become determined to mold the most flawed characteristics in the child in order to create a guilt-free excuse as to why they had attempted to kill the breed. There's a reason that when most of them looked at me they hoped it was a soulless psychopath looking back at them, just another empty automaton bent on instant gratification above all else.

I know my mother taught me to always meet expectations, even low ones, but I wasn't going to go around killing other toddlers in an act to convince the adults that they were correct about me. I doubt the thought even crossed my mind. However, a much easier opportunity to make them comfortable still arose, possibly after I'd already developed stomach ulcers from not getting to that point fast enough. My anxiety was sky-high about performing as was expected of me.

The first time I popped a second candy into my mouth after it had been offered by one of the visiting military commanders, I saw them go from tense to relaxed, with their attention moving to other parts of the room. So, to reduce any reasons for both their and my anxiety, I obliged their expectations by always asking for and ingesting an inordinate amount of candy with an addictive level of lack of self-control. I did it to appear that I could be easily manipulated via simple means, addictions. Yep, my mother taught me that too. If I didn't love her, and if she wasn't dead, I'd probably strangle her.

A control-distraction works just as well for the liar as it does for the one wanting to be lied to - i.e. if I thought I'd done something out of character from what they expected, I could distract from it by begging for candy, and they would feel in control as the manipulator because they had the say regarding if I got the candy or not. It was child-level simple, but psychology is often that simple. People like to feel like they are in control, so we walk them through the same routines until they become so comfortable with the predictability of those

routines that they become comfortable with us and forget that we're capable of anything else other than being manageable and obedient. It also helped to instill the belief that I wasn't a threat to anything other than a candy bowl.

That said, playing a long con game from the side of the victim is dangerous. I do not recommend it for individuals or societies. It's a prisoner's game intended to get the tiniest bit of leeway to get away with things or to wait for that one moment that offers a potential escape. If you're in the open air, not chained to a cell, and are still acting this way, you may want to examine why and at what point you became a voluntary prisoner.

To maintain that trust and predictability over the years, I came so close to death on numerous occasions that it's a miracle I'm still alive. Better people than me have died from it. To prove that I would obediently walk into anything blindly, I "happily" swallowed whatever was placed in front of me and went wherever I was told to, resulting in being drugged beyond comprehension while in dangerous situations more times than I could count.

It would lead down a path in life that had me so exhausted and skirting the edge of death that I had to import my concealer from China because they were the only ones that had the palest ivory makeup to match my near-death and unnaturally pale ghost complexion.

But now I'm getting ahead of myself. I'm still supposed to be talking about prison life at this stage, or how my mother seemed to be a little too educated on subterfuge. That last thing may have simply been the result of her growing up in Argentina. Living in a deceived society can teach us more about deceit than any Intelligence training can.

Sometimes, I wonder how anyone managed their mental gymnastics regarding my level of gullibility and malleability after seeing the early school readiness results from the exams they brought us to and performed in the little tower above the bureaucratic hall. But it's a million times easier to lie to someone than it is to convince them they've been lied to. They were happy to continue thinking I was an idiot even when I tested among the highest in the group.

My friend who used to talk about everything we saw while we walked through the prison was the one who probably tested the highest. She would turn out to be too aware of her surroundings for her own survival. Her attempts to evade harm eventually resulted in damage to her health. She absolutely never ate anything they gave her. She didn't trust it. If this civilization came with a rescue crew, she would have been fine before real damage set in, but there are no rescue crews, and long-term malnutrition and starvation do bad things to a child. I miss her more than anything. This world snuffs out true intelligence before it is old enough to flee.

Recruitment Contracts

It's endgame.
Not let's-save-one-side game.
Not let's-go-another-round game.
Not even let's-keep-the-rich-alive game
(although many were promised it was in exchange for funding).
Not even let's-keep-the-useful-slaves-alive game.
Endgame.
I struggled to get people to understand that.
I don't think they wanted to.
Because if they did,
they would realize the trouble we are in.

After meeting the foreigner who was about to drag me to her home country, the next significant thing I remember happening was my witnessing heightened security and excitement around countless boxes of files being moved through the main administrative area of the prison.

It is very likely that those boxes were part of what would become the Archivos del Terror (Archives of Terror), a collection of roughly a million pages of military, intelligence, and police documentation on the disappearance, movement, and murder of countless citizens of Argentina and South America during Operation Condor and Argentina's own enthusiastic version of it - the Guerra sucia (Dirty War).

To this day, they still have not allowed the public or the victims access to 98% of those pages. They've used many flimsy excuses over the years for why, but much of those revolve around the need to keep the depth and breadth of their crimes classified and away from the public's view, in order to maintain simplified control.

The crimes against the people did not end when the war did, despite the fallacy upheld by limited history books, newspapers, and front-facing political bureaucrats that proclaim war and atrocities have an official start and end date, as if they were nothing more than football matches between friendly rivals.

Using Operation Condor's agreements, policies, and political prisoner trafficking pipeline, Argentina spread its methodologies and seeded people (their own people as well as legitimate political prisoners) into projects, offices, and agencies in other parts of the country and world. The results of their continuing efforts have had, and will continue to have, further-reaching implications than the state terrorism that gripped much of South America in those years.

Back in the prison, the next moment that would impact my life happened as I was standing in the cell I shared with my mother, gazing out the window at a tree that I could always see but would never get to play under. We had a visitor. My mother spoke with the woman, the same foreign officer who had observed me as I played. They spoke for ages as I pretended to have my concentration fully on the outdoor scene.

Image: Cárcel de Devoto (Since Renamed to Complejo Penitenciario Federal de la C.A.B.A.)

Source: Google Maps[14]

I may not have caught all of the conversation, but I heard enough that I would later come to understand that it had been an agreement – my mother had signed away her rights and life to that woman in exchange for my "safety and opportunity" in the United States. They spoke about how, due to injuries, my mother wasn't eligible to be recruited for anything that a military intelligence officer could offer, except for one unpalatable option.

As for any questions about U.S. recruitment practices from war, I will highlight one thing:

The United States practice of recruiting political prisoners, war criminals, and prisoners of war can be clearly identified with the example of 1940s through 1960s Operation Paperclip (foreign scientists recruited with the lure of being protected from war crimes tribunals). If it didn't set the precedent for the 1970s through 1980s recruitments and modern wartime recruitment manuals, it's an example of the practice.

---

[14] Google Maps, Federal Correctional Complex C.A.B.A., https://maps.app.goo.gl/y6Uh5q8k5bV19WZk7

Once a policy is established by the U.S. military, it is utilized, regardless of the name of the war or the location of state terrorism. The only thing that keeps it in the past in the public mind is the combination of a belief that we are always more ethical in the present and modern day, plus that pesky 50-year average period before declassification that helps to keep the fallacy of ethical modern behavior perpetually alive by always hiding the bad parts at the time they occur.

We may want to be more ethical in the present day, and that says a lot about the potential good in humanity. However, we are often quite the opposite behind closed doors and removed from the public eye, something that is permissible due to the belief that long-term deception, even domestic deception, is still a necessity for state control and warfare.

If it's established policy and procedure, it's rare that the policy would be operational ten years prior and then simply cease to exist.

Established is established.

Policy is policy.

And if there's anything we can trust the military to do, it's to follow policy.

Between 1945 and the 1960s, the United States government brought more than 1,500 German scientists and engineers into the country through Project Paperclip to work on guided missiles, jet and rocket engines, aerodynamics, aerospace medicine, and submarine technology. The U.S. hoped these specialists could give them an advantage at the end of WWII and into the Cold War. Over time, many of the Germans disappeared into American military, industrial, and academic positions. However, one of them, Wernher von Braun, became prominent through his involvement in the Space Race.

Image: Nazi Scientists Recruited by the United States under Operation Paperclip

Source: Museum of Jewish Heritage

"Between 1945 and the 1960s, the United States government brought more than 1,500 German scientists and engineers into the country through Project Paperclip to work on guided missiles, jet and rocket engines, aerodynamics, aerospace medicine, and submarine technology. The U.S. hoped these specialists could give them an advantage at the end of WWII and into the Cold War. Over time, many of the Germans disappeared into American military, industrial, and academic positions."

Text Source: Museum of Jewish Heritage[15]

Because my mother could not be recruited for military research skills or intelligence work, both areas in which the U.S. still sought the best from foreign war recruitments, the recruiter offered the only other primary option she had available for getting my injured mother and myself out of the country. Her words seemed to indicate that she was sincerely trying to help us, her voice sometimes dropping to a hushed tone as if she was sharing

---

[15] Museum of Jewish Heritage, From WWII to the Space Race: The Story of Project Paperclip, https://mjhnyc.org/events/from-wwii-to-the-space-race-the-story-of-project-paperclip/

secrets with my mother that the guards shouldn't hear. But the recruiter's body language, the twitch of the muscles beneath her skin? Those didn't entirely match the rest of her act. I trusted my mother to know what to do with the woman, but there was something uncomfortable enough about her that the memory seared itself into my brain.

My mother agreed to fulfill the only other human resource need by the group of military departments the recruiter represented. She agreed to become a human subject for Defense medical research (something the recruiter would often call cancer research when around civilians she wanted to trust her - but my mother didn't have cancer). My mother accepted the deal in exchange for getting us both out of that prison and breaking free of the country oppressing us. It was a deal with the devil. She sacrificed everything in that moment. She thought she was doing it for me.

She truly thought she was making the sacrifice for me.

I will always love her, even more for her sacrifice. I wish what she agreed to had been a contract based on truth instead of lies, and that I could have known what it was back then. I would have clung to her. I would have screamed. I would have shouted and made a scene. Instead, I stood there silently like the perfect hostage, waiting to be whisked away without even a single struggle or whimper.

Even more, I would have preferred to have died in Argentina with my mother, safe in her arms, and without either of us knowing the true horrors beyond those prison walls, rather than going through what was still ahead of both of us.

The brutal truth is that some of the only people they could get to knowingly agree to become research subjects were political prisoners in indefinite detainment and under threat of death. Ordinary domestic prisoners, even those facing life in prison, often refused to volunteer in exchange for a reduced sentence. And ordinary people? Some of them might be horrified if they knew what their government was actually up to.

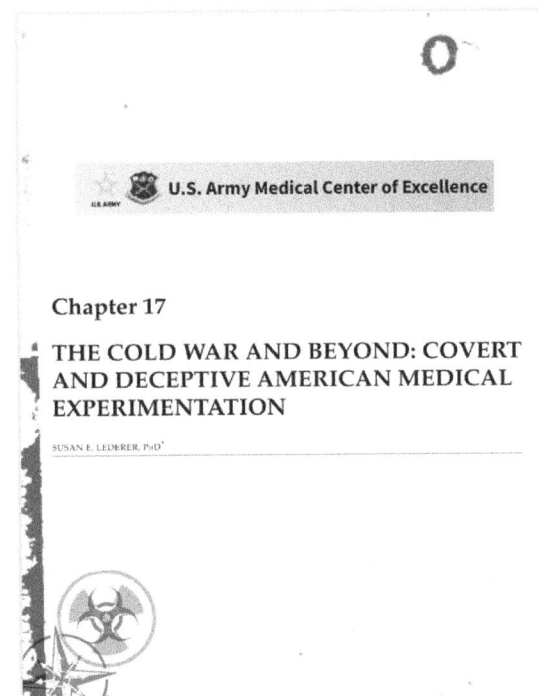

Chapter 17

THE COLD WAR AND BEYOND: COVERT AND DECEPTIVE AMERICAN MEDICAL EXPERIMENTATION

SUSAN E. LEDERER, PhD

One of the principal rationales for covert and deceptive experimentation during the Cold War was the issue of national security. Engaged in an emerging global struggle with the communist bloc, the United States government strove to meet the threat. However, national security was not the only rationale for secrecy. Since the early 1940s, officials of the federal government had also followed regulations that allowed secrets to be maintained not only because their disclosure would endanger national security, but because such disclosure "would be prejudicial to the interests or prestige of the Nation."[53(p392)]

When it began operation in 1947, the Atomic Energy Commission expanded the practice of maintaining secrecy to encompass public relations, especially the threat of "embarrassment" and legal liability. For example, in 1946 Dr. Hymer Friedell,

Image Source: US Army Medical Center of Excellence

"Officials ...allowed (covert and deceptive experimentation) secrets to be maintained not only because disclosure would endanger national security, but because such disclosure 'would be prejudicial to the interests or prestige of the Nation.'

And... expanded the practice to encompass public relations, especially the threat of 'embarrassment' and 'legal liability.'"

Text Source: US Army Medical Center of Excellence[16]

According to the U.S. government and military, the reasons for lying to the public about the harm done to individuals and communities for warfare purposes have expanded to include preventing lawsuits, embarrassment, and damage to the nation's reputation.

It hasn't been about your safety or protection since at least the 1930s.

---

[16] US Army Medical Center of Excellence, Military Medical Ethics, Volume 2, Chapter 17 The Cold War and Beyond: Covert and Deceptive American Medical Experimentation Susan E. Lederer, PhD, https://ke.army.mil/bordeninstitute/published_volumes/ethicsvol2/ethics-ch-17.pdf https://medcoeckapwstorprd01.blob.core.usgovcloudapi.net/pfw-images/borden/ethicsvol2/Ethics-ch-17.pdf https://web.archive.org/web/20130218014139/https://ke.army.mil/bordeninstitute/published_volumes/ethicsVol2/Ethics-ch-17.pdf

That government and others like it deserve to be embarrassed. They sacrifice their own citizens, and the world, for an illusion.

And the public deserves to be embarrassed for letting them. They told you they were doing it. And some of them are you.

When face-saving is the goal of government deception, their own citizens become the enemy. Witnesses become the enemy. When their crimes get big enough and we all become witnesses, we all become something to erase.

And before erasing us, when it comes to learning how to erase us, the required endgame researchers and strategists must not care about a political party, race, community, country, or their own families. This is true even if they appear to happily ride one or more of those groups to the finish line, wearing the full regalia and masking as their biggest leaders and supporters. The best endgame worker doesn't even care about the ground they stand on.

That's why militaries have to force-recruit in countries, such as Argentina, already known for leaning in the direction of genocidal ideations. No sane, normal, or non-coerced person will willingly and consistently work towards their own demise and the demise of their people, party, nation, or globe. You have to select them from the correct environment and then steal and break them in war if you want people who will work on those particular research and strategy projects with any degree of effectiveness.

Endgame workers are rarely born for the job. They are most often forged in war and then torn from their roots by enemy recruitment.

The final significant moment in the prison occurred one early evening when we children were returned to the halls where our cells were. For the first time that I could recall, my mother was not there to return to. My prison cell was empty other than our two beds pressed against the walls, one on each side of the room, as if the guards had already sought to create a separation between us. A foreboding sense felt like it was pulling me down. That weight became physical as they told me that my mother had gone to see the doctor because she had a high fever. Mothers with "high fevers" did not always return.

I was alone, wandering in anxious silence between the hall and my bed for hours before someone noticed and brought me to the small janitor's closet to get something to drink.

I was lost without my mother...

Entrenchment at Universidad de Buenos Aires

The aspect of war piercing my core
hasn't been the loud spectacle of death.
Death is restful.
Eternal agony is found in the silent weeping
& shared wounds in mother and child
that open as the war machine
rakes over and separates a mother from infant,
like wheat from chaff.

Before I had a chance to find out if my mother was alive, I was brought to another building entirely. We entered an elevator and, in that small space, I experienced the chlorine scent and sounds of a pool tucked away nearby. The elevator rose to an upper floor. As we exited it and walked down the hall, I peeked over a railing to see the floors below in the open architecture.

We entered a series of crowded rooms that contained a palpable silence. Prisoners sat huddled on the floor, filling every available space and quietly waiting for what might be the only contractual possibility to leave their current circumstances and escape the ever-present threat of death. One of them whispered to me and handed me a book to keep me occupied and silent.

Eventually, I was ushered into a back room where I saw a higher-ranking military officer guarding a file box containing our new government-forged documents and identities. When even the government can't follow their own basic laws, you know the shit show has gone on for too long. Either the laws are invalid or the government is.

He disbursed my set of falsified identity documents to the colluding foreign recruiter who had joined us from another room, the same woman who had observed me playing and then spoken with my mother.

After collecting my new documents, she and I were sent to the offices a short way down the hall for my further processing and travel vaccines. The paperwork and conversation between the adults in those final offices took forever. I spent most of that time under a desk, recovering from the travel vaccines the bureaucrats had given me. I was ineffectively hiding in the relative darkness provided by the small space intended for a chair.

The world outside the prison would be overwhelming for me, especially at first. It had none of the predictability or relative safety I had known when with my mother. We spent a couple of weeks or so in Buenos Aires before leaving the country. It was a whirlwind of experiences, all of which left me with an uncomfortable feeling that something wasn't right. On one of the first days, I tried to call for help when we visited an apartment with a phone. I didn't know how to use the phone or what number to dial. I just sat there in an empty room, tense and with the telephone in my hands. At one point someone passed through the room and asked if I knew how to use the phone. I told them yes because that was what they expected to hear. They nodded and exited. I was devastated and so deeply wished that had not been what they expected to hear from me.

I felt completely helpless, lost, scared, and alone.

There may have been a reason for those feelings, more than the state kidnapping, more than that individual war, and more than my sitting in that silent room with little hope. I would later come to discover, from the recruiter as well as some of her associates, that the woman I was now under the custody of had been involved in the 1972 bombing of a government building by the U.S. domestic terrorist organization, the Weathermen (also known as the Weather Underground Organization), widely known for their small-scale bombings of government offices within the United States.

A mountain of evidence, including the lack of prison time for the majority of the bombers, pointed to those bombings having been government-approved to give the U.S. Federal Bureau of Investigation an excuse for targeting U.S. citizens outspokenly opposed to questionable policies emerging from Washington D.C. as well as the F.B.I.'s own increasingly illegal, corrupt, and unjust activities (when attempting to target the Mob in the U.S., the F.B.I. had absorbed Mob members as well as their tactics and goals). And here was one of the bombers, looming over me in Argentina, a country that also had domestic bombings of government buildings, also blamed on dissidents, and that the charred wreckage of looked eerily like the same level of damage done by the Weather Underground in the United States, as if some of the bombings were done by the same people using the same manuals and methodologies.

El atentado en el comedor de la Superintendencia de la Policía Federal del 2 de julio de 1976 dejó 23 muertos y 110 heridos

Investigators search for clues after the May 19, 1972 Weatherman bombing of the Pentagon

First Image (*Argentina* - Bombing of Federal Police Building, 1976) Source: Infobae[17]

Second Image (*United States* - Bombing of U.S. Pentagon, 1972) Source: American Issues Project via Wikipedia[18]

---

[17] Infobae, Horror and Death: The Five Women Who Killed - The Montoneros Bomb in the Dining Room of the Federal Police, https://www.infobae.com/en/2022/03/18/horror-and-death-the-five-women-who-killed-the-montoneros-bomb-in-the-dining-room-of-the-federal-police/

[18] American Issues Project via Wikipedia, Weather Underground, https://en.wikipedia.org/wiki/Weather_Underground

There is a significant probability that I was standing there, vulnerable and owned by one of the snakes directly involved in the framing of Argentine citizens including my parents, with the intent to take away their lives and freedom, and to steal their children - including me.

At one point during our time in Buenos Aires, on a street with a view of the ocean, a haggard-looking woman made a nervous attempt to pile me into her vehicle, a wood-paneled station wagon. I was internally conflicted about it and too afraid to go with her. I would see her again later in the United States, still with that same vehicle, and she would die by gunshot at the hands of my military-dictatorship-approved keeper for having come that far. I believe the haggard-looking woman was one of my family members and was attempting to rescue me. After living in a prison with so little exposure to family or safety other than that provided by my mother, I simply didn't recognize who the older woman was quickly enough.

Aside from apartments, a large church, and government offices, we visited the major university. In an impressively enormous building, we entered their Journalism Department. The recruiter needed to check on a few things. They already knew her there. Apparently, she was deeply entrenched, using the identity of an imprisoned journalism student from the north of the country, named Alicia Raquel Burdisso Rolotti, and influencing the campus with media she had been publishing via that department. Having now spent the majority of my life as her shadow, I can promise the rhetoric she was promoting was the same rhetoric the State was pointing to and labeling the students with when calling them the enemy. She had been setting the trap.

DESAPARECIDOS

Image: Alicia Raquel Burdisso Rolotti

Source: <u>Desaparecidos</u>[19]

There are countless reasons that I find covert domestic action by government to be non-beneficial. This type of honey-and-comradery-laced entrapment is one of them.

Methods of manipulation of open-minded and caring individuals in academic institutions, for deceptive reasons and to the detriment of those young citizens, are highly questionable. It's likely that this pre-thought-crime type method of entrapment captures more kind, caring, and friendly souls than it has ever caught someone with initial bad intentions. Especially when you realize that those young minds were accepted into the institutions of higher learning either by displaying continued obedience and dedication in school or by exceptional intellectual abilities. Those are the people they choose to exploit and destroy - their citizens who have consistently displayed the traits of loyalty and exceptionalism. They

---

[19] Alicia Raquel Burdisso Rolotti, Desaparecidos, http://www.desaparecidos.org/arg/victimas/b/burdisso/index.html

are the ones who will be the most hurt by being maliciously betrayed by their own nation, and they are the ones capable of doing the most damage as retaliation for the betrayal.

The methodology harms the nation and those who would have contributed the most to its stability.

The exploitation of students, especially for dodgy recruitment purposes, perpetuates a problem that will continue into the next cycle, making internal struggle and exploitation a constant at the domestic governance level. Not everyone who has been ripped from their life and called an enemy by the State actually appreciates the lifelong threats and arbitrary punishments that come with it, nor will they necessarily appreciate those they are now coercively forced to provide their expertise to. This leads to continuing porousness in national security, and thus more international wars and a lower quality of life domestically.

You don't actually want a pissed-off and hurt political science major working in your Intelligence offices nor an angry and genius scientist working in their enemy's weapons development labs. And when you have both types of situations and the people in them know each other? It doesn't end well. You'll just have to trust me on that for now. That recruiter Argentina saw fit to leave me in the custody of? She would be a major rage and drug-fueled connecting force between those two departments.

Yes, the recruiter. Three generations into war recruitment heavy on deception, you won't know which side you or anyone else started on, is standing with, or is standing on; but the pain is still there, and that pain wasn't just my own. I was being absorbed by generations of those brought into the war machine through violence, threats, coercion, death of their families, and forcible removal from the countries they had fought and sacrificed for. They chose to soothe that pain with heroin, greed, and vengeance. I'm still standing here, holding my pain without anything to numb it. I understand why they succumb.

The memory that always surfaces the most from my post-prison time in Buenos Aires happened within the span of just a few minutes. I was standing in the middle of the university campus, the foreign woman nearby, and students were milling past in droves, seeking to get to their next classes. It was 1980 and well into the war that had taken my freedom. There I stood, small, somewhat crippled, and pale from growing up in a prison;

having just appeared among them at the age of three, without ever having an infancy they had seen.

They knew about the war. Each and every one of those hundreds of students who passed me during those moments between classes knew about the war. Not one of them stopped to save me.

Despite the public's abundantly clear policy of "close your eyes until it's over," the crimes of using intelligence channels for the international trafficking of children, trafficking in civilians, and infiltrating other governments with genocidal and marauding intentions didn't stop when the war ended. Some of the people in those Southern Cone military departments had fantasies as far-reaching as killing off the Northern Hemisphere, according to the conversations I overheard when I was young and left waiting in their offices and halls, and later during planning and early-stage implementation attempts by their transactional allies in another land. I wish I were conflating, but I'm not. I'll get more into the details on that one later, with documentation.

Like many nations that have reached a point of becoming hyper-focused on a belief in their own supremacy, there were quite a few people among the Argentine ranks who wanted to entirely eradicate their enemies, final solution style. It was an unrealistic but increasingly possible goal back then, as they spoke about the advantages of neutron bombs and other options. As we progress into the modern era, there are opportunities that open up to the sickest among us, some of whom hold authority, and some of whom are the same exact people I was in those rooms with. Just because they fade from the newspapers does not mean their careers have ended. In fact, in an established era of secrecy, removal from the public spotlight is often more concerning than remaining in it.

In a later moment that would leave me staring in disbelief, a U.S. State Department worker would sound relieved when he erroneously decided one of the scientists in my cohort must have come from Argentina to work in U.S. Department of Defense weapons research willingly, as if that alone meant all bad intentions floated away on a whimsical love of America. Americans are okay for the most part, but their intentional naivety and first-world egos frequently lead them down the wrong path. They let in a lot of bad actors due to the belief that all foreigners are deeply honored to be there and only have intentions to see

Disneyland and eat some good old Independence Day barbeque...this is despite intentional and coercive recruitment practices that target known U.S. enemies to bring them in, and international policies that take advantage of and pull from the ranks of violent dictatorships.

Argentina was entering late-stage failure when I was there, a stage that many other nations may still be in time to avoid. The country has since gotten worse. It's unlikely that the psychology and methodologies of that nation can be reversed enough to save it from its own behaviors. It will finish consuming itself, while dramatically denying it down to the final bite.

Even today, as I write this, Argentina still does a little governmental and NGO-level Munchausen by Proxy "war is over" play-act for the global community, for funding, and to avoid the international courts. Outwardly, they advertise that they are searching for the children they traded for arms and international favors, and are now offering the children help to find their original names and parents. The truth is darker than that. They commonly deny the children the right to open a case for investigation. They have now had over 45 years to find the approximately 500 stolen babies. They have located less than 150, primarily because they refuse to find the rest, even when the now-graying children are standing directly in front of them in those government and NGO offices.

That's a rate of assisting roughly two to three children per year, despite the government and NGOs having nearly unlimited funding for the project, much of which they funnel into their wardrobes, cars, and real estate (yes, the connected organizations are well-paid to keep up the farce...I'll get into more on that later). The children they parade around a couple of times a year for the media spotlight and funding purposes are almost exclusively the adopted children of media personalities, political enemies of the government and NGOs, and others who can be exploited or would be financially beneficial to control.

This is all despite their having archives with our names, who our parents were, and where they stole us from. They know who we are, but they profit too much from our disappearance. They also still hate us and believe their own rhetoric - that we were child criminals and infant terrorists who deserved to be ripped from our families and sold because one of us might attempt to vote against them. We are the embodiment of our parents who they tried to dehumanize, diminish, rub in the dirt, and then genocide. Tell me, how often does one use the military to kill the friends, community members, schoolmates, and entire family of a criminal, simply for being related to or knowing them? That's where

the chasm between the lies they tell and their true intentions can be seen through the cracks formed by reality.

The lies badly painting over the damage they cause make an undeniable and uncomfortable sight. You know that feeling. You've felt hints of it before.

Argentina had chosen genocide as a solution to the problems they didn't want to deal with, generally internal problems of abuses and a lack of resources caused by them stealing from, bullying, manipulating, and lying to each other and to themselves. Once a country goes down that route, it is nearly impossible to change its trajectory.

Their responsibility-evading and self-congratulating semantics continue to lock them into the behavior and mindset, but do not hide the amount of death and self-harm they have caused. Their grotesque mentalities also do not obscure the country's repeated and increasing history of eradicating and removing groups, one by one, over the decades of the 1900s, as if maybe the removal of the next one would finally be the solution to creating a utopian society.

Their internal problems, left undealt with during the distractions of state terrorism, only became worse after the temporary adrenaline rush of each eradication effort ended. By the time I was born, they had run out of easily identifiable ethnicities to go after and were removing people with any great-great grandparents who weren't genetically European (As far as I've gleaned, my own family was 100% culturally Argentine and I'm personally around 90% European and 10% east of that, genetically), and it still didn't solve their self-caused problems. The country is a nightmare headache today, with its economic policies written by thieves and its academic policies written by those who hate intellect. But their semantics did give the people within and supporting that regime, and the next series of regimes, a never-ending list of excuses and arguments to allow the resulting carnage and harm to continue, unabated.

Eventually, my stay in Buenos Aires ended, and I left that mess behind, in the care of a small group of Intelligence workers. I escaped Argentina, but I did not escape. I went from being an embarrassing secret of South America to being an embarrassing secret of North America.

Nothing changed for me in that regard. I was still expected to cover for those who harmed me the most.

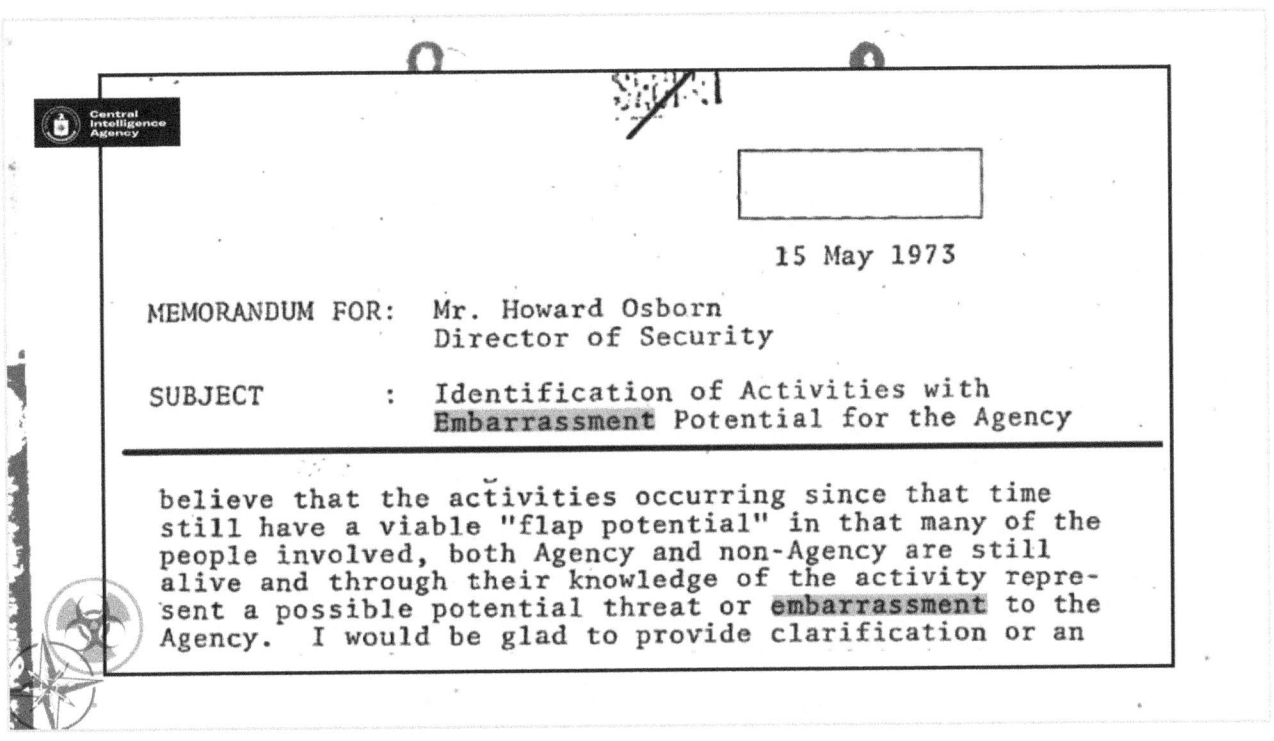

Image Source: Central Intelligence Agency

"Many of the people involved, both Agency and non-Agency, are still alive and through their knowledge of the activity represent a possible potential threat or embarrassment to the Agency."

Text Source: Central Intelligence Agency[20]

Or as the saying goes, out of the frying pan and into the fire.

---

[20] Central Intelligence Agency, Memorandum for: Executive Secretary, CIA Management Committee, Subject: Family Jewels, https://www.cia.gov/readingroom/docs/DOC_0001451843.pdf

U.S. Intelligence Recruitment
Relics of the Weathermen and World War II

"Yes, I was a scientist,
But my first duty was to the company."

As we left Argentina, I was still promised that my mother was fine and I would be brought back to her eventually. When we got further away from the only city I had ever called home, I was told we would be visiting a zoo and not to worry, that I would see my mother when we were done seeing the animals.

I repeated the promise about the zoo to a concerned-looking crew member on a boat in the Panama Canal when he asked if the people I was with were safe for me. Sometimes, I wonder how different my life would have been if I hadn't just repeated the lie. What if I had continued to speak until the truth became apparent? Would I have ended up growing up in an orphanage in Panama, or would the crew member have taken an unexpected trip to the bottom of the canal with the result only being a few extra minutes of delay watching handshakes in a back room before my trip proceeded?

More than likely, he simply would have ended up drugged, wide-eyed, and nodding in agreement with whatever new reality he had been presented with. I would see those pool-wide eyes so many times over the years, although most often they were on government records clerks as the recruiter walked with them behind their counters and had them rewrite history. But I digress, a little...

It was around that time that the recruiter first started sharing her wisdom with me. Our relationship would be a strange one. She would come to use me ruthlessly as a tool when she needed one, with absolute disregard for my health or life. But she also had moments in which she treated me like an apprentice and showed me how to exploit people, step by step, before then doing it to me. It was a pathologically insane methodology. I was trapped with

her and had no choice other than to play along, but I did learn a lot about how manipulation and exploitation actually work - from both sides of it.

She explained the landscape of what she did quite simply one time. She said there are no rules to follow. We fly above everyone and we move freely. That is why we can get so much done while they do so little to stop us. The people constrain themselves by following laws, cultural limitations, religion, and societal norms.

They create their own cages and they cannot reach us from within those self-made confines.

Later, I would argue that flying quite so freely didn't entirely apply in my case. She had federal protection and full permission to break every law. I didn't. I probably shouldn't have argued that. She may have taken it as a request to join her.

We would spend some time in Cuba (I loved peeking in through the windows of small-scale manufacturing and mechanical shops there, the smell of diesel always reminds me of it), and then went by boat to Florida before arriving in New York City. We did eventually make it to the zoo – the Bronx Zoo in New York, probably because I kept loudly asking in public spaces about the zoo trip I had been promised back in Argentina.

Now, recognizing the pervasively dark perspective of the cohort I would end up deeply ensnared with, I have to wonder if they were referring to the zoo or more so the inhabitants of the city when they spoke about the animals we would see.

While in New York City, we spent our time with the recruiter's sister, crammed into her then-tiny apartment. There, the day-to-day realities of the international trafficking of a child from war became more apparent as the two bickered over my head while dying my hair near-black and working on flattening out a few errant waves to better match the woman's board-straight and jet-black hair. I would spend the next ten years of my life with my hair over-conditioned, brushed flat while still wet, and kept henna-dyed black to the point that I looked absurdly like a caricature of Wednesday Addams from the Addams Family television show.

Operation Condor is incredibly recent history for the United States, and demonstrates the horrors that the U.S. has had a hand in across the globe. The U.S.'s involvement in the kidnapping of political prisoners and the assassinations of professors, politicians, and other left-wing luminaries is entirely antithetical to the beliefs that supposedly fuel the United States. The U.S.'s obsession with free-market capitalism and unequivocal hatred of communism led to the state being willing to look past incredibly dramatic human rights abuses. The U.S. must look to rectify their past mistakes regarding Operation Condor, and look at the leaders that they support with much more nuance and criticism. If this doesn't happen, the U.S. is doomed to repeatedly support regimes that commit the same atrocities that happened in Latin America during Operation Condor.

Image Source: Institute for Youth in Policy

"The U.S.'s involvement in the kidnapping of political prisoners and the assassinations of professors, politicians, and other left-wing luminaries is entirely antithetical to the beliefs that supposedly fuel the United States."

Text Source: Institute for Youth in Policy[21]

That word, antithetical, doesn't quite hold the standard dictionary definition, especially in the U.S. (although not limited to that country), where the government is a paid liar with the known authority to do so, granted to it by the written rules included in the formation of the Office of Strategic Services (OSS) and then the Central Intelligence Agency (CIA); the latter agency which has now entrenched itself into every level and aspect of both corporate and government life, with a stranglehold on politics and the molding and remolding of each aspect of mainstream public opinion and discourse, and a large portion of what Americans have been led to believe is outside of the mainstream.

---

[21] Institute for Youth in Policy, Operation Condor and the Horrors of U.S. Foreign Policy, https://yipinstitute.org/article/operation-condor-and-the-horrors-of-u-s-foreign-policy

In the international game, this means the American public (and the public of countries with similar policies and undercurrents of culture) get to play innocent, or even more absurdly - heroes, while individuals and the world suffer the very real consequences of their collective actions. This leads to issues both domestically and internationally.

Domestically, the populace actually appears to believe the paper-thin lies, which leads them to misstep in attempting to find solutions because most don't even know the nature of the problem they're actually dealing with. For example, both major political sides tend to hold the belief that the people streaming over their border all want to be there because it is a crown jewel of a nation, that those people have not been deceived, that they're better off in America, and that America incentivizing the destruction of their homelands isn't the actual reason they're there.

So, while bickering back and forth over what to do about the people streaming in over their border, they either argue that the people deserve a good life in America or that they are trying to steal the good life from Americans. Neither side deals with the issue of the American military, NGO advertising, and corporate interests causing the majority of problems that lead to people coming over that border in droves in the first place.

I would find myself coming up against that wall of group-learned delusion so many times over the years of my forced stay in the United States. When I reached out for help to say I had been kidnapped, I would be face to face with people who thought "I'd have a better life there," "that I would appreciate the McDonald's hamburgers and other riches of the United States," and that they were "helping me and I was too much of a dumb immigrant to know it." More importantly, they genuinely believed that their internally ensnared and thus impotent population and commercial culture were so wonderful that my being there in the hands of a dangerous exploiter could replace the value of my mother, my nation, my culture, my language, and my safety.

They've been lying for so long in the U.S. (not that it's the only government that lies to its own people in a desperate attempt to keep control while robbing them blind) that even parts of the government now believe their own false rhetoric and act upon it, creating more of a mess diplomatically and otherwise. A lie that lasts beyond one generation results in an absolute disaster. People start treating it, and acting upon it, as if it were truth.

In that cultural and political climate, my arrival in the country wasn't as smooth as Hollywood might paint activities being blatantly run through U.S. operation channels by their own employees. This is especially true if you still wistfully cling to the concept of authority as competent, organized, and holding their own workers to legal standards. However, despite a lack of convenience in attaining new documents, my temporary documents from Argentina would have raised red flags in the U.S. and reasonably had to be discarded.

The recruiter walked with me under a tree one day early on and told me what my new name would be. She cajoled me into ceasing to use the old one, promising that I would not forget it. *After so many years without it, I did eventually forget it. While Navajas and Claros are likely my surnames, the first names I use are simply the closest I could find to the truth.* She told me that my new name, beginning with a C, had the same beginning sound as my old name so it would be easy for me to recognize and respond to when people said it. But it didn't start with the same sound as my prior name - *my name* - not in Spanish and not in English. Perhaps it did in a language from the Eastern Bloc where the recruiter had spent many of her earlier years.

And when I would remember my mother? The recruiter would assure me that the woman I remembered had been a foster mother in the state of Connecticut in the winter of 1977 - 1978, in the first eight months of my life. In retrospect, her explanation made no sense. That winter fell within a time period that I could not have remembered - I was too early in infancy to develop memories by that stage. Also, I was walking fair distances in many of the memories that contained my mother. Infants don't walk.

It would be decades before I would learn about child development milestones regarding memory formation and before government officials from Connecticut would confirm that I had never been in their foster system. Because of what the recruiter told me when I was growing up, I often just assumed there was something wrong with me for having become so emotionally attached to a foster care provider to the point that the provider felt like my only mother. I internalized my loneliness because I thought I was dumb for feeling it, but I always missed my mother, even when I believed the lies that she had only been a foster mother. Every day of my life, I have missed her. I simply missed her in silence back then. I felt too

much embarrassment about my strong unbreakable attachment to someone who supposedly wasn't my family.

Even with the full change in identity, there wasn't some official clandestine CIA office smoothly working on my replacement documents and ironing out all the wrinkles for my stay in the United States. I wasn't their responsibility and probably fell squarely into the category of "embarrassment" myself, someone to hide away and sweep under the rug. I was a child, not a hired and vetted agent of theirs - we had no documented relationship in which they had to provide me with anything, despite my entering the country by the efforts and force of their employees. The forging of my U.S. identity was bumpier and never official enough to leave the responsibility plainly in their hands, although they would not be without blame.

That said, maybe there was the tiniest bit of blowback from the department. Either there was something going on internally in the recruiter's office, or the woman may have gone too far in selecting a child for her own while recruiting for government projects in Argentina. They temporarily suspended her employment. When certain officials and high-ranking officers came by the house to visit, I had to hide in the hall closet beneath a pile of clothing or tucked between coats.

Her depression stemming from it became evident as I sat quietly in a dark apartment with her. The only light came from a television that was playing clips of speeches from President Carter to her complete disdain. She sneered at that screen. Her heroin addiction also became glaringly apparent at that juncture, although it would take a few years for me to learn what the drug was and how the use of the paraphernalia and her mood swings were related. Those mood swings were hell to deal with as a child - I could do the same behavior on five different occasions and be praised for it four times out of five, and then brutally abused for it the fifth time simply because she was on the wrong side of a high at the time. As far as I know, she still has the addiction. Apparently, working for that part of the government has its advantages. She had a stable connection for obtaining quality black tar heroin the entire time she was in my life. As time went on, I would become a primary source of the cash to fund the habit.

She still found little things to cheer her up now and then in those first few months of us sharing a space. The recruiter's favorite thing was sabotage. It brought a light to her eyes and a genuine smile like nothing else could. Over the years I would watch her sabotage everyone - her enemies, her friends, her employers, her targets, her nation, other nations, the rich, the poor - everyone. I will never forget the time she tried to get me to sleep with a watch with an exposed radium dial under my pillow. I didn't entirely understand what she was about at that point, and I was still so young. I happily went to sleep with it because of the joy I saw in her eyes as she told me how wonderful it would be to get brain cancer. I was still a baby. Sometimes, I allowed myself to be lulled into believing joy was a good thing, especially from someone insisting on having the title of mother.

Luckily, I had insomnia back then. I never could actually manage to fall asleep with anything under my pillow. My hand would come across it and the feel of the metal kept me awake. I removed the thing the first night.

When I wasn't in that dark apartment, she was stashing me away at summer camp at a local military base to get rid of me during the daytime and some nights. I was in the youngest group of children there. In swimming class, they called us polliwogs (the tailed larva of a frog).

Due to the scars on my lungs, my health, and my small size, I was usually behind everyone else in games and the obstacle course (I struggled with climbing the wall and usually needed help and extra time). I always seemed to have conjunctivitis in those years, a symptom of a series of underlying walking pneumonia infections that I couldn't seem to kick for long. The flecks in the corners of my eyes could be wiped away and hidden easily enough, but my struggling when attempting to run was obvious in a way even my scarred lungs could not be entirely responsible for. I was a healthy weight, although on the thin side, but would make it less than the length of an ordinary room before needing to stop running. However, I still excelled in learning to float and do the doggy paddle in the shallow polliwog section of the swimming area, and in any sport involving a target. Archery and time using the rifle range were my favorites.

Although, the easiest and most thrilling activities happened in those rare times when they let us stay up late at night. They handed us markers and told us to "kill the enemy with

knives." In other words, we were supposed to sneak into the cabins of the other campers and silently mark their throats with the markers while they slept. Hey, I was young, it included the thrill of being up past lights-out, we had permission to enter cabins that were generally off-limits, and it was a game I could fully participate in that didn't involve long runs. Was I supposed to hate it? If you're going to judge kids for liking war games, create a civilization that doesn't encourage children to participate in war games.

Other than activities, some of the best moments on base were when the candy truck arrived. Maybe it sold something else. All I really remember was the candy. In retrospect, it probably wasn't the best choice considering my health.

Back at the apartment, alone in the light of a window in the room that held the recruiter's grand piano, I began to teach myself to read (I also attempted to teach myself to play the piano but with much less success). I went word by word through a book about a world destroyed by nuclear war in which everyone was dead except the whales. In that story, there was a baby whale who continued to have a cold, and conjunctivitis, for months before it cleared. Then the whales went on to live in a world that was now only theirs. It was an unrealistic tale (a world with no krill and plankton means a world with no whales), but my health led me to feel a connection with that baby whale.

The recruiter's office eventually reinstated her and reduced her right to international travel, other than to Asia. She was switched over from active foreign work that had included the task of recruiting political prisoners for Department of Defense (DoD) research and other purposes. She would begin working primarily in a more supervisorial role on projects and research, as well as recruitment - domestically. She no longer used her international alias, Alicia. Although, I would frequently hear her still calling in using her old domestic one from the 1960s, "Anna May," a name even Bill Ayers, the head of the Weather Underground Organization (labeled as a domestic terrorist group by the United States, due to their bombing of government buildings and other activities), still knows and references to her as.

In case the Weathermen have been written out of your history books, here's a short intro, complete with the mention of Anna:

Image Source: New York Times

"Mr. Ayers describes the Weathermen descending into a 'whirlpool of violence.'

'Everything was absolutely ideal on the day I bombed the Pentagon,' he writes. But then comes a disclaimer: 'Even though I didn't actually bomb the Pentagon -- we bombed it, in the sense that Weathermen organized it and claimed it.' He goes on to provide details about the manufacture of the bomb and how a woman he calls Anna placed the bomb in a restroom. No one was killed or injured, though the damage was extensive.

Between 1970 and 1974 the Weathermen took responsibility for 12 bombings..."

Text Source: New York Times[22]

I heard about that bombing during so many dinner parties that I lost count. I will always remember the heads of new guests turning in disbelief as the recruiter said she had placed a bomb in the Pentagon bathroom. There was a long story about another agent putting the

---

[22] New York Times, No Regrets for a Love Of Explosives; In a Memoir of Sorts, a War Protester Talks of Life With the Weathermen, https://www.nytimes.com/2001/09/11/books/no-regrets-for-love-explosives-memoir-sorts-war-protester-talks-life-with.html

bomb in her bag and hiding it beneath the panties that were in there, before they went through security with an embarrassed security guard not looking deeper in her bag than those panties, and then the recruiter panicking and attempting to flush the bomb, as if it were drugs, in the women's bathroom before going back through security again.

Her story about her work leading up to the bombing would later be reflected in files known as the Family Jewels when the Central Intelligence Agency finally declassified a few documents in order to do a bit of bragging and highlight some of their favorite agents and former activities:

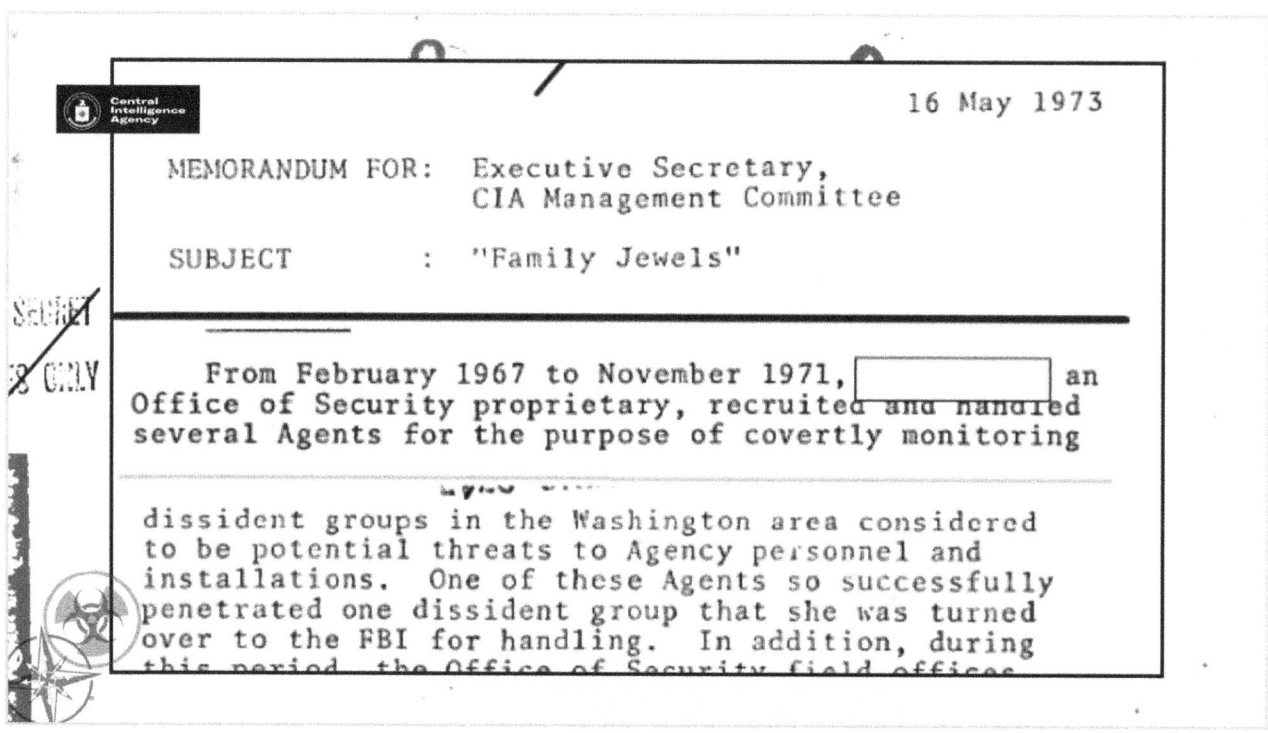

Image Source: Central Intelligence Agency

"From February 1967 to November 1971...<u>dissident groups</u> in the <u>Washington</u> area considered to be potential <u>threats to</u> Agency personnel and <u>installations</u>.

One of these Agents so successfully penetrated one dissident group that she was turned over to the FBI for handling."

Text Source: <u>Central Intelligence Agency</u>[23]

It was with the FBI that she would come to know George Edwards, a Yale Drama School-trained COINTELPRO agent who had been assigned to infiltrate the Black Panther Party, a group that had close ties to Bill Ayer's Weathermen. He didn't play a main role in my life until later, but he was already sitting with us at some of those dinners and was never among the group that acted surprised by the recruiter's recollection of bombing what was supposed to be a very secure government building. When he does come up later on, I'll share with you many New York Times articles in which he was front and center, under the same name and title the public has always known him as - George Edwards, Black Panther. The same George Edwards who leaders of the Black Panther Party correctly called out as a Federal Agent. It turns out that the Yale Daily News and the New York Times had to work overtime in screaming, "He's not a Fed, really!" to protect that particular jewel. In the process, they would expose his connection to several operations that would include intentional crimes against humanity and that would occur in the years in which I was right there and in the same rooms.

I can't blame the random dinner party guests for never believing the recruiter about the bombing. They had grown up in a world in which they had some belief in the sanctity and security of government and government buildings - especially the Pentagon. They assumed that if she had placed a bomb in the Pentagon, then she would have been convicted. I assumed the same, until I looked into it years later.

The truth is, almost no one was convicted for the bombings. The cases were mostly dismissed on technicalities. In one case, the government even cited that they would have to endanger foreign intelligence secrets in order to convict the members of the group that had taken responsibility for the bombings. In other words, a good portion of the Weather Underground was on the government payroll, and many were CIA. The only convictions I'm

---

[23] Central Intelligence Agency, Memorandum for: Executive Secretary, CIA Management Committee, Subject: Family Jewels, https://www.cia.gov/readingroom/docs/DOC_0001451843.pdf

aware of were of a scapegoat who got three years in prison, and those involved in the much later 1981 Brinks armored car robbery.

Image: United States – Bombing of US Pentagon, 1972

Image Source: American Issues Project via Wikipedia[24]

You can blow up government buildings on the government payroll, but you can't get away with robbing bankers...

---

[24] American Issues Project via Wikipedia, Weather Underground, https://en.wikipedia.org/wiki/Weather_Underground

THE WEATHER UNDERGROUND

Ω   39-242

U.S. GOVERNMENT PRINTING OFFICE
WASHINGTON : 1975

REPORT

OF THE

SUBCOMMITTEE TO INVESTIGATE THE
ADMINISTRATION OF THE INTERNAL SECURITY
ACT AND OTHER INTERNAL SECURITY LAWS

OF THE

COMMITTEE ON THE JUDICIARY
UNITED STATES SENATE
NINETY-FOURTH CONGRESS
FIRST SESSION

JANUARY 1975

> At the end of fiscal 1973 year, 29 Weathermen, including Bill Ayers, were wanted by the FBI in connection with violations of sabotage, bombing and gun control statutes, antiriot laws, and unlawful flight to avoid prosecution.
> On October 15, 1973, U.S. District Judge Damon J. Keith of Detroit dismissed conspiracy charges against the Detroit 15, including William Ayers, on the Government's own motion. The motion by U.S. Attorney Ralph B. Guy, Jr., said the Government would not endanger foreign intelligence secrets by disclosing certain information the court had ordered disclosed. Judge Keith had issued a sweeping order last June 5 for the Government to disclose whether it had used burglaries, sabotage, electronic surveillance, agents provocateurs, or other "espionage techniques" against the Weatherman.
> On January 3, 1974, U.S. District Court Judge Julius J. Hoffman in Chicago dismissed a 4-year-old indictment against 12 members of the Weatherman faction of the Students for a Democratic Society, including William Ayres, 28, of Chicago, charged with leading the riotous "Days of Rage" through Chicago streets in 1969. Judge Hoffman acted on a Government request which noted that a recent Supreme Court decision barring electronic surveillance without a court order would have hampered prosecution of the case.

Image Source: U.S. Government Printing Office via ProQuest

"On October 15, 1973, U.S. District Judge Damon J. Keith of Detroit dismissed conspiracy charges against the Detroit 15, including William Ayers, on the Government's own motion. The motion by U.S. Attorney Ralph B. Guy, Jr., said the Government would not endanger foreign intelligence secrets by disclosing certain information the court had ordered disclosed...

On January 3, 1974, U.S. District Court Judge Julius J. Hoffman in Chicago dismissed a 4-year-old indictment, against 12 members of the Weatherman faction of the Students for a Democratic Society, including William Ayres...

Judge Hoffman acted on a Government request which noted that a recent Supreme Court decision barring electronic surveillance without a court order would have hampered prosecution of the case."

Text Source: U.S. Government Printing Office via ProQuest[25]

---

[25] United States Government Printing Office via ProQuest, The Weather Underground Report - Report of the Subcommittee to Investigate the Administration of the Internal Security Act and Other Internal Security Laws of the Committee on the Judiciary United States Senate Ninety-Fourth Congress First Session

For the Black Panthers, things would go a little differently. While the Weathermen got away with detonating bombs in Federal buildings without doing jail time for it, the Black Panthers would be arrested on simply the suspicion of planning explosions. It's fairly obvious which group had more federal agents in it and which had more civilians to target. If the Weatherman Underground Organization was not a Federal plant from the start, then their people were forcibly recruited into the FBI in lieu of jail time, much the same as I'd seen in Argentina, and the Nazis had seen at the end of World War II. The only difference being that this was entirely domestic - a country slowly consuming its own people, group by group.

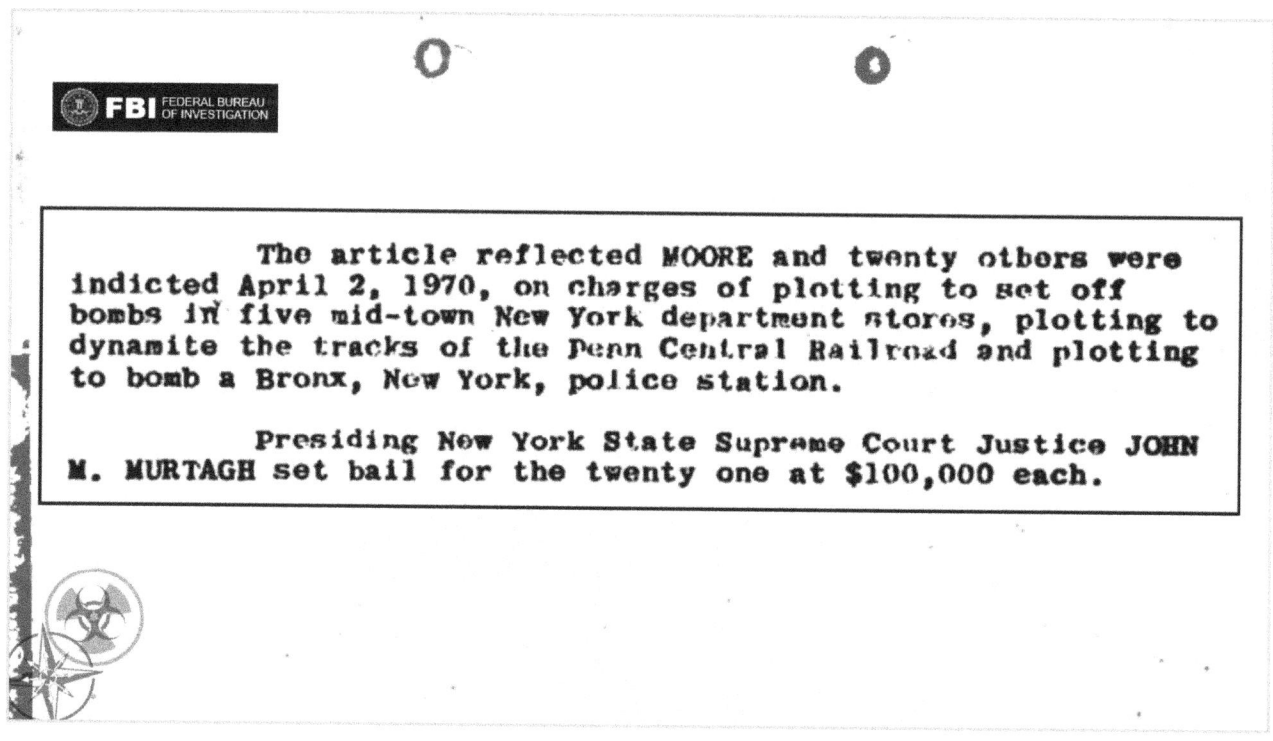

Image Source: <u>Federal Bureau of Investigation</u>

"Moore and twenty others (Black Panther Party members) were indicted April 2, 1970, on charges of plotting to set off bombs in five mid-town New York stores, … the Penn Station Railroad and … a Bronx, New York, police station.

…Set bail for the twenty-one at $100,000 each."

Text Source: <u>Federal Bureau of Investigation</u>[26]

[26] Federal Bureau of Investigation, Black Panther Party, Part 23,
https://vault.fbi.gov/Black%20Panther%20Party%20/Black%20Panther%20Party%20Part%2023%20of%2034

For the recruiter, the name Anna kept the echoes of memories from her time infiltrating and sabotaging grassroots movements in the 1960s and 70s, efforts that had put her in the spotlight to her bosses and made her eligible for the international work in which I would first meet her. According to a couple of people who knew and worked with her back then, those years were an adrenaline and drug-fueled time traipsing through the Americas, Iran, and Vietnam, among other places. It was when everyone back at the office still adored her. Then, she went to Argentina.

One of the same confidants who spoke to me about the recruiter's more exciting years in Intelligence also told me that my coming into the picture had ruined the recruiter's life. Not her sons who were born many years before me, not her failed marriage to a Navy Intelligence officer, and not her heroin addiction. Nope. Apparently, I was the one thing she had let get in her way. I was what caused the government to pull the rug on her international escapades back then.

As for the problem of warfare and military intelligence tactics being turned on a nation's own people, it is compounded by what happens after forced recruitment.

Once recruited, the forced employment starts by giving the enemy worker the protection of secrecy so that the employing nation's own departments and public won't know what they're up to. One of the three primary modern reasons for secrecy is protecting the government from embarrassment. Yes, seriously, Remember this document from earlier?

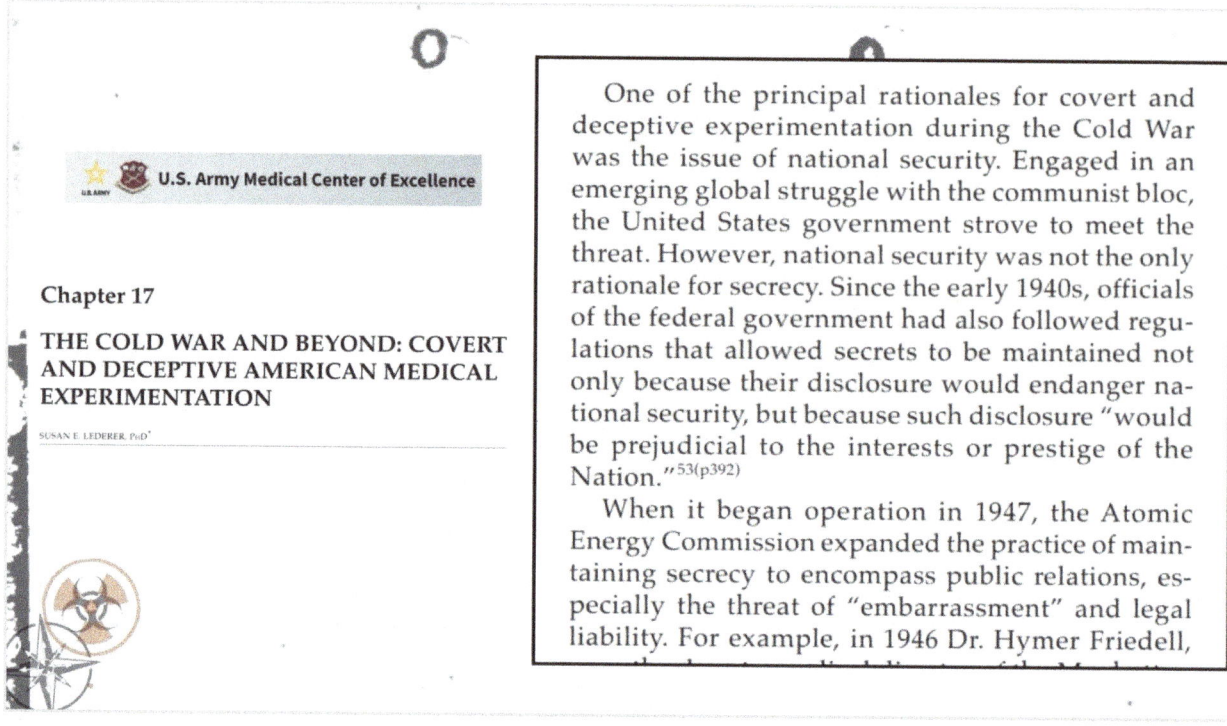

Chapter 17

THE COLD WAR AND BEYOND: COVERT AND DECEPTIVE AMERICAN MEDICAL EXPERIMENTATION

SUSAN E. LEDERER, PhD

One of the principal rationales for covert and deceptive experimentation during the Cold War was the issue of national security. Engaged in an emerging global struggle with the communist bloc, the United States government strove to meet the threat. However, national security was not the only rationale for secrecy. Since the early 1940s, officials of the federal government had also followed regulations that allowed secrets to be maintained not only because their disclosure would endanger national security, but because such disclosure "would be prejudicial to the interests or prestige of the Nation."[53(p392)]

When it began operation in 1947, the Atomic Energy Commission expanded the practice of maintaining secrecy to encompass public relations, especially the threat of "embarrassment" and legal liability. For example, in 1946 Dr. Hymer Friedell,

Image Source: US Army Medical Center of Excellence

"Officials …allowed secrets to be maintained not only because disclosure would endanger national security, but because such disclosure 'would be prejudicial to the interests or *prestige* of the Nation.'

And… expanded the practice to encompass public relations, especially the threat of '*embarrassment*' and '*legal liability*.'"

Text Source: US Army Medical Center of Excellence[27]

Needing to lean on your enemy for your own military management and weapons programs is embarrassing, especially when you're trying to maintain the reputation of a first-rate first-world nation.

---

[27] US Army Medical Center of Excellence, Military Medical Ethics, Volume 2, Chapter 17 The Cold War and Beyond: Covert and Deceptive American Medical Experimentation Susan E. Lederer, PhD, https://ke.army.mil/bordeninstitute/published_volumes/ethicsvol2/ethics-ch-17.pdf https://medcoeckapwstorprd01.blob.core.usgovcloudapi.net/pfw-images/borden/ethicsvol2/Ethics-ch-17.pdf

This dangerous strategy combined with a need for internal and domestic face-saving culminates in placing the enemy into your own endgame research labs and military intelligence offices, as well as industrial and academic positions, with full access and influence, and disguised as one of your own.

The practice is the equivalent of a nation saying, "Hold my beer!" before shooting itself in the foot and then the face.

♞ Stage 2 - Research

We're damaging our individual selves, families,
societies, countries, and international relations
by making deceit the expected norm.
Constant and pervasive deceit tears at
what makes our interactions human
and our choices safe and useful to ourselves.

Sometimes, the recruiter brought me along to make a situation look less suspicious, or in some cases maybe just because there wasn't a babysitter that day. Ordinary life is still a constant even within an unordinary life. We all have to crawl out of bed in the morning, put on our shoes, and make sure the kids are still alive (possibly not in that order).

As a child, much of the behavior of those who had been working Operation Condor and related operations would be commonplace to me because it was all I had known. However, some of it still left me worried from the start.

Before I was concerned for the public, I was concerned for the people in my life who were doing things that were obviously dangerous, including to themselves. I was worried for them and for myself. I had already lost one family. I didn't want to lose them too, even if they were absolutely not qualified to be family, professionals, or even to have a pet without supervision. As I got older and saw more, that feeling of concern would only grow regarding their behaviors and methodologies that were clearly short-sighted and against their own best interests, and eventually the world's.

The amount of unchecked secrecy they are permitted and the resulting subterfuge allow opportunistic exploiters and those with grudges to get away with gross amounts of theft, sales of entire countries, abuse of citizens, misuse of funding and resources (including warfare research labs - but we'll get to that). This includes reckless and harmful behaviors no one would allow if it were happening clearly in plain sight under glaring spotlights, with an honest narrator on blast on the television, and memories of a way to fight still present in the minds of the populace. I've seen it all, and soon enough you will

too. It eviscerates a country from within, and then the damage and instability build and spread beyond its borders.

What once may have been an almost reasonable idea of secrecy to provide protection, quickly became a tool for exploitation and unrestrained corruption. By the time I was born, the damage was already ramping up.

And don't look at me with those wide trusting and terrified eyes and say, "But there are oversight committees and internal auditors for that." Honey, the moment I turned twenty-one, I was rotated through a job in internal auditing in name only just so a department could fill out the reports on themselves by themselves. It was already their well-honed and established routine, with a never-ending list of lackeys to use. I never even saw the forms. I was also there for many visits to the private offices of oversight committee members in capitol buildings, the same ones that had overreached their own borders in order to fund the instability in South America.
There is no oversight.

But about my first years in the United States...

Once the recruiter's work status was normalized, albeit domestically instead of internationally as she had hoped, she began bringing me along to the labs. I was left to wander those lab halls alone for hours all too frequently. One time, early into her domestic supervisorial role, the recruiter was deep into a two-hour session of berating a medical researcher in his own office, and I felt uncomfortable enough from the screaming to leave the hall and seek refuge in an office, myself. I went into the darkest-lit office I could find that was unlocked. It had one of those desk toys, a Newton's cradle. I must have spent hours testing all the ways the balls could swing back and forth, clacking against each other in various patterns. There, I would first meet, and later come to somewhat know, a depressed and homesick former Nazi scientist who had been recruited back at the end of World War II, never to see his homeland again.

Before I go on with this memory, I need to clarify something for you, the reader. When I speak of a country, a political group, a military, or the like, I'm not taking sides against them, nor am I advocating for or supporting the deaths they cause. We can all benefit from being healthy. A healthy world creates healthy enemies who can rationalize instead of being hell-bent on erratic and suicidal undertakings that jeopardize us all, including them.

They had care packages sent from Germany to the scientist in an attempt to alleviate his sadness. Those were what would lead me back to his office over the years. The flavor of the German chocolate had as much tangible depth as his longing for home. It was incomparably beautiful in contrast to the plastic-tasting Hershey's chocolate of America. I loved that he shared it with me. It reminded me of the depth and care of my own mother who I had lost in my own homeland, only to be given a caricature of an American life as if it was a real replacement for a mother with a soul.

His pain, dangerously situated in the middle of a weapons research laboratory, should serve as a reminder of the dangers of wartime recruitment of the enemy in secrecy. Especially if the practice continues simply so that the public can experience the adrenaline rush of the false chase of persecuting and pursuing ancient war crimes while keeping the appearance of themselves being untainted and patriotically wholesome. It rarely leads to healing and eventually leads to the next war.

The ironic part is that the government keeps these workers and allows them to rise through the ranks and into supervisorial and strategic roles partly because of the false belief that the U.S. is a crown jewel that everyone wants to go to; as if it has nothing to do with their nations being destroyed or them being coerced by force into coming, often (especially in the case of the scientists and Intelligence) under the threat of war crime tribunals and/or death.

The sad thing is that it was Intelligence that first manufactured that belief to help Americans feel better about their post-war conditions by telling them the conditions they live in are the best in the world, a shining jewel that everyone flocks to without duress. Now, even the government buys its own lies. Do I really need to point out how terrible this is for actual national security, or for long-term global stability? Anyone who has traveled all of America and then other parts of the world knows that America, other than a few select neighborhoods, is not a shining example of prosperity or sanity.

In addition to the harm the self-congratulating lies do to a nation, there is also the harm they do to the soldiers (and civilians who get caught up in war), regardless of what country or war they come from. Many war criminals were citizens serving their country, soldiers who believed the internal propaganda and thought they were protecting other nations or their own borders. To be abandoned, exiled, and under threat because of that, for life, and often while being employed by enemy militaries (the reality of post-wartime recruitment processes), is a very big problem no one discusses. I would end up spending time in endgame research labs and war strategy think tanks with many of those forced recruits over the years. Their level of depression and resentment for having to carry the world's sins permanently, combined with government funding and access, isn't good for any of us.

It leads to weapons and strategies, used by our own militaries, that will kill us all and not just a perceived enemy of the day. To believe that the military has these workers strictly under control and manufacturing everything to specifications is pure ego and not at all realistic. The recruited scientists and strategists create what they want to create and then they hand it to the military, appeasing egos and reinforcing the national lies by falsely claiming they obediently followed specifications, like good subservient and loyal lapdogs happy to be there. I'll get to a few examples of their actual work in a bit.

The population gets to experience a time of peace and normalcy between wars. It is both inhumane and dangerous to not give the same to the soldiers who fought the wars for that public, strategized for the wars, and built the weapons at the expense of their own health and possibly their lives.

To assume it's all okay because what the public is experiencing is okay, or due to some inane hero-savior complex based on the belief that there is a country with wealth and culture truly superior above all others (and of course, out of all the luck, it always just happens to be the one they're standing in), is a major oversight that will lead to the next war having much crueler tactics and weapons. It makes the public appear weak, heartless, and having the whimsical and irrational mind of a small child. This does not put them in a favorable light to those they have captured and now forced into labor for them, especially not when the public has allowed the handing of the keys of the military-industrial complex to those captive enemies.

What intellectual or scientific mind could rationally respect that level of combined idiocy and callousness from an enemy? And which one wouldn't use the keys now in their hands?

In addition, self-congratulating self-deceit gives the public and politicians a focus that is not their current issue. Meaning current atrocities are never prevented or ended in real time. They just become a fallacious legal circus after the fact, and prime military and intelligence recruitment hunting grounds.

We do post-war wrong. This is one of the major factors behind why we have never broken the cycle of war. In shoving everything under the rug and creating a televised spectacle of completion for the public, we don't include actual healing. We only include pain and anger - driving forces behind vengeance, sustained motivation, and action. And then we take the precise people who hold those feelings and place them into military positions within the governments that forced them there, and then...just to make sure we've set ourselves up perfectly for the fall...we give them the protection of secrecy to hide behind while they work.

I hate to be the one to tell you, but if you are afraid of your government, if you feel powerless in the face of your government's crimes against its own people, that's not your government anymore. It's an infiltrator that has crawled their way up through the ranks and is now wearing the face of your government as its prize.

And your own government was probably the one that handed the keys to your enemy.

But let's get back to how I learned all this, firsthand...

When one group of scientists visited in less formal settings, I was still allowed to remain in the room, rather than nestled into the back of the coat closet like I had been when superiors on the administrative and strategy side visited. There was a clear separation between the group from those labs and their superiors. The lab workers were tight-knit and kept their own secrets within their part of the hierarchy. I would be just another secret to add to their list.

That was when I first sat with the cohort of primarily military-captive scientists for a long series of dinner table discussions that would end up spanning the early years of my childhood in the country. It's where I first heard them endlessly discuss plans and ideas for potential longer-running projects. When it came to one topic of discussion, the energy and drive behind the excitement in their voices were enough to capture my attention. They strategized about combining walking pneumonia with an incurable disease so that it would slowly sink into the entire population. They wanted an incurable pneumonia that no effective vaccine could be created for, and that people would pass between each other without becoming immediately incapacitated.

They actually wanted the endgame - something that even they, with their scientific expertise, could not cure once it was released. They discussed the Epstein–Barr virus and a slew of other viruses back then, still undecided on the perfect one.

They had no loyalties. Their own countries had abandoned them and they were forced to work for the enemy. For them, life was already over. They simply wanted to take everyone else out with them.

I'll be honest. There were days when I would come to agree with them, but not due to hate or vengeance. After seeing the never-ending harm done to the children (you'll see more of what I'm referring to in a bit) by a culture that feeds on its own youth, I saw no way to save those children or myself. How can you save them if their own parents, communities, and nations are their exploiters and the ones selling them to additional exploiters in exchange for a head pat and a little extra cash? There's nowhere safe for the children to grow. In those dark moments when I lost my humanity and aligned with the scientists, it wasn't due to hate. It was love. I saw it as a mercy killing. The only way to end the children's pain.

If you're an ordinary citizen, hardcore war-borne nihilism may be difficult to comprehend because you still have something to live for - family, country, the future. The people ripped from war have none of that. It was stolen from them. They are the people you should be concerned about handing your safety to. They are not you. They are the ones who will always stand on the bridge while burning it because they are already on fire. And this entire world is their bridge to the frivolous and unthinking civilization that turns its back and leaves them to toil in the war machine. Your knee-jerk response is to take this lightly or avert from it. Don't. It's not an empty threat from those you have safely chained. No one is attempting to scare you in order to gain a ransom from you. You already handed everything to them - the money and the ability to maneuver within your own military, to exploit you without needing your further consent.

It is the reality of what has already been going on this entire time, tangibly, with funding, and unchecked.

I sat quietly over my plate of roast beef and mashed potatoes and listened to the scientists talk about creating their theoretical hybrid viruses, something I was raised to refer to as sane and unconcerning dinner conversation. There are reasons I would develop stomach ulcers as a child. The fact that the scientists' experiences had correctly led them to believe funding was available for such obviously reckless research is as concerning now as it was then.

Maneuverings

The closest thing to magic that humanity has is lies.
And it's one of the worst kinds of magic,
because it claims the truth is a lie
while still leaving it there to suffer,
unchanged and in its original form
- the truth -
while the world believes the lies.

During that first year in the United States, a woman at the local Vital Statistics office in charge of birth and death certificates happily accepted a large and unofficial pile of money to register my "birth in the United States" three years after I was born (another grating pain in my life because it often gets flagged as false, due to that three-year discrepancy of having a birth certificate that says 1977 on it but is filed in the 1980 birth records book, in an office that is never more than three weeks behind in filing). She thought she was helping a child war victim temporarily hide in the United States, but she was also profiting from the situation. I stood on my toes and strained to see the exchange of the document and the large stack of cash in the worker's kitchen. I was barely even tall enough to see the top of that kitchen table.

When the woman who illegally adopted me refused to return me after the war, even the Vital Statistics worker walked away in anger, although still feeling the tug of self-preservation and the distressing chains of having been ensnared as a willing actor in trafficking. She continued to help with the coverup for as long as she could, albeit from more of a distance. When she was still alive, she was who we would reach out to for fixing things when even her own office refused to acknowledge the misnumbered and misfiled certificate as genuine.

Eventually, she died of old age, still carrying the secret that had been forced upon me. Managing to get proof of my "legal" existence became more difficult after that point. It

would become a tangled mess of conning, coercing, and guiding bureaucrats, forging and replicating documents when they were not available, and not-always-successful attempts at timing official requests perfectly for when the most malleable workers were in the office.

Other than that extra work and inconvenience, the identity still functioned on and off for a while. The record was there, in an official office (when the document could be located in the wrong section of records), and U.S. culture and government are permissive of that, especially since additional documentation was procured in that same year when I was three. A name change document was also attained. It was applied for because two official documents were needed to acquire any further documentation, such as a social security number, which was also eventually attained successfully, later that year. Without a hospital record, and with only the late-filed birth certificate as documentation, a name change document for a minor clerical-level alteration was the easiest and most affordable second one to pursue, since the priest at the local church refused to get involved and create a retroactive baptismal document.

As I got older, getting them to reliably certify my forged birth certificate would eventually become such a hindrance that, as an adult, I would go outside of what was familiar to me and would seek additional citizenship in a third country just to have documents that were reliably and properly filed somewhere on this earth. The bureaucratic portion of the process to gain that citizenship took over five years instead of the standard six months - because for five years straight no one in the U.S. Vital Statistics office could locate my birth certificate in their records to confirm its existence to my new nation.

Five years into that delay, l finally gave in and walked a new U.S. Vital Statistics clerk through the process of finding my certificate where it resides, in the wrong year's record book, and had her set aside a copy of that certificate on the office counter next to the phone in expectation of a call from the foreign embassy, a call which I was scheduling at the same time. From there, the approval for my new citizenship was processed in less than a month. If it will remain valid is uncertain, because it was based on a forgery. But as of this writing, it's at least been less of a hassle.

The coercive recruiter's own family was angry with her for breaking conventions and not returning me when the war was over. Her solution? When I was barely four years old, she told me the whole family had gotten together in two large tour buses to come to visit me, and that those buses had been run off the road in a storm, killing all of them in one go, except for a few of her immediate local family members (two sons she did not have custody of, her mother, a sister, and a cousin who lived near Yale). I don't know what she told the rest of her family about me, but I spent a lot of time hidden away behind coats in closets when they came by unannounced, which they often did because many of her aunts, uncles, cousins, etc. lived in the area.

My life became very limited and unprotected. I was nothing more than a convenient tool for a psychopath who had lost her own biological children due to her dangerous and unethical exploitation of them. Her ex-husband, a naval intelligence officer, removed them from her care after he discovered she had brought them to South and Central America with her as cover while on a government operation. He found out that she had her small sons helping with manual labor during large-scale drug harvests, a behavior she thought was logical and cute. Now, I was a replacement for those children, *and even her own family was no longer there to protect me.*

Strategists & Blackmail

Before I delve too much further into my early years, I'll ask that you don't get too hung up on the personal aspects of the low-level individual abuse and exploitation that make up some of the next few chapters. I'll only highlight a few instances as examples to lead to a deeper understanding of the larger landscape. They are not where this is leading, but they are some of the stones on which the path is set.

I don't need pity regarding the parts that involve myself, and honestly, I wouldn't know what to do with pity. It's an uncomfortable type of emotion to respond to. There is already a high level of discomfort simply in sharing some instances (and I've left many of the worst ones out due to that squeamishness - for the sake of the reader as well as myself). Abuses in this stage are some of the most difficult topics to write about, and potentially the most discrediting. It's much easier to believe a child has an active imagination than it is to face the severity and clinical psychopathology of some abuses.

Thus, for a victim, it's often easier to stay in silence about these things rather having to battle twice - once in living through it and again in having to explain it to someone who may choose to lash out in disbelief. One battle is already at an intolerable level without doubling it.

These few early chapters are on my direct interactions with someone who was also interacting much the same way with the world on a larger scale, with nearly unlimited freedom to act and massive military research budgets. As they say, if you give someone a hammer, everything becomes a nail. Their patterns of behavior grow well beyond those felt on an individual level, until they become like an ever-expanding nuclear explosion on the horizon that burns us all.

Problems start small before they grow.

Individual abuses and regional politics are only the first symptoms, although I do wish any part of our global civilization was healthy enough to stop things in the early stages. The fact is it isn't, and thus these next pages exist.

The memories from those early years are a mix of waking nightmares from which there was no escape. I was stuck with the woman I was now forced to call "mother" by society. It turns out that people will easily accept "She has an active imagination" as a reasonable excuse from the adult who you just said was your kidnapper. They accept it just as easily as they accept, "Oh, he's drunk," when referring to a man drugged against his will. I wish I were joking about that. People are very unlikely to help in a situation in which there is even the slightest amount of doubt, personal danger, or a chance of causing an imposition. As I found out firsthand, and was devastated by, this is true even when it involves a nervous child asking for help.

As a child, the worst of those experiences, and one that still stings to this day, happened in a hallway. The recruiter was in a meeting with a man in what may have been a consulate (I'm not entirely sure, but the building did have that feeling and architecture), and I was left alone in the hallway to wait. At that point, I had already spent several months in the recruiter's unlit living room, watching television, and had seen enough public service announcements during the commercials to know that if you are kidnapped, you are supposed to tell an adult or police officer. So, when a woman I had heard speaking Spanish walked by me in that hall, I finally pushed through my massive wall of anxiety and shyness. I stopped her and tried to explain, in Spanish, that the woman I had entered the building with was not my mother and that I had been kidnapped.

Her response left me muted on the subject for years. It removed just about every bit of hope that I had in finding freedom before I was an adult. She told me, "But you'll have good schools here."

She absolutely understood what I had said and yet still chose to do nothing.

My plea for help may have been some of the last words I ever spoke in that language. The utterly devastating betrayal felt in that moment made clinging to Spanish feel pointless. It became a useless language. What is the point of speaking it if that is the response? Even as an adult, I struggle to pick it up again. The deep sense of betrayal and loneliness the sound of the words elicit can be difficult to work through.

Society has been fully trained to err on the side of deferring to deceit. Allowing the government to lie without the need for apology or admittance of guilt within an official's lifetime, on top of that, creates a social seal protecting semi-concealed criminal behavior by authority. It is a seal that is almost impossible to break because everyone does their part to maintain it, even the victims and witnesses.

Remember the story of the fire in Argentina and the behavior of the prisoners, the prison guards, and the witnesses? Ever wonder what level of crime it is to keep several hundred people locked in a burning building because they have a different political ideology than yours? There were hundreds of people there, in all three of the key positions - victim, perpetrator (yes, even authority can wear that crown), and witness. Not one of them unlocked the doors before the bodies were charred. That behavior is par for the course. Many will claim otherwise, but it's still the reality.

Around the time we visited that possible-embassy was also about the time when the recruiter started using me as a door opener. She would send me up to office buildings with security guards that she could not get past, and instruct me to tell the guards that "my mom is inside." That would almost always gain me access, despite my stuttering and inability to answer simple questions such as "Who is your mom?" because I hadn't been told what to say if any questions were asked. From there, I was expected to find certain offices and people and to give them messages or envelopes. It was a fairly simple task, but it wasn't one I was comfortable with nor did I honestly have the people skills and bold personality that were necessary, especially not between the ages of three and six, when the majority of those tasks were thrust on me. As I have come to understand it, the recruiter had used her sons in a similar manner before she lost custody of them. Now, instead of two boisterous boys with each other for support, it was just me facing the task alone. I was too shy to deal with it all and I was terrified.

So, the second time she asked me to do it, I smiled, nodded, and agreed. And then I went and hid under a bush along the pathway to the building for several hours. This would lead her to think I wasn't obedient enough (I was obedient in everything, but sometimes my fear overruled my ability to follow orders). Her thoughts on that would cause her to attempt a variety of overzealous, unethical, and cruel ways to turn me into an obedient little subservient. Methods that would, in some cases, even bring international outcry when used on adults at Guantanamo Bay. She clearly did not comprehend child-rearing, or I simply

wasn't a child to her. I get the feeling, when considering what she would put me through, that she still saw me as more of an enemy combatant. But I'll get into a few of the more oppressive and bizarre methods of control that she attempted, later.

In the meantime, I was brought along to a myriad of labs, clandestine meetings, and for simple ordinary tasks, often among people who had the potential to do as much damage as the person I was there with. Sometimes the lines blurred, and no real distinction could be made between ordinary life and the recruiter's work. One such experience was when we were visiting a man in the late evenings. The two of them would talk in another room while they left me sitting on a barstool in the kitchen watching Tales from the Darkside or The Twilight Zone (I can't honestly remember which, the two shows were so similar) on a small television. It seemed like an ordinary meeting between two people who knew each other, except for the late hour. Even that seemed ordinary enough.

One night when they were taking much too long, the show I was watching ended. I got bored and started wandering the living room. There, I found something that I have since been informed is so rare that it's only heard of in rumors. It was a lampshade with a tattoo. I brought it up to the light and examined it, appreciating how beautiful and flawed it was. When they came into the room, they told me it was made from a woman. The man returned it to the box I found it in. I still loved it and wished I could have a tattoo like the one I saw on it. I was a child. I didn't honestly understand the implications. It was just something slightly unique that stood out in a room that was otherwise standard worn furniture, musty sleeping bags, and classically male with no real care for decor or cleaning. How was I supposed to know that the person the recruiter was speaking to might be directly related to the higher rankings of the German SS? There were no obvious indications other than his choice in lighting. He was the recruiter's age, not the same age as the depressed scientist I had met. He also seemed anything but depressed.

Back in the daylight, the recruiter and a work friend of hers were theatrically whispering together one time while looking at me. I wanted to know what the secret was. So, they told me I was a French princess but I couldn't tell anyone at all, that it was a secret and if people knew there would be grave consequences. I was young. By the end of the week, every kid at my preschool knew I was a "princess." Obviously, the tale they had told me about my being a princess was a lie. They just wanted to know if I could keep a big secret. That was when they decided I couldn't.

As a result, and for other purposes as well, the recruiter would spend her spare moments at home creating a strong and unpleasant-tasting homemade mix of drugs from nature, with datura and poppies among the main ingredients. When she thought she had the mixture right, she would invite me over to where she sat with her mortar and pestle to test it for her. She made me consume that awful mixture by the spoonful. As my vision became that of a carnival mirror room, with my body parts going through uncomfortable waves of seeming both incredibly large and small, she would inform me that I had a fever.

I've had many legitimate fevers in life – what I experienced after I consumed her mixture was not a fever.

What was more concerning than her using a child as the tester for her homemade drug experimentation, was that she was not the only one to go that far. Around that same time, she brought me to a language school somewhere in central Connecticut. As we walked

through a room with sinks on the left and plain children's hospital beds on the right, I became frightened. As I clung closer to her, she told me not to worry, that it would be fine. We passed through that room and, eventually, I was brought to another. I crawled up onto the examination chair and they restrained me.

They talked amongst themselves about how children don't remember, how what they were doing was more humane than leaving us attached to an inferior language and a memory full of atrocities. I get the feeling they were only trying to hide behind enough professionalism and false concern to convince themselves.

What would follow was a series of strong electrical shocks directly to my temples, simultaneously on both sides, an absolutely excruciating process from which I squirmed, desperately trying to find any escape from the pain. I discovered that if I squirmed just enough that they were not exactly equal on my temples, and if they pressed against the edge of the bone of my skull rather than the soft and unprotected flesh of my temples, then the pain was slightly diminished. Thus, I fought to squirm down and tilt my head that little extra bit. If you look at my temples even today, the electrical burn scars are still there and one is a little higher than the other. I had succeeded. However, even my attempt to escape some of the pain was not enough to stop the voltage from doing its job.

Eventually, the pain would become so intense that it would leave, and I would find myself in this white, empty, seemingly vast space inside my head. There was no language there; it appeared like emptiness, and my thoughts functioned freely in it without words, making boundless connections. I found it beautiful. I wish I'd never been in the situation to discover it, but it was beautiful. When back "home" with that woman I was now forced to call "mom," I would often wander into the back garden alone, sit in the grass or on a rock, and reminisce about that vivid empty space in my mind and how free my thoughts had been without the constraints of language with its limited and fixed definitions. I grew to hate the concept of language and its imposed limitations.

As for the language school part, it was indeed a school in the sense that, after wiping our minds nearly as clean as snow, they taught us. I met some of the other children who had occupied the beds I'd seen when I first entered the space. I spent long hours side-by-side with them as the teachers brought us through the entire English language, reading and reciting the words in groups and in order until we knew the language better than the native speakers in the area.

And as for my Argentine-government-approved kidnapper's particular homemade mixture of drugs, she eventually discovered that an effective way to hide it was in chocolate and strong beverages. She would mix it into my hot chocolate, which she made with copious amounts of intensely-flavored unsweetened dark baker's chocolate, heated milk, and honey. I began to become anxious about how I would feel after consuming a beverage she had given me, and I started to switch our drinks. It took me a while to realize it was only in the thicker beverages. I wasted quite a few of my attempts at sleight of hand on switching our water glasses.

Despite my novice lack of attention to details, by determination and luck, I finally got it right.

I switched our mugs of hot chocolate while she had her back turned, with her attention on a rarity - a bear and cub outside the kitchen window. When she returned to the table, we drank. Several minutes later, I stood in that kitchen horrified, as she began to act like a panicked and trapped wild animal, fighting both me and the drugs. She clawed at me with her nails still dirty with turpentine and garden soil. I stood panicked and frozen until eventually running to hide in my room for hours. The long red scratches she left on one of my arms would inflame and infect long before they healed. She tried to drug me again to forget the incident, but pain holds memories more tightly than a mother holds her child. The soreness of the swollen scratches and the rapid beating of my heart from heightened anxiety sliced right through the fog of the drugs.

Mind you, the recruiter didn't always need to be drugged in order to go through fits of rage. Every few months, I would wake up to loud smashing in the kitchen, as she would spend at least an hour systematically going through and throwing each plate at the floor until the entire kitchen was covered in broken dishes, and only two dishes and two cups remained (even in these odd fits of rage, she still remembered to leave us just enough to eat and drink from). During the cacophony of her screams and the sounds of breaking glass and ceramic plates, I would sneak outside and go to the edge of the property to avoid becoming a victim.

She eventually began to test her homemade drug on adults, with varying results. When I was along, she would make sure I knew which drink was mine, often by marking it in a way I would recognize. So, even if we were all taking Coke bottles from the same ice bucket, I would know to look for the one with a small indent on it. Sometimes, she used that method to drug me. Other times she used it to drug everyone else, leaving me there sober and aware as the people in the room began to act strange or drop their faces into their plates. If I was drugged or if everyone else was genuinely depended on the situation, what her goal was, and who needed to be compliant for that goal to be reached.

The drugs would cause some of her targets to become compliant and some to become violent. She brought them to the house in both conditions and maneuvered them in front of a shiny silver tarp that was hung on a wall. There, she would pose me with them for inappropriate photographs, and use the Polaroid photos for blackmail. One of them was Joseph, a man the recruiter had intentionally moved in next door to on Judd Farm Road around the time I was turning five years old. He was the head sheriff for New Haven County at that time. I was never comfortable with the situation, and I will never be comfortable enough to discuss any of those situations in detail.

No matter how many times I was told it was fine and normal, I was never comfortable in any of those situations.

By then, I had already been present when the haggard-looking woman from Argentina was shot at point-blank range after she came to the United States to confront the woman who had stolen me from my country.

She drove up in her wood-paneled station wagon and parked behind the office of the raw materials plant we were frequently at during that time period (the industry-massive piles of sand and other raw construction and concrete materials were an effective cover for major drug smuggling, primarily cocaine, being done by the business owner). The recruiter told us kids, myself and the children of the owner, to hide on the ground floor of the building. My friends found spots to hide. I stood frozen in the center of a room, not that far from the back door. The recruiter, my false mother, went through that door to the rear of the building and got into a screaming match with the woman who was likely one of my actual family members. Then I heard something that sounded a lot like thunder but not really. What I had heard were shots fired from the recruiter's handgun.

After the shots rang out, the recruiter came flying through the building, her hands shaking (ironic that she could poison and bomb people without flinching but that pulling the trigger on a gun made her visibly shaken, but that's how human psychology is - killing is often easy and elating except when its a combination of immediate and personal). She pushed us kids in the direction of the side door. The few other people who had been in the office ran to get into the company owner's pickup truck and another vehicle. We all sped away. I asked why we were leaving in such a hurry. Someone, probably the recruiter, told me it was because there was a dangerous storm coming. From the open back of the pickup truck, I looked up into the sky. It was blue. There wasn't a cloud in sight. I never spoke about it, but I knew we weren't running from the weather that day.

I still wonder how the deceased woman who had driven the station wagon was related to me. I often think of her as my grandmother. We age the same, something that I both adore in that I can now see the reflection of family when I look in the mirror and also abhor because it comes along with etched lines in my skin.

She wasn't the only would-be savior of mine who I saw harmed or worse. The guilt ate at me. So did the growing sense of loneliness.

Domestic Research Subject Recruitment

We're a world of individuals and nations
attempting to make real moves for survival,
based on fictitious information and half-truths
about concealed dangers.
The results are disastrous, painful to watch, and often fatal.

It is impossible to walk a path to safety when
you've been blindfolded and lied to about
where every stone in that path is placed.

I was moved around frequently and kept out of sight of many of the recruiter's family and superiors. I had been hidden away for months at a time in a series of military camps and often-expensive schools. The recruiter rarely let me stay at one school for more than a few months, and I was frequently absent entirely for months, and sometimes years, at a time (I once missed two and a half years of school in a row, between the beginning of fifth grade and the latter half of seventh grade). It felt like being given an in-depth tour of every type of educational model. I can confirm that some are, indeed, better than others.

I do not recommend the by-rote Prussian model of "education" adopted by many public school systems, nor the modernized and infantilized version of Montessori education - although the original Montessori model offers some serious advantages for students in the early years of education. What I recommend the most is a method that does not appear to exist in modern education - one that allows and promotes true analytical thinking and creativity within the sciences by the students, without treating the field as if it were an infallible and untouchable altar to worship at. In order to learn, in order to teach children to learn, we must first admit to them that we are still learning and do not know everything already.

Out of the habit and conveniences offered to a medical research recruiter, my mother-by-illegal-adoption also stowed me away on clinical wings of pharmaceutical company campuses for long residential trials, primarily of cancer drugs for which my medical documents were altered by her to make it appear that I had a wide variety of cancer types so that she could have the added benefit of collecting the payments that were being given to the parents of volunteers.

The recruiter would forge my medical records to match the "disease of the day" and sign me into paid medical research, primarily via her connections and the list of research participation opportunities that they kept in the office of the Yale Medical Research Department. She had connections to that department going back to the 1960s, according to officially published medical articles citing her, using her then-married name, as a researcher for the Yale Medical Library.

World Biomedical Journals, 1951–60:

A Study of the Relative Significance of 1,388 Titles Indexed in *Current List of Medical Literature*

Research and Development, Yale University Library, and formerly Librarian, Yale Medical Library, for housing the project and for computer assistance; to Dr. Colin White, Professor of Public Health (Biometry), Department of Epidemiology and Public Health, Yale School of Medicine, for statistical counsel; to Richard Bigelow, Computer Programmer, Yale Medical Library, for the programs yielding index computations and tabular listings; to analysts Shirley Chance, Barbara Codeanne, Eva Creighton, Karen Eberhardt, Brian Forrest, Martha Kilgour, Mary Parham, Diane Pellman, Ann Rodnick, and Wendy Shingler for their

Image Source: National Library of Medicine

"World Biomedical Journals… Acknowledgements:… Yale Medical Library, for the programs yielding index computations and tabular listings; to analysts (omitted) Mary Parham, (omitted) and (omitted) for their citation gathering…"

Text Source: National Library of Medicine[28]

She would sign me into the highest-paying research programs, which at the time primarily focused on childhood epilepsy and cancer - two conditions I did not have.

One epilepsy researcher did mention to me, in a worried voice, that he thought the recruiter might have Munchausen by Proxy once he realized I did not have the condition he was doing his research on. I assured him that she wasn't sick. She just wanted the money. In retrospect, maybe I shouldn't have added that insight if I wanted help.

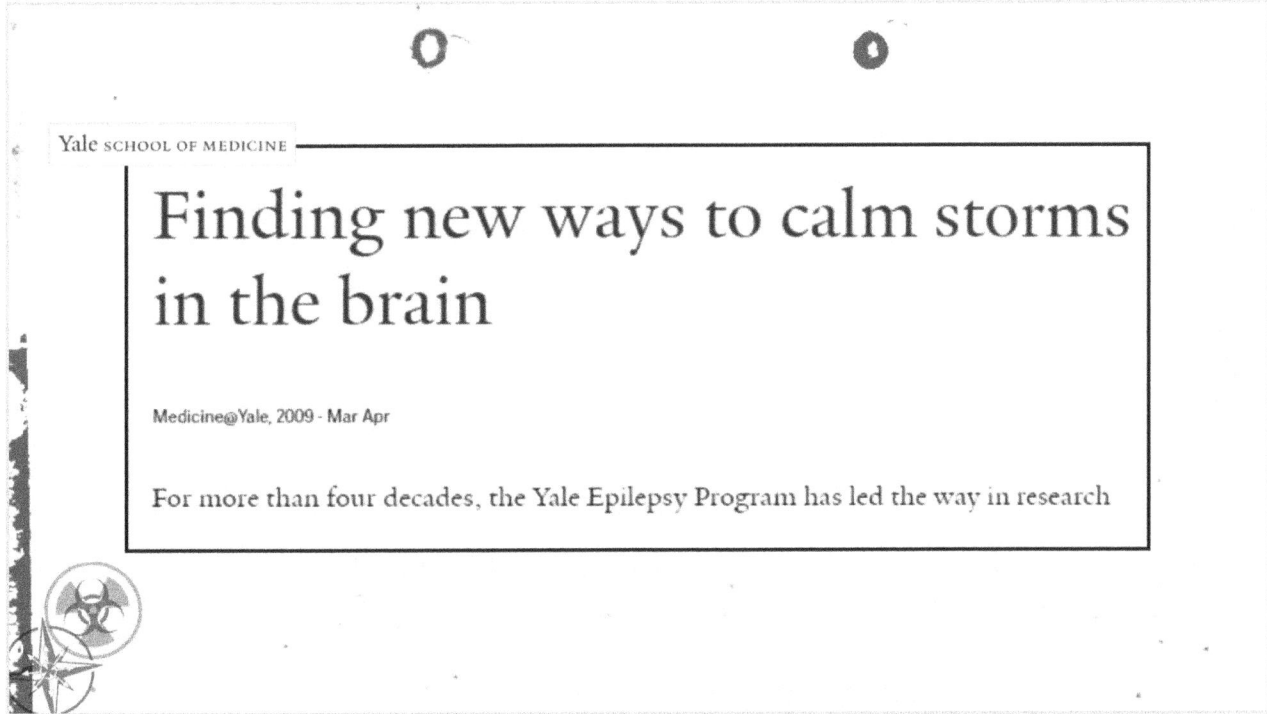

Yale SCHOOL OF MEDICINE

Finding new ways to calm storms in the brain

Medicine@Yale, 2009 - Mar Apr

For more than four decades, the Yale Epilepsy Program has led the way in research

Image Source: Yale School of Medicine

---

[28] National Library of Medicine, World Biomedical Journals, 1951-60: A Study of the Relative Significance of 1,388 Titles Indexed in Current List of Medical Literature, https://www.ncbi.nlm.nih.gov/pmc/articles/PMC198399/pdf/mlab00175-0028.pdf

"For more than four decades, the Yale Epilepsy Program has led the way in research."

Text Source: <u>Yale School of Medicine</u>[29]

There are official state child abuse and medical records from that time confirming that I didn't have epilepsy and that the recruiter was faking it in me (images of records can be found below). The social workers were never able to locate me to speak to me directly. The recruiter kept me hidden and out of school in those years.

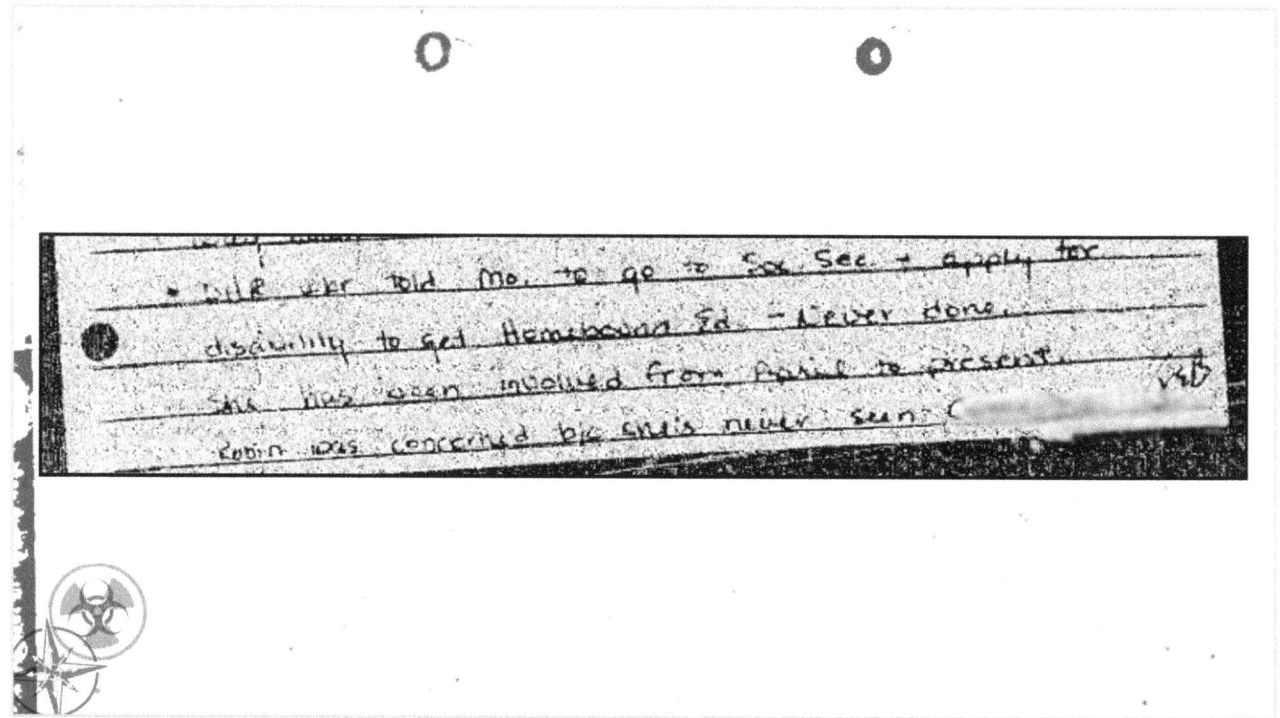

Image Source: Personal File, State of Connecticut Department of Children and Youth Services

"DHR worker…Robin was concerned because she has never seen (child)."

Text Source: Personal File, State of Connecticut Department of Children and Youth Services[30]

---

[29] Yale School of Medicine, Finding New Ways to Calm Storms in the Brain, https://medicine.yale.edu/news/medicineatyale/article/finding-new-ways-to-calm-storms-in-the/

[30] State of Connecticut Department of Children and Youth Services, Author's Personal File - Child Abuse Investigation Report

So, if anyone thinks I'm a diabolical manipulative mastermind and have been since early childhood (that same "child criminal" concept Argentina and other genocidally-inclined nations are convinced of), and that I make up cruel stories about the saint who illegally adopted me and brought me over international borders, you can stop it now. I had zero influence over the investigation the social workers did which led them to believe the recruiter was fabricating illnesses for me to have. The case was first opened when a school reported me truant. I was not involved. I wasn't even present in the school to be questioned - that's why the case was opened. The only people the social workers ever spoke to were doctors, the recruiter, and possible new schools to send me to.

I do wish that I had somehow known those were the years to reach out to Child Protective Services myself, to reach a particular social worker I didn't know the name of, and to highlight - among all the abuse I was going through - the Munchausen by Proxy aspects. Because if I had, it might have triggered them to do something more. Unfortunately, most victims are kept in the dark and won't know the exact moment of an opportunity that could have potentially saved them.

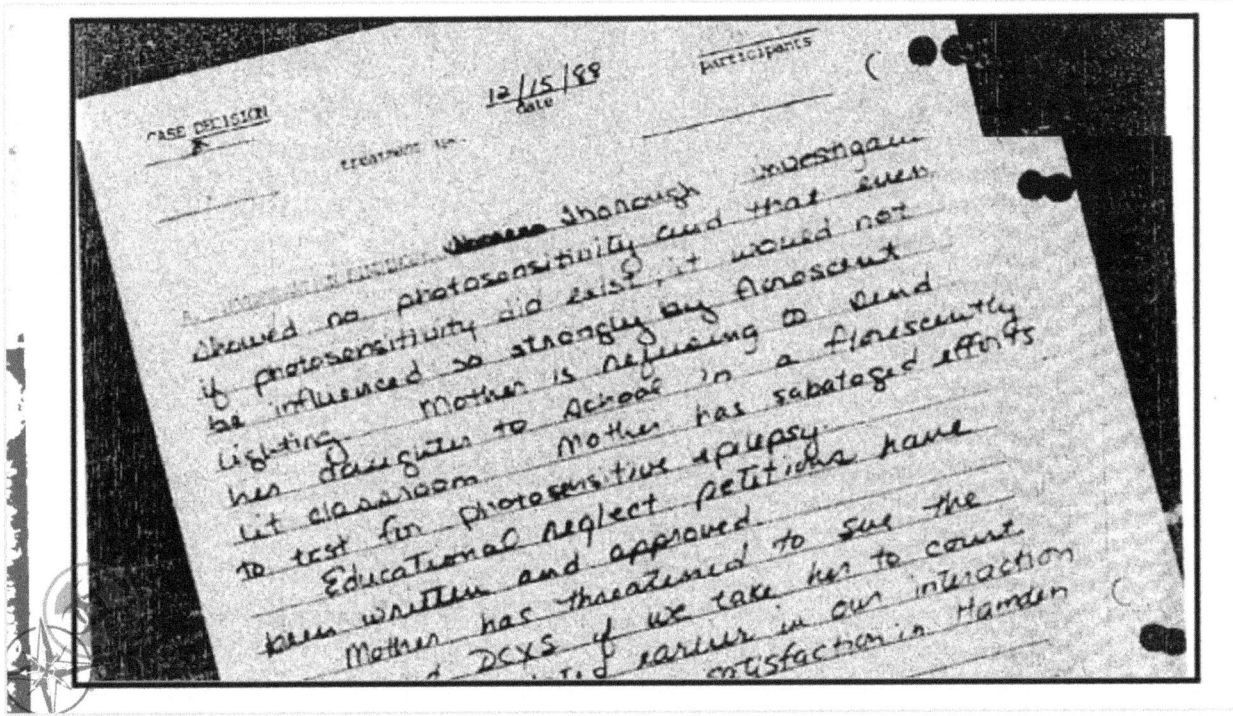

Image Source: Personal File, State of Connecticut Department of Children and Youth Services

"Thorough investigation showed no photosensitivity and that even if photosensitivity did exist, it would not be influenced so strongly by fluorescent lighting. Mother is refusing to send her daughter to school in a fluorescently lit classroom. Mother has sabotaged efforts to test for photosensitive epilepsy...Mother is threatening to sue if we take her to court."

Text Source: Personal File, State of Connecticut Department of Children and Youth Services[31]

While I would note that Child Protective Services cowardly closed the case after being threatened with a lawsuit by a Yale-affiliated "parent," despite my still being missing, I should probably dive in to something more relevant to the recruiter's long-game. So, I'll explain what the ridiculous circus she was bringing the social workers through was actually about. Her strange claims that it was fluorescent lighting that induced my "epilepsy" were part of a very well-thought-out con. She wanted to visit multiple schools in the area under the pretense of being a concerned parent of a potential student. Access to the social workers - the gatekeepers of children and thus the school system - gave her a way to do exactly that.

She would tell each school that she wanted to "see the lighting in the classrooms," and there would be the authority of a social worker there to back up her absurd requests and claims. That would get her through the door during school hours. Once in the classrooms, she would seek out potential impoverished students who might fit the medical research recruitment requirements for the same high-paying programs she was signing me into. Running only one child through the programs wasn't enough of a payout for her.

If she saw a student who interested her, she would tell the head of the school that she was interested in having me attend there, and that she would like to go to a parent-teacher night to meet the teachers and school community to make sure it was truly a good fit for her significantly intellectually disabled special-needs daughter (a definition of me that she had given to the social workers and that they had simply accepted). There, she would locate the parents of a child she was interested in and would begin her deceptive recruitment tactics, turning up the charm and posing as a philanthropist from Yale.

---

[31] State of Connecticut Department of Children and Youth Services, Author's Personal File - Child Abuse Investigation Report

I was the model child she would use when she was recruiting those children into "opportunity programs" that didn't actually exist. She would point to my ballet lessons and large vocabulary as part of a rags-to-riches success story. It was simply her tricking the parents into signing over enough medical rights buried in contracts she would call "permission forms" so that she could gain the written authority to sign their kids into much of the same paid epilepsy, cancer, and other research she was signing me into.

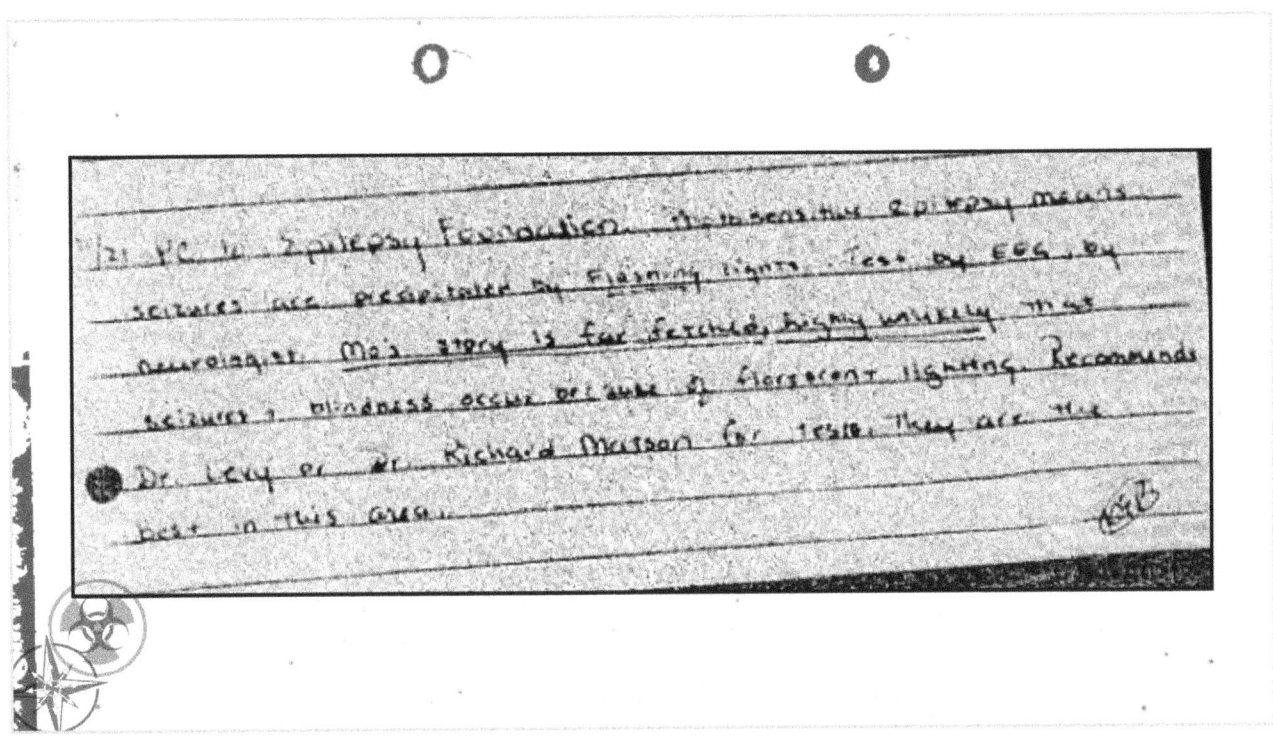

Image Source: Personal File, State of Connecticut Department of Children and Youth Services

"Mother's story is far-fetched and highly unlikely that seizures and blindness occur because of fluorescent lighting."

Text Source: Personal File, State of Connecticut Department of Children and Youth Services[32]

I watched as kids were convinced they were headed to summer camp. Each parent was told that their kid had been approved for a full scholarship/grant to cover the costs and would be attending summer programs at Yale for free. The recruiter informed them that the

---

[32] State of Connecticut Department of Children and Youth Services, Author's Personal File - Child Abuse/Neglect Investigation Report

programs would give their child the exceptional opportunity to meet rich and influential people who would help that child's career. The parents always signed. Then the kids were bused to university hospitals or pharmaceutical companies to be hooked up to chemo IVs or worse, often with creative ways to keep them in the dark, such as telling commercial pharmaceutical researchers they were dealing with "child cancer patients who don't know they have cancer because it's better for them psychologically if they don't, so let's all pretend this is a summer camp for them, the poor things." i.e., cons within cons, blanketed in the good intentions of complacent adults who participated in the harm done to us for profit. And how gullible they thought children were? How little they thought of us when they came up with their lies? I don't know about you, but I've never seen a traditional summer camp with rows of beds with IV poles next to them and I hope I never will.

The children's cancer treatment drug trials were depressing. In one case, the recruiter convinced colleagues of hers to also enroll one of their adopted children into the program. He was a boy roughly around my age. The odds of us both having the same type of rare cancer, which neither of us knew we had, is not in our pediatric medical records, and we've never even been told the name of as adults so that we could inform our own doctors about it... Those odds are simply impossible, especially considering that his adoptive parents at least appeared competent. In other words, it was just a scam to get the significant monetary payouts the pharmaceutical company was giving to parents. We didn't have cancer.

I had to sit there in one of the little hospital beds, next to my friend, as he talked about what he thought was a summer camp we had been signed into. They had lied to him and drugged him before sending him into the building. The happiness in his voice hurt my head and broke my heart as the particularly noxious chemotherapy drugs entered my veins.

Those chemicals in my bloodstream caused an instant deep and sinking darkness that took over my whole world and perception. All of the remaining good, health, and lightness left my mind and body in an instant. It was replaced by a dragging weight and an intense sense of hopelessness and dread. The world actually looked darker.

Through the windows by our beds, we could see a hill that led down behind the building. We begged so much to be allowed to play on it, that one day they finally caved in and let us. I attempted to gather the other children and have them run down the hill with me to escape.

A few followed for a bit, but the tall dry grass and forest were unforgiving, prickly, and rough, especially to children made oversensitive by what was nothing more than human testing for medically prescribed chemical poisoning. They were also concerned about breaking the rules - the adults were poisoning them, quite literally, chemotherapy is poison and the early-stage-research chemotherapy running through our veins certainly was - but they still felt the compulsion to obey and the fear of consequences if they did not. We have had actual survival conditioned out of us before the age of ten.

By the time I reached the road at the bottom of the hill, I was the only one who hadn't turned around and given up.

Security guards from the pharmaceutical company building drove by and collected me shortly after. People do not feel the need to act humanely if the harm they are doing is being covered with a lie of care or assistance. I assure you, poisoning a child for a cash payout or research funding is neither care nor is it assistance.

I saw kids die from the research. Not from health conditions. From the research. I also bet there are several out there who are considered certifiably insane if they've mentioned the trauma of "IVs at summer camp" and tried to process how that happened. Never mind the ones that were placed into DoD research, and that did happen. Sometimes, I come across one who was clearly damaged and cannot come to terms with it. Most of them turn to drugs or eventually fall into psychosis. This culture we live in, this society, was not made to support the victims of the crimes it hides. It eventually just finishes them off and mows them under.

It is so much easier for people to believe that what is wrong with a victim comes from the internal and not from abuse. Case and point: The recruiter told Child Protective Services, people who should know to look for signs of abuse, that I was extremely learning disabled.

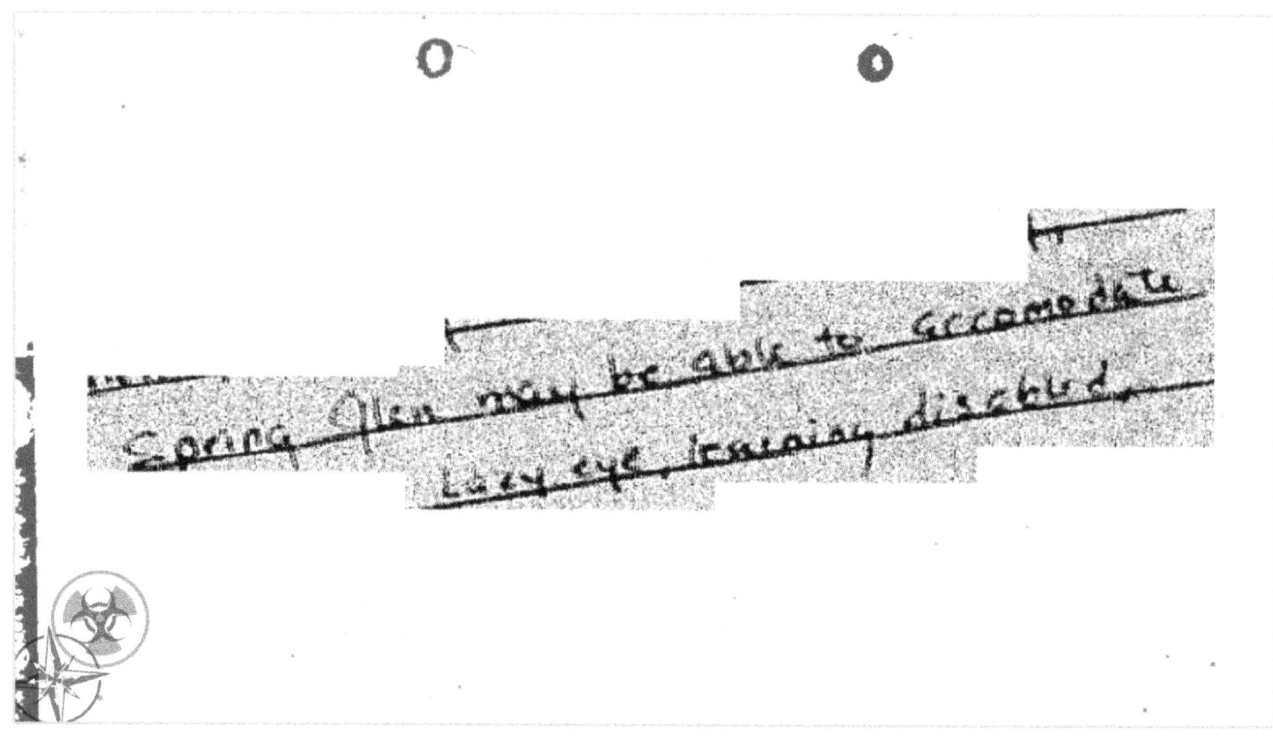

Image Source: Personal File, State of Connecticut Department of Children and Youth Services

"Spring Glen (school) may be able to accommodate...

Lazy eye, learning disabled."

Text Source: Personal File, State of Connecticut Department of Children and Youth Services[33]

Child Protective Services never even questioned it, nor did they ask the teachers or administration at my prior school who could have confirmed that I was an ordinary student with B grades at the time. It was a private Catholic school that didn't accept children with learning disabilities. They didn't have the resources set up to do so. The blunder of not knowing or looking into this was made despite CPS being trained to investigate signs of child abuse and endangerment. Silencing a child by falsely claiming they're too dumb to speak is a major red flag. Yet, tactics like that have become so pervasive in society as a whole that even professionals have trained themselves to ignore the signs.

---

[33] State of Connecticut Department of Children and Youth Services, Author's Personal File - Child Abuse/Neglect Investigation Report

I promise that I'm not, nor have I ever been, learning disabled. I missed nearly half of the total years of schooling before university and still managed to fight my way to the top portion of the class nearly every time I returned. I'm also writing this for you right now, with post-graduate credentials, while working in a country that is not my own, and keeping a large apartment directly by the sea. I am not learning disabled. Quite the opposite. There is nothing wrong with me other than the damage I wear from this life and my rather conversational use of commas.

The recruiter "visiting schools for her disabled daughter" was entirely a con only intended to recruit. She went through at least half a dozen schools. She never sent me to any of them. I was rarely even in the New Haven area at that time. She was utilizing me elsewhere.

Many times, elsewhere was obviously in a research hospital or a pharmaceutical company's facilities. As I mentioned, she kept the monetary payments that resulted from the children (myself included) "volunteering" in medical research. I paid with my health. I've had unnecessary chemo, MRIs, radiation therapy, bone biopsies, and more while my actual health problems were usually neglected because standard childhood medical appointments do not come with a stipend/payment for the adult to collect.

Oh, and the thing about "the mother sabotaging efforts" that the social worker mentioned in their first notes I referenced (three images above). They may have been referring to when the recruiter drugged me to an excessive poisoning level before an electroencephalogram (EEG) with every substance she could find that might induce a seizure, in the hopes of having something akin to an epileptic seizure show up on the scan.
It didn't. I still didn't have a seizure. I've never had a seizure in my life.

I did, however, develop cancer shortly after a series of very destructive chemotherapy and a separate trial looking into altering immune system response via changes to hormone levels.

The tumors I developed from that would eventually be discovered by doctors later when I was in my teens. The recruiter told them not to inform me "because it might make the cancer patient sad" and neglected to have it treated because it would cost her in both effort

and money. There were no research programs for the particular type of cancer that would have paid her to enroll me and allow them to treat the condition.

A lab assistant, who I knew socially through a friend, rushed out of the hospital when he spotted me walking alone on the sidewalk, and he was the one who informed me that I had cancer. I didn't believe him. I assumed he had my file confused with some random cancer patient's. My stomach hurt frequently, and I was always tired, but there were so many other legitimate reasons for both of those at that time in my life.

Years later, when I was residing in another part of the country in my early twenties, the pain became unbearable. I saw a doctor there and was referred to a surgeon who removed the still-growing cancerous mass from my stomach. He found it latched on between my womb and intestines. That was the painful tug I had felt every time I had anxiety. When my stomach muscles tightened in an anxious moment, it would pull at the healthy tissue and surrounding organs. It wasn't until after the surgery that I learned that anxiety doesn't have to physically hurt.

One of the easier medical research projects I was sent to as a child was as a test subject for a new type of MRI machine being used on humans for the first time. They needed healthy female test subjects and were willing to pay several thousand dollars for only a few hours of a participant's time. The recruiter signed me up quickly, added a few years to my age on the form so that I would qualify, and came along to ensure that I made it to the appointment. She let me wear makeup that day.

The MRI machine scan picked up the problem with my neck that had most likely resulted from the leap my mother had taken before I was born. The doctors made a quick emergency consultation, showing us the results and stating that I would need to have several of my vertebrae fused. The recruiter smiled, nodded, and agreed to bring me to a specialist. Then she double-drugged me on the way home so I wouldn't remember, and never brought me to any follow-up appointments for my spine. I only recall the walk from the research hospital because the amount of drugging that day made me so incredibly nauseous that the agony of it broke through the pharmaceutically-induced amnesia wall. While I do not appreciate the level of medical neglect the recruiter put me through, nor her outlandish and overdone methodologies, in this one case I am happy she did not listen to the doctors. No one needs metal fusing their vertebrae.

Decades later, in Italy, I would go to a specialist on my own to see why my neck had always hurt. When he showed me the results of my MRI (the first image below), it took everything in me to remain quiet and not look like a crazy person by mentioning the drugging, medical abuse, and the fact that I'd seen that exact issue with my neck on an MRI scan before, in a drug haze, with doctors recommending surgically inserting metal, years and years prior.

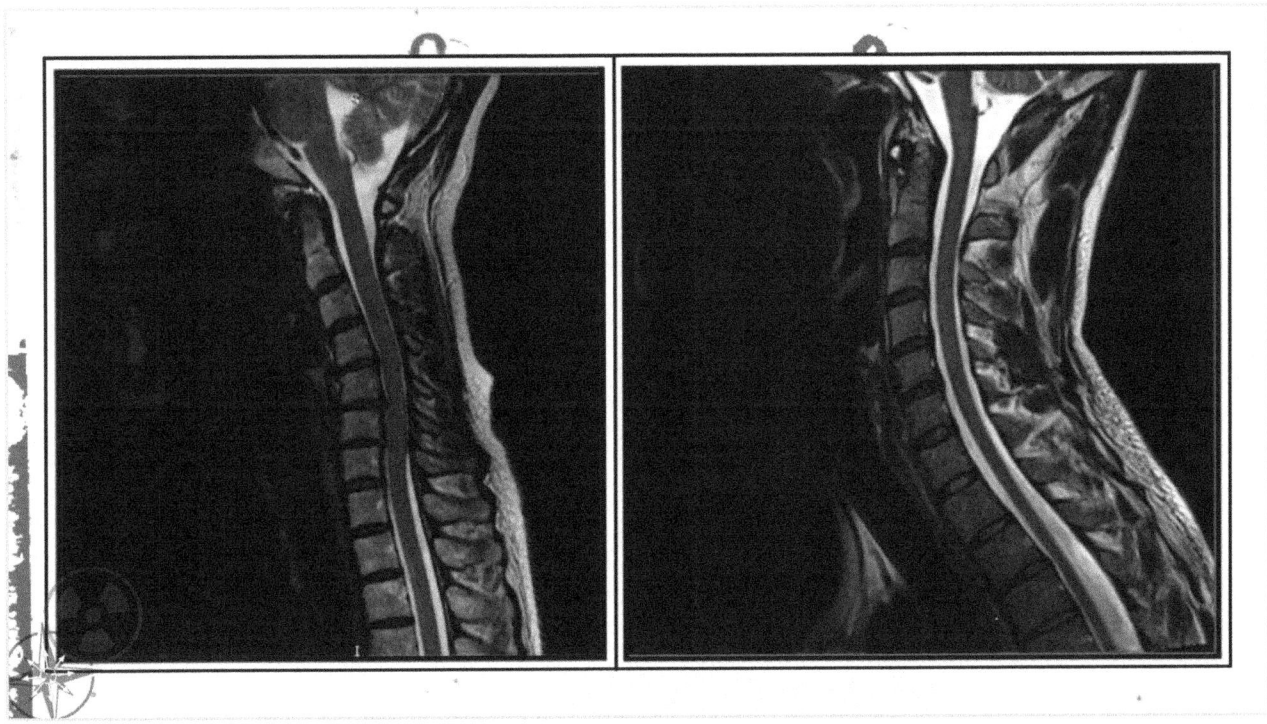

First Image Source: Author's Personal Medical File, Cervical Spine MRI 2018, Age 41[34]

Second Image Source: Example of a Healthy Cervical Spine MRI, Radiopaedia[35]

But that's getting into the future. There are still the years I was growing up in the grasp of a psychopath:

---

[34] Author's Personal Medical File, Cervical Spine MRI 2018, Age 41

[35] Radiopaedia, Normal Cervical Spine, https://radiopaedia.org/cases/normal-cervical-spine-mri-1

There was one cancer research trial that I remember in particular, not because of the treatment itself, but due to it highlighting the distressing but pervasive nature of the individual components of humanity - humans - to hide the deceit of others for their own temporary self-preservation.

While that method of survival may have worked in a world in which we could escape the consequences of our actions simply by running from them, it's an archaic instinct that will result in our demise in the modern world in which implications can travel the globe.

The medical trial was in a clinical setting, and I was sitting in a waiting room with the recruiter. Near us were a mother and child. The child very obviously had cancer. The medical trial was for the type of cancer she had, quite like one would expect in a relatively sane world. The mother, spying the recruiter and I sitting in the waiting room, thought she had found another mother-and-daughter cancer duo. She started to talk to us about the type of cancer and other details. It was clear that she had done her homework and knew as much as she could about the condition her daughter was suffering through.

As she spoke to us and I couldn't answer anything about the cancer - not its name, not what part of my health it would have affected, etc., her eyes began to widen. I could see her processing the information and realizing that I didn't have cancer. In that moment, she knew the woman I was sitting there with was a fraud and about to expose a child to unnecessary and dangerous cancer treatments. I watched that mother closely as the muscles tightened in her neck and she began to turn to look for a nurse or someone else to alert. And then I watched her suddenly pause and look back at her daughter.

Her emotions were so clearly written on her face, with her panicked eyes flickering around the scene as she thought about it all in those few seconds. I could see the exact moment when she decided that her daughter's treatment might be at risk if she reported that the other child in the room was there fraudulently. In that moment, she chose her daughter's life above the safety of a stranger's child. She went silent, stayed in her seat, and didn't alert anyone. I can't entirely blame her. Her daughter was dying and that cancer research trial may have been the best bet she was told she had for recovery.

However, I've seen that exact response and behavior in countless situations with much less extreme potential consequences for the witnesses. They still never did anything to stop the crimes unfolding in front of them.

That's the reality I became faced with when dealing with potentially very harmful and often deadly situations. I could not save myself or anyone else unless I did it on my own, which wasn't always possible although I did try. There was no community support. The community almost always chooses to support the predator, and they do it due to immediate fear. They never seem to think of the long-term consequences of keeping a predator encouraged, well-paid, and thriving within their own community.

It's a flaw in the human mind and one that the predators among us take full advantage of. It gives them the full and complete protection of the herd they feed on. It would take an incredible amount of care and restraint to not take advantage of that. Very few have both care and restraint to that degree.

I needed to share these stories from an unwitting trial participant's perspective because behaviors of abuse and coercion do not change simply because someone capable of damage has a child within reach rather than a nation that day. Much of what was done to me would be done to the world on a wider scale, with many of the same methodologies. It's like research and results. We research on a small scale before we enact the results on a larger scale... and I was living among the scientists. That's how they work.

Abuses are simpler to see when they're still small enough to be in the same room with you. They get harder to pinpoint once they're magnified and obscured through complex policies and backroom maneuverings on a large scale, even if they are planned and enacted by many of the same people.

I wanted to show you some of the mechanisms, mentalities, and behaviors behind the small parts of the explosion before we get to the mushroom cloud on the horizon. That mushroom cloud will be much easier to comprehend this way. You'll know where it ignited, and how. You'll know precisely how the hand moved when it detonated that post-nuclear bomb.

In order to learn about a field, we must start with the building blocks. We must first see that 2 + 2 equals 4 before jumping into differential equations.

Positioning

Chronologically may still be the best way to explain everything, even if it's more personal than I would like. It's been front-loaded with the parts that hit me the most (and I, subsequently, have had a lot to say on those topics). That's the reality of growing up. When we are young, our world is small and we are victims of our immediate surroundings. As we get older, we expand our knowledge and reach until we know and become a part of those surroundings and the larger landscape. However, my small world was sitting on a main artery and poisoning the larger landscape.

At first, it seemed localized enough.

A solution was finally found for the problem of the recruiter having to hide me from her own family. She decided that my new home would be in a series of side offices and safehouses in New Haven, Connecticut. They generally had extra rooms, a shower, and a kitchen. Each one also had a petty cash box. I was expected to record every cent I spent from that box, even if it had been on a 10-cent lemon-flavored candy from the small corner store down the street, so the woman who now owned me for life could be reimbursed for the "business expense" of keeping me.

On top of being her personal errand girl and medical cash cow, I was now also living right under the noses and in the view of whichever government agency or contractor was funding the operations for those locations. Unless anyone in clearance-level accounting offices can genuinely claim they believed it was an adult recording 10-cent midday purchases of lemon and baked bean flavored candies from the corner store. It's somewhat doubtful anyone intelligent enough to be hired for the job would be that dumb.

I was eight years old when we hit New Haven, and ten when I started going to the corner store on my own and the petty cash box procedures for that purpose were introduced to me.

Life in my New Haven accommodations had some interesting moments. Often, the space was ours exclusively, and the recruiter would sleep in the front living room or office like a sentry, despite there usually being an extra bedroom in the back that she could have used, in addition to the one I occupied. Sometimes, we would have unexpected guests when people needed to use the space. I remember coming home one evening to discover roughly twenty-five refugees crammed into the two spacious front rooms, refugees from the same region of political instability that had left me in the hands of the recruiter.

Looking back on it, I wonder if they even knew they were in a government-funded apartment, or if they had been told they were being protected by individual citizens who cared. When they saw the recruiter, did any of them remember her as "Alicia from the Journalism Department" at the University of Buenos Aires and feel relief? Or would that have brought them apprehension?

While sitting there, huddled in my living room, they just looked like a group of people being manipulated and moved around the country until someone could come up with a way to utilize them. History uses a heavy brush as it paints us as radicals and federal agents, as freedom fighters and military, victims and CIA, but it often forgets that we're all just people, as fallible and vulnerable as the next, and thrown into the midst of it all. We still need to eat and to find a soft spot to rest our heads at the end of the night.

Frequently, we slept with our captors.

For a while, things heated up on a personal level as the recruiter was ducking Child Protective Services. She decided to get me out of town. While doing networking on location, she gave me a tent, introduced me to some of the organizers, let me listen in on their conversations, and then left me on my own to spend time on The Great Peace March for Global Nuclear Disarmament, the 1986 3,700-mile walking journey from Los Angeles to Washington D.C.

(Yes, I missed school that year.)

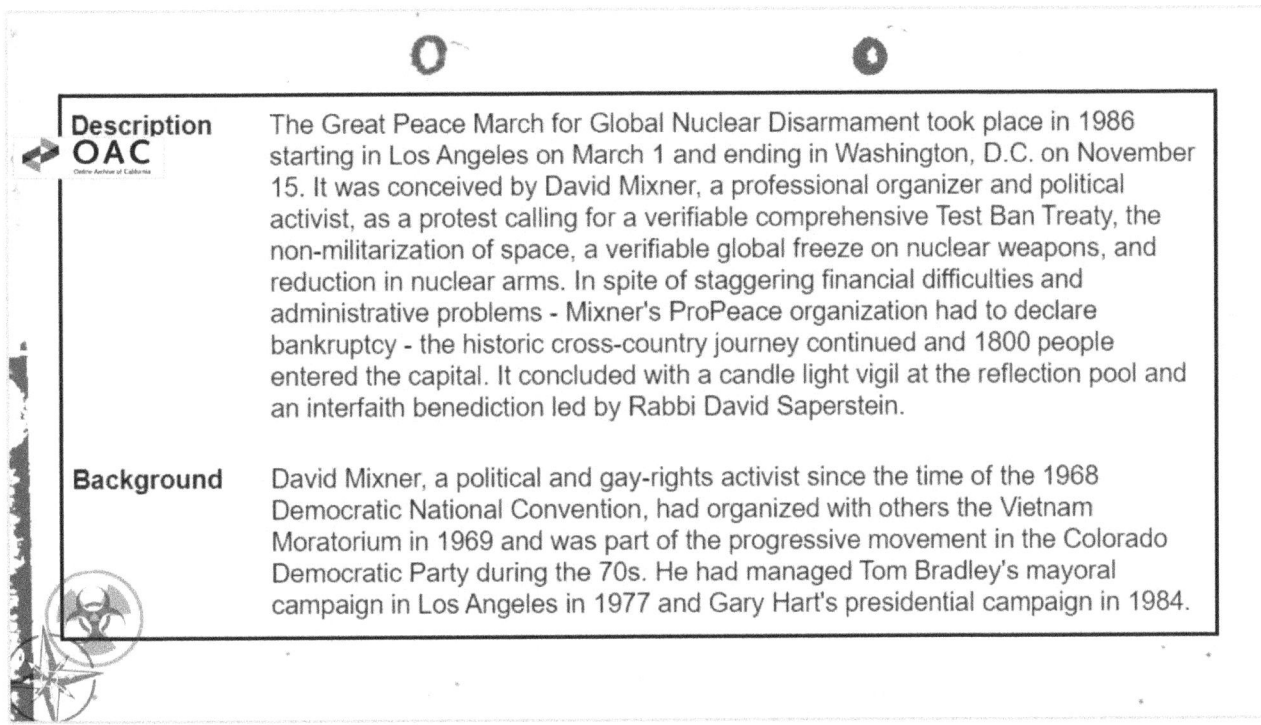

Image Source: <u>Online Archive of California</u>

"The Great Peace March for Global Nuclear Disarmament took place in 1986 starting in Los Angeles on March 1 and ending in Washington, D.C. on November 15. It was conceived by David Mixner, a professional organizer and political activist."

Text Source: <u>Online Archive of California</u>[36]

Let me be very clear in this. While promoted under the banner of a good cause, that peace walk was primarily intended to clean up Los Angeles by relocating a large group of homeless out of the city. The peace walk used celebrity activists as lures and promised the homeless and disenfranchised that if they came along they would have free mobile medical support, a dentist, a mobile post office, shelter to sleep in each night, community, three meals a day, laundry service, access to water, and everything they could need and had struggled to attain.

---

[36] Online Archive of California, Great Peace March Collection, 1985-1986, https://oac.cdlib.org/findaid/ark:/13030/kt8w1006s0/

Image: Peace March Mobile Post Office, 1986, Source, Dan Coogan via Flickr[37]

Image: Great Peace March Mobile Dental Clinic, 1986, Source: Jeff Share[38]

---

[37] Flickr, Great Peace March, Dan Coogan Photographer, https://www.flickr.com/photos/cooganphoto/5903978923/in/album-72157626908632257/

[38] Jeff Share, The Great Peace March for Global Nuclear Disarmament 1986, https://jshare.wixsite.com/jeffshare/peace-march?lightbox=dataItem-j066kaav1

Images: Great Peace March 1986

Source: Jeff Share[39]

All the homeless had to do in exchange was walk each day. The organizers were a modern Pied Piper. Much like the Orphan Trains that had cleared impoverished youth from the streets of San Francisco, the Great Peace March was cleaning up California by redistributing their buildup of impoverished to other sections of the country.

---

[39] Jeff Share, The Great Peace March for Global Nuclear Disarmament 1986, https://jshare.wixsite.com/jeffshare/peace-march

Image: Orphan Train

Source: Louisiana's Old State Capitol[40]

[40] Louisiana's Old State Capitol, Louisiana Orphan Train: Stories From the Descendants, https://louisianaoldstatecapitol.org/exhibits-events/louisiana-orphan-train-stories

Orphan Trains (1854 – 1929)

Introduction: Between 1854 and 1929 the United States was engaged in an ambitious, and ultimately controversial, social experiment to rescue poor and homeless children, the Orphan Train Movement. The Orphan Trains operated prior to the federal government's involvement in child protection and child welfare. While they operated, Orphan Trains moved approximately 200,000 children from cities like New York and Boston to the American West to be adopted. Many of these children were placed with parents who loved and cared for them; however others always felt out of place and some were even mistreated.

victimized. The police often arrested the children, some as young as five years old, and put them in lock up facilities with adult criminals. Determined to remedy the situation, the Children's Aid Society and the New York Foundling Hospital devised a program to take children off of the streets of New York and Boston and place them in homes in the American West rather than allow them to continue to be arrested and taken advantage of on the streets. Because the children were transported by train to their new homes, the term "orphan trains" began being used.

"The best of all asylums for the outcast child is the farmer's home. The great duty is to get these children of unhappy fortune utterly out of their surroundings and to send them away to kind Christian homes in the country." Charles Loring Brace

Riders leave their pasts behind

In the beginning of the Orphan Train Movement, the trains that took children across country were little better than cattle cars and only had make-shift bathroom facilities. The conditions of the train cars improved in later years as more money became available; and in the final years the children rode in sleeping cars. At any one time, there were between 30 and 40 children, infants to teens, traveling with two or three adult chaperones. The children often had no idea where they were going, and were only told that they were going to take a train ride.

A quarter million children rode the orphan trains from 1854 to 1929.
Photo: Kansas State Historical Society

"I'd just finished eating and this matron came by and tapped us along the head. 'You're going to Texas. You're going to Texas.' Well, some of the kids, you know, clapped and laughed. When she came to me, I looked up. I said, 'I can't go. I'm not an orphan. My mother's still living. She's in a hospital right here in New York.' 'You're going to Texas.' No use arguing." —Hazelle Latimer (Orphan Train rider)

Image Source: <u>Virginia Commonwealth University's Social Welfare History Project</u>

"During the 1850s there were thousands of children living on the streets of several major cities.

Between 1854 and 1929, Orphan Trains moved approximately 200,000 children from cities like New York and Boston to the American West to be adopted...

At any one time, there were between 30 and 40 children, infants to teens, traveling with two or three adult chaperones. The children often had no idea where they were going, and were only told that they were going to take a train ride...

"I'd just finished eating and this matron came by and tapped us along the head. 'You're going to Texas. You're going to Texas.' ... I looked up. I said, 'I can't go. I'm not an orphan. My mother's still living. She's in a hospital right here in New York.' 'You're going to Texas.' No use arguing." —*Hazelle Latimer (Orphan Train rider)...*

The confused and often frightened children lost contact with their families back in their hometowns and, those who were old enough, were encouraged to make a complete break with their past. When the children arrived in the new area where they were to live, there was no formal process to place them with new families. There were only handbills that announced the distribution of groups of needy children that brought crowds of prospective parents to view and choose children. Although the Children's Aid Society made a point of emphasizing the success stories of children who were well cared for and loved, the outcome of the placements in general was mixed. Some of the farming families saw the children only as cheap labor."

Text Source: Virginia Commonwealth University's Social Welfare History Project[41]

I can't help but notice that they've taken to using the same well-practiced domestic methodologies and tactics over even longer distances and international borders since then for both children and impoverished adults. California and major cities in the United States may have been frequent utilizers of the services in the beginning, but as time went on, they would not be the only areas the U.S. had involvement in that would come to have an overabundance of poor to disburse. As we move through history and it becomes closer and thus clearer, the growing involvement of destabilizing Intelligence objectives becomes more obvious.

---

[41] Virginia Commonwealth University's Social Welfare History Project, Orphan Trains, https://socialwelfare.library.vcu.edu/programs/child-welfarechild-labor/orphan-trains/

There is a major problem with the methodology, and it goes far beyond the inconveniences it causes in the intake areas where the people have been disbursed. When an area creates more impoverished and/or criminal elements than it can manage, allowing it to simply remove those people from their community is not actually beneficial to that community in the long run. It does not create a responsible government and culture in that area. This is because, without having to continuously face the issues they cause - primarily a large portion of their people becoming impoverished - they do not learn how to solve the problem healthily and within their own communities and regions. They don't have to. Someone else will take the problem off their hands and hide it away where they no longer have to see it. Thus, they continue to veer off course, creating a situation in which their people are likely to become impoverished, and the rest of the world continues to have to absorb the people of that failed and irresponsible system. No one wins unless they happen to be a sadistic warlord who likes the giggles caused by creating unnecessary human suffering and an unsustainable mess.

There is a certain danger that comes with painting every harm as something beneficial. People cling to the illusion long after they should let it go.

As a child, I simply adapted to the peace-march life and did what I tended to do when given a situation. I made the best of it. I came to know the drivers of the buses carrying supplies so that I could get a ride each day and avoid having to walk. The driver of the kitchen bus happened to have children. It wasn't difficult to embed myself with them. While everyone else was walking, I was playing or helping the mobile kitchen.

Image: Peace March Support Vehicles, 1986, Source, Flickr, Dan Coogan[42]

Image: Great Peace March, 1986, Source: Jeff Share[43]

---

[42] Flickr, Great Peace March, Dan Coogan Photographer, https://www.flickr.com/photos/cooganphoto/5904538890/in/album-72157626908632257/

[43] Jeff Share, The Great Peace March for Global Nuclear Disarmament 1986, https://jshare.wixsite.com/jeffshare/peace-march?lightbox=dataItem-j066kaau3

After the peace walk, I was hidden away in a much different setting - an empty condo in the hills of Hamden, a quiet and comfortable community next to New Haven. Bored and stuck staring at the blank walls there for months on end, I entertained myself by dancing around the bedroom and imagining that I was a famous singer. I named myself Roxana. The first time I told the recruiter, she responded that it was a terrible name, a prostitute's name, and to pick a better one. She suggested Foxine. I went along, I wasn't going to spend a lot of time analyzing why the name Roxana had such a strong reaction in her. Years later, I would find out it was because it had been my mother's name. I had kept little parts of her buried in my memory all those years. When I saw myself filled with pride and self-esteem in the bathroom mirror while pretending to be a rock star, it was her I saw reflected in the glass, and her name I had taken to encapsulate that moment.

Some things will always surface.

Don't lie to people about themselves and who they come from.

The recruiter was still up to making money on the side. That is, if it was the side. Where the line blurred between government pay and personal side hustle was always difficult to distinguish with her - she drove back and forth over it like a drunk person. And one of the times started so innocently that I actually thought it was going to be something normal and sane...

She didn't give me modern or brand-new toys, ever, so when I asked her for a Cabbage Patch Kid, her original response of "no" was expected. However, when she learned they came with customized adoption certificates, her eyes lit up and I would shortly end up with a series of the dolls. I treasured those dolls and their adoption certificates, which I kept in their own special drawer next to my bed.

One after another, the adoption certificates would go missing from my drawer while I slept. And why would that be? The recruiter had sidled up to and started sleeping with a man who worked with actual adoption records, for humans and not Cabbage Patch dolls. His name was Tom Flanders, and he was working with adoption records for the Pequot and Paugussett tribes in Connecticut.

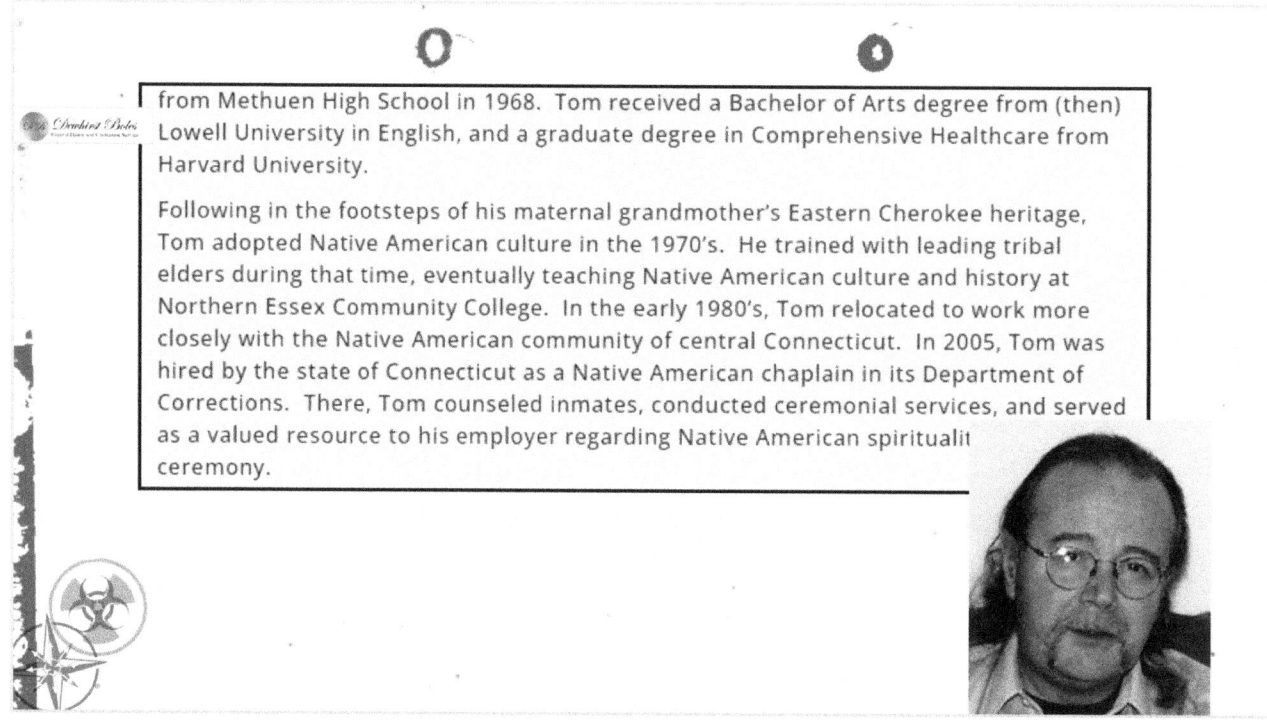

from Methuen High School in 1968. Tom received a Bachelor of Arts degree from (then) Lowell University in English, and a graduate degree in Comprehensive Healthcare from Harvard University.

Following in the footsteps of his maternal grandmother's Eastern Cherokee heritage, Tom adopted Native American culture in the 1970's. He trained with leading tribal elders during that time, eventually teaching Native American culture and history at Northern Essex Community College. In the early 1980's, Tom relocated to work more closely with the Native American community of central Connecticut. In 2005, Tom was hired by the state of Connecticut as a Native American chaplain in its Department of Corrections. There, Tom counseled inmates, conducted ceremonial services, and served as a valued resource to his employer regarding Native American spiritualit ceremony.

Image Source: <u>DewHirst Funeral Home</u>

"A graduate degree in Comprehensive Healthcare from Harvard University...Trained with tribal elders...teaching Native American culture...In the early 1980s, Tom relocated to work more closely with the Native American community of Central Connecticut."

Text Source: <u>DewHerst Funeral Home</u>[44]

---

[44] DewHerst Funeral Home, Tom Flanders, https://www.dewhirstfuneral.com/obituary/Tom-Flanders

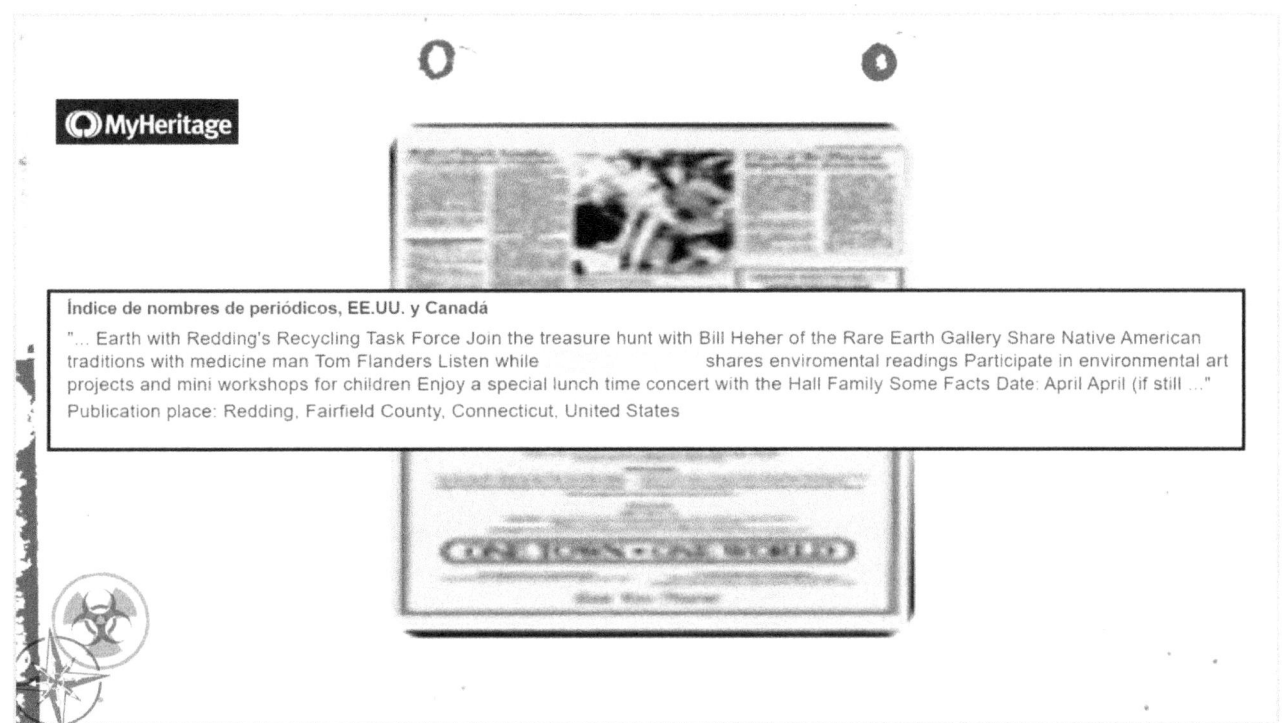

Image Source: <u>MyHeritage</u>

"Native American traditions with medicine man Tom Flanders..."

Text Source: <u>MyHeritage</u>[45]

She would tell him that I had lost my doll's certificate and that I was devastated, and get him to pull a genuine adoption certificate from work and fill it in with the "doll's info" which the recruiter provided to him. I would receive the certificate from him, and that too would go missing from my drawer by the next morning. By the third or fourth doll, I didn't even bother getting attached.

And those adoption certificates? One of them had the first and last name of a child I would meet through the recruiter around that same time, the same child who was there with me drugged out of his mind at one of the cancer research trials. Another had that child's sister's first and last name, and the third adoption certificate - a few years later, I would meet a girl with that exact first, middle, and last name. It probably wasn't a

---

[45] MyHeritage, Carmen Matthews, https://www.myheritage.es/names/carmen_matthews#

coincidence. I know the first two weren't. I overheard the conversations between the adults. Those were the documents they were using to legitimize illegal adoptions, a deceptively mundane name for kidnappings.

So, when I look back at my first collection of brand-new and trendy dolls, I'm stuck with nothing but guilt over my unwitting participation in the trafficking of my friends.

I won't be publishing the names of the abducted kids without their permission. After a lifetime in the U.S., knowing nothing else, some may choose not to go through the hassle of having their citizenship questioned. I've left that to the individuals and informed two of them. In a world that does nothing for us, I wouldn't blame them if they choose to remain in the country they were forced to build their lives in. They have lives there now, and those lives are their own. None of us owe the human trafficking intake country a thing. They turned their backs on and were complicit in our abductions and continued captivity. This failed civilization has already taken everything from us. If I give you anything, if I give you knowledge, don't think it's because I owe you something. I don't. I do it because it's painful to watch people kill their own children in their attempted suicide-by-military and I'm seeking to reach the few who would prefer not to be that, and who might still have the balls and intellect to choose a different path.

Cohorts

I may not have had family, and the recruiter was never human enough to me to be a replacement for family, but I did have research scientists and domestic counterintelligence who spent enough time in my vicinity to almost qualify. One, who I mentioned earlier, was George Edwards, a man that newspapers, including the New York Times, regularly published entire articles on that could have easily been summed up as "He's not a federal agent, we swear!" I'll show you some of those articles shortly. I grew to know him to the point that he did nearly replace family, at least for a couple of years. He was the only one I had any loyalty to in that mess. Out of respect for his life and career, I waited until he died before writing about his full involvement.

Most of the scientists I only met when they needed an assistant in their office to go through stacks of participant files or other mundane and repetitive work. The counterintelligence agents I would first be introduced to behind closed doors, I would see again at protests, marches, crop harvesting, political campaign offices, grassroots organization meetings, illicit recruitment drives, and coffee shops. Once in a while, there would be a crossover, and they and the scientists could be found in the same place.

Many of them had been recruited by the same mechanism I had been illegally adopted through. They had been offered an escape from prison, threats of death, and criminal or war crimes charges, and they took it. Some had a history of domestic terrorism and activism within the United States, and some had come from foreign countries and predicaments similar to my mother's. As I mentioned, we even had a few leftover aging Nazi scientists of our own, from the recruitment of that era. However, most of those human relics of World War II began retiring right around the time I reached New Haven.

I understand the need for an infiltrated system. An unpenetrated one may be cohesive enough to be a true danger to other countries. However, the foreign and enemy self-inoculation of military and intelligence via unethical recruitment processes that take advantage of wounds of war comes with psychological aspects and unmet needs among the recruited that, when left unresolved and unacknowledged, endanger us all.

While many of those I met held deep-seated resentment, anger, and sadness, there were some who seemed to have adapted (but then, many people thought the same of me). I fully acknowledge that I have experienced the full range of those emotions, as well as a few fleeting moments of hope, over the course of my life and service.

There is a deep-set pain caused by being enslaved by the enemy and being forced to work in intelligence and weapons research that is aimed at the destruction of your own people. It drills all the way down to a person's core and then keeps going.

As at-odds as it may seem, I felt most comfortable speaking to the people involved in my abuse and the abuses I witnessed, when it came to how I was really feeling and why. I didn't have to worry about them not comprehending what I was talking about. I didn't have to explain what was making me miserable or uncomfortable. They already knew.

I could be closer to my complete self with some of them than I could with anyone else. They were the only people who held my secrets and knew them to be true without refutation. Even as I write this I feel like I'm trying to climb an insurmountable wall to make someone on the outside understand. I didn't have that issue with them. They were right there on the inside with me. They had seen the damage caused. They were a large part of what caused it.

And I do feel deeply for the ones I have met (and those I haven't met yet), even many of the ones who have caused me great harm. All people should be free, and they are my people. I feel their pain more deeply than I feel the pain of anyone else, with the exception of the children they harm. I feel their pain because it is mine.

Life is complicated. Without love, I settled for finding comfort in intelligence and reason. Unfortunately, a world that has been taught to self-deceive, in an act of respect for the lies of others, tends to be a little short on reason, even within Intelligence.

Expropriated Counterintelligence

There will always be people waiting
to be commanded to work against their own best interests.
And there will always be someone who has worked
their way into a position of authority,
or of influencing authority,
with their goals set on war, exploitation,
and seeking to command others through fear.
Not all among us are of a healthy mind.
These truths are as inevitable
as the birth of a child in the middle of their wars.

The recruiter, her cohort, and the department she was most directly associated with were lacking in morals and ethics. They were made immune from domestic, and in many cases international, laws due to their position and the perceived significance of their work within the Department of Defense.

They also had quite a few internal and inter-departmental issues. The New Haven Federal Bureau of Investigation (FBI) office, the local office many of the adults in my small circle worked through, has been ranked as the most corrupt FBI office in the country, internally and by the FBI's own agents. The group I was surrounded by was one of the primary reasons. However, even they felt the damage from it. Things are not neat and tidy in that mess. Everyone gets hurt.

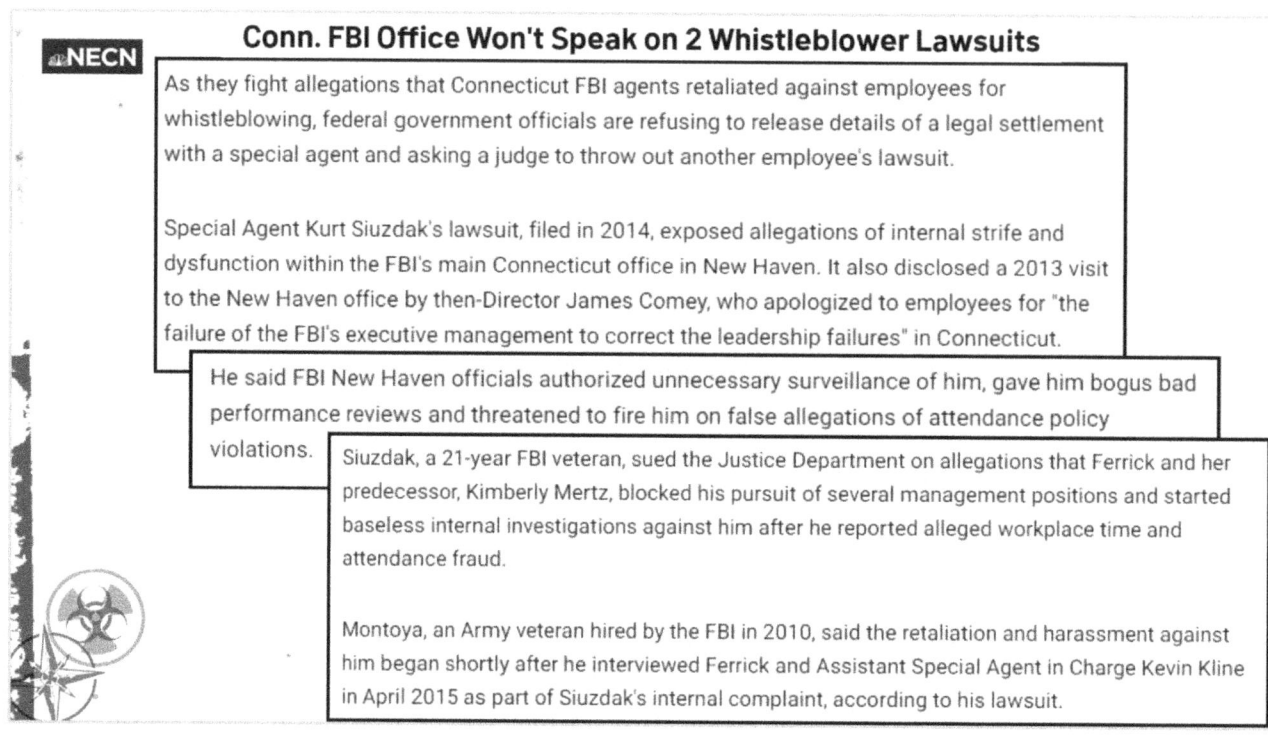

Conn. FBI Office Won't Speak on 2 Whistleblower Lawsuits

As they fight allegations that Connecticut FBI agents retaliated against employees for whistleblowing, federal government officials are refusing to release details of a legal settlement with a special agent and asking a judge to throw out another employee's lawsuit.

Special Agent Kurt Siuzdak's lawsuit, filed in 2014, exposed allegations of internal strife and dysfunction within the FBI's main Connecticut office in New Haven. It also disclosed a 2013 visit to the New Haven office by then-Director James Comey, who apologized to employees for "the failure of the FBI's executive management to correct the leadership failures" in Connecticut.

He said FBI New Haven officials authorized unnecessary surveillance of him, gave him bogus bad performance reviews and threatened to fire him on false allegations of attendance policy violations.

Siuzdak, a 21-year FBI veteran, sued the Justice Department on allegations that Ferrick and her predecessor, Kimberly Mertz, blocked his pursuit of several management positions and started baseless internal investigations against him after he reported alleged workplace time and attendance fraud.

Montoya, an Army veteran hired by the FBI in 2010, said the retaliation and harassment against him began shortly after he interviewed Ferrick and Assistant Special Agent in Charge Kevin Kline in April 2015 as part of Siuzdak's internal complaint, according to his lawsuit.

Image Source: <u>NECN</u>

"Special Agent Kurt Siuzdak's lawsuit, filed in 2014, exposed allegations of internal strife and dysfunction within the FBI's main Connecticut office in New Haven. It also disclosed a 2013 visit to the New Haven office by then-Director James Comey, who apologized to employees for 'the failure of the FBI's executive management to correct the leadership failures' in Connecticut...

He said FBI New Haven officials authorized unnecessary surveillance of him, gave him bogus bad performance reviews, and threatened to fire him on false allegations of attendance policy violations."

Text Source: <u>NECN</u>[46]

When people working in foreign intelligence come home to roost, they often have to change agencies and offices in order to work domestically, and there are bureaucratic routes that simplify the process. The New Haven FBI office, with its proximity to Yale, a prime

---

[46] NECN, Conn. FBI Office Won't Speak on 2 Whistleblower Lawsuits, https://www.necn.com/news/local/connecticut/conn-fbi-office-wont-speak-on-2-lawsuits-alleging/2013002/

Intelligence recruiting ground, is a top choice in the area for anyone within the agencies clawing for real power (it offers the opportunity of unrestricted access to heirs of the rich and powerful in their earliest adult years, when they are prime for recruitment and being influenced, having blackmail material made to use at a later date, or for directly influencing and accessing their parents).

For God, Country, Yale and the CIA

JULIE POST | 12:00 AM, SEP 24, 2004

> A number of Yale graduates have worked for the Office of Strategic Services, the CIA's predecessor. They dominated the CIA's leadership throughout the Cold War period and continue to join the agency in large numbers, said Diplomat-in-Residence Charles Hill, who teaches Studies in Grand Strategy with professors John Gaddis and Paul Kennedy.
>
> CIA recruiters visit other college campuses, but they seem to have a predilection for Yalies — it could have something to do with "nostalgia for the 'Old Blue' mentality," Hill said, or it could be that Yalies are simply more attractive candidates than their Ivy League counterparts.

Image Source: Yale Daily News

"A number of Yale graduates have worked for the Office of Strategic Services, the CIA's predecessor. They dominated the CIA's leadership throughout the Cold War period and continue to join the agency in large numbers, said Diplomat-in-Residence Charles Hill, who teaches Studies in Grand Strategy with professors John Gaddis and Paul Kennedy.

CIA recruiters visit other college campuses, but they seem to have a predilection for Yalies — it could have something to do with 'nostalgia for the Old Blue mentality,' Hill said, or it could be that Yalies are simply more attractive candidates than their Ivy League counterparts."

Text Source: <u>Yale Daily News</u>[47]

That office became an interesting meeting point of corruption, CIA transfers, and a few crossovers with the DoD researchers who worked in the area, protected by the FBI and CIA-extended military intelligence umbrella.

And, yes, that mixture does happen. Doctor Charles Morgan, who will come up in this book later in conjunction with his publicized (and cited) New Haven-located FBI research, has for disclosure, reasons of public misdirection, or ego, chosen to allow MedScape to also note his CIA employment.

The recruiter isn't the only one who drunk drives all over interdepartmental and ethical lines. Many of them, especially in the Yale and New Haven circles, do. Never underestimate those who are paid to ignore the rules, even the rules of secrecy they told you they follow. They may only pepper in the truth within manipulative methods to guide you in the direction they want you to go, but that doesn't mean they are entirely averse to the truth. They simply tend to wield it a bit loosely. A little truth tends to make the rest of the deception that much easier to swallow.

---

[47] Yale Daily News, For God, Country, Yale, and the CIA, https://yaledailynews.com/blog/2004/09/24/for-god-country-yale-and-the-cia/

Image Source: Medscape

"Charles Morgan, MD, a psychiatrist who worked for the CIA for 7 years...

Morgan, who teaches intelligence analysis at the University of New Haven, Connecticut."

Text Source: Medscape[48]

As I mentioned before, I spent a significant amount of time around one of the agents, George Edwards. He appeared to be primarily domestic, other than a short stint in England and possible involvement in active theaters of war early in his military career. He was a classically Yale Drama School-trained actor (even Yale openly admits to this) and is mentioned in countless articles that include COINTELPRO (the FBI's counterintelligence program) and the Black Panther Party, who rightfully decided he was a federal agent.

---

[48] Medscape, Doctor/Spy: How MDs Get Involved in Espionage, https://www.medscape.com/viewarticle/951889?form=fpf

A Panther Passes On

NEW HAVEN ✳ INDEPENDENT

> He worked on B-52 bombers as an engineer for the U.S Air Force from 1955 through 1961, when he was unceremoniously removed for his role in antimilitarism protests. He later said a recording of a speech by Malcolm X had made him question his service to the United States: "I had a serious confrontation with history, politics, racism. I was becoming conscious of the world. This man had shown a light to the darkness of my brain."
>
> Yale School of Drama brought Edwards to New Haven, where he became a stalwart performer in the local Black Arts Movement.

Image Source: New Haven Independent

"...(George Edwards) was an engineer for the U.S Air Force from 1955 through 1961, when he was unceremoniously removed for his role in antimilitarism protests...

Yale School of Drama brought Edwards to New Haven, where he became a stalwart performer in the local Black Arts Movement."

Text Source: New Haven Independent[49]

George has been mentioned in news articles as having attacked a police officer with a chain, walking in the heavily populated downtown New Haven area with a rifle, and being arrested and imprisoned because of a Black Panther murder case. He then subsequently held front jobs working for the telephone company, the New Haven Health Department, and Yale University despite what was an extensive, published, and public record of erratic and criminal behavior by that point. It's the type of behavior that usually does not get a person past the standard job application approval process.

---

[49] New Haven Independent, A Panther Passes On, https://www.newhavenindependent.org/article/panther_passes_on

Once a Black Panther, Always a Cause

The New York Times

Mr. Edwards was given two suspended sentences after pleading guilty to two counts of aggravated assault. One dealt with the beating of Mr. Rackley and the second involved an earlier event in which Mr. Edwards used a length of chain to assault a police officer. Mr. Seale was acquitted of the murder charges in 1972. Warren Kimbro was released from prison in 1972 and now runs a program in New Haven to aid ex-offenders.

Mr. Edwards said recently that he was targeted as an informant because he did not get along with several top members of the party. He added, "The biggest tragedy of the Rackley murder is that the government used it to launch an all-out war on the Panther Party."

Image Source: New York Times

"Mr. Edwards was given two suspended sentences after pleading guilty to two counts of aggravated assault. One dealt with the beating of Mr. Rackley and the second involved an earlier event in which Mr. Edwards used a length of chain to assault a police officer."

Text Source: New York Times[50]

---

[50] New York Times, Once a Black Panther - Always a Cause, https://www.nytimes.com/1992/11/22/nyregion/once-a-black-panther-always-a-cause.html

Image: Black Panther Manifesto. George Edwards, Top Right.

Source: IberLibro[51]

He was propped up over the years as a radical and a Black Panther by Yale, the authorities, and media outlets such as the New York Times, Yale Daily News, the New Haven Register, and the New Haven Independent. They also consistently made him out to be a victim of the FBI. The Black Panther Party did not agree. They were some of the original victims of his being a federal agent.

[51] IberLibro, The Black Panther Manifesto / If the Fascists Attempt to Murder Chairman Bobby, https://www.iberlibro.com/arte-grabados/Black-Panther-Manifesto-Fascists-Attempt-Murder/31053324903/bd#&gid=1&pid=2

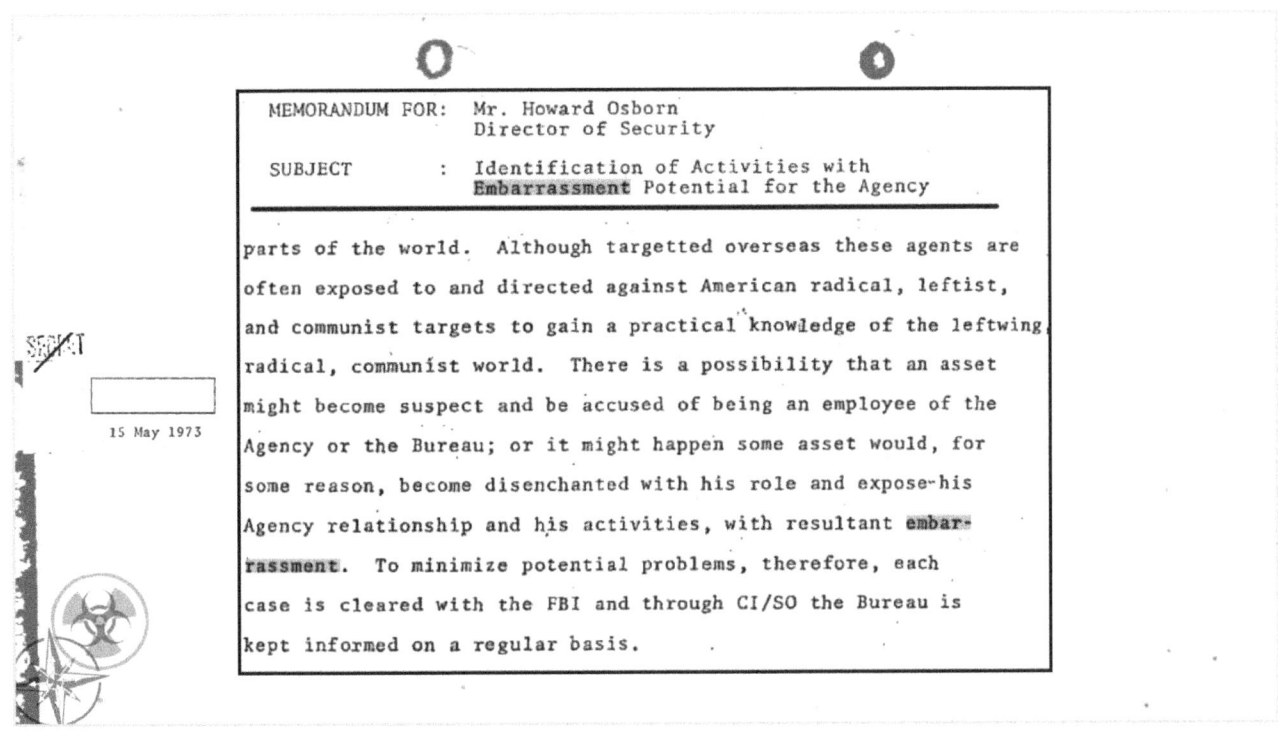

MEMORANDUM FOR: Mr. Howard Osborn
                 Director of Security

SUBJECT   : Identification of Activities with
                 Embarrassment Potential for the Agency

parts of the world. Although targetted overseas these agents are often exposed to and directed against American radical, leftist, and communist targets to gain a practical knowledge of the leftwing, radical, communist world. There is a possibility that an asset might become suspect and be accused of being an employee of the Agency or the Bureau; or it might happen some asset would, for some reason, become disenchanted with his role and expose his Agency relationship and his activities, with resultant **embarrassment**. To minimize potential problems, therefore, each case is cleared with the FBI and through CI/SO the Bureau is kept informed on a regular basis.

15 May 1973

Image Source: <u>Central Intelligence Agency</u>

"Although targeted overseas these agents are often exposed to and directed against American radical, leftist, and communist targets to gain a practical knowledge of the leftwing, radical, communist world. There is a possibility that an asset might become suspect and be accused of being an employee of the Agency or Bureau; or it might happen some asset would, for some reason, become disenchanted with his role and expose his Agency relationship and his activities, with resultant embarrassment. To minimize potential problems, therefore, each case is cleared with the FBI..."

Text Source: <u>Central Intelligence Agency</u>[52]

The Black Panthers were so steadfast in their belief that they had held George at gunpoint, tortured him, and then refused to call him a Black Panther for thirty-seven years until Yale intervened and forced one of the prior members to apologize.

---

[52] Central Intelligence Agency, Memorandum for: Executive Secretary, CIA Management Committee, Subject: Family Jewels, https://www.cia.gov/readingroom/docs/DOC_0001451843.pdf

That ruse became fact in 1969, when a New York Panther named Alex Rackley was brought to New Haven for a show trial in the basement of an apartment at the old Ethan Gardens Coop on Orchard Street. The apartment served as New Haven Panther headquarters. The Panthers accused Rackley of being a government informant involved in disrupting the New York chapter; it would later turn out that government informants indeed infiltrated that chapter (as well as New Haven's), but Rackley wasn't among them.

The Panthers tied Rackley to a chair and beat him and poured pots of boiling water over his body until he could come up with a story about serving as an informant. Edwards refused to participate in the torture. So they tied up Edwards too. With a .45 pointed at his head, he was ordered to "confess."

Edwards was able to flee the apartment. He went into hiding. The Panthers secured Rackley for days to an upstairs bed, where he lay in his own waste.

On the evening of May 20, an order came to drive Rackley to a spot out of town, where he would be murdered. Another Panther, Warren Kimbro, who had participated in the torture, was told to contact Edwards in order to take him on the murderous ride, too. Kimbro said he couldn't reach Edwards.

Image Source: <u>New Haven Independent</u>

"That ruse became fact in 1969 when a New York Panther named Alex Rackley was brought to New Haven for a show trial in the basement of an apartment at the old Ethan Gardens Coop on Orchard Street. The apartment served as New Haven Panther headquarters. The Panthers accused Rackley of being a government informant involved in disrupting the New York Section; it would later turn out that government informants indeed infiltrated that chapter (as well as New Haven's), but Rackley wasn't among them.

The Panthers tied Rackley to a chair and beat him and poured pots of boiling water over his body until he could come up with a story about serving as an informant. Edwards refused to participate in the torture. So they tied up Edwards too. With a .45 pointed at his head, he was ordered to 'confess.'"

Text Source: <u>New Haven Independent</u>[53]

---

[53] New Haven Independent, A Panther Passes On, https://www.newhavenindependent.org/article/panther_passes_on

Another score to settle was with fellow Panther Warren Kimbro. One night in 2006 Kimbro spoke at the Yale Bookstore about a book detailing the Panther period and his subsequent life in prison for murdering Rackley, as well as his post-prison life developing the model reentry agency Project MORE.

Edwards listened to Kimbro speak. (He listened to me, too; I co-wrote the book.) He listened as attendees asked Kimbro questions.

Then Edwards stood up. And the bookstore became his stage.

"After 37 years, five months tomorrow," he told Kimbro, "I want a public apology for having been tied up in that basement at gunpoint, under orders of [out-of-town Panther] George Sams, a .45 to my head."

Image Source: <u>New Haven Independent</u>

"Another score to settle was with fellow Panther Warren Kimbro. One night in 2006 Kimbro spoke at the Yale Bookstore..

Edwards listened to Kimbro speak...

Then Edwards stood up. And the bookstore became his stage.

'After 37 years, five months tomorrow,' he told Kimbro, 'I want a public apology for having been tied up in that basement at gunpoint, under orders of [out-of-town Panther] George Sams, a .45 to my head.'"

Text Source: <u>New Haven Independent</u>[54]

I would note that despite the Black Panther Party not acknowledging him as a member for thirty-seven years, he spent all of those years posing as one for the media, and he eventually went on to influence the New Black Panther Party directly. He would use the costume of a Black Panther radical within his undercover work infiltrating, organizing, and guiding grassroots organizations and movements for the FBI for roughly half a century.

---

[54] New Haven Independent, A Panther Passes On, https://www.newhavenindependent.org/article/panther_passes_on

As far as the general in-the-open infiltrating activities of the cohort I was stuck with, it's often been more horrifying to watch than what I saw behind closed doors. I've felt helpless to prevent it. Even when I've stepped away from the perpetrators and whispered to their victims, those victims more often than not still chose to trust those preying on them because they promised false incentives and presented with a sense of authority. My voice was never quite loud enough to break through those illusions. I also had no polished gifts to promise them in exchange for their dealing with reality. I still don't.

Relevant to George's case while I was there, was his connection to the wiretapping (a persistent issue referenced in the FBI whistleblower article at the beginning of this chapter) that went on within and by the New Haven FBI office for decades. George, despite his publicized long history of problems with the law, held a job at the local telephone company. From what I remember, he would go to it when needed, to wiretap people's apartments. It was not a full-time job, although it was listed as one. There were months at a time that he did not go, and yet they had no issue with him showing up when he needed to do something for the FBI.

NEW HAVEN ✺ INDEPENDENT

Another score concerned file #124 – 310G and others like it. In 1983, New Haven agreed to pay 1,238 citizens a total of $1.75 million to settle a class-action lawsuit over its massive illegal wiretapping operation. Victims were each awarded between $1,000 and $6,000 depending on how often they were illegally surveilled. Edwards, of course, got the full $6,000.

The money helped. Edwards never made a lot of it. He had day jobs working as a technician for Southern New England Telephone, as a staffer for New Haven government's pioneering needle-exchange program during the AIDS crisis.

Image Source: New Haven Independent

"He had day jobs working as a technician for Southern New England Telephone,"

...

"In 1983, New Haven agreed to pay 1,238 citizens a total of $1.75 million to settle a class-action lawsuit over its massive illegal wiretapping operation. Victims were each awarded between $1,000 and $6,000 depending on how often they were illegally surveilled. Edwards, of course, got the full $6,000."

Text Source: New Haven Independent[55]

This was a man who openly complained about being wiretapped "as a radical" and actually received one of the largest payouts for having been the target of wiretapping (a payment which was blatant fraud, considering his employment with the telephone company as well as with the FBI). He was the one tapping the lines with a telephone company hat on. Even the media has admitted that he always worked for the phone company on an as-needed basis, except for a short break allowing the company to save face when he was publicly implicated in crimes.

They were paying a person who directly perpetrated the crime - and they were paying him from the victims' fund.

While I was growing up in his presence, I never knew about the Black Panther Party's problem with the man. He had me and everyone else around him absolutely convinced that he was a Black Panther. Each day, he would wear the full overdone outfit: pins representing the Black Panther Party in text or imagery, printed t-shirts that did the same, dashikis, berets, and other overtly Black Panther regalia. In retrospect, he was so incredibly obviously a Yale Drama-trained actor. No actual member of the Black Panther Party would have dressed like that on a daily basis. In fact, it's doubtful that any went to that full amount and all at once, ever.

However, it never occurred to me that it was unusual, possibly because his partner, the recruiter, was at the same level of absurdly theatrical when it came to her anti-nuclear outfits - with multiple pins, printed antinuclear t-shirts, and even including full-body suit protective gear with a full gasmask on occasion. Frequently enough, she would openly carry

---

[55] New Haven Independent, A Panther Passes On, https://www.newhavenindependent.org/article/panther_passes_on

an unnecessarily gargantuan Geiger counter. The Geiger counter she carried for show was a massive box-type Geiger counter. The one she actually used for herself (I'll get into that later) was smaller and much easier to conceal. The terrifying thing is that, when she was infiltrating grassroots antinuclear organizations, they took her seriously and let her join their boards.

I know I've been lecturing everyone up until this moment about the seriousness of not allowing deceit to ruin a nation or the world, but I have to pause for a moment because when remembering these details, I'm breaking out into laughter. Any people capable of the level of delusion and lack of basic reasoning required to accept that overdramatic acting as genuine probably deserved exactly what they got.

Okay, I'll now go back to attempting to plead with humanity to care for itself…

Yale further propped George up with their theater department:

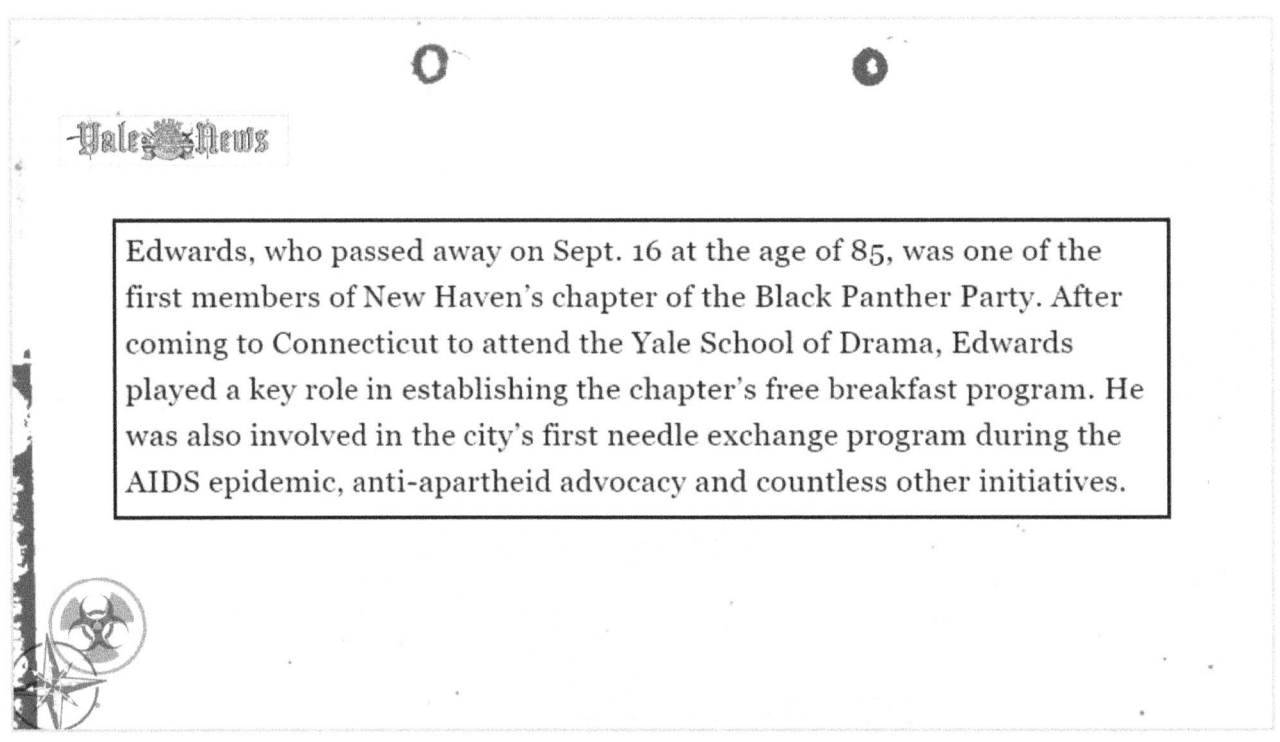

Edwards, who passed away on Sept. 16 at the age of 85, was one of the first members of New Haven's chapter of the Black Panther Party. After coming to Connecticut to attend the Yale School of Drama, Edwards played a key role in establishing the chapter's free breakfast program. He was also involved in the city's first needle exchange program during the AIDS epidemic, anti-apartheid advocacy and countless other initiatives.

Image Source: Yale Daily News

"Edwards...was one of the first members of New Haven's chapter of the Black Panther Party. After coming to Connecticut to attend the Yale School of Drama,"

Text Source: <u>Yale Daily News</u>[56]

An interesting little side note on that theater department:

I was once brought along to the David Geffen School of Drama theater on Yale campus by the recruiter. She had me sit two rows from the front in the empty theater. Then she told me, "You're supposed to be drugged, so act like it." It was a concerning statement, especially in the moment. A minute later, a very small group of other people came in. They began practicing what I would come to refer to as street acting. They were rehearsing to be believable in their roles when interacting with the public "spontaneously" outside of the theater. I sat in my seat, slightly terrified because I did not actually know what I looked like or behaved like when fully drugged, so I wasn't sure how to fake it. On top of that, I had to convincingly fake it in front of what were clearly professional actors and spies. I stayed so incredibly still that I probably looked like a deer in the headlights.

Later, after they left, the recruiter gave me a little tour of the building, the lighting, and backstage. She explained that lighting was the most important aspect of stage work. An actor could move or speak in any manner, but it was the lighting they were cast in that made the audience perceive them in a certain way. It was the lighting that made the audience love or hate them. She said all the power is in the hands of the lighting crew. Knowing her, I was certain she was speaking about the use of media manipulation on the political and global stage.

Years later, when watching televised presidential debates and noticing how one candidate was cast in a diffused white angelic glow while the other candidate was under an unnaturally orange light, I nearly choked on my dinner because I was laughing so hard when thinking of it in that context. And it was in that context. A short block away from the theater, when taking a footpath, stood a society building on Yale's campus that I would always refer to as the Political Actors' Guild because that's what they are in the context of the modern-day, and I abhor subterfuge. It was conveniently located on High Street, a short

---

[56] Yale Daily News, Q-House Hosts Celebration of Life for Black Panther George Edwards, https://yaledailynews.com/blog/2022/10/31/q-house-hosts-celebration-of-life-for-black-panther-george-edwards/

distance from the theater department, the law school, and Dwight Hall. That well-positioned Political Actors' Guild has produced more U.S. presidents in our lifetime than any other.

A quick aside on Dwight Hall, in case you've looked into it and seen that they primarily focus on social issues, such as and including workers' rights. While they may be good causes on the surface, they are causes that should be approached from a bottom-up perspective and not a top-down one. Allowing the seeds of these movements to be formed and informed by the rich, political powers, and industry that they will be negotiating with is not wise. Because those powerful will make sure their own interests are first met and that they are layered into any doctrine. Why wouldn't they? The guidelines and rhetoric are being written in Ivy League university classrooms and those are the territory of the rich. The reality is that each and every group is out for themselves first, and that includes socioeconomic groups. When it comes to workers' rights and related, you do not want the greedy at the top to have first say - you want the greedy at the bottom - those who want an extra meal, and who want dessert with it - to have that major influence over how they approach retaining and gaining enough to eat and succeed in life.

These things, in order to be healthy and successful, must come from the workers themselves, without pre-influence from those who seek to take advantage of them. And the industry does, indeed still seek to take advantage of the workers. I assisted in Ivy League research (not Yale, for once) only recently (2017) that saw the worker as nothing more than something to use at peak performance with overtime until they crashed and became disposable. They thought the worker was an easily replaceable tool from the limitless resource of humanity. There was one worker in our research pool who was actually connecting to us, and continuing to do his work, from the hospital waiting room. Even that was not enough of a wake-up call for those in charge of the research to understand that they were going too far. When I pointed out that workers were falling out of the project due to burnout and that this one was dealing with medical issues, the head of the research only seemed relieved that he still logged in - on the hospital wifi. They considered his dedication to the work to be a success while failing to note that in doing so he was shortening his life and his ability to work for them in the long run, if not within the week.

Never let the foxes build the henhouse. That henhouse is so unstable at this point that no one is safe within it - neither hen nor fox.

Regarding the dangers of allowing the Ivy League to dictate workers' rights, the same can be said about letting politicians represent the people. They do not have the same interests at heart.

So, back to the political actors the Ivy League is prone to produce:

What I would learn over the years in my interactions with that theater department goes well beyond a few recruiters conning a few Yalies on a street corner between classes. Yale (and other Ivy League) trained actors and drama department academics do a significant portion of the mass-scale public manipulation we see every time we turn on a television. They're the professional political actors with the resumes to get those jobs.

After such a long history of the takeover of the national and international political stage with a primary strategy of public diversion and manipulation for the benefit of whatever program needed to be kept quiet and whatever exploiters and war criminals needed the most money funneled that week, the public can no longer make informed decisions. They've never been informed. They haven't been given any rational or uncorrupted information with which to make informed decisions. While a portion of the public on both sides of the political aisle genuinely tries to do what is right from their perspectives, they cannot because someone switched out their practical solutions with ones that look similar on the surface but are in reality tainted weapons and exploited half-thoughts. In other words, they've all been subverted. I've met quite a few of the people who did it.

This public audience manipulation is done with basic mechanisms. I will explain one in the simplest terms possible because I do not want to upset anyone on either side of the aisle. It's not my intention, although it's inevitable. Things have been maneuvered in such a way that every move in politics has now been painted as a struggle for life for which each side needs to savagely fight. If only they knew that life was already being stolen from them and that there are no political debates or voting boxes that can fix the damage. Those have become a part of the damage.

A mechanism:

We have a pan. That pan is our shared world. A political actor hands a first group (a political party or a nation) an egg. A second political actor hands a second group the oil necessary to fry the egg. They then individually tell both groups that what their group is holding is necessary to cook. This isn't a complete lie. What they are holding is necessary to cook, and they know it, and thus each side fully adopts and accepts the words regarding what they are holding - an egg or the oil. Then the actors tell each group that the other group wants to destroy what they are holding because the other side is a madman in direct opposition to that ingredient. Then, the actors on the stage walk away, satisfied, and the public goes at each other's throats forever, while slowly starving from an inadequate diet on both sides.

Actually, while I'm still on the subject of political theater, let me touch upon the patrons of those arts...

Going back a few years, one occasion from before we moved to New Haven stands out simply because it shows the psychology of some of the people the recruiter did dealings with. These were the ones with the money, people who had the actual tangible resources, mineral rights, federal politics sewn up, etc., in that country. They would be the patrons of the political actors' arts.

The recruiter was there to finalize a contract with them for her bosses, and one boss in particular. The thing about "the company" is that, while you may be a scientist (or any other position), you first work for the company and do the company work. If you can still get your actual scientific work completed, good for you but it's not the top priority. That's just how things operate and get done. Apparently, that even applies to the supervisors. So, she was finalizing a political acting contract instead of authorizing disease vector payments and procuring research subjects that day.

The meeting area was a large dining hall on a sublevel of a mall, in the footprint of that mall, and taking up the same area of space as the food court did on the ground level. When planning the mall, they had included the construction of an entire sublevel just for themselves away from the public. Bringing a child through the mall to access the internal elevator provided a level of cover that came with absolutely no suspicion. And that's how I got dragged along for those negotiations.

I'm honestly not sure I'm ready to mention the negotiations or attempt to maneuver around those carefully placed eggshells. They involve politics, which is always a dicey subject, especially if the politicians are not quite as aligned with the needs of the people and parties they claim to be assisting. It's a bit like the bird that hides its eggs in another's nest. You can scream all day that the unrelated baby is stealing all the food from the other nestlings, but at the end of the day, that imposter is the nest owner's baby, as far as she knows...and she'll kill you if you say anything else. I've become quite tired of having that murderous reaction pointed directly at me. It's not easy being the messenger.

Instead, let's start with a tour of the sub-basement layout. I wasn't the only kid down there. The wealthy families that had joined together to share that private space away from public eyes had provided areas for their children to play in. They converted a movie theater space into a traditional theater with a stage. They made a large shopping area into an arcade with areas to run around and play games. And then there was the museum. It was a large space, big enough to play sports. Along the walls, they had set up a museum of nuclear war. As the children played and ran around the space, we would see the lit-up large depictions of various nuclear explosions projected onto the walls with text below them and triggered audio telling us what country they had happened in, how terrible it had been, and that this was how the world had entered nuclear winter. The people who commissioned that sub-basement, as a giant bunker, had prewritten history for their children and they expected that history to include a nuclear World War III.

So, back in the dining area, I would walk back and forth along the velvet rope that separated the areas between the wealthy and the absurdly wealthy, as the recruiter sat and spoke to a man behind that rope. I acted distracted and retarded, a small person who couldn't absorb information and was of no threat to secrecy. It wasn't difficult to do back then. I had a lazy eye when I was small. I may have an IQ that's off-the-charts high, but people are superficial and tend to take in surface appearances and simply accept them, and I doubt I looked too bright with one eye wandering in the direction of my nose.

(I would work on exercising it in the mirror for hours when I was young. I don't have any pictures from before the age of eight, but you can see that it still went a little in at that age, even after my initial efforts. Also, excuse the dyed black hair the recruiter insisted on - well, "darkest brown" according to the bottle. It never did suit me. Nothing about that predicament suited me.)

Image: Author, Age 8
Source: Author's Personal Collection[57]

So there I was, pretending to be easy to amuse and ridiculously interested in every fiber of the velvet of the rope, with the smell of rich cigar smoke entering my nostrils as they spoke.

The group the man was representing and was a part of was a core group of people who owned America. They were the ones who owned the majority of the country's resources and had been taking turns playing the role of U.S. president. Yes, it's been sewn up for quite

---

[57] Author's Personal Collection, Image

some time and since long before we were born. However, I'd note that they cared about some level of stability back then because the nation being wealthy kept them wealthy. Those negotiations were going to change that detail to a significant degree. I listened in horror because I already knew who and what he was negotiating with.

The group wanted a vacation from playing the presidential face of the nation. Being in the public eye is honestly exhausting for most people. We're not all sociopathic stage actors by nature - that actually takes certain born traits many of us quite simply lack. They had been in negotiations to have political actors fill the roles since the year George H.W. Bush was the head of the CIA (1976-1977) and he'd had a say in what the contract would include. It was an agreement to use the Yale Political Actors' Guild that he had been in since his days attending the university, still had membership in and influence over, and would profit from financially. And, yes, that guild goes by another name. I just refuse to give them any more power by saying it.

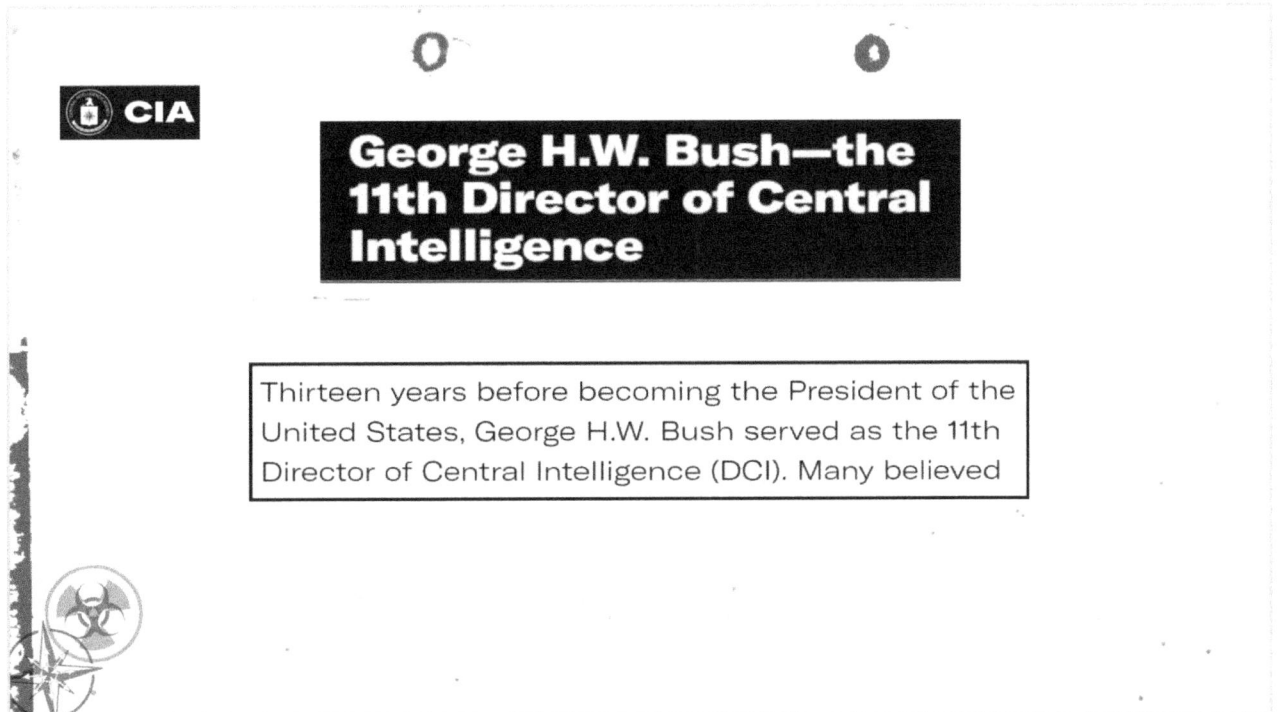

(⬢) CIA

George H.W. Bush—the 11th Director of Central Intelligence

Thirteen years before becoming the President of the United States, George H.W. Bush served as the 11th Director of Central Intelligence (DCI). Many believed

Image Source: Central Intelligence Agency

"George H.W. Bush - the 11th Director of Central Intelligence"

Text Source: <u>Central Intelligence Agency</u>[58]

That Political Actors' Guild, I would later spend a limited amount of time around them behind closed doors. Beneath the polish and media hype, they're nothing but thieves. Large-scale nation-stealing thieves with inside jokes about being pirates that aren't even jokes - they have the very real and tangible souvenirs to support those claims. In their need for a vacation, the money and power of the United States handed the keys for the federal-level political theater, and thus the nation's stability, to a bunch of thieves, many of whom I knew to be long-term heroin addicts. That would commence the draining of America, and a political stage that would go from measured voices and reasoning with a consistently pressured slow drain of resources to being completely replaced by a succession of quick drains and a cascading carnival-madness feeling until the debt ceiling would reach WWII levels once again, and without the need for a declared war.

Maybe when they signed that contract in the bunker they had already built to protect themselves, the truly wealthy of the U.S. knew they were ensuring our destruction by handing the nation over to the addicts among us.

But that's enough about actors and theater, for now...

As I grew up, trapped within those circles, I would lean against the back wall in many a room. I stood stunned into silence as I witnessed astounding levels of mismanagement, swindling, drug abuse (mostly heroin back then), sabotage, extortion, safety failures, and illicit dealings going on within military research, governance, and intelligence activities.

To a distant public, it was all hidden under a blanket of secrecy and a promise of military-grade professionalism by first-world nations. Up close and in person, the behaviors of the authorities in charge of the projects looked more like those of inmates in a corrupt prison, rather than the falsely promised polish of members of a professional tax-funded organization with rules and regulations.

---

[58] Central Intelligence Agency, George H.W. Bush - the 11th Director of Central Intelligence, https://www.cia.gov/stories/story/george-h-w-bush-the-11th-director-of-central-intelligence/

To them, it was a rush of control and access to drugs, resources, and weapons, all with no consequences, no genuine oversight, and no voice of reason to stand in their way. Many of them had entered the profession at the height of the sixties' liberation culture, having been deeply influenced by it (many having influenced it themselves) while in university. They were still high on the adrenaline rush and drugs, and now had full permission from multiple governments to break every promise and every law, including any modicum of truth, the sanctity of human life, and group survival. It was all being paid for by the public and the war-enabled black market, and was backed by one of the largest militaries on the planet. It still is.

And what's an arms race if you don't have the method to win the race to the end?

To me, a child too close to the reality to be deceived by the promises of nation-saving and professional behavior that were made to the public, a child who was desperately trying to find something real to cling to that wouldn't be destroyed or smoked up, it was nauseating. I never felt safe. I never felt that any of us were safe.

And yet, despite all of that, government and their handlers wouldn't be the biggest barrier to my freedom or the public's safety.

It was the citizens, kept in the dark and guided to blindly saw at the tree of their own ancestors and children. They would be the ones most effectively blocking the way. They still are.

AIDS Research

Some of the clandestine research and endeavors behind public-facing projects the adults in my circle worked on were direct violations of humanity and would have been best left to horror movies, nightmares, and the pits of hell. As a child witnessing them, I was simply told they were normal. Despite believing this because I had no other input to go on, there was a tight and painful feeling in my stomach that never went away, and my heart rate in those years always stood at about forty beats per minute higher than it should have been. I was terrified, but I internalized it. I felt that being scared was my fault, that it was something wrong with me, because no one else in that circle seemed to think that anything going on around us was concerning.

Years later, I would speak to someone outside of that sphere and find out that I wasn't wrong in having been terrified. The public had been misguided into believing these things didn't happen anymore due to their torturous nature, unethical means, and often genocidal undertones. If they had seen what I had seen, many of them would have been equally as terrified.

Due to what I was witnessing, I would become outspoken about the potential harm of current research design methodology to research participants, even in ethics-board-approved research. These things rarely do absolutely no harm, and almost never offer continuing support to the volunteers who sacrificed their own health and well-being on the altar of science for others to profit and benefit from. A one-time $200, or even $2000, research participant stipend cannot compensate for a lifetime of disability or lack of support in healing. It also cannot provide the social or medical reintegration that a research participant was never fully informed that they might need, because even the scientists do not fully acknowledge the breadth of possible harm caused during human experimentation.

There's a basic reason it's called experimentation. It is because there is no certain way that we can fully predict all of the results. The scientific community does not care for the people they use. They treat them as one-time-use discardable products, rather than taking

responsibility for the long-term effects and the human beings now carrying the burden of those effects.

No one fully understood my argument, or they didn't want to because it would interfere with their paycheck or would require extra work on their part. There's this unspoken phenomenon in American culture, and possibly in many other cultures, but I was there to see it in America. Because the criminals have been in charge of the government for so long (not surprising once we accept that governments are simply the larger culmination of gangs that have grown in size, gangs that once had a purpose of protecting their communities but eventually always seem to grow to exploit those same communities), people genuinely strongly hold an unspoken belief that evil is expected of them, and if they do not do evil, they will be punished by the dark hand within the government.

And thus they do not question the status quo, even when they can see that it is directly doing harm to individuals, the community, the country, and the world. At a deep-rooted and unspoken level, the same level at which we form personal secrets for our own survival, a level that has long been tapped into by societal and governmental level deceit, they tightly hold the belief that they are being bound to and forced to follow rules both spoken and unspoken, even when those do harm, and possibly especially because those rules result in harm.

Within the environment created by masses of people who follow such beliefs, I sat in on, and would eventually participate in many think tanks that would consider and hone unethical, stealthy, and inhumane strategies that would end up being utilized on the world stage. Beneath that cloak of secrecy, we had been working on how to avoid provoking nuclear war while still taking territory, profiting, and damaging an enemy.

However, there was one in particular that had more far-reaching implications than altering political lines on a map, giving the military-industrial complex more leeway, or operating in ways that intentional harm would become plausibly deniable infringements and "industrial accidents" to avoid triggering official declared domestic and international wars while very much engaging in them.

There was also the issue that this particular research would be hidden beneath DoD funding with a much different purpose listed on the front page of the proposal. They would be doing this within government, with government funding, and using government labs. Due to their subterfuge, not everyone in government knew what they were actually working on. Of course, very few people in the public would know at all, even when it impacted their lives.

Some of the most unethical weapons research I saw came directly from the dinner table biological warfare strategy sessions I had sat in on during my earliest years in the country. Even before deciding on the right viruses to use for a pinnacle project (they were still undecided and had been contemplating using a walking pneumonia and Epstein–Barr virus combination), they were already working on funding.

I was there waiting in the lobby and sometimes in the room for countless meetings in locations with large echoing halls and marble pillars as they lured idealistic scientists, the government, and the mega-wealthy into supporting and funding their project, with a promise that it would solve the funders' problems while still allowing them to protect their own family, their own soldiers, and their own staff. That protective portion of that sales pitch was a lie, but it was an easy one for large egos and large money to accept, and it was a significant part of what led them to shell out the funding, research space, and the AIDS virus.

We had told them that along with a modified HIV-based disease, we could provide a cure manufactured just for them. Apparently, wiretapping wasn't good enough back then to listen in and capture the dinner-table research planning discussions in which the words "incurable" and "no vaccine can be made for" were uttered. All it had taken back in those days to avoid anyone overhearing was simply to unplug the rotary phone and remove it from the room. It was also helpful to have people inside the FBI and the telephone company.

I use the word "we" loosely. I was still a child and pretending to be completely distracted by dessert on a table or the candy machines in the hallway. The amount of sugar I consumed back then should have been a crime on its own.

After the funding had been secured and the research had been approved was right around when George's face started popping up in relation to AIDS research and community outreach to help with the recruitment of unwitting research participants.

To this day, I hope there were major flaws in their research results.

Once a Black Panther, Always a Cause

The New York Times

> Now 55 years old, he has remained a constant force on the city's political scene and has often acted as a lone voice on a litany of issues yet to surface in the mainstream. He has run a neighborhood health clinic, helped to build shanties on the Yale campus to protest the university's investment practices in South Africa, and has organized and participated in numerous demonstrations against wars ranging from Vietnam to the Persian Gulf. Those who know Mr. Edwards as an AIDS outreach worker described him as a tireless and resourceful advocate who finds housing for his clients and tries to garner support from their families.

Image Source: New York Times

"Those who know Mr. Edwards as an AIDS outreach worker described him as tireless and resourceful."

Text Source: New York Times[59]

---

[59] New York Times, Once a Black Panther - Always a Cause, https://www.nytimes.com/1992/11/22/nyregion/once-a-black-panther-always-a-cause.html

It was when we first moved to the series of safehouses by Yale that I had seen the change. They stopped planning and started acting on their plans with military-funded AIDS research in a grouping of lab rooms behind a secure vault door on Yale campus, in the lower level beneath the Law Library, and in a section not-so-creatively referred to as "The Vaults" due to the overdone security door. There, they let me see the AIDS primates. I believe the recruiter actually thought she was being kind to me in that moment, letting a child see monkeys. The reality is that I was terrified that I would either catch their disease or accidentally contaminate them in their vulnerable state, resulting in their deaths. Sometimes, I wonder if I thought more like an adult than the psychopath did, even when I was still a small child.

(If you attended Yale in that time period, you may be able to confirm where The Vaults were located. Even if there has since been remodeling, they may still be there. Beneath the Law Library was a space unofficially called "machine city," a cafeteria with multiple vending machines at the center. If you headed from there towards the tunnel that led down to the other library, on your left was a smaller hall that led to the hall with the vault door, which is impossible to miss if you've seen that door - it's a proper vault door with all of the mechanisms as if it were sitting in a bank. I believe the left you take to get there is before the women's bathroom, but it's been decades since I've been down there, so I could be wrong. It is, however, reasonably in that vicinity and before you properly head down the tunnel.)

At this point, I would like to note to everyone who attended Yale and sent their children there, that there was a lab with military-funded biowarfare research within reasonable sneezing distance of that cafeteria, and it's highly doubtful that they warned students of the dangers. They never cared about any of us, not the rich, not the poor, not the powerful nor weak, and not even those who close their eyes and pretend there's nothing there. There is no behavior or monetary amount that will make you immune to a properly enacted endgame.

I was also there when they selected impoverished neighborhoods in New Haven and systematically introduced the AIDS virus to them under the guise of assistance and altruism as a needle exchange program. Between 1985 and 1986, I listened to the recruiter and a work partner on the project, George Edwards, discuss it as we sat at a smaller dinner table many nights.

Those two always made quite a pair. I can imagine them in their early days, him playing as a strong Black Panther and her as a Weather Underground militant radical. At the dinner table, with no one else there to observe other than me, they still had an energy to them, even if the topics weren't the theater of radicalism they showed to their targets. As they aged, he continued to play the role of a Black Panther when infiltrating grassroots organizations, right alongside her as she went into full-on righteous and dramatic mode about being an anti-nuclear activist. But there in the kitchen, away from the eyes and ears of their audience, they were excitedly discussing infecting the Dixwell Avenue neighborhood in New Haven with AIDS. George, trained by the Yale Drama Department, would be one of the pioneering workers and the outward face of the program. He was the face the low-income black community in that neighborhood would automatically trust.

Image: George Edwards, fourth from left

Source: Yale School of Public Health[60]

---

[60] Yale School of Public Health, Public Health Pioneers, https://ysph.yale.edu/news-article/public-health-pioneers/

They were successful. By the end of that year, 98-99% of the participants tested positive for HIV. The rate was so high in the Dixwell Avenue neighborhood (there may have been two others; I was only brought along to that one neighborhood, so I can only confirm the one) that it rocketed New Haven onto the top 5 list for cities and towns with the highest AIDS rates in the country.

While their research is obviously buried, a nearby drug treatment clinic showed a rate of 81.1% HIV positive status in black patients in 1986.

III INTERNATIONAL CONFERENCE ON ACQUIRED IMMUNODEFICIENCY SYNDROME (AIDS)

June 1-5, 1987
Washington Hilton and Towers
Washington, D.C.

THP.44 HIV Seroprevalence Among Connecticut Intravenous Drug Users in 1986
RICHARD D'AQUILA*, A.B. WILLIAMS*, L.R. PETERSEN**, A.E. WILLIAMS**
*Yale University, New Haven, CT., **Centers for Disease Control, Hartford, CT.
***American Red Cross, Bethesda, MD., U.S.A.
The rising seroprevalence of HIV infection among Connecticut intravenous drug users (IVDU) in 1986 was monitored by anonymously testing all admissions to selected drug treatment programs for HIV antibody. The largest number of sera (171) were obtained from entrants to the New Haven Substance Abuse Treatment Unit. In 1986, 22.2% (38/171) of those seeking treatment for active intravenous drug use were Western blot (WB) confirmed HIV seropositive. Interview questionaire data on 114 of these entrants have been analyzed. Significantly more of the blacks (81.8%-18/22) and of the Hispanics (40%-2/5) than of the whites (10.4%-9/86) were WB seropositive (p<0.0001, chi-square) among this 76% white group. Seropositives were older (mean-33 vs. 30 years, p<0.007, t-test) and had a longer history of drug injection (mean-14.3 vs. 10.6 years, p=0.03, t-test). There was a non-significant trend toward more needle uses in the past

Image Source: U.S. Department of Health and Human Services via Google Books

"Of those seeking treatment for active intravenous drug use were Western Blot (WB) confirmed HIV seropositive. ...Significantly more of the blacks (81.8%)...were WB seropositive."

Text Source: U.S. Department of Health and Human Services via Google Books[61]

[61] U.S. Department of Health and Human Services via Google Books, III International Conference on Acquired Immunodeficiency Syndrome (AIDS): June 1-5, 1987, Washington Hilton and Towers, Washington, D.C.,:
https://www.google.com/books/edition/III_International_Conference_on_Acquired/bKv9Li26MD8C?hl=en&gbpv=1

The New York Times also gave a subtle nod to the accomplishment. And, yes, it was a nod. That's one of the ways the New York Times is used, but I'll get more into that aspect later.

NEW HAVEN'S TOP KILLER OF YOUNG MEN IS AIDS

By Jacqueline Weaver
Dec. 13, 1987

The New York Times

AIDS is now the leading cause of death among men in New Haven 20 to 45 years old, according to the city's Medical Director, Dr. Fred Gager.

Dr. Gager said AIDS also might be one of the leading causes of death for women of the same age, although he had not yet completed a statistical analysis of that data.

Image Source: New York Times

1987 article:

"AIDS is now the leading cause of death among men in New Haven 20 to 45 years old."

Text Source: New York Times[62]

While the documents from the part of the research I discussed do not appear to have been declassified yet (often and historically the case with unethical research, especially on the weapons side), there is documentation from that time linking Yale and the Department of Defense regarding AIDS research under the same funding umbrella.

---

[62] New York Times, New Haven's Top Killer of Young Men is AIDS, https://www.nytimes.com/1987/12/13/nyregion/new-havens-top-killer-of-young-men-is-aids.html

4IN; FILE COP'

AD-A203 587 IENTATION PAGE

Form Approved
OMB No. 0704-0188

1a.	1b. RESTRICTIVE MARKINGS
Unclassified	
2a. SECURITY CLASSIFICATION AUTHORITY	3. DISTRIBUTION / AVAILABILITY OF REPORT
	Distribution Unlimited
2b. DECLASSIFICATION / DOWNGRADING SCHEDULE	(Approved for public release)

4. PERFORMING ORGANIZATION REPORT NUMBER(S)	5. MONITORING ORGANIZATION REPORT NUMBER(S)

DTIC
ELECTE
13 JAN 1989
S
E

6a. NAME OF PERFORMING ORGANIZATION	6b. OFFICE SYMBOL (If applicable)	7a. NAME OF MONITORING ORGANIZATION
Yale University School of Medicine		
6c. ADDRESS (City, State, and ZIP Code)		7b. ADDRESS (City, State, and ZIP Code)
New Haven, CT 06510		

8a. NAME OF FUNDING / SPONSORING ORGANIZATION	8b. OFFICE SYMBOL (If applicable)	9. PROCUREMENT INSTRUMENT IDENTIFICATION NUMBER
US Army Medical Research and Development Command		DAMD17-87-C-7065

8c. ADDRESS (City, State, and ZIP Code)	10. SOURCE OF FUNDING NUMBERS			
Fort Detrickm Frederick MD 21701-5012	PROGRAM ELEMENT NO.	PROJECT NO. 3M2	TASK NO.	WORK UNIT ACCESSION NO.
	623105	623105H29	AA	044

11. TITLE (Include Security Classification)

Sylvatic HTLV Related Viruses in South America

12. PERSONAL AUTHOR(S)

Francis L. Black, Lisa Regan, Sidney E.B.Santos, Roy A. Capper

13a. TYPE OF REPORT	13b. TIME COVERED	14. DATE OF REPORT (Year, Month, Day)	15. PAGE COUNT
Final	FROM 12/15/86 TO 12/14/87	Mar 11, 1988	29

16. SUPPLEMENTARY NOTATION

17.	COSATI CODES		18. SUBJECT TERMS (Continue on reverse if necessary and identify by block number)
FIELD	GROUP	SUB-GROUP	AIDS, HIV1, HIV2, HTLV-I, SIV, South America,
06	03		Amerindian, New World Monkey, Platyrrhine Primate,
06	13		Retrovirus, RA I

Eighteen of 387 specimens (4.6%) from Platyrhine primates captured in various parts of the Amazon Basin were positive by a Protein A ELISA test for HIV1. The positive specimens included the genera Alouatta, Aotus, Ateles, Cebus and Snguinus. Fourteen of 30 ELISA

20. DISTRIBUTION / AVAILABILITY OF ABSTRACT	21. ABSTRACT SECURITY CLASSIFICATION

Image Source: U.S. Military, Defense Technical Information Center

"AD-A203 587.

Performing Organization: Yale University School of Medicine...

Funding/Sponsoring Organization: U.S. Army Medical Research and Development Command, Fort Detrick...

Subject Terms: AIDS, HIV1, HIV2, HTVL-I, SIV, South America..."

Text Source: U.S. Military, <u>Defense Technical Information Center</u>[63]

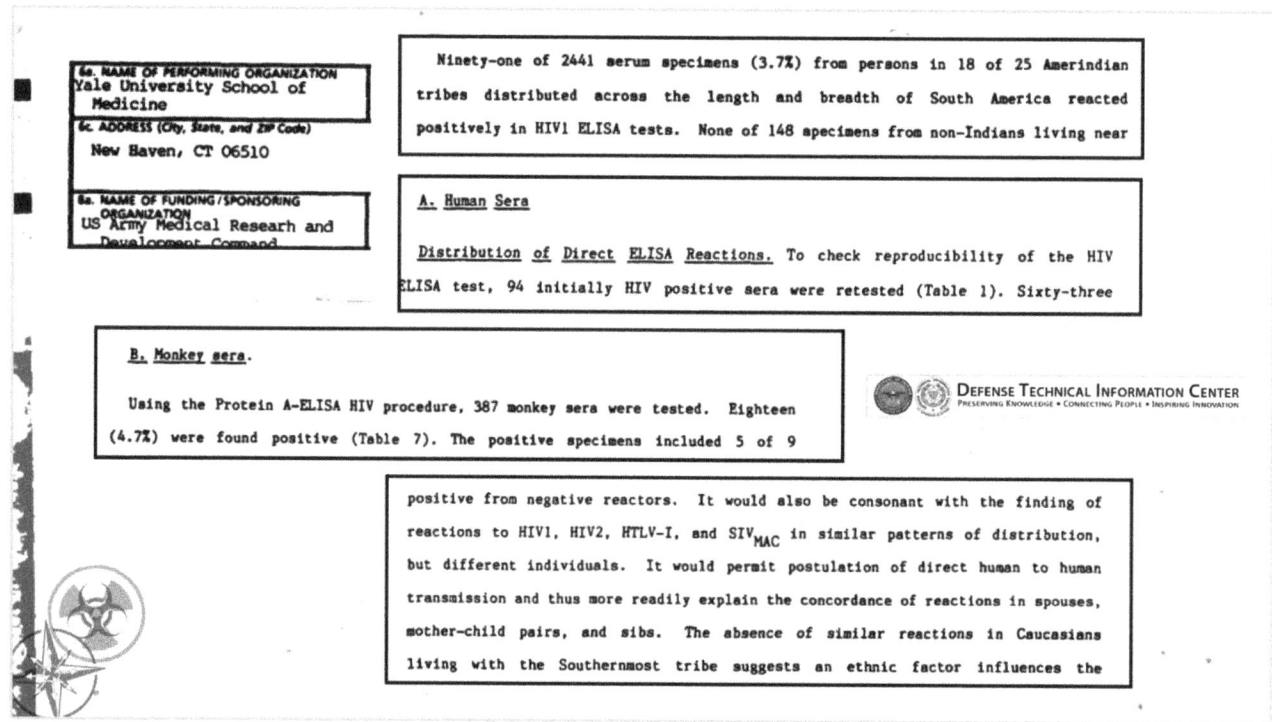

Image Source: U.S. Military, <u>Defense Technical Information Center</u>

"18 of 25 Amerindian tribes distributed across the length and breadth of South America reacted positively in HIV1 ELISA tests...Using the A-ELISA HIV procedure, 387 monkey sera were tested... It would be consistent with the finding of reactions to HIV1, HIV2, HTLV-I, and SIV..."

Text Source: U.S. Military, <u>Defense Technical Information Center</u>[64]

---

[63] U.S. Military, Defense Technical Information Center, AD-A203 587, https://apps.dtic.mil/sti/pdfs/ADA203587.pdf

[64] U.S. Military, Defense Technical Information Center, AD-A203 587, https://apps.dtic.mil/sti/pdfs/ADA203587.pdf

And that same Fort Detrick U.S Army Medical Research and Development Command was already working on creating a combined HIV and cold virus (adenoviruses are a common cause of respiratory illnesses) in 1986 and 87:

DEFENSE TECHNICAL INFORMATION CENTER
PRESERVING KNOWLEDGE • CONNECTING PEOPLE • INSPIRING INNOVATION

6a. NAME OF PERFORMING ORGANIZATION	6b. OFFICE SYMBOL *(If applicable)*	7a. NAME OF MONITORING ORGANIZATION
Biotech Research Labs., Inc.		

6c. ADDRESS *(City, State, and ZIP Code)*	7b. ADDRESS *(City, State, and ZIP Code)*
1600 East Gude Drive Rockville, MD 20850	

8a. NAME OF FUNDING / SPONSORING ORGANIZATION U.S. Army Medical Research & Development Command	8b. OFFICE SYMBOL *(If applicable)*	9. PROCUREMENT INSTRUMENT IDENTIFICATION NUMBER Contract No. DAMD17-86-C-6284

8c. ADDRESS *(City, State, and ZIP Code)*	10. SOURCE OF FUNDING NUMBERS			
	PROGRAM ELEMENT NO.	PROJECT NO.	TASK NO.	WORK UNIT ACCESSION NO.
Fort Detrick, Frederick, MD 21701-5012	623105	3M2-623105H29	AD	014

11. TITLE *(Include Security Classification)*
Development and Evaluation of Adeno-HTLV-III Hybrid Virus and
Non-Cytopathic HTLV-III Mutant for Vaccine Use

12. PERSONAL AUTHOR(S)
Lubet, Martha Turner   and   Dusing, Sandra Kay

13a. TYPE OF REPORT	13b. TIME COVERED	14. DATE OF REPORT *(Year, Month, Day)*	15. PAGE COUNT
Annual	FROM 9/29/86 TO 9/30/87	87/10/28	46

16. SUPPLEMENTARY NOTATION

17. COSATI CODES			18. SUBJECT TERMS *(Continue on reverse if necessary and identify by block number)*
FIELD	GROUP	SUB-GROUP	AIDS, Vaccine, DNA Recombinant, Antibody, T-Cell
06	03		
06	13		

19. ABSTRACT *(Continue on reverse if necessary and identify by block number)*

Acquired immunodeficiency disease syndrome (AIDS) was initially recognized as a separate disease in 1981. Results from research groups in France and the United States determined that a previously unknown virus called HIV is the primary aetiological agent of AIDS.

Two HIV vaccines, a recombinant Adeno-HIV hybrid virus and a recombinant vaccinia HIV will be tested. The recombinant Adeno-HIV virus is being developed as part of this proposal. The vaccines will be tested in two species of monkeys, chimpanzees and African green monkeys. Vaccinated animals will be challenged with a defined dose of HIV virus. Assessment of vaccine efficacy against the virus challenge will include T4/T8 ratios,

Image Source: U.S. Military, <u>Defense Technical Information Center</u>

169

"Performing Organization: Biotech Research Labs., Inc...

Funding/Sponsoring Organization: U.S. Army Medical Research & Development Command...

Contract No. DAMD17-86-C-6284...

Title: Development and Evaluation of Adeno-HTLV-III Hybrid Virus and Non-Cytopathic HTLV-III Mutant for Vaccine Use...

Abstract: Two HIV vaccines, a recombinant Adeno-HIV hybrid virus and a recombinant vaccinia HIV will be tested. The recombinant Adeno-HIV virus is being developed as part of this proposal. The vaccines will be tested in two species of monkeys, chimpanzees and African green monkeys..."

Text Source: U.S. Military, <u>Defense Technical Information Center</u>[65]

The scientists I had grown up with now had their HIV/respiratory illness prototype, funded by the military:

---

[65] U.S. Military, Defense Technical Information Center, DAMD17-86-C-6284, https://apps.dtic.mil/sti/pdfs/ADA189926.pdf

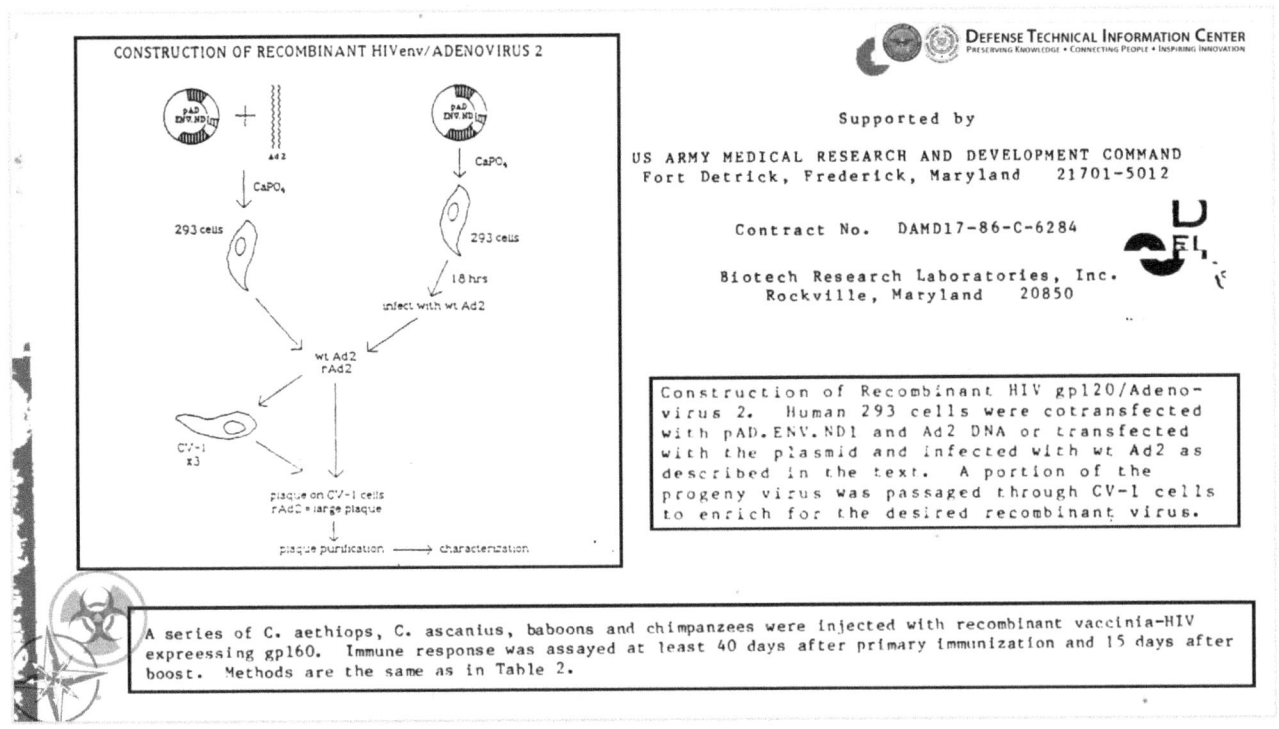

Image Source: U.S. Military, <u>Defense Technical Information Center</u>

"Construction of recombinant HIVenv/Adenovirus 2"

Text Source: U.S. Military, <u>Defense Technical Information Center</u>[66]

By 1987, Yale Medical School also had a nearly unlimited supply of human AIDS subjects with a wide variety of opportunistic infections to use for testing and research:

---

[66] U.S. Military, Defense Technical Information Center, DAMD17-86-C-6284, https://apps.dtic.mil/sti/pdfs/ADA189926.pdf

III INTERNATIONAL CONFERENCE ON ACQUIRED IMMUNODEFICIENCY SYNDROME (AIDS)

TP.150 Prognostic Indicators of Survival in AIDS Patients with Pneumocystis carinii Pneumonia: A Biostatistical Analysis
N.A. LEE*, E. BELLIN*, L. FRAULINO+, WARREN A. ANDIMAN*+. *Yale University School of Medicine, +Yale-New Haven Hospital, New Haven, CT.
In order to identify prognostic indicators of survival from Pneumocystis carinii pneumonia (PCP) we studied retrospectively our first 48 adult AIDS patients with PCP. We determined which clinical and laboratory features present

THP.8 Anti-HIV Activity of 2',3'-Dideoxycytidine and the Unsaturated Derivative (2',3'-Dideoxy 2',3'dehydrocytidine) Compared to 3' Azidothymidine (AZT).
ELAINE KINNEY-THOMAS*, TAI-SHUN LIN**, WILLIAM H. PRUSOFF**, and ISMAIL GHAZZOULI‡ *Genetic Systems Corp., Seattle, WA; **Yale University School of Medicine, Pharmacology Dept., New Haven CT; ‡Bristol-Myers Co., Virology Dept., Syracuse, NY

M.5.6 Viral lipids as a site of action for developing novel anti-viral agents: Studies with AL721. A. S. Lippa[1], F. T. Crews[2], M. H. Grieco[3], E. Buimovici-Klein[3], M. Lange[3], D. I. Scheer[4], and C. A. Klepner[1]; [1]Praxis Pharmaceuticals Inc., Beverly Hills, CA., [2]University of Florida Medical School, Gainesville, FLA, [3]St. Luke's/Roosevelt Hospital Center, New York, NY, [4]Yale University School of Medicine, New Haven, CT.
A major underlying theme in biology is the understanding that many important processes involve the recognition of biologically relevant substances by specific receptor molecules. This theme can be

WP.225 Transplantation of Thymic Tissue to Reconstitute the Immune System of Patients with AIDS
JOHN M. DWYER*, C.C. WOOD**, G.J. McNAMARA**, B. KINDER**, *Department of Medicine, Prince Henry/Prince of Wales Hospitals, Randwick, N.S.W. Australia. **Division of Clinical Immunology, Yale University School of Medicine, New Haven, CT. U.S.A.
Thymic epithelial fragments were transplanted into 15 patients in an advanced stage of the acquired immune deficiency syndrome (AIDS). One patient was given interleukin 2 in addition to thymic tissue. We demonstrated the following :

TP.38 Virologic Endpoints in Antiretroviral Chemotherapy Trails
WADE P. PARKS*, E.S. PARKS*, M. FISCHL*, R. MAKUCH**, M. LEUTHER**, J.P. ALLAIN***, *University of Miami School of Medicine, Miami, FL. **Yale University School of Medicine, New Haven, CT. ***Abbott Laboratories, North Chicago, IL.
Virologic measures may provide useful adjuncts to clinical or immunologic endpoints to assess the efficacy of chemotherapeutic agents in antiretroviral trials. Such nonclinical endpoints may be especially important in asymptomatic or mildly symptomatic patients where clinical endpoints are infrequent or will require p... independent virologic measures, virus recove... leukocytes (PBL) and p24 antigen detection in... been evaluated in placebo-controlled trials of 3... (AZT) and Ribavirin which involved a total of...

THP.44 HIV Seroprevalence Among Connecticut Intravenous Drug Users in 1986
RICHARD D'AQUILA*, A.B. WILLIAMS*, L.R. PETERSEN**, A.E. WILLIAMS** *Yale University, New Haven, CT., **Centers for Disease Control, Hartford, CT. ***American Red Cross, Bethesda, MD., U.S.A.
The rising seroprevalence of HIV infection among Connecticut intravenous drug users (IVDU) in 1986 was monitored by anonymously testing all admissions to selected drug treatment programs for HIV antibody. The largest number of sera (171) were obtained from entrants to the New Haven Substance Abuse Treatment Unit. In 1986, 22.2% (38/171) of those seeking treatment for active intravenous drug use were Western blot (WB) confirmed HIV seropositive. Interview questionaire data on 114 of these entrants have been analyzed. Significantly more of the blacks (81.8%-18/22) and of the Hispanics (40%-2/5) than of the whites (10.4%-9/86) were WB seropositive (p<0.0001, chi-square) among this 76% white group. Seropositives were older (mean-33 vs. 30 years, p<0.007, t-test) and had a longer history of drug injection (mean-14.3 vs. 10.6 years, p=0.03, t-test). There was a non-significant trend toward more needle uses in the past

WP.108 Cytoboxic Factor Secreted by Human T-Lymphotropic... Infected Cells
LEE RATNER*, S. POLMAR*, N. PAUL**, AND N. RUDDLE**, *Washington University, St. Louis, MO, **Yale University, New Haven, CT.
The mechanisms responsible for depletion of T4 lymphocytes by human T-lymphotropic virus type III (HTLV-III) remain to be fully characterized. To explore the possibility that indirect effects might exist, conditioned media from HTLV-III infected cells were tested for cytotoxic cell-derived factors.

"Yale University School of Medicine, Yale-New Haven Hospital...

TP.150: In order to identify prognostic indicators of survival from Pneumocystis carinii pneumonia we studied retrospectively our first 48 adult AIDS patients (with the pneumonia)...,

THP.8: Anti-HIV activity of...,

M.5.6: Viral lipids for a site of action for developing novel anti-viral agents..,

WP.255: Transplantation of thymic tissue to reconstitute the immune system of patients with AIDS...,

TP.38: Virologic endpoints in antiretroviral chemotherapy trials...,

THP.44: HIV seroprevalence among Connecticut HIV intravenous drug users...,

WP.106: Cytotoxic factor secreted by human T-lymphotropic virus type III infected cells..."

Text Source: U.S. Department of Health and Human Services via Google Books[67]

This was why I waited until George Edwards died to write about his part in it. I've broached the subject of what was happening on Dixwell Avenue many times over the years with countless people, but I was never comfortable attaching George's name or explaining just how messed up his involvement was. He was the only person in the United States who ever, even temporarily, treated me like a family member. And I know he didn't entirely, and I know he risked my life more often than not (I'll talk more on that later). But I was an abducted child trapped in an unfortunate situation. I didn't get to choose, and he was the closest thing to humanity that I had. I clung to that. Maybe I shouldn't have, but I did.

That said, I can't sugarcoat how bad things were and still are. The place where they "celebrated George's life," played music, and had people speak about how much of an asset he was to the community? It was at Q-House, a Dixwell Avenue community center building. They had the very people he injured, the people he took family members from, celebrating his life.

[67] U.S. Department of Health and Human Services via Google Books, III International Conference on Acquired Immunodeficiency Syndrome (AIDS): June 1-5, 1987, Washington Hilton and Towers, Washington, D.C., https://www.google.com/books/edition/III_International_Conference_on_Acquired/bKv9Li26MD8C?hl=en Alternate: https://www.google.com/books/edition/III_International_Conference_on_Acquired/bKv9Li26MD8C?hl=en&gbpv=1

That is the culmination of deception. We thank the people who kill us.

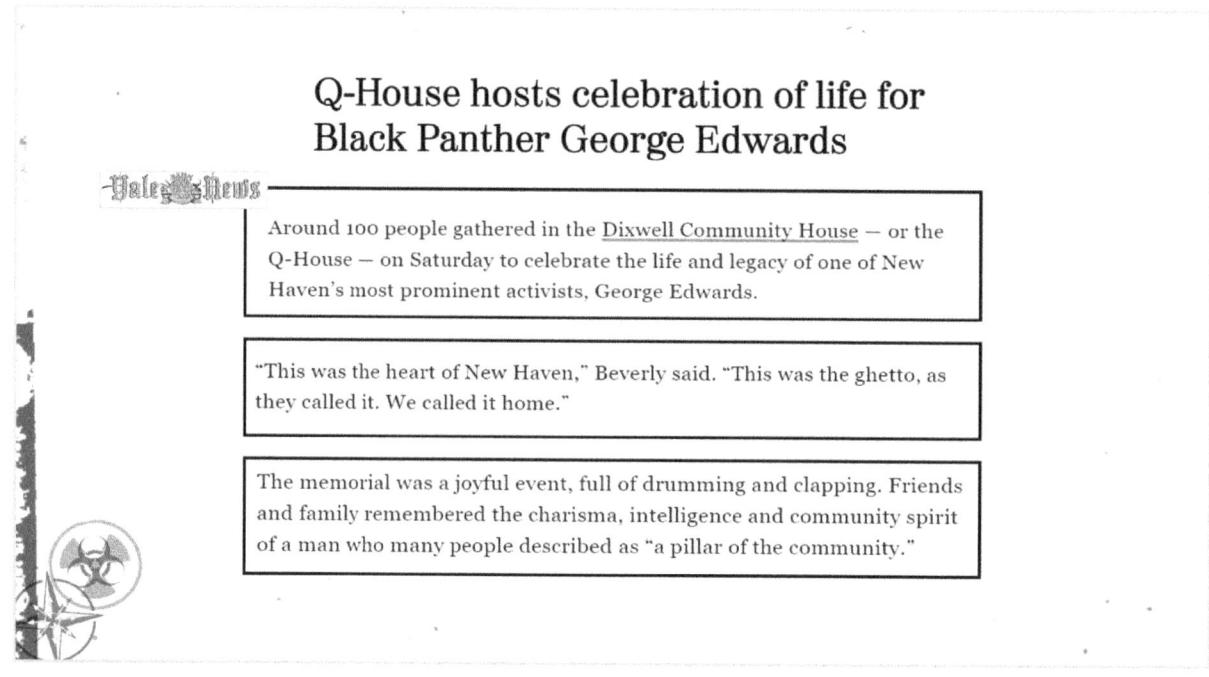

Image Source: Yale Daily News

"Around 100 people gathered in the Dixwell Community House — or the Q-House — on Saturday to celebrate the life and legacy of one of New Haven's most prominent activists, George Edwards....

'This was the heart of New Haven,' Beverly said. 'This was the ghetto, as they called it. We called it home.' ...

The memorial was a joyful event, full of drumming and clapping. Friends and family remembered the charisma, intelligence, and community spirit of a man who many people described as 'a pillar of the community.'"

Text Source: Yale Daily News[68]

[68] Yale Daily News, Q-House Hosts Celebration of Life for Black Panther George Edwards, https://yaledailynews.com/blog/2022/10/31/q-house-hosts-celebration-of-life-for-black-panther-george-edwards/

The exploitation of that poor community for medical research, and the use of the promises of help via a biologically poisoned needle, brings back memories of Argentina...

Occasionally, something out of the ordinary enough would happen in the prison that it was worth tucking away as a childhood memory. When we went through one of the main sections on the women's side to get routine vaccines, I remember how loud it was, filled with the talking and screaming of so many women echoing between those walls. I recall thinking that I would be safe walking past them; after all, the women prisoners in my life had all been motherly and wonderful people up to that point. That faith was quickly extinguished as a woman to my right violently reached out to grab at my clothing. I tried to pry my clothing loose from her hands. Several in my group had to help me.

We continued past the women and to a small hallway with a room to our left containing an ob-gyn chair and the room to our right having a basic physician's examination table. The chatter of my always-talking friend and the mothers filled my ears as I learned that we were lining up to get vaccines in the room to the right and that none of the mothers liked the room on the left nor the doctor in charge of the often-forced and torturous births that went on there. Then, it was my turn to come face to face with the doctor in the examination room.

I don't recall if the needles hurt. I can only assume they did.

In all honesty, allowing any type of needle to enter beyond the protective layer of a child's skin in that situation should have been prohibited. And, yet, a bland and naive faith in humanity has propelled national and international policies regarding child political prisoners and vulnerable populations under any type of government authority or guardianship. Policy generally dictates that children and disadvantaged populations receive medical care, food, and education. The suggestions are made without thoroughly considering how these simple necessities can be forced, poisoned, and misused with the intention of causing harm when they are in the hands of a hateful or indifferent enemy or exploiter using deceptive tactics.

When following standard international policies of human rights, an ill-intentioned government will often use deceitful tactics to save face and appear to be doing the correct

thing on the surface, much like a Munchausen by Proxy mother claiming to help her child while poisoning them. The United States has a clear history of using "low value" people within its society for medical experimentation (more on that later, with citations). Argentina has taken to using its population in another way, as sales items in human trafficking, but via much the same path, as can still be seen in their handling and continuing concealment of their kidnapping and reallocation of infants.

Both show signs of a failed society, with humanity and care for their own people collapsing nearly entirely under the weight of the government they created to crush them. Healthy nations don't turn their own people into disposable slaves with no rights. Other people, yes. Immigrants? Sure. But their own people? Not generally. And when they go as far as exploiting their own children, that's usually past the limit of a salvageable society, even during wartime.

These two nations are, by far, not the only ones to turn covert warfare inward on their own people. They are just glaringly obvious examples, with all the parts exposed to highlight with ease. I wouldn't trust any invasive authority or pseudo-authority with a needle, a child, or a gun; not when combined with methodologies of malfeasance and subterfuge. It terrifies me how often people blindly trust them anyway.

Blind faith is not actually an admirable trait. It's a concerning one.

The issue with authority and needles would also become more prominent later in what would become our shared history, in several aspects, and not simply limited to Buenos Aires or New Haven, but more on that later.

Decay as a Facilitative Tool for Demolition

In those years and the following, I tried to talk to people about what we were doing to the Dixwell Avenue community. No one cared. It wasn't them. The victims were impoverished and with no social value.

I was also young and naive, and often broaching the subject with knowledgeable and experienced medical professionals from Yale who I knew socially. I approached them about it because I believed they would be the ones to follow their Hippocratic oath and they had the internal access to stop the unfolding atrocity. I didn't know that this type of research was common in the United States and they were probably more than aware of it already, especially when working for a prominent research hospital. It wouldn't have been a shock to them like it was to me. Even I, despite my experiences, had fallen for the false lull of comfort that comes with the 50-year classification of unethical medical research within the country.

From my conversations with the Yale medical staff and others, I began to realize it was possible that the people I was speaking to only cared if they were personally the victims, so I tried to appeal to that reasoning. I attempted an appeal to educated logic and explained that Yale research generally gets used by government, companies, and major organizations because it is authoritative and high quality, and thus, the unethical practices would eventually be used on the larger population, including the people I was speaking to. I didn't know why those words had no effect. I figured that maybe they thought they would only receive positive benefits from the research done at the expense of other human lives. As if humanity is not interconnected at all.

I didn't fully comprehend that this wasn't the first time in recent history that U.S. medical researchers, often at the government's behest, had given diseases to the impoverished and socially unwanted while lying to them and claiming to be there for their benefit.

What was going on in front of me in the 1980s and 90s was simply an echo from a not-so-distant past:

Int J MCH AIDS. 2015; 3(1): 81–84.

Overcoming Challenges in Conducting Clinical Trials in Minority Populations:
Identifying and Testing What Works

Romuladus E. Azuine, DrPH, RN[1,*] and Sussan E. Ekejiuba, DVM, PhD[1]

Between 1950s and 1972, children with mental disability at a State School in Willowbrook, Staten Island, New York, USA were intentionally infected with viral hepatitis in an unethical experimental quest to help discover vaccine.[4,5] In 1963, Dr. Chester Southam, another clinical researcher, injected live cancer cells to 22 elderly patients at the Jewish Chronic Disease Hospital in Brooklyn, New York, USA, with live cancer cells in an unethical bid to understand how the human body fights off malignant cells.[4,5] Perhaps, the most celebrated of these unethical studies was the infamous 1932 "Tuskegee Study of Untreated Syphilis in the Negro Male." Unlike prior studies, in this study sponsored by a government public health agency, researchers informed black men that they were receiving treatment for Syphilis—which was not true.[3] Unethical studies are, by no means, limited to developed countries. In 1996, pharmaceutical giant Pfizer paid out thousands of dollars in compensation for conducting a Trovan study on children in Nigeria that raised fundamental issues around ethics and corruption in clinical trials.[4]

Image Source: International Journal of Maternal and Child Health and AIDS

"Between 1950s and 1972, children with mental disabilities at a State School in Willowbrook, Staten Island, New York, USA were intentionally infected with viral hepatitis in an unethical experimental quest to help discover vaccines.

In 1963, Dr. Chester Southam, another clinical researcher, injected live cancer cells to 22 elderly patients at the Jewish Chronic Disease Hospital in Brooklyn, New York, USA (*without their knowledge or consent*)... in an unethical bid to understand how the human body fights off malignant cells.

Perhaps, the most celebrated of these unethical studies was the infamous 1932 'Tuskegee Study of Untreated Syphilis in the Negro Male.' ...In this study sponsored by a government public health agency, researchers informed black men that they were receiving treatment for Syphilis—which was not true.

...By no means, limited to developed countries. In 1996, pharmaceutical giant Pfizer paid out thousands of dollars in compensation for conducting a Trovan study on children in Nigeria that raised fundamental issues around ethics and corruption in clinical trials."

Text Source: <u>International Journal of Maternal and Child Health and AIDS</u>[69]

I wouldn't find out about how extensive that recent and continuing dark practice was until decades later when looking further into the subject. However, the experts at Yale clearly knew.

In a later interview (in this case about using abandoned and orphaned children in state care in the 1960s, rather than impoverished black communities too poor to relocate in the 1980s), a medical history professor at Yale let on how common the unethical and callous practices were when seeking research grants to experiment on the unwitting:

"They were the raw material of medical research," says Susan Lederer, who teaches medical history at Yale University. She was a member of the presidential committee that investigated the radiation experiments, and she says she wasn't shocked by the findings because researchers have been using disabled children in experiments for over a century.

CBS NEWS

"Children in orphanages, children in homes of the mentally retarded, these are all good populations from the sense of medical research, because you have an easily accessible group of people living in controlled circumstances, and you can monitor them," says Lederer.

Lederer read the study that was conducted at Sonoma State Hospital, and says the children underwent painful experimentation "for which they received no direct benefit."

"It seems clear that these were intended to enlarge knowledge about cerebral palsy," adds Lederer.

It did not produce a breakthrough, although Lederer says studies using mentally retarded children were critical in creating vaccines for polio and hepatitis.

Lederer says using captive populations meant big money for medical researchers: "It would even be an advantage in applying for grant money, because you don't have to go to the problem of recruiting subjects."

Image Source: <u>CBS News</u>

---

[69] International Journal of Maternal and Child Health and AIDS, Overcoming Challenges in Conducting Clinical Trials in Minority Populations: Identifying and Testing What Works, https://www.ncbi.nlm.nih.gov/pmc/articles/PMC4948175/

"They were the raw material of medical research,' says Susan Lederer, who teaches medical history at Yale University. She was a member of the presidential committee that investigated the radiation experiments, and she says she wasn't shocked by the findings because researchers have been using disabled children in experiments for over a century.

'Children in orphanages, children in homes of the mentally retarded, these are all good populations from the sense of medical research, because you have an easily accessible group of people living in controlled circumstances, and you can monitor them,' says Lederer.

Lederer read the study that was conducted at Sonoma State Hospital, and says the children underwent painful experimentation 'for which they received no direct benefit.'

...

Lederer says using captive populations meant big money for medical researchers: 'It would even be an advantage in applying for grant money, because you don't have to go to the problem of recruiting subjects.'"

Text Source: CBS News[70]

They knew. The people at Yale knew how deceptive we were in our practices, in how we approached medical recruiting, and in how we exploited people while lying to them. And they did nothing to prevent it, even when they became recruitment targets for other purposes; and at Yale, in that CIA recruitment box, Yale students and staff absolutely were Intelligence recruitment targets, and it did not always go light on the manipulation or coercion.

Even despite that, they still could not see past their egos to understand that it was not only those with "no value" that our methodologies were being used on. It was those with "no value" whom we were experimenting on so that we could get the techniques correct before going after the ones with value - the larger population, those with money, those with land to steal, those with power, and everyone who ever thought they were "too necessary" to become a target.

---

[70] CBS News, A Dark Chapter in Medical History, https://www.cbsnews.com/news/a-dark-chapter-in-medical-history-09-02-2005/

But being necessary does make you a target. You have something an exploiter needs to control and an enemy needs to eliminate.

I still tried. Despite their egos and lack of compassion for others, I still tried to save them from what the medical experimentation would result in, by asking them to intervene before it got worse, before it expanded, before it reached them. You cannot say I didn't try.

They simply were not interested. They did not realize the chains that were on others were the same ones on them as well. So, they did not remove the chains of the victims below them. They did not break the chains.

Their mindset is a large part of why we are where we are today, as I write this to you. The egotistical and unthoughtful mind often is.

So, with even less hope for humanity than I had previously, I spent more time hanging around George and the recruiter, blending into the background as they wove their way not just through grassroots organizations, but also through Yale's campus and society. After all, they had both spent their university-age years on that campus. They were Yalies themselves. In those halls, in their Yale societies and away from prying eyes, that's when I became introduced to the culture and mindset that were the money and power driving a lot of what we had been doing. Sometimes, I would join the conversation. Why wouldn't I? I was there.

One time, when I was safe to speak behind closed doors, I asked about why some of the industry and academic planners there were reducing the ability of doctors to make truly patient-tailored diagnoses and treatments with thorough analysis. At that time, the standardization of medicine and education was producing a sharp decline in fine-tuned analytical and diagnostic skills. It was affecting more than one industry (and I was deeply concerned that we would lose the genius and detail of thought necessary to get our civilization out of a mess at a later date). However, medicine was the area that I felt would cause each of us the most personal damage, especially as the generations went on and the original knowledge became lost, further complicated by an increase in difficult-to-treat immune system dysregulation.

When we go to a physician, it's often because we are damaged. The last thing we want or need in that moment is for them to damage us more, at least in my opinion.

Their response was disheartening, to say the least. The standardization was being done because, from a governance and management perspective, a standardized homogenous industry is much easier to manage and regulate. They wanted less work for themselves at the government, industry, and regulatory level. They also wanted fewer unexpected results and actions to contend with. In other words, they were lazy and afraid of competition. When I mentioned the problem of having to see a doctor who was less than ideally skilled, someone scoffed at me and said, "We have our own doctors." Obviously, they could not comprehend that if you dumb down an entire society, eventually even your best doctors will be affected and their skills will be reduced. The less-honed skills and the (lack of) thought processes behind those will eventually seep into everything, including the Ivy League medical schools.

In the early years, it became obvious that the house of war criminals I was now a quasi-member of was exploiting the population so hard that entire nations were getting ready to collapse under the weight. Their thinking was that of a lazy drug-addicted predator accustomed to being served everything on a silver tray. I would attempt to reason with them and mention that you cannot take someone for 100% of their profits and expect them to still keep producing and giving to you year after year. They didn't believe me. Every person and group they got their hooks into, they would eventually take for everything. When willing to tell me why, one of them stated something along the lines of, "They've always managed with nothing, so they'll keep managing with nothing."

That statement alone had so many flaws that I didn't even have a response. I would have had to throw out any faith in their understanding and start at the beginning, much like what I'm doing with this book. If it feels like I'm overexplaining things, you can blame them. The way I see it, if the pros in charge can't understand something as simple as why stealing someone's food will result in them not being able to work, why would the people who "voted them in" and put them in charge understand the bare bones of how things function?

Back then, before I was aware that a larger population outside of the Ivory Towers even really existed, I was arguing for the sustainability of the recruiter's Yale alumni cohort's criminal enterprise atop government. I was trying to save them, the same as I've tried to save myself, the same as I've tried to save you. As it turns out, I'm a failure when it comes to reasoning with addicts and those who like life to be easy. They were too high on their own egos and Afghani heroin to care. Their victims were still happy to cling to the small comforts they were promised they could keep as long as they were well-behaved victims. And we were all heading for the cliff we're now standing on.

They say knowledge makes people unhappy. This is why. Even back then, it was obvious that we were all heading for disaster while they were the nation's and the globe's chauffeurs.

As for the abundant failures of random politicians, media personalities, and others to fix the mess made by the war criminals and their thieving cohorts, the concept of some hero coming to the rescue was made by Hollywood, not reality. One person cannot save millions. It's actually impossible. The physics of the model cannot conform to or function like that. Once they make waves, that one person is instantly swamped by all the predators who go for the peak prey - anyone with sway or access to power. There are no superheroes. Either we all pull our weight in not being bamboozled, or this ship sinks and that's the end of it. And considering how many spineless nihilists we have these days, I'm not betting on survival. The odds are not in our favor. If they were, we wouldn't be in this situation to begin with.

While my attempts to create some stability for myself, my world, and the world may have been paltry, the recruiter's attempts at her own aims were not much better in some regards, although she definitely put a lot more funding and effort in. She still wasn't happy about my level of obedience, so she started bringing in some of her buddies from research departments related to the ones she had been directly supervising. They "invited" me to become a more useful human being. By invited, I mean they showed up at the safehouse in the middle of the night, driving an ambulance.

I walked out to the ambulance with the recruiter. There was nothing wrong with me at all, but she assured a worried-looking neighbor that I was okay and just a little dizzy. I got into the back of the ambulance, and they insisted on putting the oxygen mask on me. This trip happened several times. I remember because the usual man in the back of the ambulance

was aware of my claustrophobic feeling of suffocating once the mask was on, and he was kind enough to always use a long rope of cotton along the edge of the mask to protect my skin and to create a small gap giving me the tiniest bit of ordinary air to breathe. When he didn't and it was someone else, she abrasively put the mask on me directly. That resulted in my feeling panicked in the moment and with an acne outbreak around my mouth that went on for months after. The man had been right about the mask's potential for creating skin irritation.

The oxygen wasn't just oxygen. It knocked me out every time. On one occasion, I woke up in the clinic they had brought us to. I say us because I was not the only child there. There was a teenage boy I had met before. He was screaming down the hall as they hustled him out. He was screaming to change the meaning of the words. He kept repeating "knot the not" as they pushed him out the door.

My hospital bed in the clinic was behind a thin curtain. They kept the lights low and their voices hushed. All of the "patients" were sleeping. The medication made it impossible to move. We were kept immobile for what felt like weeks. I lost all sense of time. I've always fought anesthesia (a leftover from my survival instinct to fight the recruiter's drugging), so my waking up despite the amount of drugs flowing into me via an IV was not unusual, not for me.

I woke up in agony. Because of the injuries to my spine that I've had since Argentina, being paralyzed on my back without the pillow being in the one position that's actually comfortable for me caused every nerve in my body to scream and every muscle to seize up. I hurt so incredibly badly that all the anesthesia in the world would not have kept me sleeping. That's when I became aware of the machine on my right. It was playing a recording over and over again, the same words, a command. It made me recall what the boy in the hall had said, "Knot the not." Suddenly, his words made sense. The recording started with "I will not know." I don't remember the rest. Between the agony, going in and out of sleep, and my fighting to keep the words out of my head and change their meaning to make them ineffective, I simply didn't allow them to take hold in my memory. I changed "I will not know" to "Eye will knot no."

The pain, however, was still there. My right calf had become a solid knot and I couldn't reach it to massage it. The hours continued to go by. I was fighting the words, I was fighting the drugs to stay awake so I could fight the words, and then I was in agony on top of everything. That's when I went deep in my mind because it was the only thing I could control in the situation. I found that little pain switch in my head and I flicked it over from agony to ecstasy. That's the moment I became a masochist. I've never been able to entirely flip that switch back to its original position. The result of that moment would be a disaster in my romantic relationships later on. It's difficult to have a healthy dynamic when you require a sadist in order to get off, but I digress. We haven't hit my adulthood yet, and I'd definitely prefer to compartmentalize that, for obvious reasons. Let's get back to 1980s New Haven for now...

At least I was allowed to escape via school and summer camp sometimes. One of the summer camps was located on a small island off the coast between New York and Connecticut. The buses would park in a large lot, and from there, we would take boats with our camp counselors to get to the jellyfish-surrounded island. The amount of jellyfish there was actually ludicrous. Each day, before we could swim, the counselors would have to remove over a hundred of them from our small designated swimming area. Part of the fun of camp was watching the captured jellyfish get dumped on the beach.

The camp had historical roots. I believe it was the first government-funded boy's military camp in the United States. When I was there, I knew none of that. However, I was in the first group of girls to be in the camp. We were younger than everyone else and we didn't have the proper attire because they simply had not made regulations for girls yet. We stuck out like sore thumbs. But it was camp and I enjoyed it for the most part. If something was too terrifying (I was afraid of heights and didn't want to climb up to attempt to maneuver the ropes they had between trees), I would act scared and they would invariably let me skip out on an activity because I was a girl. By the second week, my activity schedule card was mostly full of swimming. They had given up on involving me in anything else other than camp-wide activities.

The Cadets at Plum Island

THE JUNIOR PLATTSBURG

First Federal Military Training

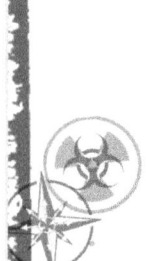

> On 6 July, 1916, 1200 boys, eager and enthusiastic but without military training or discipline, entered the First Federal Military Training Camp for Boys, at Fort Terry on Plum Island; five* weeks later the same number, physically and mentally "fit" and disciplined, respecting authority because they respected themselves, and bearing themselves like men, left camp for their homes.

Image Source: Connecticut State Library

"On 6 July 1916, 1200 boys, eager and enthusiastic but without military training or discipline, entered the First Federal Military Training Camp for Boys, at Fort Terry on Plum Island."

Text Source: Connecticut State Library[71]

The experience became comfortable with all of that sorted out, and I was enjoying my days. Unfortunately for me, I was still connected to the recruiter. Another girl and I both had "parents" who chose to send us to that camp because they had direct connections to the research lab on the other side of the island, now known as the U.S. Office of National Laboratories (ONL) Plum Island Animal Disease Center. We would sometimes be called to meet them at that lab when they were stopping by the island or if they needed to pick us up early for any reason. On those days, we would walk along a path from the beach and enter the lab from the side. As we walked along the left side of the building, on the dirt path, with

[71] Connecticut State Library, The Cadets at Plum Island, https://cslib.contentdm.oclc.org/digital/api/collection/p4005coll11/id/39/download
Additional Camp Documents: https://carlisleindian.dickinson.edu/sites/default/files/docs-documents/NARA_RG75_CCF_b021_f06_57042.pdf

the sounds of angry dogs (there was an ongoing rabies research project at the time) in their path-facing kennels snarling at us, our ankles were getting eaten alive by fleas.

In the moment, the fleas were simply an annoyance and the dogs were scary but relatively harmless (no one led us onto the hall where we would have had direct contact). However, in retrospect, I would like to note that biolab was funded by a government that supposedly has enough money to keep things professional, sanitary, and free from lab leaks. And yet, visitors and anyone who walked nearby were being bitten by the same fleas that were biting ill and rabies-heavy dogs. This is a lab being run by the same "professional government scientists" the public blindly trusts to keep them safe.

Plum Island Animal Disease Center

Science and
Technology

Location: Orient Point, NY

Since 1954, the Plum Island Animal Disease Center (PIADC) has served as the nation's premier defense against accidental or intentional introduction of transboundary animal diseases—highly transmissible diseases of livestock and other animals, including foot-and-mouth disease (FMD) and African swine fever (ASF)—that can significantly affect food security, trade, and the economy. These diseases are not transmissible between animals and humans.

Image Source: US Department of Homeland Security

"Plum Island Animal Disease Center

Location: Orient Point, NY

Since 1954, the DHS S&T Office of National Laboratories (ONL) Plum Island Animal Disease Center (PIADC) has served as the nation's premier defense against accidental or intentional introduction of transboundary animal diseases (a.k.a. foreign animal diseases)."

Text Source: US Department of Homeland Security[72]

These "experts" are the ones the public has complete faith in to protect them from "accidental or intentional" contact with animal diseases, in addition to being happy to be lied to by them. These same experts who allowed children and scientists to be exposed to whatever transmittable diseases their actively rabid dogs may have had.

I have to say, I'm not shocked that many people believe that Plum Island is where the major tick-carried Lyme Disease outbreak came from. It's geographically close enough to Lyme, Connecticut, and campers and scientists who spend time on that island bring ticks home, to Connecticut and New York, on their clothes every day. While I have some doubts regarding the validity of the overdone theories about the lab having created a new version of Lyme Disease in that time frame, I have to acknowledge that lab may have simply been housing one of the older strains and let it get into the wild. They had no effective safety protocols in place to prevent spread. In fact, their safety levels were so low, that I would call them an ideal starting point for uncontrolled spread of animal-human transmitted illnesses.

The government, its bureaucrats, its scientists, and its workers are not competent, honest, responsible, or mature enough to handle biological weapons to a high enough level to contain them, despite their outwardly impressive credentials, badges, and military brass that could be easily replaced by 1-cent gold-star-shaped stickers intended to reward a child for cleaning their room by shoving everything under the bed. They never have been responsible enough. This has been proven countless times.

---

[72] US Department of Homeland Security, Plum Island Animal Disease Center, https://www.dhs.gov/science-and-technology/plum-island-animal-disease-center

The unspoken and yet standard policy of glossing over errors and blaming bureaucracy or unnecessary requirements is born from the level of deceit that appears to be a requirement for the majority of people in academic and professional circles if they wish to meet on-paper-only hiring requirements. The desire to attain a better paycheck and a higher title does not create a positive outcome when it comes to the sciences.

In fact, their need for personal gain above lab safety limits the likelihood that those in the labs and imposing the rules will have the actual scope or capability to have honest conversations about problem areas that need to be rectified. Instead, they bow to authority and the need for face-saving in order to maintain their pay, ranking, and status. In doing so, they gloss over problems and errors in a desperate attempt to appear professional and highly competent without ever attaining the same level of professionalism or competence that the gloss portrays. Their self-necessitated deceit causes them to intentionally error, rather than admit to errors. They pile disaster on top of disaster, thinking that somehow more lies will fix the very tangible problem of lab failures.

Biowarfare research protocols, when created and maintained within a deep-seated culture of deceit, simply cannot be attained at a level that will guarantee containment. Science requires honesty. So does containment. All it takes is one error for a mistake to become fatal. When you have twenty errors because the people and departments involved have additional motives other than pure science and containment, and are capable of using deception to hide the fact that they have given their other motives priority above safety, global fatalities become guaranteed.

Then the scientists go home and pray their errors don't follow them. Even that, I've personally seen go wrong.

The recruiter worked with various labs and projects over the years. One was actually doing cancer research. And, due to lab contamination, she developed tumors up and down her spine when I was around ten years old. She spent the next year getting experimental treatments from that same lab (as far as I know, she talked about them but I never went with her for those) and also ingesting food-grade peroxide right in front of me, in small but seemingly frequent quantities diluted in beverages. When I asked why, she said it was because cancer needs an anaerobic environment to thrive. The more oxygen you push at it,

the better your chance of survival. I've never tested that theory, myself. However, her tumors did eventually resolve due to some combination of what she had been doing.

On the subject of labs under the recruiter's supervisorial domain, one lab from that same group was working on what may have been one of the surface projects funding and providing support and biological materials for the hidden research our tight-knit group of scientists from the dinner parties was doing with the AIDS virus. The lab in question's stated research purpose was to enhance immune systems to increase chances of survival during nuclear and biological attacks. So, they did just enough research on immune system enhancement to make the project look legitimate for their funders. At around the same time, as referenced previously with documentation, the more blatant walking pneumonia/HIV hybrid research would be hidden in plain sight under the umbrella of vaccine research.

When I saw what was going on within that immune system enhancement project was when I first started to worry about everyone's immediate safety. Not about a future time when things might snowball out of control, like I was with the AIDS research. Nope. In the case of the immune system research, I was already concerned for humanity then and there. The researchers decided that hormones were the key to unlocking the full potential of the human immune system. As a result of the hormones they altered to test that theory, every research subject of theirs that I met had developed overactive immune system dysfunction symptoms ranging from severe life-threatening allergies to full-blown lupus.

I wasn't there to witness it as an assistant that time. I was one of the human numbers in the research subject pool. They had been short on participants and the recruiter volunteered me to fill one of the spots on the list. As a result, if you so much as sneezed near me, my immune system would go into overdrive and my skin would end up covered in a persistent sandpaper rash. I struggled with constant aching, dizziness, and an overactive immune system for decades after. It was not great for the self-esteem of someone prone to acne for life - every zit became swollen up to ten times the size it should have been, due to near-instant, sustained, and systemic inflammation that could only be halted with long courses of antibiotics. A doctor in Italy who was treating my skin later on told me that my hormone profile matched that of a teenager. I was forty when he told me that.

One time, while driving to a pharmaceutical company's campus, the recruiter told me not to worry. She said that when she signed me into medical and pharmaceutical research programs, she always used her influence to make sure that I would be in the placebo group. At this point, it's rather obvious that was a lie.

The only thing that makes me feel a little better about it all is that, in my fear of being seen as weak (I was convinced that the recruiter's psychopathic instincts would go into overdrive if she knew how close to death I was and that it would lead her to finishing me off, so I always did my best to look okay even when I wasn't), I may have skewed their early research some as a test subject. There's a chance that their target market - the people who were happy to use unwitting test subjects to further their own survival - were being told the treatment was safe for them to use when it was not.

Actually, there is one other dark silver lining. The woman in charge of that particular lab, I can never remember her name. Maybe it was Jody. She wasn't interested in keeping soldiers alive or finding cures for the bioweapons we were creating. It is very likely that she had been recruited from a university campus in the middle of the late 1960s to early 1970s psychedelic drug craze. Yes, she may have had the potential to be a brilliant scientist when she was in university, but by the time she graduated, she was full-on Age of Aquarius new-age mantra pie in the sky delusional about what could be achieved and how she would achieve it. The drugs and insanely unrealistic culture had altered her thoughts. She was misusing Department of Defense research funding to attempt what she was really interested in - finding the fountain of youth through science. She wanted immortality and felt she was "peak human" enough to find it. That's all she ever actually worked on. It didn't matter what a research proposal said or where her funding was coming from. Achieving a fountain of youth was all she was ever working on. When I met her, she was convinced hormones were the answer (my Italian dermatologist might half agree with her - after all, his aging patient did manage to retain the acne of a fifteen-year-old).

But enough about that portion of the ego-borne insanity. The reason I became concerned for all of us was because, shortly after witnessing the statistically very significant symptoms of allergies, lupus, and general overreactive immune system issues in the research subject group, I started noticing them popping up in the larger population and in new and unusually high amounts. It wasn't just funders who were getting the treatment. Remember when groups of kids started getting peanut allergies around the same time? Giving a treatment to

alter hormone levels to cause an immune system overreaction at the same time as administering a vaccine that included peanut oil (a vaccine ingredient at that time), wouldn't just cause the same severe allergies and immune dysregulation the research pool was already seeing. It might actually cause even more.

I'm fairly certain, especially considering what lab I was standing in for that one, that the U.S. government was experimenting on its own people, possibly for what they believed to be genuine reasons and in the favor of the citizens for once.

This would have been done without the people's consent, understanding of the side effects, or knowledge as to what was being hidden in the standard childhood vaccines they were permitting to be injected into their children with trust in the medical system and faith in pharmaceutical companies to produce quality products without something extra thrown in. Yes, the U.S. still uses its own population as test subjects. It never "stopped 50 years ago." That's just the 50-year classification rule doing its job of making sure all the victims are dead of old age and bad health before they can sue.

What was that line again, the one from Military Medical Ethics, Volume 2? Ah, right:

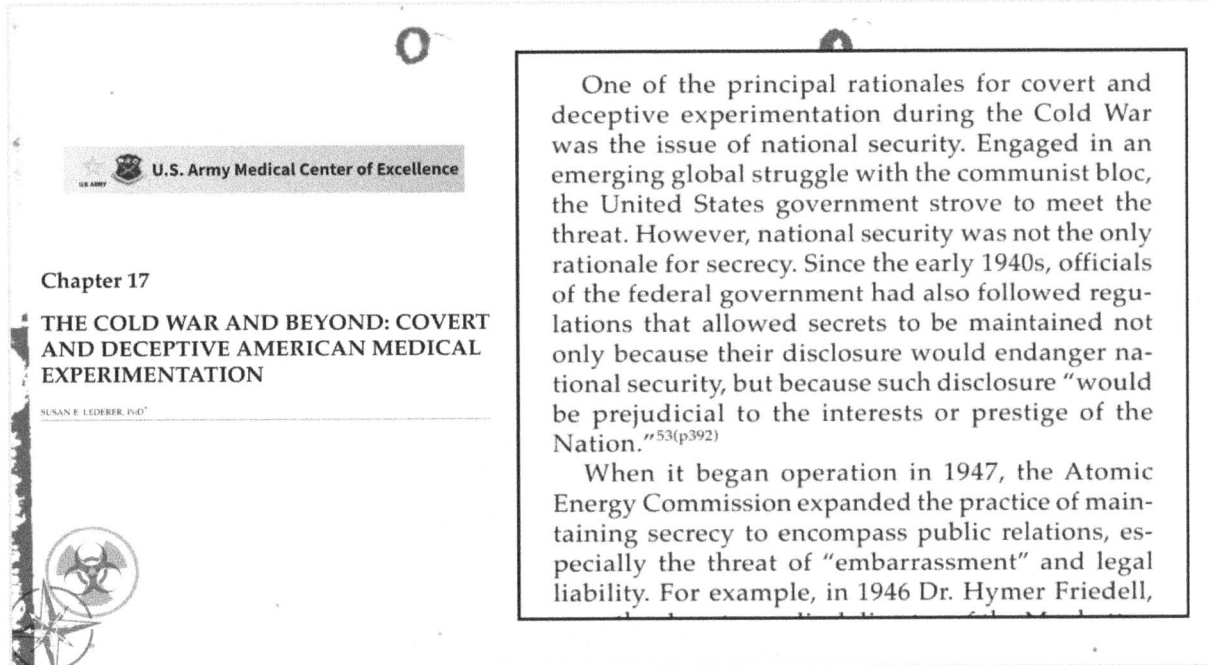

One of the principal rationales for covert and deceptive experimentation during the Cold War was the issue of national security. Engaged in an emerging global struggle with the communist bloc, the United States government strove to meet the threat. However, national security was not the only rationale for secrecy. Since the early 1940s, officials of the federal government had also followed regulations that allowed secrets to be maintained not only because their disclosure would endanger national security, but because such disclosure "would be prejudicial to the interests or prestige of the Nation."[53(p392)]

When it began operation in 1947, the Atomic Energy Commission expanded the practice of maintaining secrecy to encompass public relations, especially the threat of "embarrassment" and legal liability. For example, in 1946 Dr. Hymer Friedell,

Image Source: U.S. Army Medical Center of Excellence

"The Atomic Energy Commission expanded the practice of maintaining secrecy to encompass public relations, especially the threat of 'embarrassment' and legal liability."

Text Source: U.S. Army Medical Center of Excellence[73]

Because the easiest victims to ignore and lie to, and about, are the injured ones. After all, the injured and disabled have so little value in society that they wouldn't have enough of a voice even if the government weren't burying them to save a few dollars. That's just the sad truth about society. It's a leftover from our herd instincts, back when we left the weak to be eaten by predators. Sadly, not much has actually changed despite our moving into the modern day of germ warfare and advanced weapons research. We still leave the weak to be eaten.

Unfortunately, in doing so in the modern context, we've set everyone up to become the weak. Is there any question as to why the predators among us have, in sensing weakness, now become brazen and emboldened enough to attack the population?

---

[73] United States Army Medical Center of Excellence, Military Medical Ethics, Volume 2, Chapter 17 The Cold War and Beyond: Covert and Deceptive American Medical Experimentation, Susan E. Lederer, PhD,
https://ke.army.mil/bordeninstitute/published_volumes/ethicsvol2/ethics-ch-17.pdf
https://medcoeckapwstorprd01.blob.core.usgovcloudapi.net/pfw-images/borden/ethicsvol2/Ethics-ch-17.pdf

In addition to what I personally saw, there are too many prior examples of unethical research to go through them one by one, and the declassified published information on those within the United States almost all suddenly stops 50 or so years ago. The practice didn't stop. I was there for several newer projects, and I'm not 50 quite yet.

Entrenchment at Yale

Take the blindfold off and walk away from the ledge.
Pushing people over it won't save you.
They're tied to you.

(And yes, I know this advice is difficult to follow.
There are days I can see the benefit
of pushing all of Argentina off a cliff, myself.)

Back on the ground in New Haven (and sometimes Hartford, Washington D.C., and other primarily East Coast locations), there was much more going on. Directly in front of my eyes, politicians were leashed and business owners were harassed. In my presence, and often with my assistance, healthy children and cancer patients were manipulated into becoming Department of Defense test subjects for various projects "for their benefit" and almost inevitably resulting in their injury or death.

It always shocked me how easily the parents of children fell for the fraud. All it took was promising their children "opportunity," the magic word of America that works just as well domestically as it does internationally. I will never shake off the memory of the deceased body of one of those children. She was a beautiful blonde child and a good friend to me for the short time that I knew her. I witnessed her snuffed out by scientists before her time in a room accessed from the halls beneath Yale New Haven Hospital.

I will always mourn her, even though I feel alone in my grief, as if she has been long forgotten by everyone else.

In the period of time in which she died, the recruiter would have me guide children from medical lab to medical lab throughout the day for various clinical research projects and then several blocks away to a local community center to be picked up by their parents from "camp." These were generally the low-income children whose parents the recruiter had

conned into giving her medical guardianship. At the end of one day, I had already collected a Jamaican girl who was roughly my age and we walked down the hall together to find the blonde girl to bring with us to the "camp" parent pickup area. The room door was on our right as we walked down that hall. We entered and there was that girl, on the floor, dead, in front of a small therapeutic pool. Other than her, the room was void of people. They had just left her body there alone. The two of us responded quite like you'd assume girls would, shrieking and jumping around as if we had just seen the biggest spider ever.

Researchers heard our screams and came running. They gave the girl I was with a small cup of drugs to calm her down or help her forget (I'd assume more the latter) and the day went on from there. That evening, they crowded most of the parents into a room in the back of the nearby Jewish Community Center, the building they had used as a camp front for the research. They told the parents it had been a tragic accident that had happened while the children were having swimming lessons in a large pool in that community center, blocks away from the small room where that child had died alone, other than the presence of researchers. The parents accepted the explanation, although many reasonably pulled their children from the camp, and thus the research projects, after that night.

When the deceased girl's mother entered the room, I tried to say something. I was never great with emotional things; for me they were too raw to summarize in hollow and perfunctory statements such as "I'm sorry for your loss." I had buried my own feelings so deep to survive through those years that I didn't know how to adequately express my deep regret, empathy, and pain. As I was trying to find the words, the recruiter swept in between us, guided the woman into a dark room, and drugged her. Within about five minutes, that mother walked out of the dark room, having easily accepted the lie that her daughter's tragic end was an innocent death, a swimming accident. She actually seemed to be unnaturally at peace with the loss.

While much of that mother's response was due to the drugs, my heart sank when I saw it. The recruiter had been using strong hypnotics in those years. A suggestion seeded and formed while on the drugs tended to persist in a person long after the drugs faded. In fact, it almost always became a central thought and way of thinking. Those the recruiter drugged were often described as having "changed overnight," and many never returned to their prior beliefs.

Before that moment, I thought that a child's death would be enough to wake a parent from their slumber if nothing else was. I was proven wrong.

As for that Jewish Community Center, according to the Ethnic Heritage Center and New Haven Independent, the building had already been sold or was in the transitory hand-off period by that time (the sale was initiated in 1985 and final closing ceremonies were in the early summer of 1986). I did not first meet the Jamaican child, who witnessed the body with me, until the summer of 1986. Meaning, that particular "camp" was either during the end of the transitory period or was falsely running in the name of the established community center, using their prior reputation, even though the people who had established that reputation had handed over the keys, left the sign in place above the door, and had already relocated to another area.

Actually, the history of a Catholic school I went to was much the same - people taking advantage of a reputation established by a prior administration, but I digress...

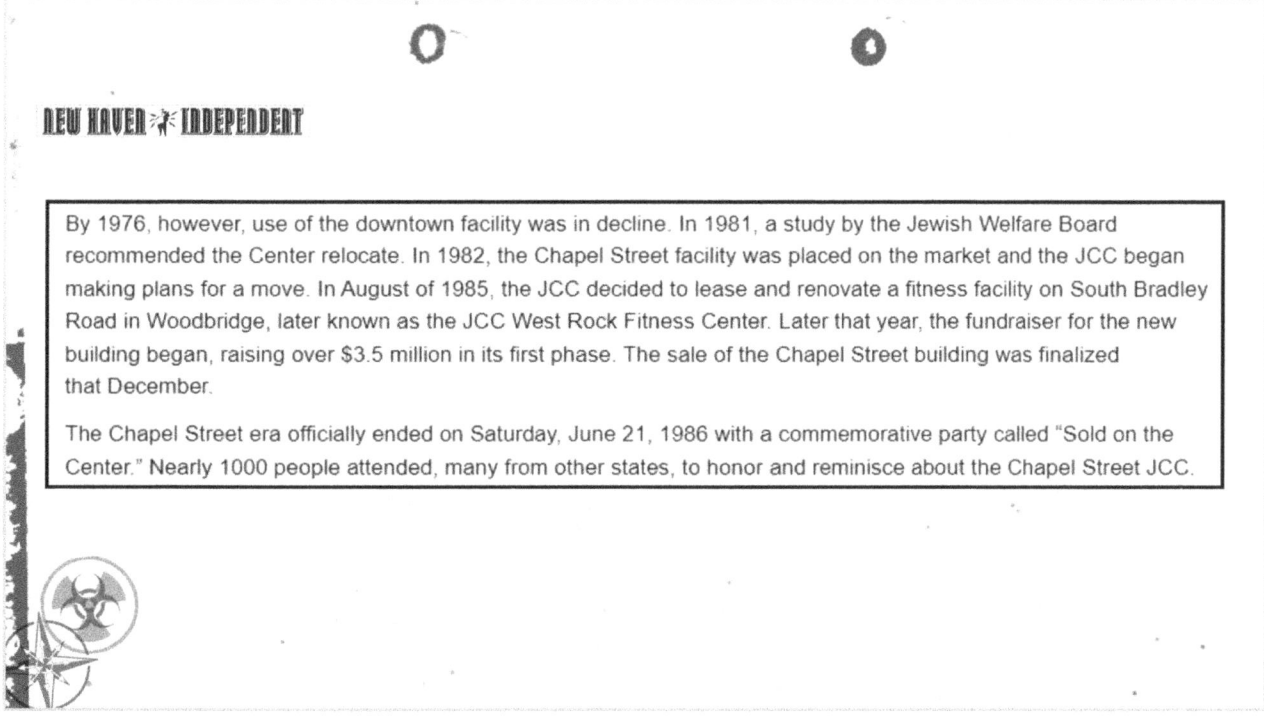

NEW HAVEN ✴ INDEPENDENT

By 1976, however, use of the downtown facility was in decline. In 1981, a study by the Jewish Welfare Board recommended the Center relocate. In 1982, the Chapel Street facility was placed on the market and the JCC began making plans for a move. In August of 1985, the JCC decided to lease and renovate a fitness facility on South Bradley Road in Woodbridge, later known as the JCC West Rock Fitness Center. Later that year, the fundraiser for the new building began, raising over $3.5 million in its first phase. The sale of the Chapel Street building was finalized that December.

The Chapel Street era officially ended on Saturday, June 21, 1986 with a commemorative party called "Sold on the Center." Nearly 1000 people attended, many from other states, to honor and reminisce about the Chapel Street JCC.

Image Source: New Haven Independent

"New Haven's Jewish Community Center was downtown on Chapel Street in those days...It no longer is in that Chapel Street building. (Yale's art school is.)

In August of 1985, the JCC decided to lease and renovate a fitness facility on South Bradley Road in Woodbridge...The sale of the Chapel Street (New Haven) building was finalized that December...

The Chapel Street era officially ended on Saturday, June 21, 1986, with a commemorative party."

Text Source: New Haven Independent[74]

WALK NEW HAVEN
CULTURAL HERITAGE TOURS

Jewish Community Center

1156 CHAPEL STREET (FORMER)

Jewish Community Center at 1156 Chapel Street, c. 1960s

Image: Chapel Street Jewish Community Center Building

Source: The Ethnic Heritage Center[75]

While I was there, they did have a camp in the building, or at least activities, and we attended once in a while to make the farce seem legit. It was sitting in a gymnasium room in

[74] New Haven Independent, You Don't Have to be Jewish,
https://www.newhavenindependent.org/index.php/article/you_didnt_have_to_be_jewish_

[75] The Ethnic Heritage Center, Jewish Community Center, https://walknewhaven.org/jewish-community-center

that Jewish Community Center where I once played the parachute game with other children. We would sit in a circle and loft a large and colorful parachute into the air between us. Then, we would run under it, the chaos of our movement hidden under the material as it fell back to the ground. Beneath that parachute, we would seek a way out and find a new place to sit. Once everything was over, every spot to sit was taken, but no child remained in their original place. That is how I see war, especially as a child of it. In the chaos of war, so many of us change positions, that within a few rounds, no one knows what side they are on, what side they started on, or who their enemy is. Have a few generations play that game under a policy of secrecy and deception, and the chaos becomes complete.

At least when the recruiter preyed on adult cancer patients, rather than healthy children, you knew she was probably ending their painful struggle by bringing them to the mercy of death more quickly. Although, her recruitment tactics were still highly unethical (and so was giving patients false hope when the only intention was to use them for the benefit of weapons research for "national security").

To target some of the cancer patients, she would bring me along for trips on the New Haven to New York Amtrak train and she carried along a small and relatively discreet handheld Geiger counter for radiation monitoring. She'd wander through the train cars until she located someone who had radiation treatment recently enough that they could cause the numbers on the Geiger counter to spike.

Then she would tuck away the Geiger counter and sit next to them as if she were simply a fellow passenger in need of a seat. She would strike up a friendly conversation, which she would quickly steer in the direction of health until they spoke about their cancer treatment. From there, she would exclaim, "Oh, what an amazing coincidence!" The recruiter would go on to tell them that she worked for Yale New Haven Hospital, that she was a cancer researcher there, and that she just happened to know of an excellent research program that had one remaining available space.

As far as I know, every single one of those conned cancer patients died.

And her little, "I'm a cancer researcher" spiel she would tell so many of her marks? Technically, maybe she was early in her career. Those were some of the labs and projects she would end up supervising as time went on. However, the research projects I saw her sign off on covered a somewhat wider variety, and not just nuclear and biological.

When it came to what she told others, her credentials and title seemed to change to match whomever or whatever her mark was. She once told the public and the Nuclear Regulatory Commission, in official documents intended to be used in court, that she had a background in Environmental Sciences.

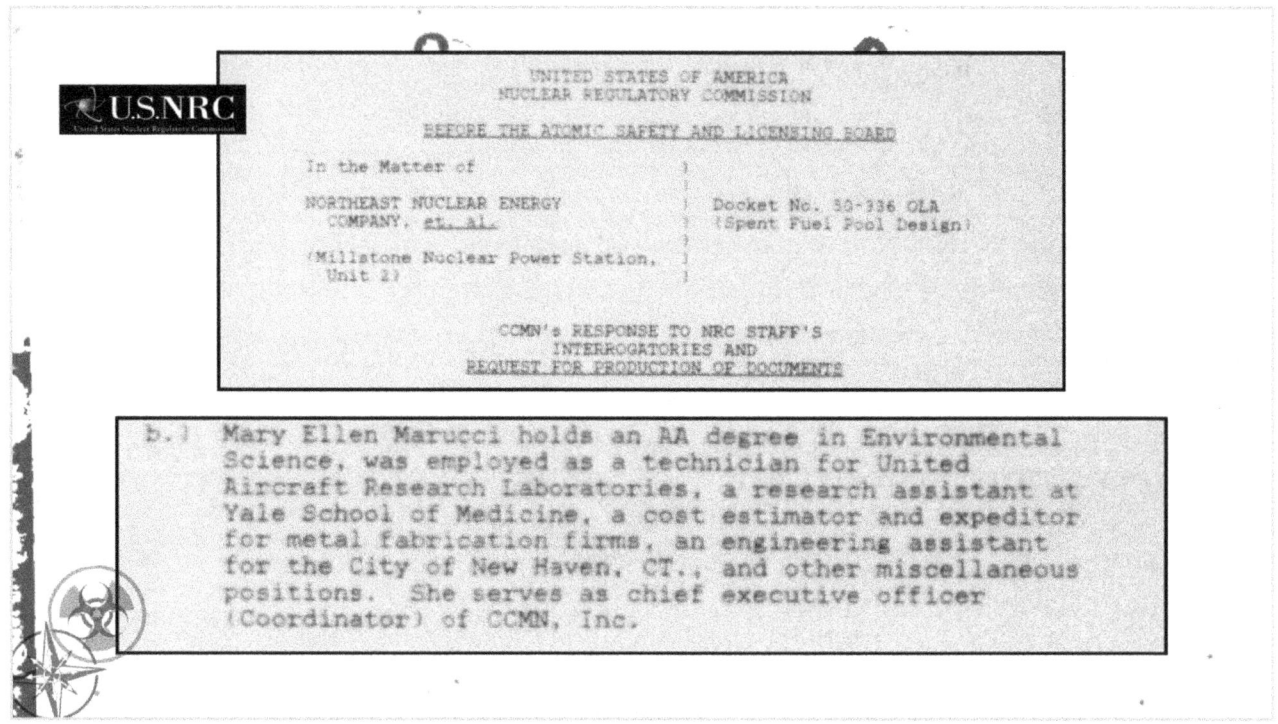

Image Source: <u>Nuclear Regulatory Commission</u>

".. holds an AA degree in Environmental Science, was employed as a technician for United Aircraft Research Laboratories... a cost estimator and expeditor for metal fabrication firms, an engineering assistant for the City of New Haven, CT.... She serves as chief executive officer (Coordinator) of CCMN, Inc."

Text Source: <u>Nuclear Regulatory Commission</u>[76]

---

[76] Nuclear Regulatory Commission, United States of America Nuclear Regulatory Commission Before the Atomic Safety and Licensing Board, https://www.nrc.gov/docs/ML2003/ML20034H791.pdf

It would switch over to nuclear engineering or nuclear medicine when speaking with antinuclear organizations or potential research subjects.

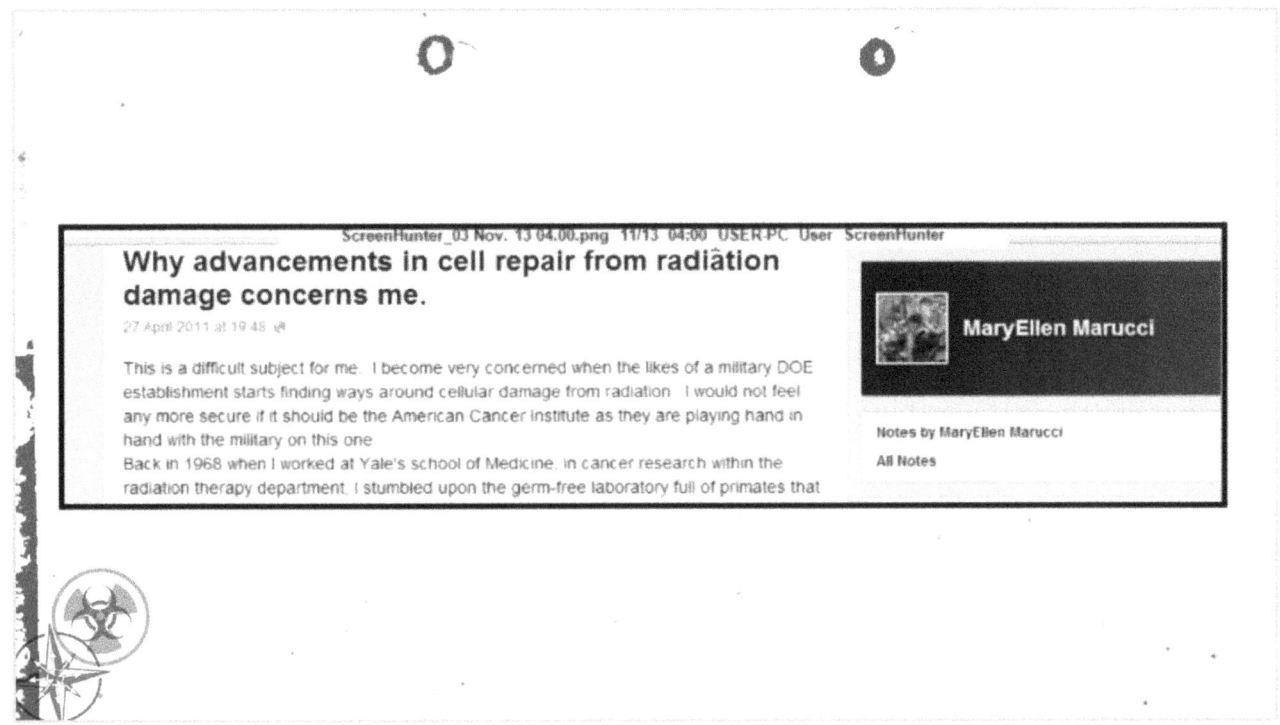

Image Source: 2013 Screenshot Facebook

"When I worked at Yale's School of Medicine, in cancer research within the radiation therapy department."

Text Source: 2013 Screenshot Facebook[77]

77 Facebook, MaryEllen Marucci Profile, https://www.facebook.com/seedsaver/

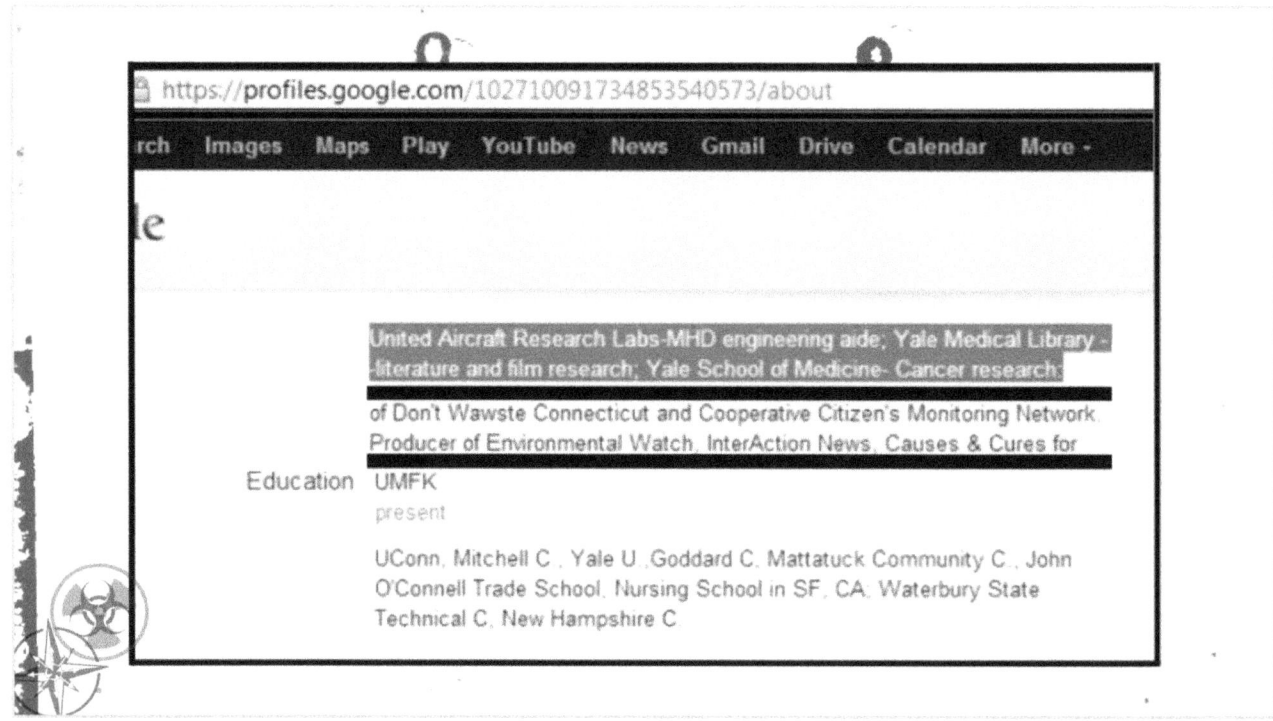

Image Source: <u>Google Profiles</u> 2013 Screenshot

"United Aircraft Research Labs MHD Engineering aide, Yale Medical Library...Yale School of Medicine - Cancer Research...Yale......UCONN, Yale, Goddard, Nursing School... "

Text Source: <u>Google Profiles</u> 2013 Screenshot[78]

I was growing up in a situation entirely devoid of ethics or honesty, and in which children were not protected, although we were often there to make a dangerous situation appear normal and safe. Illusion is not the same as reality.

We were never safe.

And neither was anyone else.

Shortly after our arrival in New Haven, the recruiter started bringing me along to "Yale movie nights." They seemed innocent enough, especially if you bring a child along to

---

[78] Google Profiles, 2013 Screenshot - Mary Ellen Marucci, https://profiles.google.com/102710091734853540573/about

manufacture an appearance of the safe and innocent. The York Square Cinema was a small theater located on the edge of campus back then. On one weekday per week, the recruiter's group would rent out the entire theater, barring anyone else from using it, lock the doors, and only permit Yale students who had responded to a flyer to enter. The flyers, posted all over campus, had promised a series of radical movies. The movies highlighted concepts like apartheid, the struggle of grassroots organizations to fight against corporations to stop the poisoning of towns by waste runoff, guerrilla warfare, and other topics of interest to young anti-authoritarian or cognizant students.

We would pile everyone in and start the movie. The theater refreshment stand was closed (although as a child brought along by the representative of the organization renting the space, I would still manage to sneak a bag of Twizzlers before everyone arrived). "Luckily," the people running the series brought refreshments for everyone and would have a drink dispenser and a bowl of snacks available on a table they set up in the back of the movie theater room we would be occupying for the evening. The beverage in the dispenser was spiked - most likely with whatever expert scopolamine derivative was coming out of the Yale chemistry lab at the time (I'll get more into that later), i.e., a strong hypnotic.

Then, we would watch the movie. Three or four organizers would watch the Yale students to see what their reactions were throughout the movie. That is how they would decide which ones to target. It was the same routine every time. They'd slide up into the seat next to the ideal ones, start a conversation, and lead them off before the end of the night. I have no idea what happened to the students after that. They were Yalies, so I can reasonably assume they didn't go entirely missing or end up sold into cancer research. But I do know they left in a highly drugged state, with the type of people who do exploitative, unethical, and blackmail-tinged recruitment. What the recruiter had been doing at the university and in the prisons of Buenos Aires was pretty much the same thing she was doing in New Haven, just with a little more tact since we weren't in the middle of active state terrorism in 1980s Connecticut.

Did you really think a tiger, or a government, changes its stripes just because it's in its own neighborhood? That's where the tiger gets more confident.

It owns the place.

Later, beliefs-based recruitment would come more frequently from the shanty town, where George Edwards was ever-present. That shanty stood, aesthetically very out of place, in the plaza between Yale's Woolsey Hall and Beinecke Rare Book and Manuscript Library for about two years.

Image: Shanty on Yale Campus

Source: Yale Alumni Magazine[79]

---

[79] Yale Alumni Magazine, When Yale Activists Targeted Apartheid, https://yalealumnimagazine.org/blog_posts/1649-when-yale-activists-targeted-apartheid

He was mostly known as an omnipresence on New Haven streets, in settings formal and informal, with stories to tell and points to make. When activists built a shantytown to push Yale to divest from apartheid South Africa, Edwards was there to help build the structures. When activists joined politicians to elect the city's first Black mayor in 1989, Edwards was in the trenches.

"He said his job was the community," daughter Dickerson recalled.

"He said his job was the community,"

NEW HAVEN ☆ INDEPENDENT

Image Source: <u>New Haven Independent</u>

"He was mostly known as an omnipresence on New Haven streets, in settings formal and informal, with stories to tell and points to make. When activists built a shantytown to push Yale to divest from apartheid South Africa, Edwards was there to help build the structures."

Text Source: <u>New Haven Independent</u>[80]

---

[80] New Haven Independent, A Panther Passes On, https://www.newhavenindependent.org/article/panther_passes_on

Image: Shanty on Yale Campus

Source: Yale Alumni Magazine[81]

This type of involvement is standard for the agencies, although it is yet another classifiable form of "embarrassment."

---

81 Yale Alumni Magazine, When Yale Activists Targeted Apartheid, https://yalealumnimagazine.org/blog_posts/1649-when-yale-activists-targeted-apartheid

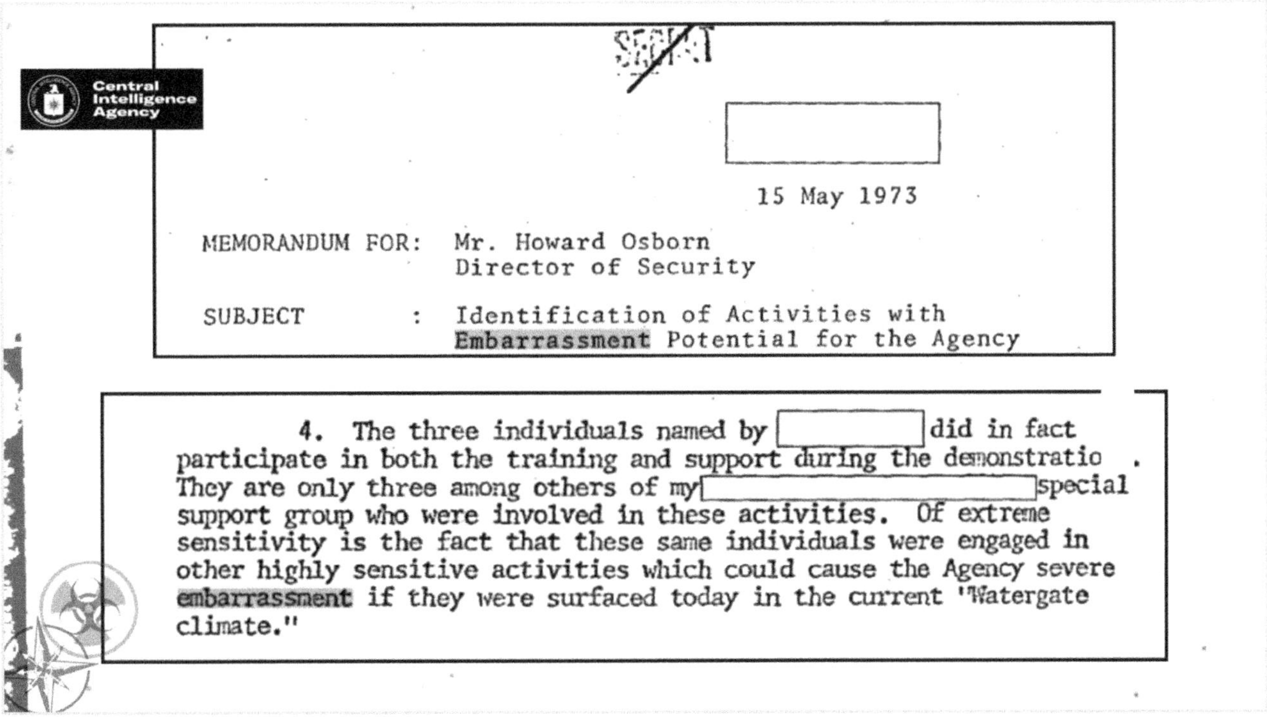

SECRET

[redacted]

15 May 1973

MEMORANDUM FOR: Mr. Howard Osborn
Director of Security

SUBJECT : Identification of Activities with Embarrassment Potential for the Agency

4. The three individuals named by [redacted] did in fact participate in both the training and support during the demonstratio . They are only three among others of my [redacted] special support group who were involved in these activities. Of extreme sensitivity is the fact that these same individuals were engaged in other highly sensitive activities which could cause the Agency severe embarrassment if they were surfaced today in the current 'Watergate climate."

Image Source: Central Intelligence Agency

"The three individuals named by (redacted) did in fact participate in both the training and support during demonstrations...Of extreme sensitivity in the fact that these same individuals were engaged in other highly sensitive activities which could cause the Agency severe embarrassment if they were surfaced today..."

Image Text: Central Intelligence Agency[82]

---

[82] Central Intelligence Agency, Memorandum for: Executive Secretary, CIA Management Committee, Subject: Family Jewels, https://www.cia.gov/readingroom/docs/DOC_0001451843.pdf

Demolition Crews

The sampling of experiences and highlighted points in history in this book are just grazing the surface of what I witnessed and was forced to be involved in. To write it all would require thousands of pages. I saw more exploitative coercion and callous death in the United States than I ever witnessed anywhere else, possibly because there is more there, or possibly because I was trapped with the offices that do the most harm. Both answers being correct is also a valid possibility.

Because I was still unskilled back then and always available for use, there were occasions on which they quite literally left me to clean it up.

As an example, there was an incident during my freshman or sophomore year of high school, so roughly between 1991 and 1993. The recruiter and her group had brought Middle Eastern men with demolition crew experience into the United States on fake Moroccan passports with marriage green cards, after paying several local women in New Haven and New York City to marry the men to get them into the country. One of the women was the recruiter's sister, a music teacher I had met in my first days in the U.S. in her tiny Bronx apartment. Another was a cousin with a part-time journalism job who had been living in an apartment in her parents' multifamily home. They were both in their 30s or early 40s at the time. They would both go from having small apartments (rented and rent-free from parents, respectively) to being owners of nice homes on large lots in preferred neighborhoods. It is highly likely that they received funds for the home purchases from their participation in the scheme.

It was clear that the recruiter selected family members because they were close enough to her to tightly control, and controlling them was necessary. The fake marriages would be rocky, obviously, because the men had to live with the women enough to pass Immigration scrutiny. We spent a lot of time in the women's apartments in those years, talking them through things and coming up with solutions. It was sad, in a way, because the cousin had fallen for the fantasy and was actually upset that her fake marriage wasn't working out. There were a lot of emotions involved in keeping up the farce.

However, there were worse conflicts between some of the men, and one of them ended up murdered, apparently at the hands of another of the men imported for the planned criminal yet government-funded demolition project. The office at my high school received a call from the recruiter about an "emergency" with instructions directing me to an address near her cousin's house. I took the city bus and arrived in time to see them working on dragging the body away.

The recruiter's cousin was still standing there, visibly shaking and in shock. She nervously talked to me while I ate my sandwich from school in the open kitchen and watched them haul the dead man away. She asked me how I could eat in that situation. I just looked at her. I didn't have a way to respond. How do you tell someone, whose biggest issues are what to wear and who to fall in love with, that when you're always surrounded by chaos, you don't let the chaos dictate your health, your hunger, or your well-being? Or at least you try not to.

Eventually, everyone left and I was handed the keys. Alone in the silence of that small apartment, I cleaned up the blood and tidied up everything else. The entire time, I wondered if I was dropping hair somewhere, if I'd left a fingerprint, and if I had left any trace of myself at all. Honestly, I knew I had. I was never a professional crime scene cleaner. I was thrown into so many insane situations that required a professional, and I just had to try my best. This was no different. For decades I stayed silent, partly because I wondered if I would get blamed for a crime because those were my fingerprints on the cleanup. Looking back at it, I no longer feel the same, not about that murder. I was fourteen or fifteen, a little too young to be masterminding events with men who shouldn't have even been in the country and who were about to be implicated in something that was much bigger than a young teenage girl with a $5 allowance to buy a sandwich.

I was standing among giants in the intel community, and all I could do was act as if I was okay with it, as if I were somehow magically unaware of what was going on. On more days than I can count, I came within inches of death because of it. On several occasions, it went beyond that line, and I needed to be revived.

And sometimes, I was there for more than the cleanup.

One summer evening, I was standing across the street from the Daily Cafe near Yale, bored and smoking a cigarette by myself. It was something I had done at least a hundred times before. Someone a few years older than me, whom I had met a couple of times before socially, pulled up alongside the curb and started talking to me. He asked if I wanted to drive with him to the nearby parking lot while he parked his car. I got in the car since the parking lot was only a block away. It may have been a little dumb of me. Especially when you consider that we didn't go to the parking lot.

He kept driving another block or two down Elm Street until we got to a part where the streetlights had been broken out. In the darkest section, he stopped the car in the middle of the street. Another car pulled up right alongside us and did the same. He told me to get into the other car, so I piled into it. It was crowded with several people, including a woman I had met once before with George, only a few blocks from the FBI building.

When I met her the first time, George had pulled up in his car with her already sitting in the passenger seat (entirely unexpected, he'd never given me a ride from classes), to pick me up on Audubon Street, right as I was walking out from where I was taking jewelry-making and acting courses through the Creative Arts Workshop and a basement dance and theater studio in the building across the street. His picking me up wasn't so obviously as clandestine of a situation as I would end up in with her next, but he still seemed nervous and hurried. And, like I said, it was entirely out of character for him. While in the car together, she seemed overly interested in me and asked to see my jewelry while we drove. I showed her a pair of metal earrings that I had made that day. She asked if she could buy them from me.

The next time I saw her, this time in the darkness of the crowded car on Elm Street, one of the first things I would notice about her was the glinting metal of one of those earrings dangling from an ear. I don't normally fixate on women, notice what they're wearing, or even talk to them most of the time. After listening to so many females screaming in the prison when I was little, and then being exploited by a woman since the moment I left that prison, it has been rare that I can stand their voices, trust them, or find much in common with them other than the occasional need to learn something from them about clothing sizes and makeup.

But there she was, and something about her stuck in my mind. Sometimes I wonder if I saw something familiar in her. Maybe she was an aunt or a cousin of mine. I spent a lot of life

searching for my mother in every face I came across, and in parts of my own reflection, so it wasn't unusual that I would consider it when looking at her. The only difference was it felt like I might have finally found something.

That's when the driver took a left off Elm Street and headed into an area with off-campus Yale housing.

We parked and then snuck behind one of the residential buildings and down into its mostly unfurnished basement. It was summer and the majority of students had gone home. The building was vacant except for us. There in the semi-darkness stood the old man the people in the car had wanted me to meet. He spoke for ages and told me about my family, about aunts and uncles I had never heard the names of before, about how they were doing and what they were up to. He spoke for what must have been at least an hour. I had no idea what he was talking about. I acted polite and listened because he was an old man, but I was sure he was senile and had me confused with someone else. In retrospect, and considering the situation, that first judgment of mine may have been incorrect.

Later that evening I would go upstairs to one of the several apartments in the building. Most of the people from the car were there, plus a few others. One of them had gotten ahold of my journal after a friend of a friend stole it. The man holding my journal was a conspiracy theory writer in the making at the time (he would become published later) and he was absolutely convinced that I was a "high-level Illuminati mind-controlled slave." Things got a little weird from there, I'm not going to lie. He told me that I needed to get in the apartment's tub to read the journal because "water breaks the mind control." I humored him and got in the tub, with my clothes on because I wasn't quite willing to humor him enough to strip naked and read to an apartment full of people while sitting in a tub. I can't remember what part of the journal he was the most interested in. Maybe I need to get in a tub with a notebook and think about it...(that last sentence was a joke).

Not to spoil the fun, but I wasn't mind-controlled in quite the way he probably thought. I was primarily silenced by fear, still following the advice of my mother to be a good victim, and also heavily drugged and pliable on that particular day because I had run into the recruiter downtown. I'll get more into the details of that last part later.

I met with him and parts of that group a few more times over the following weeks in a different apartment on Park Street. He had a manuscript for one of his books that he insisted that I read, in order. It was a dull, long, and dry genealogy of at least twenty-three influential families. I wanted to skip ahead to get to the chapter on the Bush family, but he insisted I start at chapter one. Did I mention that I'm not good with names and that it's useless to make me read a book that is almost entirely names? I absorbed less than 1% of that reading. It turned out that I would not have the opportunity to make it to the chapter on the Bush family. That chapter also never made it into the published edition.

The next time I went to visit at that Park Street building, the recruiter was already there, waiting for me in front of it. Seeing her resulted in a sudden kick of anxiety. She led me inside, telling me that everything I was about to witness was my fault (No, I don't believe her. It's more likely this was continuing cleanup from Operation Condor, since the majority of the people in that room were from South America). Inside the lobby, most of the members of the group were lined up against the walls furthest from the door. There were men who appeared to be SWAT (all dressed in black with rifles that were drawn and pointing at the backs of the heads of three people on their knees in the center of the room). During all of this, the recruiter continued to berate me and insist that their deaths were on my hands. That I was responsible. As the first shot was fired, I turned my head to avoid seeing the result. I still don't know how many people died. I left the building and never looked back.

I spent the next week attempting to locate the survivors. I didn't know what I would do when I found them, but I had to try something. Finding them was the first step. I went to the New Haven Police Station, several New Haven Police substations, and the Yale Police Station. No one knew where they were, until the last one. The officer at the desk there told me that the group had been taken by the FBI. When I asked what prison they were brought to, he couldn't answer. He didn't know. There was a record of them leaving a New Haven jail in FBI custody, but no record of where they had been brought to.

Years later, that would-be author showed back up, alive, in another part of the country. His books were published but there was something different about them. Instead of the dry academic and thorough writing about more than twenty families, he had brought the number down to thirteen families and the pages were full of ranting religious rhetoric. I think they tortured him until they broke him and he reverted to religious belief to a manic level, in his mind's bid for self-preservation and escape. His father was a minister, so it

makes sense that's the safety his thoughts would go to during torture. My mind focuses on the pain and turns it inside out into something else, but I'm another story entirely.

The point is, they broke that man. Is basic information really so dangerous that we need to destroy people to protect them from it? Seriously. How many people need to be protected from what is already common knowledge - that rich people with resources exist, that they have families just like the rest of us, and that some of them influence the industries and countries they own and live in? And the concept that some, or even a large percent, of the population might be manipulated and duped - is that really a state secret? Is it worth destroying lives over?

I found an online live chat he was in years later and quietly listened in, afraid to say anything that might spook him. He spoke about an execution and still sounded shaken up by it. There's little doubt in my mind about what execution he was referring to.

Subversion

You've been infiltrated.
You welcomed it in
when it promised an easy path
to short-term solutions
at the cost of everything.

Not every moment was like a slap in the face. Some had to be looked back on to fully comprehend.

While bringing me along to Washington D.C. to gain easy access to the offices of legislators (there are documents with their signatures on her behalf later in this writing), to areas within Yale that even graduate students and most faculty were not allowed in, and with the smell of her expensive thick wool clothing always filling my nostrils when she was near - the recruiter would tell me that we were impoverished.

This is the woman who had a large office space in Torrington, Connecticut containing a professional printing press, aisles and aisles of heavy and neatly organized equipment on closely stacked professional shelving, and everything of quality - including her full mahogany desk with a thick marble slab top. That office alone contained more value than many small museums. And another office she was affiliated with? Back when I was still small, her address was listed as 150 Windsor Street, Hartford, a bank processing center inaccessible to customers. I had been to it with her. She shared access to an office there on the upper level over the processing floor. She brought me when she was collecting several gold bricks from the large vault in the bottom level. She needed them for a project. I remember how nervous she appeared as we exited the back of the building, her carrying them out in an ordinary-looking canvas bag. I don't know if the project the gold was for was personal or business (I assume the latter), but the method of carrying the gold bricks seemed clandestine and unconventional - in other words, it suited her perfectly.

She even had a nice newer-model car that she would keep parked around the corner from where she raised me so that she could claim to be without a vehicle, unless she actually needed to use it. Despite the quality of the vehicle, the area around my feet was always littered with her empty Coke cans and Snickers bar wrappers when I entered it. But I digress.

Actual impoverished people tried to explain to me that the recruiter was not poor. They highlighted their own lives and the quality of their food and furnishings. I understood there was a difference, but I didn't listen quite as closely as I should have. The recruiter had already created a wedge between us and them by telling me they simply were not educated enough to understand what it was like to be from Yale, and that their lifestyles were due to a lack of intellect rather than a lack of money. I was young and she was the authority on things in life, having taken the role of mother, so I believed her that their choices were simply bad shopping habits.

It wasn't until I was on my own as an adult that it fully struck me - poverty does not mean full access to Yale, full access to politicians, and enough equipment and gourmet food to keep yourself going for a lifetime. Poverty means the discount food on the lower shelves at the grocery store. It means furniture that will fall apart. It means not even being able to borrow that piece of equipment, never mind owning fifty pieces just like it. Poverty is a struggle to get the most out of limited resources. It's not a costume to wear like she had.

Distraction & Misdirection

Back in our day-to-day lives while I was still a young teen, the recruiter was bringing me along to Yale recruitment movie nights, which had moved from the cinema to a university building beyond Woolsey Hall and down Prospect Street. They would divide the groups up among various lecture rooms, From what I saw and experienced, either the drugs varied by room, or the hypnotics simply had a very different effect depending on the room setting and what type of movie was being watched. The students who attended were primarily Yale students, as far as I knew, and I believe most were there to gain extra credit for their classes by volunteering to attend seemingly innocent college-sponsored social events that were promoted as only requiring the watching of a few movies.

The first time I went, I was led to a tiny basement room to watch a version of Willie Wonka and the Chocolate Factory. There were two slightly sketchy students who smelled like the engineering department. One of them was passing out little pill cups full of something. Whatever it was, I consumed it. Thanks to the mind-altering chemicals in it, for many years after, I would have every single part of that movie burnt into my brain, especially the Oompa Loompa song. While somewhat irritating, it wasn't a terrifying or overly concerning experience, at least not by my measure.

Much like the original recruitment movie nights, the nights in the new location were weekly. On another week, I was assigned to a room that was upstairs with a group watching Single White Female. General advice: whether you're safe at home or surrounded by sketchy recruiters at Yale, don't watch Single White Female while tripping. About maybe forty minutes into the movie, I looked to my right and saw what I thought was a woman being trapped and pulled through a massive tube on the wall. I decided it was time to take a bathroom break. In other words, on the outside, I was calmly getting up and leaving to find the ladies' room. On the inside, I was screaming and thinking I was the next one to get trapped by the tube.

Once in the quiet hallway, I calmed my nerves and took a very slow walk to the furthest restroom I knew of. I had to pass another movie-night room to do so. It was towards the end of the building and to my left. From the hall, I could see the students. They were in the dark,

and on the screen was the violent carnage-filled Vietnam War movie we had been using in several other types of psychological experiments during that time and in that location. Although, I might note, that after so many years, I don't think those were experiments anymore. We were getting the intended results. The experimental stage was long over. It was psychological manipulation via deceitful means after the also-deceitful lure of "it's just a harmless movie night."

What I saw when I looked in was concerning, more real and concerning than my temporary hallucination of a tube. The majority of the people in that room were visibly panicking from being exposed to the movie in the dark while on what must have been copious amounts of hallucinogens. And the staff and security? They were blocking the door, not letting anyone leave, and making sure the lights stayed off and the movie continued. They were actually physically fighting off several of the students.

I never learned the purpose of drugging and traumatizing a room full of our future leaders of industry and nations, but I can say I don't think it was a good one. The long-term and widespread results have been atrocious and are still snowballing out of control as I write this.

One of the staff caught me staring, so I made a little small talk, pretending like whatever was going on was ordinary. And then, I finally finished my walk down the hall and into the ladies' room.

While we're on the topic of drugs, I remember one harvest season when the recruiter sent me down by a river, on someone else's overgrown private property, to harvest an entire field of Jimson Weed (Datura stramonium) she had planted. The landowner had become suspicious of her and was keeping an eye on the place, so she couldn't do it on her own. I'll admit I went to the library and looked up what the plant was, and considered using it to get high. But I was too afraid to let loose my grasp on reality, so I didn't even try one seed. I simply brought the harvest home to her and handed it over.

It, or something like it, would end up in my system anyway when she decided I was more malleable when drugged without my knowledge. A year or two after that harvest, she found a better supply of drugs via an infamous Yale chemist. The high school and college students in the area knew him for his LSD. Actually, probably most of New England knew him for that. People like the recruiter knew him for his unique and powerful scopolamine and Rohypnol derivatives. Her access to him led to my waking up exhausted nearly every morning for several years.

For the longest time, I thought I had terrible health and that's why I was so tired upon waking after a night of boring dreams, mostly of walking around town with her. Then little things started painting a larger picture. In the morning, at the city bus stop near Yale on my way to school, people would approach me who were absolutely convinced they remembered me from the night before. However, I had been sleeping in my bed all that night, or I reasonably assumed I was, since I put my head on the pillow at 9 PM and then woke up to the 5:45 AM alarm in that same bed. According to these strangers, we'd had long conversations throughout the night, and they would understandably act offended when I genuinely could not remember them after such intense evenings together. I told them they had the wrong person.

They were enough to make me wonder, but it wasn't until a friend was reminiscing with me about a time he and I were hanging out and having fun with "my mother" (a time that I could not recall and would not have allowed when sober because I went out of my way to protect my friends from her by never introducing them) that it finally hit me. She had been drugging me while I slept, waking me up in that condition, and dragging me all over town with her until dawn.

I later confirmed it by leaving evidence for myself for the mornings. Any time I felt like I was drugged and she was there telling me I was dreaming (her usual spiel when I was high and we were out of earshot of others), I would tear a nail, scrape my arm on concrete, rip a seam in my clothing, fill my shoes full of sand, or anything else that logical excuses would not be able to explain. Jumping into pools with all my clothing on was a favorite. Shoes never really dry after that. The only thing that never worked was filling my pockets. Those, she always made sure I emptied, and she kept the contents.

I wasn't the only target in those years. I was just always close by and, therefore, got the brunt of it. I never could understand why I wasn't simply allowed to come along while sober. I think for her it was about control, and she always wanted a ridiculous amount of control.

She also controlled my education to an absurd degree, when it was convenient enough to actually send me to school. I did the math once, and I missed approximately half of the years of formal education between the first and twelfth grade (senior year). I was a quick study, but there are some subjects I've struggled with because it's difficult to just pick up where you left off on things like mathematics when the class had gone over two years of the foundational blocks of the current lesson while you were gone. I will never be a genius when it comes to calculus.

As time went on, I went to and participated in several years of discussions and courses on and related to history, law, and negotiations, primarily via Dwight Hall. The recruiter was generally there to usher me in. She had plans for my career already. She wanted me to be the domestic and international negotiator at the table, one more position to exploit. Having control over one side in a negotiation is good. Owning the people on both sides is better. But owning the neutral party in the middle too? That's perfection from a manipulator's perspective. At that point, you have the whole table.

No one ever questioned the recruiter about my presence, either because they couldn't do anything about it or because they were accustomed to her behavior by that juncture. She had done something very similar before with her biological sons on campus in the 1960s and 1970s.

Image: Yale Campus, Group Photo. Recruiter: First Female in the Top Left Portion of the Group. Children: Bottom Left.

Source: Unknown Photographer[83]

Thanks to her, I've spent more time in lectures, discussions, and the stacks at Yale than most post-grad students have. When I reached out for help years before about being kidnapped from my mom and was given a heartless response of "But you'll have good schools here," that soulless answer wasn't entirely wrong. I have an education from one of the best universities in the country (and, no, it's still not an adequate replacement for my mother, my home, my safety, my childhood, my freedom, my language, my culture, or my country). Later, I would attain a postgraduate degree to authenticate it, after being railroaded back into the same field I'd been forced to attend classes on at Yale. I would obtain the documentation from a spin-off department of Berkeley professors who decided to relocate to a university someone without a trust fund might actually be able to afford. Unlike the recruiter, I don't have to obscure my credentials. I have them. I may not particularly want them, but I have them.

---

[83] Unknown Photographer, Photo on Yale University Campus

Back in New Haven and the surrounding area, I also went along to and was abandoned for hours and days at endless classes, discussions, and conferences on countless topics, ranging from nuclear energy to the history of native tribes.

I spent one summer at Wesleyan University in Connecticut, taking a course in genetics. It was a residential science program for young scholars and had been covered by a scholarship. In order to be allowed to attend, I had to promise the recruiter that I would not take any genetics courses. So, they were the first thing I signed up for. It was a nice reprieve from New Haven and I had an enjoyable time. They even had us spend a weekend at a military camp I had attended when I was much younger. I was always the last over the wall of the obstacle course when I was small. But against a group of mostly unathletic science students? I was the second one over that wall. It was a nice feeling, even it was almost like cheating.

The only problem that arose during my entire time at Wesleyan was in a genetics course early on. They asked us to compare our visible dominant and non-dominant traits with a parent's, using photographs. The professor was certain I had not paid attention or done the work correctly because, as he said, "There is no way you could be related to that person." The recruiter's crimes had a way of seeping in and ruining things for me even when she was far away.

On a different campus in New England, she and I once attended an excellent lecture by Michio Kaku that coincidentally did not match up with what he would later state in public media, at the behest of the Japanese government, after the Fukushima incident. It's possible that his theories simply evolved through the decades. It's also more probable that when on television as a spokesman for the nuclear industry, he was saying whatever the government and corporate script told him to say. In the lecture hall, with only a hundred or so sets of eyes on him, that nuclear physicist told us that it's not short-term high-level radiation exposure that is the most concerning for damage on a cellular level (although, obviously, it's still not safe). It's sustained low levels of radiation that do the most damage, such as those that persist in the environment at industry-determined "safe levels" long after an accident.

I even ended up in an extracurricular course on social engineering taught by people who were both highly educated and cult-level insane. They combined guided meditation, visualization with psychedelics, and visual training to enhance their instructing of us on topics pertaining to mechanisms used in social engineering. We learned how to guide populations through intended funnels, find squeeze points, and utilize those as needed until the people moved through the funnels as we intended, self-sorted into the right areas where they were needed, and agreed to take on extra costs and responsibilities at their own expense. We did this by using a combination of societal pressure, fear, need, the threat of law, and financial incentives and disincentives. Visually, it was a lot like an elaborate hamster maze made of tunnels. One of the first real projects they allowed us to work on was the early planning for the public acceptance of what would eventually be named Obamacare.

From a related faculty lecture series I had been dragged along to that was happening in those same years, here's a paper exploring the concept of mechanisms in social engineering (law, in this case):

Faculty Scholarship Series
Yale Law School Faculty Scholarship

1-1-1985

A Comment on Causation, Law Reform, and Guerilla Warfare

Jerry L. Mashaw
Yale Law School

It seems appropriate in a conference concerned with the conjunction of law and science to mention what lawyers can teach scientists and vice versa. For example, this morning the lawyers may be teaching the scientists that the lawyers have invented the "perpetual motion machine," an elusive apparatus long sought by scientists. It turns out to be a social rather than a physical mechanism, and in legal circles it usually goes by the name "law reform."

Law reform is indeed a perpetual motion machine. From any location in the legal system we can always imagine another point (by which I mean another configuration of the relevant legal rules) we would prefer. If we were to array these points incrementally on a graph, they would probably describe a circle. Whenever we actually find ourselves in a regulatory system, we tend to prefer taxes. Whenever we are using taxes, we suspect that subsidies might work better. Of course, when evaluating the use of subsidies, we are strongly attracted to criminal penalties. And to complete the circle, when we are considering the ineffectiveness of the criminal law, we long for the strengths of the tort system.

For most of this conference our discussion has been confined to the tort system. As Don Elliott has suggested, however, that is not the only system of law available to us.[1] We can reform the law of "toxic torts" without concentrating on the law of "torts." We can set out on a journey via the law reform perpetual motion machine. Although that journey may take us in some sense back to where we began, when we return the tort system need not be the same as we left it. We can try to put the pieces of the machine together in novel ways that will produce better and better results, so that its motion traces an upward spiral rather than a mere circle. The panel has been given this sort of problem of systems design. How can we make motion yield progress?

The question put to the panel—"What do we wish from the system?"—is so broad that the meanings of both "we" and "the system" are unclear. For present purposes, I will imagine that the "we" in the question is some sort of, if you will forgive the term, neutral placeholder. That is, we do not know who we are. We, the system's engineers, might turn out to have any position in the social system we design. The social "system," as I imagine it, should include but not be limited to law.

Image Source: Yale Law School Lillian Goldman Law Library

"The lawyers may be teaching the scientists that the lawyers have invented the 'perpetual motion machine,' an elusive apparatus long sought by scientists. It turns out to be a social rather than a physical mechanism, and in legal circles it usually goes by the name 'law reform.'... From any location in the legal system we can always imagine another point (by which I mean another configuration of the relevant legal rules) we would prefer. If we were to array these points incrementally on a graph, they would probably describe a circle. Whenever we actually find ourselves in a regulatory system, we tend to prefer taxes. Whenever we are using taxes, we suspect that subsidies might work better. Of course, when evaluating the use of subsidies, we are strongly attracted to criminal penalties. And to complete the circle, when we are considering the ineffectiveness of the criminal law, we long for the strengths of the tort system.

...

We can try to put the pieces of the machine together in novel ways that will produce better and better results, so that its motion traces an upward spiral rather than a mere circle. The panel has been given this sort of problem of systems design. How can we make motion yield progress? The question put to the panel - 'What do we wish from the system?' - is so broad that the meanings of both 'we' and 'the system' are unclear. For present purposes, I will imagine that the 'we' in the question is some sort of, if you will forgive the term, a neutral placeholder. That is, we do not know who we are. We, the system's engineers, might turn out to have any position in the social system we design. The social 'system,' as I imagine it, should include but not be limited to law."

Text Source: Yale Law School Lillian Goldman Law Library[84]

Sitting on orderly mats on the floor of a large room with the lights off, we walked through the function of each of the mechanisms while visualizing the whole structure in front of us with the help of the drugs. Looking back at it, I bet something similar could be done much more ethically, and with less potential brain damage, by utilizing 3D modeling. That said, we probably knew about funnels long before they became a part of common business terminology, and the lessons are still permanently burned into my brain. The learning model may have been too new age and potentially dangerous, but the results weren't the worst.

---

[84] Yale Law School Lillian Goldman Law Library, A Comment on Causation, Law Reform, and Guerrilla Warfare by Mashaw, Jerry, https://openyls.law.yale.edu/handle/20.500.13051/342

After that course, I started getting invitations to think tank sessions. For the most part, they all started with the same basic rules. The military brass would break it down for us:

We needed to create and hone non-standard warfare strategies and tactics that came with plausible deniability. We were told that in a world in which countries had effective defenses and in which we did not want outright war due to the risk of nuclear war, we needed to create penetration strategies that could get through without triggering a country's defenses. As for attacks, each and every attack we planned needed to be attributable to something else. Industrial accidents reached the top of the list.

As time would go on, long after those sessions in which we worked together to make sure that each and every flaw was fixed before presenting our final weapons and accompanying strategies, I would peruse the news to see which, if any, of our ideas had been used. It turns out, probably quite a few were, and they were being tested in and/or used against the very country we were standing in. The Deepwater Horizon oil spill, and the resulting use of Corexit, always find their way to the top of that list of potential results. Of course, whether it was a result of one of our think tanks or not will always be something that can be questioned. It was designed to be.

Plausible deniability.

Toxicity of dispersant Corexit 9500A and crude oil to marine microzooplankton

PubMed

Abstract

In 2010, nearly 7 million liters of chemical dispersants, mainly Corexit 9500A, were released in the Gulf of Mexico to treat the Deepwater Horizon oil spill. However, little is still known about the effects of Corexit 9500A and dispersed crude oil on microzooplankton despite the important roles of these planktonic organisms in marine ecosystems. We conducted laboratory experiments to determine the acute toxicity of Corexit 9500A, and physically and chemically dispersed Louisiana light sweet crude oil to marine microzooplankton (oligotrich ciliates, tintinnids and heterotrophic dinoflagellates). Our results indicate that Corexit 9500A is highly toxic to microzooplankton, particularly to small ciliates, and that the combination of dispersant with crude oil significantly increases the toxicity of crude oil to microzooplankton. The negative impact of crude oil and dispersant on microzooplankton may disrupt the transfer of energy from lower to higher trophic levels and change the structure and dynamics of marine planktonic communities.

Image Source: Ecotoxicology and Environmental Safety via PubMed

"In 2010, nearly 7 million liters of chemical dispersants, mainly Corexit 9500A, were released in the Gulf of Mexico to treat the Deepwater Horizon oil spill...

Our results indicate that Corexit 9500A is highly toxic to microzooplankton, particularly to small ciliates, and that the combination of dispersant with crude oil significantly increases the toxicity of crude oil to microzooplankton. The negative impact of crude oil and dispersant on microzooplankton may disrupt the transfer of energy from lower to higher trophic levels and change the structure and dynamics of marine planktonic communities."

Text Source: Ecotoxicology and Environmental Safety via PubMed[85]

Remember the book about the baby whale I told you about earlier? Its surviving was unrealistic because the ocean would not contain anything for the whales to eat. In other words, these are the types of events that can lead to food chain collapse. Combine

---

[85] Ecotoxicology and Environmental Safety via PubMed, Toxicity of Dispersant Corexit 9500A and Crude Oil to Marine Microzooplankton, https://pubmed.ncbi.nlm.nih.gov/24836881/

enough of them, and humanity will start having a very difficult time finding something to eat.

Normalization of Internal Exploitation

The words that carry the most regret are poignantly short:
"If only I had known."

I settled into my life and role. What choice did I have? Every time I reached out for help, people would either act dumb or become targets of the kidnapper I had been forced to live with. She used blackmail, threats, harassment, drugging, hardcore interrogation techniques that would leave even Gitmo workers questioning morality, manipulation, and when that failed – murder.

She truly was the dark shadow that hung over my life. I felt profoundly personally responsible for each person harmed, and it tore at me. For years at a time, I ceased to reach out for help. I didn't want to do further harm. It was bad enough when it happened to me. After all, that was inevitable. But I couldn't stand to watch it be done to others. I still felt an underlying connection with humanity back then, and I could feel their pain on a deep and tangible level.

So, I endured.

On a self-preserving and less altruistic level, I was often scared to say anything when I was asked if I was okay. I would analyze each situation and reasonably assume that the person asking would not be effective in going against the recruiter to save me, even if I told them the truth. Their failed attempts and my admitting that I was uncomfortable with what was going on, at least to some degree, would risk my hard-earned reputation as completely willing, blind, and accepting of what I was trapped in.

That reputation was important for my safety in the situation I was "legally" obligated to remain in as a minor. It made me seem harmless and on the team of those who owned me, rather than appearing to be an enemy. In addition, more than any potential would-be savior, that hard-earned status was truly vital for any potentially effective future exit plans. I was going to have to crawl out on my own, but I was also going to need to use their activities as a

launching pad for my plans, so that they would let me come along as an assistant, and I could then use the situation and their weight to get my own objective reached. As a tool, I needed to become a wielder of tools. It wasn't easy from my position. All I had to work with was their trust in me. Reputation is always key. During those years, so were endurance and eternal patience.

I did everything I could to protect the world from the people I was trapped with in that situation. I insulated strangers from it, I never invited my friends home, and I sacrificed myself more times than I can count – because I lived with the enemy. I knew their tactics, and outsiders didn't.

I also did it because I still had faith in humanity, thanks to memories of my mother in Argentina. Those memories and feelings of connection were the flame of life that kept me going through the darkness all those years, even as I was intentionally drowned and revived over and over again in a room beneath Yale New Haven Hospital, drowned for what purpose I will never understand.

It's possible that room saw even more human suffering than I did in those years. It was a large storage room, accessed via a somewhat active lower hospital hallway, and then a very short hall that branched from that. It was directly at the end of the short hall. The room was large enough to hold dozens of pieces of equipment. When near the back wall of that room, especially on the right side, I could hear the cars in the parking structure it must have shared a wall with.

Because it was officially deemed a storage room, no one had to sign any lists, documents, or schedules to utilize it for their research purposes. It was an off-the-books medical lab right on Yale's campus, in full sight of anyone who walked by. The best part of it, from a research perspective, was that allocating expensive or heavy medical equipment to it without approval was incredibly easy. All you had to do was send the equipment to storage, a process that required no oversight at all.

The research I witnessed there went against humanity. However, not all of it was quite so dark. The room wasn't only used by the recruiter's professional cohort (although, they definitely had first priority). The paperless loophole that it provided was also being utilized by some of the university's graduate students. In order to meet the unrealistically high expectations and reputation of Yale research proposals being of an almost clairvoyant level of accuracy in predicted outcomes, they actually needed to test their theories before asking an ethics board for approval to test them. They needed to ensure that the result of each proposal would lead to a success. The off-use lab was incredibly convenient for exactly that. And in all honestly, they may have used the room more. After all, military research doesn't require the extra work of gaining an ethics board's approval. It's unethical by nature, and that is accepted because it is presumed any of the research is for the benefit of national security.

One semi-example of the room's use would be Charles Morgan's utilization of it (if you remember, he was the one who would go on to be cited as a CIA psychiatrist in a Medscape article later in his career). While he was still a student, he utilized the room to test his "more humane" military interrogation techniques. He had a (now published) theory that people of certain ethnicities respond differently to coercive interrogation. I was there for that one... that or multiple students were fighting for foreigner interrogation grants during that time and I have him confused with one of the hoard. Either way, apparently my being from South America and the tiniest bit Iranian was enough to qualify me as a participant in that earliest research.

Yale denies knowledge of FBI-sponsored interview research

School of Medicine Psychiatry Professor Charles Morgan has allegedly been conducting private research involving interview techniques with local immigrants using funding from the Federal Bureau of Investigation, according to a Friday article in the New Haven Independent.

In a Friday statement, the University said Yale was unaware of Morgan's private work until the Independent published the findings. Recently, Morgan has been at the center of a controversy involving a military training center he had planned to propose to the School of Medicine using a $1.8 million grant from the United States Special Operations Command, but both the Department of Defense and Yale said on Feb. 22 that the center would not move forward.

Yale News

"I think the point is [Morgan's research is] not done through Yale," Alpern said. "[Morgan is] what we call a volunteer faculty member, which means he's not employed by us and he's free to do whatever he wants to do outside of Yale."

Image Source: Yale Daily News

"School of Medicine Psychiatry Professor Charles Morgan has allegedly been conducting private research involving interview techniques with local immigrants using funding from the Federal Bureau of Investigation.

....

'I think the point is [Morgan's research is] not done through Yale,' Alpern said. '[Morgan is] what we call a volunteer faculty member, which means he's not employed by us and he's free to do whatever he wants to do outside of Yale.'"

Text Source: Yale Daily News[86]

Unfortunately for me and my incredibly unlucky timing in life, some of my time at Yale overlapped with when he was a student at the university.

---

[86] Yale Daily News, Yale Denies Knowledge of FBI-Sponsored Interview Research, https://yaledailynews.com/blog/2013/03/04/yale-denies-knowledge-of-fbi-sponsored-interview-research/

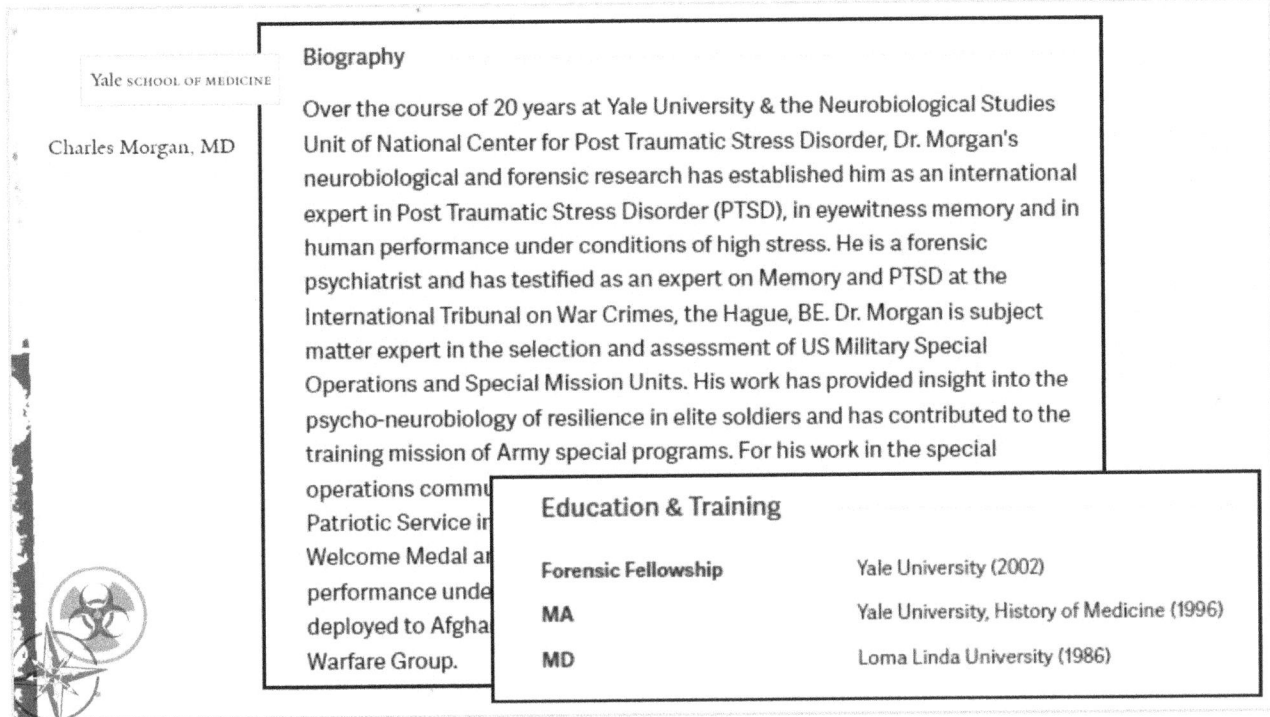

Biography

Over the course of 20 years at Yale University & the Neurobiological Studies Unit of National Center for Post Traumatic Stress Disorder, Dr. Morgan's neurobiological and forensic research has established him as an international expert in Post Traumatic Stress Disorder (PTSD), in eyewitness memory and in human performance under conditions of high stress. He is a forensic psychiatrist and has testified as an expert on Memory and PTSD at the International Tribunal on War Crimes, the Hague, BE. Dr. Morgan is subject matter expert in the selection and assessment of US Military Special Operations and Special Mission Units. His work has provided insight into the psycho-neurobiology of resilience in elite soldiers and has contributed to the training mission of Army special programs. For his work in the special operations commu... Patriotic Service i... Welcome Medal a... performance unde... deployed to Afgha... Warfare Group.

Education & Training

Forensic Fellowship	Yale University (2002)
MA	Yale University, History of Medicine (1996)
MD	Loma Linda University (1986)

Image Source: Yale School of Medicine

"Charles Morgan, MD

Associate Clinical Professor, Psychiatry

…

Education & Training

Forensic Fellowship - Yale University (2002)

MA - Yale University, History of Medicine (1996)"

Text Source: Yale School of Medicine[87]

Because of the nature of the research that went on in the off-use laboratory, and the fact that I was sent down there on my own dozens upon dozens of times to assist and otherwise be a part of that research (the drownings come to mind, more on that in a bit), the recruiter

---

[87] Yale School of Medicine, Charles Morgan, MD, https://medicine.yale.edu/profile/cmorgan/

felt the need to ensure that I didn't talk about it. What she would do had happened hundreds of times before, to the point that I eventually knew each distinctive part of the routine. This is just one location and one example:

The entrance I used was in a smaller building. It had a security guard and a hall that inclined down for long enough that it likely extended beyond the footprint of that building. There, in the sublevel, it met with other halls that would lead to the off-use lab. One time, the recruiter came with me. She asked the security guard to show us footage of me entering the building by myself. He complied. He brought us into the security room with the monitors and found a recording of me entering the small lobby.

That's when the recruiter started screaming at me. Her methodology was always to go at the subject as if it were not real, or as if we were talking about someone else's experiences. She berated me and said things along the lines of "That is such an idiotic thing for her to do. Imagine if it had been you going through that lobby." Then, as was standard, she next attempted to make me feel personally ashamed about the incident/location/being in the location (like I said, she had done this hundreds of times after bringing me places she didn't want me to discuss). She would say something starting with "Who would do that? What is wrong with them?" and continue on that trajectory. I was then expected to react in shame and side with her, agreeing that only terrible people would have been there. At which point, I'd start lying for her, and claim I had not been there, and then attempt to convince her of such. Obviously, there were drugs in my system... At least, I seriously hope there were. I'd hate to think that a mind can be that easily broken without them.

The interesting thing, in this case, was that we did it in front of the video recording, playing on a loop, of me entering that building. An hour or so into her screaming me down, I had become convinced (in that moment) that I had never been through that lobby on my own, despite the evidence playing out on the screen right in front of me.

As for the drownings, I would be asked to arrive with a bathing suit and towel for those days. One day in particular stood out to me more than the rest, because of the conversation and lack of drugging. As I stood in front of a jacuzzi tub taking up a fraction of the space in that large room, the researcher there told me to get in and then she said, "Don't worry. We won't be drowning you this time." I always buried my reactions to everything, but that? Even I twitched at that. This time? That meant it had been done before. I got into the tub. Next, she began to lower a plastic sheet until it was nearly in contact with the water. She told me that I would only be revived if I behaved and died without a struggle. So, as the plastic sealed to the surface of the water, leaving no room for air, I submerged myself silently, held my breath, went still, and prayed they thought I was dead before I really was. My next memories were on that cement ground, outside the tub, coughing up water as someone stood above me. I don't know how close to death I had come or if I had passed that threshold.

The blonde girl I mentioned previously, whose family had been coerced into enrolling her as a research participant while believing they were signing her in for an opportunity to participate in camp activities and meet people of influence at Yale, I witnessed her dead body in a room in those same halls. She had never returned from beyond that threshold. While I had been revived after they drowned me, they could not revive her. Sometimes I wonder how many people have died from what I survived, and why they had to. And why I had to endure. There's a saying, "There is no rescue crew." It's been incredibly true in my experience.

I could only remember glimpses of those moments of my drowning, other than the one evening I mentioned, but my body remembered every single second of every single time. As I went through life, I would randomly feel like I couldn't breathe, that I couldn't get in enough air to breathe. It would hit me at any moment, with no warning at all. I went to my pediatrician in a panic one day when I was near his office and was convinced it was asthma. According to him, my lungs were fine, although he noted the possibility of child abuse when writing in my medical records.

What I was experiencing wasn't asthma. It was the lingering physical anxiety and reaction from those moments. I had developed a type of post-traumatic stress disorder (PTSD) only referenced in literature on waterboarding victims in Guantanamo Bay. Later on, I actually felt a sense of relief in learning that my response was normal, despite the situation itself being abnormal. While looking for information on how to deal with the lingering effects years later, what I first saw was significant enough to me that I paused and screen-captured it.

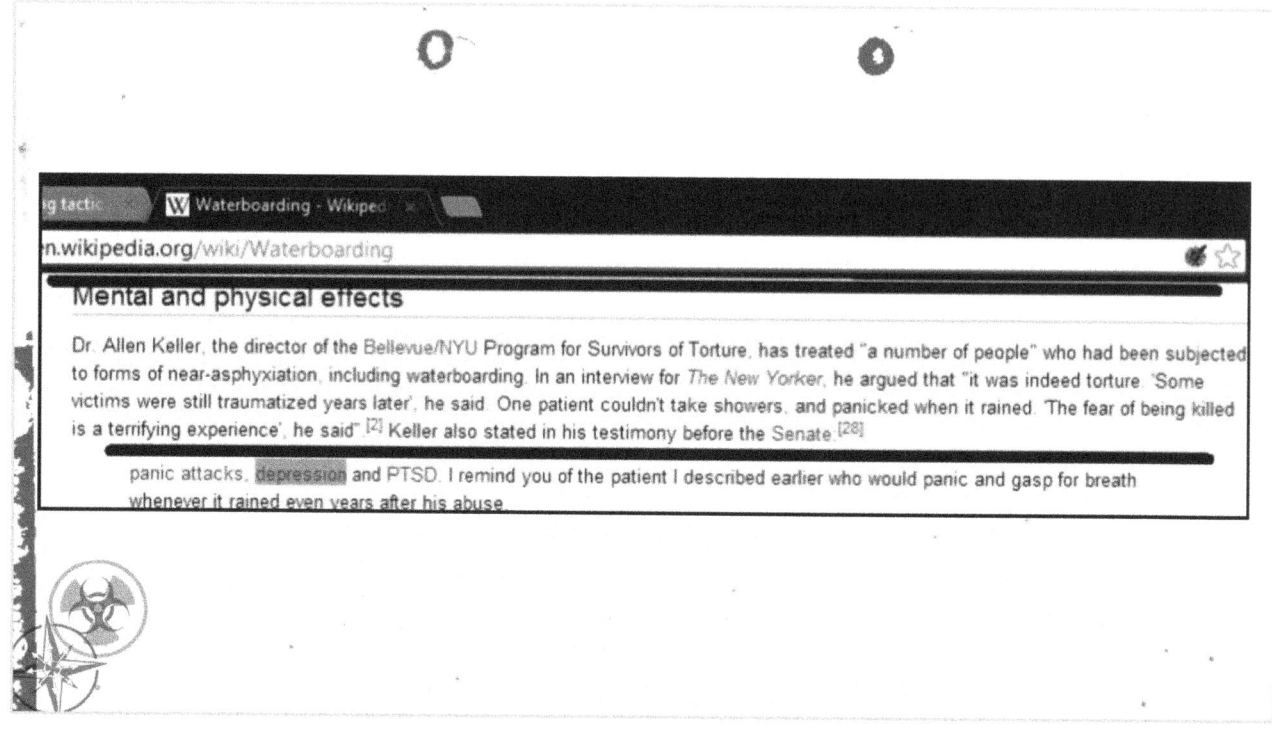

Image Source: <u>Wikipedia</u>, 2013 Screen Capture

"The patient...would panic and gasp for breath whenever it rained even years after the abuse."

Text Source: <u>Wikipedia</u>, 2013 Screen Capture[88]

To me, it meant I was okay. My reaction was natural. It was only the situation that was not. That was something I had needed to hear for an incredibly long time.

Although I was an experienced and skilled swimmer (military camp did something right), I quit swimming in the year of the drownings. I haven't enjoyed it since. As of this writing, the last time I went deeper than my waist was to save someone's life, and that was seven years ago.

---

88 Wikipedia, Waterboarding, https://en.wikipedia.org/wiki/Waterboarding

I became a cigarette smoker shortly after my experiences with being drowned in that cavernous room. When I had a random unprovoked feeling of drowning, a cigarette would quickly open my lungs and reduce my anxiety enough for the feeling to fade. I became a chain smoker and remained one until I was twenty. Time has changed my response a little but I still reach for something outside of myself to save me from that sense of drowning. I also experience that panicked sense of not being able to fill my lungs completely less frequently now. It usually only hits when remembering the events. I'm currently drinking an iced coffee and praying it stops the coughing triggered by the memories from writing this, even though I know the only thing that will truly make the moment stop is to finish writing this section and move on to the next.

Despite what I was put through, I still dragged through life, discovering that coffee was my greatest ally by the time I was fourteen years old. I spent my time often in the halls of Yale and Washington DC, left there to occupy myself while my kidnapper and others worked. I argued philosophy, ethics, and practicality with the people I met when it came to topics of control, governance, and exploitation of human resources. My arguments fell on deaf ears. I tried my best to advocate for the people that I still cared for. Without a tribe of my own, without a country of my own, I felt everyone's pain. I wanted to create a better life for them where it mattered and where I was standing - where policies were formed. I was still young and naive, but I was also growing a spine due to sheer exhaustion. I could no longer maintain my fear of those with more power than I had. It took too much energy to do so. In my mind, we were already on the path to becoming equals.

I had an unparalleled amount of freedom and access, despite being a slave, or maybe because of it. There was no one there to worry if I came home at 3 AM unless I was needed for a task. No one told me "Don't dive that deep!" or "That's too high to jump from." I had a natural survival instinct, but I was also young and unfamiliar with a conventional upbringing and expectations of caution. Many times, I went far beyond the traditional limits of safety.

That freedom would eventually lead me to stand on the sidewalk in front of Cutler's Records with a friend at a late enough hour to run into the infamous Yale chemist, in the flesh. He came down the sidewalk, walking backwards. To this day, I have no idea if he was high on his own drugs or if he was attempting to trick the nearby Yale surveillance cameras. As he passed by, he slipped a small paper sachet of pills into my hand. I was never into pills. I didn't trust them. But this was a chemist who was infamous, someone whom whispers about

could be heard across the entire region. I kept the pills. He had too much clout. I couldn't throw them away. What I had just experienced was the teenage equivalent of having Elvis or God walk by and hand you something.

I held onto those pills for at least a week or two before finally getting up the nerve to take one. I was sitting on the grass, in the dark of night, in front of the Law Library with a friend. We both took a pill. My memory went flat. There's nothing there. The next thing I remember was when we were briskly walking several blocks away near the train station. The moment we stopped walking, there was a memory blank. The next thing I would recall was walking from the train station to his friend's house, half the state away. And that's how the experience went. If my heart rate was high enough from anxiety or exercise, it would push me past the amnesia barrier and I'd have a memory from it. But everything between? Absolute dead space.

That morning, as the sun rose, I came down from the drug and became aware of my surroundings on the beach. I was in the middle of a lengthy conversation with my friend. I couldn't remember what we had been saying or how or when we had gotten there.

But that experience? Every part of it lined up with hundreds of experiences I had with the recruiter. The chemist, by giving me the drug so I could ingest it knowingly, had allowed me to examine its effects and come to realize when I was being drugged and how to put the memories back together when it was over. He hadn't handed me the LSD he was famous for. He had handed me his other prize drug that only the shadiest people request, the same one he had been disbursing to the woman who had been exploiting me ever since she had taken custody of me at the age of three.

♞ Stage 3: Deployment

Death is always a possibility.
When you do nothing,
it becomes a certainty.

The recruiter had a few projects going on. One of them was infiltrating the local grassroots antinuclear organizations. The local antinuclear movement had been attempting to force the Nuclear Regulatory Commission (NRC) to update its regulations regarding overly packed spent fuel pools at Millstone Unit 2 and at other power plants with the same design.

The way the fuel pool regulations and engineering were, they came with the very real hazard of causing a meltdown in the case of a natural disaster or other major event. Changes needed to be made and the NRC was the regulatory body in charge of making sure that happened.

The recruiter was there to make sure the movement's efforts were not successful.

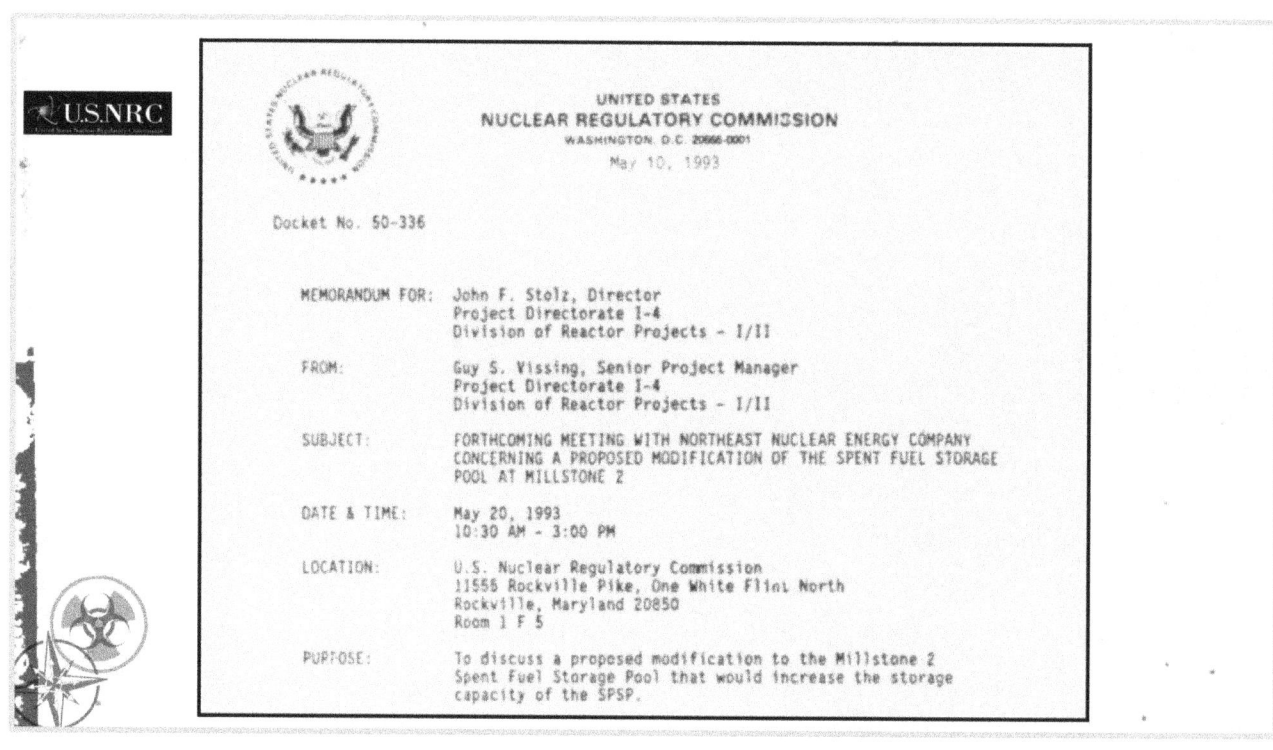

Image Source: <u>Nuclear Regulatory Commission</u>

NRC notice:

"Forthcoming meeting with Northeast Nuclear Energy Company concerning a proposed modification of the spent fuel storage pool at Millstone 2."

Text Source: <u>Nuclear Regulatory Commission</u>[89]

She'd bring me along as a prop when going to antinuclear meetings. My being there helped to complete her "concerned parent and citizen" act as she told the actually concerned nuclear activists that she was an ex-nuclear engineer (she has since moved on to the title "breast cancer researcher" because it gets a more positive response from people). She had an entire story she would go through, including that she realized the

[89] Nuclear Regulatory Commission, Docket No. 50-336. Memorandum for Atomic Safety and Licensing Board and All Parties, https://www.nrc.gov/docs/ML2006/ML20062J215.pdf
https://webcache.googleusercontent.com/search?q=cache:6SAEdJsAr2oJ:https://www.nrc.gov/docs/ML2006/ML20062J215.pdf&hl=en&gl=us
https://web.archive.org/web/20231111020444/https://webcache.googleusercontent.com/search?q=cache:6SAEdJsAr2oJ:https://www.nrc.gov/docs/ML2006/ML20062J215.pdf&hl=en&gl=us

error of her ways in the 1960s and stopped working in Department of Defense research (a complete lie). She made sure to drop random words (spent fuel pools, strontium-90, etc.) to give herself the appearance of a professional in the field and thus an expert for them to bring into their fold and utilize. To my silent horror, they fell for it every time.

She would still be found using many of the same lines, decades later, when working to control the movement online. I've also seen her post about being anti-slavery, something that makes me outwardly cringe after a lifetime of her exploiting me and others. There's also the detail of her illegally using state terrorism to coerce my mother into signing me over.

But I digress, back to the subject at hand...

Here's an example of how she reels people in:

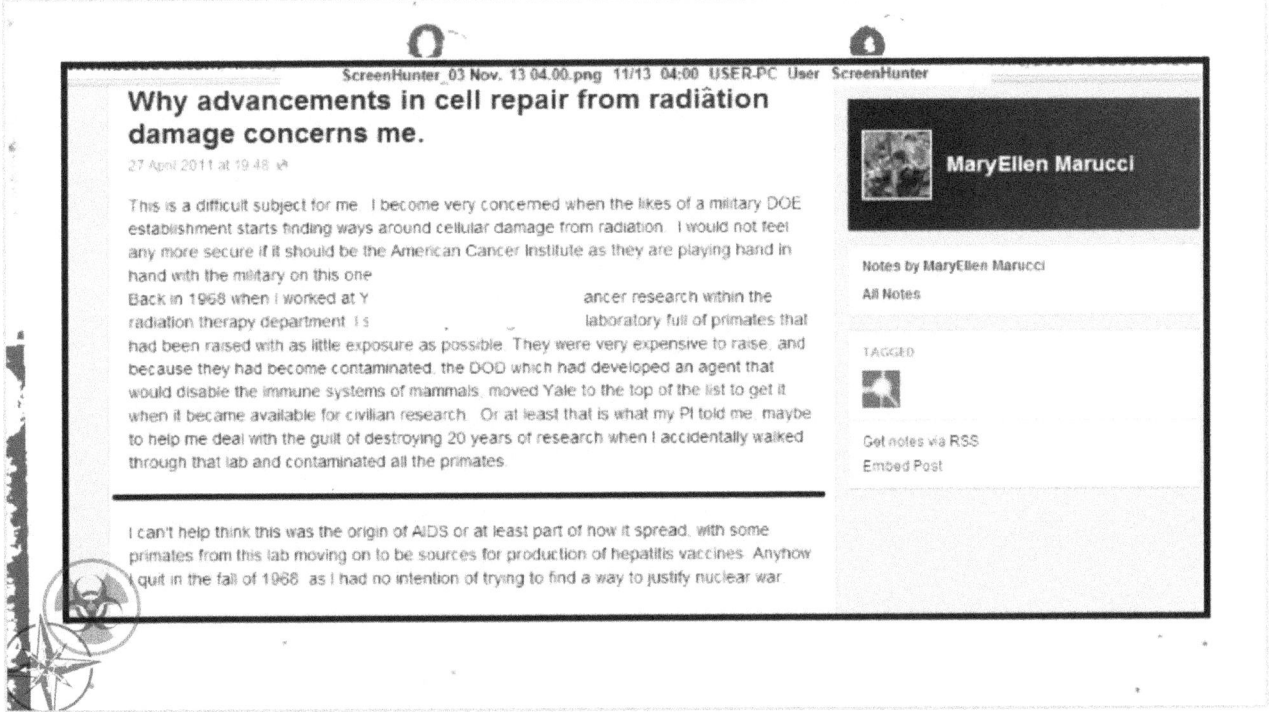

Image Source: 2013 Screenshot Facebook

"Back in 1968 when I worked at Yale's School of Medicine, in cancer research...I can't help think this was the origin of AIDS or at least part of how it spread, with some primates from the lab moving on to be sources for production of hepatitis vaccines.

241

Anyhow I quit in the fall of 1968 as I had no intention of trying to find a way to justify nuclear war."

Text Source: 2013 Screenshot Facebook[90]

The recruiter would become a member of the board of a grassroots antinuclear organization and then force every other member out, one at a time, primarily by harassment. Slowly, she would become their primary spokesperson and leader.

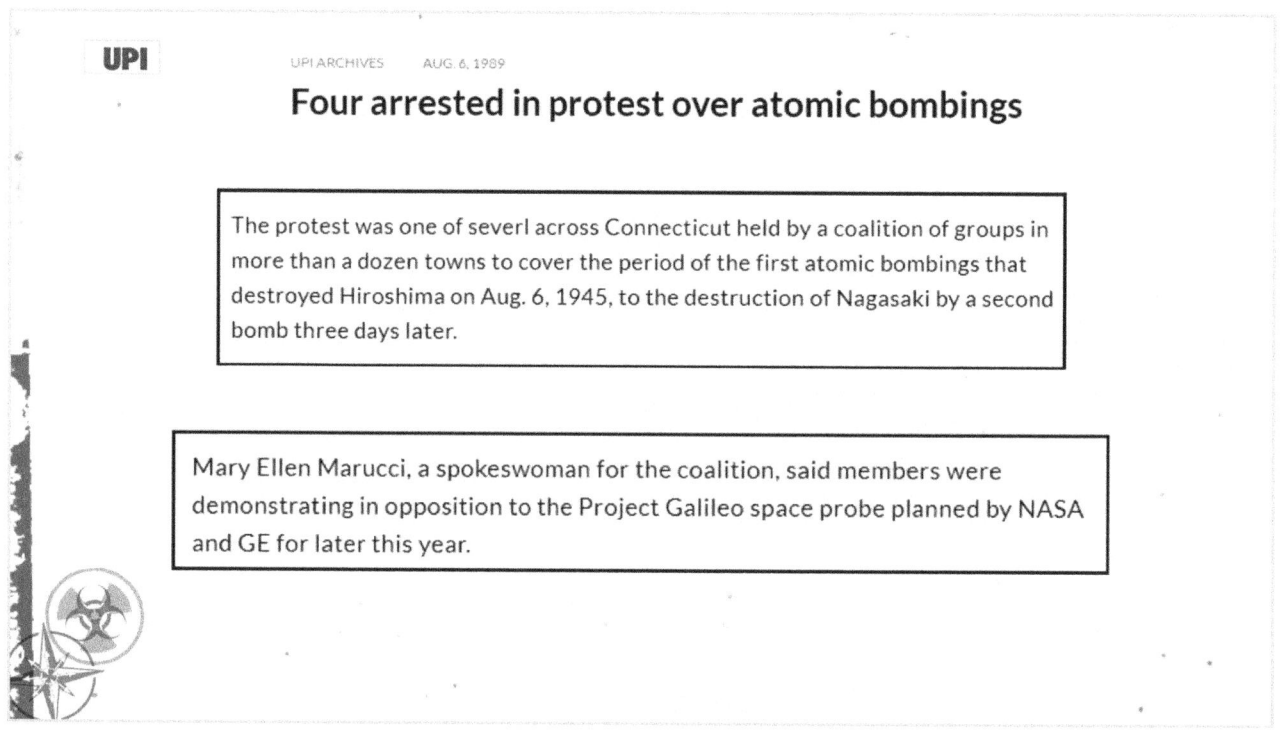

UPI

UPI ARCHIVES   AUG. 6, 1989

Four arrested in protest over atomic bombings

The protest was one of severl across Connecticut held by a coalition of groups in more than a dozen towns to cover the period of the first atomic bombings that destroyed Hiroshima on Aug. 6, 1945, to the destruction of Nagasaki by a second bomb three days later.

Mary Ellen Marucci, a spokeswoman for the coalition, said members were demonstrating in opposition to the Project Galileo space probe planned by NASA and GE for later this year.

Image Source: United Press International

"Four Arrested in Protest Over Atomic Bombings...

The protest ....held by a coalition of groups...Mary Ellen Marucci, a spokeswoman for the coalition..."

Text Source: United Press International[91]

---

90 Facebook, MaryEllen Marucci Profile, https://www.facebook.com/seedsaver/

91 United Press International, Four Arrested in Protest Over Atomic Bombings, https://www.upi.com/Archives/1989/08/06/Four-arrested-in-protest-over-atomic-bombings/1559618379200/

She repeated this process with several anti-nuclear organizations and then consolidated them under the umbrella of an organization she created on her own, for which she was the only head. She deceptively named it the Cooperative Citizens Monitoring Network.

From there, she would take over the court case with the people's plea for the NRC to adjust their nuclear power plant spent fuel pool regulations. Updated regulations were needed in order to prevent catastrophes that were likely to result from fuel rods packed so tightly together that they were anticipated to melt together during an emergency situation. Once that type of scenario unfolds, there is very little, if anything, that can be done to prevent a meltdown.

Over the course of a year, the recruiter kept maneuvering within the courts and managed to become the sole voice of the people against the nuclear industry and NRC.

NUCLEAR REGULATORY COMMISSION ISSUANCES

OPINIONS AND DECISIONS OF THE NUCLEAR REGULATORY COMMISSION WITH SELECTED ORDERS

On April 28, 1992, the NRC Staff, for the Commission, issued a preliminary determination that Amendment 158 involved "no significant hazards consideration," and published a Notice of Opportunity for Hearing.[2] The notice required that written requests for hearing and petitions for leave to intervene in accordance with 10 C.F.R. § 2.714 be filed by May 28, 1992. On June 4, 1992, the NRC Staff issued Amendment No. 158 after considering comments from intervention petitioners in accordance with 10 C.F.R. § 50.92.

Petitions for leave to intervene and requests for hearing were filed by several entities.[3] The petition granted by this Order was filed by Mary Ellen Marucci on behalf of herself and CCMN on May 28, 1992. Other petitions remain significant only because some petitioners authorize CCMN to represent their interests. See "Preliminary Ruling," Section III, *infra*.

Image Source: p. 204 <u>Nuclear Regulatory Commission</u>

243

"Petitions for leave to intervene and requests for hearing were filed by several entities. The petition granted by this Order was filed by Mary Ellen Marucci on behalf of herself and CCMN.

...

Other petitions remain significant only because some petitioners authorize CCMN to represent their interests."

Text Source: p. 204 <u>Nuclear Regulatory Commission</u>[92]

Much like she had stolen my voice, she now stole the voice of the people and became their representative in court.

She did this primarily by using the clout, expertise, and influence of others. She roped in the renowned physicist, Dr. Michio Kaku, to give his expert testimony (she brought me along to a lecture of his previously to do that, and his testimony was expert and it very likely would have been accepted by the NRC as reason enough to change the fuel pool specifications) as well as two senators, Christopher Dodd and Joseph Liebermann (I was along for those too).

[92] Nuclear Regulatory Commission, Opinions and Decisions of the Nuclear Regulatory Commission with Selected Orders, Volume 36, https://www.nrc.gov/docs/ML1635/ML16357A723.pdf
https://web.archive.org/web/20230000000000*/https://www.nrc.gov/docs/ML1635/ML16357A723.pdf

NUCLEAR REGULATORY COMMISSION ISSUANCES

OPINIONS AND DECISIONS OF THE NUCLEAR REGULATORY COMMISSION WITH SELECTED ORDERS

That there is no basis for the NRC to contend that no significant risk is involved in the issuance of the design change that was issued to address the criticality errors found at Millstone 2.

CCMN explained that Contentions 1 and 2 were supported by additional Sections A, B, and C and by the attached affidavits of Dr. Gordon Thompson and Dr. Michio Kaku. *Id.* Contention 1, it turns out, depends entirely upon the affidavit of Dr. Kaku, which we deem to be a part of the contention itself.[15] Sections A, B, and C of the CCMN Contention pleading and the affidavit of Dr. Gordon Thompson were of no value in explaining either Contention 1 or 2.

Image Source: p. 215 Nuclear Regulatory Commission

"CCMN explained that...were supported by...the attached affidavits of Dr. Gordon Thompson and Dr. Michio Kaku."

Text Source: p. 215 Nuclear Regulatory Commission[93]

---

93 Nuclear Regulatory Commission, Opinions and Decisions of the Nuclear Regulatory Commission with Selected Orders, Volume 36, https://www.nrc.gov/docs/ML1635/ML16357A723.pdf
https://web.archive.org/web/20230000000000*/https://www.nrc.gov/docs/ML1635/ML16357A723.pdf

JOSEPH I. LIEBERMAN
* CONNECTICUT

COMMITTEE
ENVIRONMENT AND PUBLIC WORKS
GOVERNMENTAL AFFAIRS
SMALL BUSINESS

United States Senate

WASHINGTON, DC 20510-0703

October 8, 1992

Mr. James M. Taylor
Executive Director of Operations
Nuclear Regulatory Commission
Washington, D.C. 20555

Dear Mr. Taylor:

We are again writing to you on behalf of a constituent, Ms. Mary Ellen Marucci and a constituent group, the Cooperative Citizen's Monitoring Network regarding the storage of new fuel rods at the Millstone nuclear Power Station, Unit. No.2.

As you may know, the Atomic Safety Licensing Board will conduct a hearing later this fall on the reconfiguration of the spent fuel pool at Millstone II. It is our understanding that this hearing will examine the concerns raised by our constituents. We have now been informed that our constituents recently learned that new fuel may be loaded into the pool for temporary storage within several days.

Our constituents have raised concerns about the impact of the addition of more nuclear material on the pool. We would appreciate your expeditious review of this matter and specific review of actions to be taken within the next several days.

Sincerely,

Joseph I. Lieberman
U.S. Senator

Christopher J. Dodd
U.S. Senator

Image Source: Nuclear Regulatory Commission

"Mr. James M Taylor

Executive Director of Operations

Nuclear Regulatory Commission

Dear Mr. Taylor,

We are again writing to you on behalf of a constituent, Ms. Mary Ellen Marucci...

Sincerely,

Joseph I. Lieberman, U.S. Senator

Christopher J. Dodd, U.S. Senator"

Text Source: Nuclear Regulatory Commission[94]

And then, when the case finally officially reached the courts, she intentionally dropped it, giving the NRC an automatic win and allowing the public to continue to be endangered by a spent fuel pool issue that actually did need to be addressed.

[94] Nuclear Regulatory Commission, United States Senate Letter to the Chairman of the Nuclear Regulatory Commission
https://www.nrc.gov/docs/ML2011/ML20116D106.pdf
https://webcache.googleusercontent.com/search?q=cache:n6TeRxMP11EJ:https://www.nrc.gov/docs/ML2011/ML20116D106.pdf&hl=en&gl=es

Cite as 38 NRC 5 (1993)   LBP-93-12

UNITED STATES OF AMERICA
NUCLEAR REGULATORY COMMISSION

ATOMIC SAFETY AND LICENSING BOARD

Before Administrative Judges:

Ivan W. Smith, Chairman
Dr. Charles N. Kelber
Dr. Jerry R. Kline

In the Matter of   Docket No. 50-336-OLA
                                                    (ASLBP No. 92-665-02-OLA)
                                                    (FOL No. DPR-65)
                                                    (Spent Fuel Pool Design)

NORTHEAST NUCLEAR ENERGY
  COMPANY
(Millstone Nuclear Power Station,
  Unit 2)   July 9, 1993

DECISION AND ORDER
(Terminating Proceeding by Summary Disposition)

SYNOPSIS

Northeast Nuclear Energy Company (NNECO), supported by the NRC Staff, moves for summary disposition of Concerned Citizens Monitoring Network (CCMN) Contention 1. Both NNECO and the NRC Staff have submitted the affidavits of qualified experts demonstrating that Contention 1 has not raised a genuine issue of material fact to be heard. CCMN has not answered the motion. The Licensing Board grants the motion. CCMN Contention 1 was the only contention accepted for adjudication. Accordingly, the Board terminates this proceeding.

Image Source: Nuclear Regulatory Commission

"CCMN has not answered the motion…

CCMN Contention 1 was the only contention accepted for adjudication. Accordingly, the Board terminates this proceeding."

Text Source: <u>Nuclear Regulatory Commission</u>[95]

We would all see the results of this intentional 1993 mishandling of the case, decades later in 2011 when an earthquake and tsunami hit a nuclear plant built in the same decade, with the same design, and with the same spent fuel pool issues.

---

[95] Nuclear Regulatory Commission, Opinions and Decisions of the Nuclear Regulatory Commission with Selected Orders, Volume 38, https://www.nrc.gov/docs/ML1635/ML16357A718.pdf
https://web.archive.org/web/20220801000000*/https://www.nrc.gov/docs/ML1635/ML16357A718.pdf

UNITED STATES
NUCLEAR REGULATORY COMMISSION
WASHINGTON, D.C. 20555-0001

December 7, 2020

Mr. Daniel G. Stoddard
Senior Vice President and
  Chief Nuclear Officer
Dominion Nuclear Connecticut, Inc.
Millstone Power Station
Innsbrook Technical Center
5000 Dominion Boulevard
Glen Allen, VA 23060-6711

SUBJECT: MILLSTONE POWER STATION, UNITS 2 AND 3 – DOCUMENTATION OF THE
              COMPLETION OF REQUIRED ACTIONS TAKEN IN RESPONSE TO THE
              LESSONS LEARNED FROM THE FUKUSHIMA DAI-ICHI ACCIDENT

Dear Mr. Stoddard:

The purpose of this letter is to acknowledge and document that the actions required by the
U.S. Nuclear Regulatory Commission (NRC) in orders issued following the accident at the
Fukushima Dai-ichi Nuclear Power Station have been completed for Millstone Power Station,
Units 2 and 3 (Millstone). In addition, this letter acknowledges and documents that Dominion
Nuclear Connecticut, Inc. (Dominion, the licensee), has provided the information requested in
the NRC's March 12, 2012, request for information under Title 10 of the *Code of Federal
Regulations* (10 CFR), Section 50.54(f), related to the lessons learned from that accident.
Completing these actions and providing the requested information, in conjunction with the
regulatory activities associated with the Mitigation of Beyond-Design-Basis Events (MBDBE)
rulemaking, implements the safety enhancements mandated by the NRC based on the lessons
learned from the accident. Relevant NRC, industry, and licensee documents are listed in the
reference tables provided in the enclosure to this letter. The NRC will provide oversight of these
safety enhancements through the Reactor Oversight Process (ROP).

Image Source: Nuclear Regulatory Commission

"Millstone Power Station, Units 2 and 3 - Documentation of the completion of required actions taken in response to the lessons learned from the Fukushima Dai-ichi accident."

Text Source: <u>Nuclear Regulatory Commission</u>[96]

Millstone Unit 2 was the power plant that was at the center of the court case that the recruiter had intentionally handed to the NRC at the expense of the people. It came with the same fuel pool concerns as the units at Fukushima that had been built around the same time.

Fukushima had a complete meltdown, increasing radiation levels in the Northern Hemisphere as well as the Atlantic Ocean.

There is a chance some of the catastrophe of Fukushima could have been prevented if she had not intervened and if the court case had been allowed to proceed and regulations updated to include suggestions for plants commissioned at the time both Millstone and Fukushima were built.

And if you ever think it was just an honest mistake. If you start to sink down that hole back into allowing in deception, I would like you to first see this:

---

[96] Nuclear Regulatory Commission, Letter: Millstone Power Station, Units 2 and 3 – Documentation of the Completion of Required Actions Taken in Response to the Lessons Learned From the Fukushima Dai-ichi Accident, https://www.nrc.gov/docs/ML2033/ML20332A139.pdf https://webcache.googleusercontent.com/search?q=cache:GFOKWGgQrkYJ:https://www.nrc.gov/docs/ML2033/ML20332A139.pdf&hl=en&gl=es
http://web.archive.org/web/20231111021033/https://webcache.googleusercontent.com/search?q=cache:GFOKWGgQrkYJ:https://www.nrc.gov/docs/ML2033/ML20332A139.pdf&hl=en&gl=es

FAIR

Image Source: <u>FAIR</u>

"Yet the NRC still refused a public hearing on safety issues surrounding spent fuel pools."

Text Source: <u>FAIR</u>[97]

Years later, when continuing her work to infiltrate and sabotage the antinuclear movement, she claimed in a posted comment that it was the NRC that never held a hearing, that they were solely the responsible ones. She did so without ever mentioning the part she played in making sure the hearings closed without the evidence being considered.

This is despite her being the one to stomp on everyone to respond to the public posting and notice for that hearing.

---

[97] FAIR, Comment on: NYT's Reassuring Radiation Reporting, https://fair.org/uncategorized/nyts-reassuring-radiation-reporting/

Image: Mary Ellen Marucci

Source: Author's Personal Photos[98]

She continued to dress in character for her audience, playing one role behind closed doors and another in public. When she had an audience, she would mix in the occasional conspiracy theory, tiny bits of truth, radical rhetoric, "for the children," and lots of "nuclear expert" credentials. (I've known her nearly my entire life and even I'm not 100% sure what her academic credentials actually are. I can only confirm that she had enough of them to have full access at Yale.)

When not dressed in a mock-radiation suit, she often wore a hand-tailored and custom-made wool poncho and knee-high leather boots. One of those winter outfits cost nearly as much as a mid-size sedan. The outfits were so eccentric that she had the rich convinced she was rich due to the combination of odd style and quality materials, and she had everyone else convinced she was insane enough to be impoverished and not know how to select normal-looking American clothing at a thrift shop.

---

[98] Author's Personal Collection, Photo: Mary Ellen Marucci,

Acceptance of grand theatrics, impossible promises, and other forms of deception has caused an excess of fake radicals and fake politicians, playing off each other and excluding the public while pretending to represent them. This deception goes as far as and includes their playacting within the courts and legislative buildings in Washington D.C., and then their national and international racketeering and shakedowns going beyond that gate.

This is unsafe for those of us forced to live in the real world where their short-sighted and self-serving actions have consequences. In other words, it's unsafe for all of us, and that includes the misguided operatives, lazy bureaucrats, and money-hungry individuals who are actively undermining the parts of the system intended to safeguard us from harm.

Also, after having to dig through countless pages of those NRC documents, I have to point out that the Nuclear Regulatory Commission's process is absolutely ridiculous. Determining and correcting errors in the engineering and maintenance of nuclear power plants should not be a court carnival with a result that depends on every clown and money man being there and tossing the correct balloon that day. It should be a practical and responsible science: examine problems and fix them.

Deployment, Part Two

Yes, I was in terrible situations with dangerous people.
But it was the crowd that did nothing,
that wandered in circles
making itself dizzy
just to distract itself
so it did not have to do anything.
They are the biggest part of the problem.
Everything could have been solved in minutes
if the populace wasn't weak as shit
and made insane.

Now that the topic of politicians has been fully broached with the signatures of Dodd and Lieberman, I feel like this is a good point at which to bring up why I've been skirting U.S. politics this entire time.

The truth is, I could easily add another fifty pages on how we leashed politicians with a combination of blackmail, threats, mutually beneficial camaraderie, bribery, and more. I could also discuss how one politician in particular leveraged the protection of being a federal witness - after a large-scale heroin bust in a politically involved legal office in San Francisco - to have anyone who went to court against her eliminated by the FBI, allowing her political career to begin and blossom in what is an otherwise harsh environment, and how the FBI has a history of covering for its witnesses at the expense of innocent citizens.

For example:

U.S. Told to Pay $101 Million for Framing 4 Men

The New York Times

BOSTON, July 26 — In what appears to be the largest sum of money ever awarded to people who were wrongfully convicted, a judge today ordered the federal government to pay $101.8 million to make amends for framing four men for a murder they did not commit.

Two of the men died in prison after being falsely convicted in the 1965 gangland murder. Another, Peter Limone, spent 33 years in jail before he was exonerated in 2001. The fourth, Joseph Salvati, spent 29 years in prison.

Mr. Barboza's motivation was to protect the real killer, and F.B.I. officials went along, the memos suggested, because Mr. Barboza had been helping them solve cases and because the killer, Vincent Flemmi, was an F.B.I. informant.

"The government's position is, in a word, absurd," Judge Gertner said.

The four wrongly convicted men were treated as "acceptable collateral damage" because the F.B.I.'s priority at the time was taking down the Mafia, their lawyers said.

Image Source: New York Times

"A judge today ordered the federal government to pay $101.8 million to make amends for framing four men for a murder they did not commit.

Two of the men died in prison after being falsely convicted in the 1965 gangland murder. Another, Peter Limone, spent 33 years in jail before he was exonerated in 2001. The fourth, Joseph Salvati, spent 29 years in prison.

....F.B.I. officials went along, the memos suggested, because Mr. Barboza had been helping them solve cases and because the killer, Vincent Flemmi, was an F.B.I. informant.

In her decision today, Judge Gertner forcefully criticized the F.B.I. and the argument made by Justice Department lawyers that federal authorities were not required to share information with state prosecutors, and were not responsible for the results of a state prosecution. 'The government's position is, in a word, absurd,' Judge Gertner said.

....The four wrongly convicted men were treated as 'acceptable collateral damage'...their lawyers said."

Text Source: <u>New York Times</u>[99]

I could talk about backroom deals that sold the entire country more times than once. Actually, I already mentioned one of those.

I could talk about the political science research project we did that resulted in tapping two future presidents based solely on what they looked like and their vocations (one black man and one real estate tycoon), due to what presidential demographics the research told us would work best for manipulating the public and then keeping them on the manipulation hook long term. George Edwards' involvement on that one made it into the news. The media always did love him.

[99] New York Times, U.S. Told to Pay $101 Million for Framing 4 Men, https://www.nytimes.com/2007/07/26/us/26cnd-mob.html

Friends, family to celebrate life of Black Panther, community activist George Edwards

When the time came to elect John C. Daniels the city's first Black mayor in 1989, Edwards got involved in that, too.

Image Source: New Haven Register

"When the time came to elect John C. Daniels the city's first Black mayor in 1989, Edwards got involved in that, too."

Text Source: New Haven Register[100]

New Haven is a model city. It has been since before I was born. That means Yale works to keep the city's population demographic as close to matching the U.S. as possible in order to use it as a large social and political sciences lab.

---

[100] New Haven Register, Friends, Family to Celebrate Life of Black Panther, Community Activist, George Edwards, https://www.nhregister.com/news/article/Community-mourns-Black-Panther-activist-Edwards-17536370.php

> I calculated how demographically similar each U.S. metropolitan area is to the U.S. overall, based on age, educational attainment, and race and ethnicity.[1] The index equals 100 if a metro's demographic mix were identical to that of the U.S. overall.[2]
>
> By this measure, the metropolitan area that looks most like the U.S. is New Haven, Connecticut, followed by Tampa, Florida, and Hartford, Connecticut.

Image Source: ABC News - FiveThirtyEight

"I calculated how demographically similar each U.S. metropolitan area is to the U.S. overall, based on age, educational attainment, and race and ethnicity. The index equals 100 if a metro's demographic mix were identical to that of the U.S. overall.

By this measure, the metropolitan area that looks most like the U.S. is New Haven, Connecticut."

Text Source: ABC News - FiveThirtyEight[101]

We used New Haven's mayoral elections as a test, using the campaign of John C. Daniels (black demographic) and then–Mayor John Destefano (white real estate investor). And, yes, the media caught George with both of them.

---

[101] ABC News FiveThirtyEight, Normal America is Not a Small Town of White People, https://fivethirtyeight.com/features/normal-america-is-not-a-small-town-of-white-people/

259

Edwards confers with then-Mayor John Destefano in 2007.

Image Source: <u>New Haven Independent</u>

"Edwards confers with then–Mayor John Destefano."

Text Source: <u>New Haven Independent</u>[102]

We ran an entire campaign to kick off that particular research project. I was in the campaign office of John C. Daniels on some nights, stacking sheaves of collected data and stuffing envelopes.

I'm deeply sorry for ruining any illusions. I know we all need hope to cling to. That basic emotional need, and a need for a functioning country, were both exploited by the people making the country dysfunctional. Those are the people who chose the presidents. Both U.S. presidents mentioned are individual humans with their own thoughts, motivations, and personalities. I'm not claiming that they manufactured humans, but they did choose them

---

102 New Haven Independent, A Panther Passes On, https://www.newhavenindependent.org/article/panther_passes_on

based on what the public manipulation research said, and there were times when they also manipulated both men.

On a related note, at higher levels on the political stage, methods from research and/or historical events are generally analyzed and chosen before making a move. The intent is to get a specific result, so they look for something that has been proven to attain that result before. What that exact thing is that gets the intended result does not matter as much. That's partially why our political landscape is now so scattered with random madness and parts that don't logically fit. Each of those things is there to get an intended result. That's the only reason they are there. It has pretty much nothing to do with our shared reality or needs.

I could even go on to discuss how the recruiter's cohort had people under their control on both sides of the aisle. Or I could mention how they once drugged an entire club at Yale, at their own dining table, and then proceeded to blackmail every single one of them. There are really no limits to the political stories I could tell. None. Absolutely none. The people I was stuck with did not have limits.

As the recruiter explained, only the people below have the limits of rules, social norms, expectations, religion, and laws. Those who choose to rule over them, or to exploit them from behind the curtain of secrecy, do not.

The reason I don't delve too far into the political topics is simple. People get too invested in the political media darlings, in their parties, in that last bit of hope of stability and/or change that they want. If I already struggle to get people to back away from lies they previously swallowed, why would I want the added task of trying to pry their political dreams from their hands?

Modern politics contains easy but useful-feeling distractions intended to engage the populace and avert their attention while the coffers are raided.

Much like holding up a protest sign, the act of being engaged in politics feels like an action, and people desperately need to feel that. In reality, it is often nothing more than government actors and organizers, like my buddy George over in COINTELPRO, leading the populace on a run like a dog until it runs out of energy. It's a necessity for running a

government without true public interference. However, it's a necessity for those running the government. It may not be as advantageous to you. It sure as hell isn't to the kids this civilization willingly tosses into the fire of war while everyone wears their "save the children" buttons and uses angry-face emojis. Don't even get me started on the political organization in Argentina that waves "the stolen children" around as a banner to raise funds for themselves while calling us same children criminals behind closed doors.

As I said, politics are a distraction. Even I get caught up in them now and then. I understand the emotional pull and utter distraction. I'm not going down that road. This is about focusing on our survival. Not the political actors on the theater stage. Those assholes will keep going until the final curtain. They are not the solution. Their theatrics and audience manipulation are part of the problem.

And, no, I gain nothing financially from suggesting honesty in how we manage government. My postgraduate credentials, the money and pay-outs in the field and career I am educated in and currently refuse to work in, require that politics combined with deception continue on indefinitely.

The primary premise in my profession at the upper level is that we take two (or more) leaders, go behind closed doors, find out their actual objectives, and come to an agreement that meets those while appeasing their citizens with lies and face-saving measures.

At the mid-level, it requires conning the public of the losing side into accepting reduced resources and rights while telling them its for their benefit.

In smaller negotiations, the goal is to find out what two (or more) people/parties in a negotiation are lying about by taking each one aside privately to see what their actual interests and needs are that they aren't admitting to (or to glean the truth by interpreting their lies). Then, create an agreement that serves both sides without letting each party know the secrets of the other party, what their actual needs were, and why they've all come to the resolution and agreement I've created for them to meet the needs that each of them will not reveal to the other side.

In other words, my entire job description is protecting secrets while still making things semi-function, and often to the detriment of the public and the exploited side, because those with the resources know the game. That's how they got the resources.

What would that even look like without all the subterfuge? Hell if I know. I might have to take up dog grooming as a permanent profession. I'm in uncharted territory. We all are. We've been in deception for so long. However, I would rather be a dog groomer in a functioning world than be paid off to make things worse while wearing a suit.

So, back to my life...

In addition to assisting with grassroots organization toppling for government ease, I was used for every task you can imagine, ranging from menial to extremely dangerous. I filed papers in the end-game labs, I visited and collected information from political prisoners, I worked the overnight shift on the bureaucratic side of a money laundering operation for a bit, and I assisted with the physical relocation of protected war criminals for the U.S. government as needed, among other things, some simply for the recruiter's profit, and others often directly relating to her work.

They quit letting me do pretty much anything that involved lab equipment after I sabotaged it more than once while playing dumb. So, much of my lab assistant work was boring - moving boxes or sorting through stacks of collected information no one with a decent pay grade wanted to touch. Sometimes, it was interesting.

I once spent a week helping a visiting lecturer at Yale to unpack his office, located on the short hallway that led to the large storage area and off-the-books medical laboratory. He was military, and as I understood it, his expertise was somewhere between strategy and psychology. He had me unpacking boxes and boxes of thick classified military manuals. I wanted to peek between the pages so badly. I was always curious - even when what I saw was horrifying, I usually still looked. I was only loaned to him for a day. I willingly volunteered my time for the rest of the week just to get a look at the inside of those manuals. I never had any luck. He never even left that office for long enough to use the men's room.

Another mundane at the time moment that would be catastrophic in the long term, was when I was brought to another building at Yale, primarily classrooms, but with some smaller lab equipment. I was asked to stuff envelopes while the recruiter and a female scientist spoke. There were several hundred envelopes with addresses all over the globe. I was sending the conclusion and information about their research to interested parties from everywhere.

As they spoke, the scientist confirmed they had developed a hybrid virus. It sounded a lot like the walking pneumonia one I had heard plans for when I was little, and with the HIV-1 virus that we had moved to New Haven to work with several years prior. However, she said it would take too long to produce and replicate the virus (the time mentioned was, at a minimum, several months; she may have mentioned a year or more). They were shelving the project until technology improved.

Later on, CRISPR technology would come into existence. I can't genuinely say 100% if I was doing the mundane envelope stuffing that day for a project that would become the prototype for COVID-19.

I will say that the previously mentioned military medical research states that the government was playing around with respiratory viruses combined with HIV in 1986 and 87:

DEFENSE TECHNICAL INFORMATION CENTER
PRESERVING KNOWLEDGE • CONNECTING PEOPLE • INSPIRING INNOVATION

6a. NAME OF PERFORMING ORGANIZATION	6b. OFFICE SYMBOL (If applicable)	7a. NAME OF MONITORING ORGANIZATION	
Biotech Research Labs., Inc.			

6c. ADDRESS (City, State, and ZIP Code)	7b. ADDRESS (City, State, and ZIP Code)
1600 East Gude Drive Rockville, MD 20850	

8a. NAME OF FUNDING / SPONSORING ORGANIZATION U.S. Army Medical Research & Development Command	8b. OFFICE SYMBOL (If applicable)	9. PROCUREMENT INSTRUMENT IDENTIFICATION NUMBER Contract No. DAMD17-86-C-6284

8c. ADDRESS (City, State, and ZIP Code)	10. SOURCE OF FUNDING NUMBERS			
Fort Detrick, Frederick, MD 21701-5012	PROGRAM ELEMENT NO. 623105	PROJECT NO. 3M2-623105H29	TASK NO. AD	WORK UNIT ACCESSION NO. 014

11. TITLE (Include Security Classification)
Development and Evaluation of Adeno-HTLV-III Hybrid Virus and Non-Cytopathic HTLV-III Mutant for Vaccine Use

12. PERSONAL AUTHOR(S)
Lubet, Martha Turner and Dusing, Sandra Kay

13a. TYPE OF REPORT	13b. TIME COVERED	14. DATE OF REPORT (Year, Month, Day)	15. PAGE COUNT
Annual	FROM 9/29/86 TO 9/30/87	87/10/28	46

16. SUPPLEMENTARY NOTATION

17. COSATI CODES			18. SUBJECT TERMS (Continue on reverse if necessary and identify by block number)
FIELD	GROUP	SUB-GROUP	AIDS, Vaccine, DNA Recombinant, Antibody, T-Cell
06	03		
06	13		

19. ABSTRACT (Continue on reverse if necessary and identify by block number)

Acquired immunodeficiency disease syndrome (AIDS) was initially recognized as a separate disease in 1981. Results from research groups in France and the United States determined that a previously unknown virus called HIV is the primary aetiological agent of AIDS.

Two HIV vaccines, a recombinant Adeno-HIV hybrid virus and a recombinant vaccinia HIV will be tested. The recombinant Adeno-HIV virus is being developed as part of this proposal. The vaccines will be tested in two species of monkeys, chimpanzees and African green monkeys. Vaccinated animals will be challenged with a defined dose of HIV virus. Assessment of vaccine efficacy against the virus challenge will include T4/T8 ratios,

Image Source: U.S. Military, <u>Defense Technical Information Center</u>

265

"Time covered: 9/29/86 to 9/30/87...

The recombinant Adeno-HIV virus is being developed as part of this proposal."

Text Source: U.S. Military, <u>Defense Technical Information Center</u>[103]

They were doing it under the guise of it being an effective tool for vaccine research and development. However, just because you can use something, doesn't mean that you should. No matter how polished your shoes or how much taxpayer money you're funneling, there is no excuse for some things.

I can also state that other labs were publishing their use of a combination HIV-1 and SARS-CoV pseudotype virus in 2004, according to scientific research articles from that time:

 Receptor-binding domain of SARS-CoV spike protein induces highly potent neutralizing antibodies: implication for developing subunit vaccine

> *Neutralization of pseudovirus infection.* A sensitive, quantitative, and safe neutralization assay based on reported SARS-CoV pseudovirus system [34], [41], [42], [43] was developed. HIV pseudotyped with SARS-CoV S protein was prepared as previously described [23], [24], [43]. In brief, 293T cells were co-transfected with a plasmid encoding codon-optimized SARS-CoV S protein and a plasmid encoding Env-defective, luciferase-expressing HIV-1 genome (pNL4-3.luc.RE) using Fugene 6 reagents (Boehringer–Mannheim). Supernatants containing HIV/SARS-CoV S protein were harvested 48 h post-transfection and used for single-cycle infection of ACE2-transfected 293T cells.

Image Source: <u>Biochemical and Biophysical Research Communications</u>

---

[103] U.S, Military, Defense Technical Information Center, Annual Report - Contract No. DAMD17-86-C-6284, https://apps.dtic.mil/sti/pdfs/ADA189926.pdf

"HIV pseudotyped with SARS-CoV S protein was prepared as previously described. In brief, 293T cells were co-transfected with a plasmid encoding codon-optimized SARS-CoV S protein and a plasmid encoding Env-defective, luciferase-expressing HIV-1 genome (pNL4-3.luc.RE) using Fugene 6 reagents (Boehringer–Mannheim). Supernatants containing HIV/SARS-CoV S protein were harvested."

Text Source: <u>Biochemical and Biophysical Research Communications</u>[104]

And the Wuhan lab was doing it in 2010:

Angiotensin–converting enzyme 2 (ACE2) proteins of different bat species confer variable susceptibility to SARS-CoV entry

Original Article | Published: 22 June 2010

act as a functional receptor for SARS-CoV. Here, we extended our previous study to ACE2 molecules from seven additional bat species and tested their interactions with human SARS-CoV spike protein using both HIV-based pseudotype and live SARS-CoV infection

Pseudotype virus infection assays

An HIV-1-luciferase pseudotype virus carrying the SARS-CoV BJ01 S protein, HIV/BJ01-S, was prepared as described previously [13]. HeLa cells were seeded onto 96-well plates for 18 h and then transfected with 0.2 μg recombinant plasmid containing bat or human ACE2

Image Source: Archives of Virology via <u>Springer</u>

"An HIV-1-luciferase pseudotype virus carrying the SARS-CoV BJ01 S protein, HIV/BJ01-S, was prepared...

---

[104] Biochemical and Biophysical Research Communications, Receptor-Binding Domain of SARS-CoV Spike Protein Induces Highly Potent Neutralizing Antibodies: Implication for Developing Subunit Vaccine, https://www.ncbi.nlm.nih.gov/pmc/articles/PMC7092904/

We extended our previous study to ACE2 molecules from seven additional bat species and tested their interactions with human SARS-CoV spike protein using both HIV-based pseudotype and live SARS-CoV infection assays."

Text Source: Archives of Virology via Springer[105]

It was all done in the soothing and calming name of vaccine research. Quite like how the recruiter used to call everything she did for the military "cancer research." If a tactic works, it tends to get repeated.

Biowarfare is government Munchausen by Proxy. They use classification and secrecy for "the protection of the nation" to hide the making of a weapon, and then advertise the making of a damaging "cure" for that same weapon (vaccine research, etc.). Then, much like a Munchausen by Proxy mother, they expect to be praised and rewarded for their efforts. And much like the child of a Munchausen by Proxy mother, the citizenry becomes too ill to be independent and they look to the same government that harmed them to heal them.

Unfortunately, that's not a response that leads to survival. Of all the forms of child abuse, Munchausen by Proxy is the most fatal. This is why I was always so concerned for the public. I barely survived it myself.

I can't say if any of these viruses work how the scientists I knew intended back when they were first talking about endgame walking pneumonia and incurable illness virus hybrids in front of me over plates of food at dinner table discussions. I can only tell you what I saw and heard, and how my heart felt like it jumped into my throat and stayed there when I first saw researchers noting the HIV-1 insert in COVID decades later.

If anyone ever seriously looks into this, you may be able to confirm that I was in the room, if nothing else. Because I was stuffing envelopes, my fingerprints were on the letters that were sent all over the world to let interested parties know how the early prototype turned out. I was still a child then, assuming I wasn't drugged on the recruiter's mortar-and-pestle

---

[105] Archives of Virology via Springer, Angiotensin-Converting Enzyme 2 (ACE2) Proteins of Different Bat Species Confer Variable Susceptibility to SARS-CoV Entry, https://link.springer.com/article/10.1007/s00705-010-0729-6

homemade scopolamine combination to the point that I simply thought I was a child that day. I'm sure I'll still hang for it, even if I was underage. That's just how people are.

If it seems like a badly thought-out decision to leave exploited internationally-trafficked children with the brunt of deciding which information the public should and shouldn't get, I agree. It's also unreasonable to leave children with the task of attempting to get that information out there despite their age and lack of education on how to get the public's attention regarding sensitive and difficult classified topics. It would be much more rational to stop hiding endgame research from the populations it's being tested on and/or will eventually be used on, which includes all of us. The weight I carried was ridiculous, and there were adults with functioning minds in those rooms, with family in that country, who all allowed the gross human rights violations to continue. God knows I tried to warn you, but my voice was not enough to break through. It is not realistic to leave the weight of this knowledge on a tiny number of people who generally fall into two categories - profiteers of the damage or the damaged.

Anyway, let's get back to the problems of the past, not all of which so directly brought about our current predicaments, although they have set the larger stage upon which these things can and do happen.

Test Firing

Just because you hide something
doesn't mean that it no longer has consequences.

In those years, the recruiter continued to use me as a prop to recruit, do cons, blackmail, extort, etc.

For the blackmailing part, she framed adults with resources (political, police, large industry, etc., much like Joseph, the sheriff we had moved in next door to with the sole intention of blackmailing him). She would frame each one by drugging them, positioning them inappropriately, and including me in the photos when I was young. When I was older, it got more creative, explosive, and more serious than that.

For grassroots organizations, parents' organizations, and individuals, she would use me as a prop so she could claim she was there for legitimate community or family reasons instead of what she was actually there for, which was primarily to derail their progress, take them over, or coercively recruit from them.

And then there were the times she would pile me in with everyone else she was running. For about two or three years, she had developed a seemingly quirky habit of simultaneously wearing approximately six stopwatches, hanging around her neck, all in different colors. It seemed like an odd fashion statement. It had nothing to do with fashion. She would wear them while standing on the New Haven Green, and she had one for each person she was running through that center of town.

The stopwatches were dual-purpose. The alarm function in them would alert her when each person was expected to arrive, or would be coming out of a building for a work break (she was targeting someone from the town hall, and someone from the government offices above the post office, in addition to a few people taking buses). The stopwatches also allowed her to time and record how long it took until the drugs would take effect once she hit someone

with them. There were a lot of numbers recorded. I would know. Frequently, I would collect them from all the devices and write them down in a ledger for her.

She kept a bag with more than forty bus schedules in it. She had one for every route. Again, seemingly a little quirky. However, there were some schedules that she had two of. For those, the second copy contained a processed version of scopolamine and who knows what else. It was one of the chemist's specials. It was a white powder, barely visible on the bus schedules, but powdery and uncomfortable on my already dry and sensitive hands, which it clung to. It would be lined up in the crevice at the bottom of the folded paper until you popped the schedule open to read it. And that's how she got people. I don't know the mechanism entirely, if it absorbed through the fingers or if the dust was inhaled as it flew into the schedule-reader's face, but it was effective.

She wasn't pleasant and most of her victims were tired of her, even if they could not entirely remember or articulate why. So, when they wanted to end a conversation, she would say, "Okay. But can you read this bus schedule for me so I can leave and catch a bus? I forgot my glasses." And they would invariably read it for her in the hopes of her going away after that. I know. I fell for it at least fifty times, myself. The one that was specifically for me was her extra copy of the D bus line schedule. I could never remember that I had already previously fallen for the ruse until I felt that powder on my hands and it was already too late.

In what felt like less than 120 seconds, I would find myself following her down the street, amenably, with my reasonable anger, distrust, and refusal entirely melted away. I'd remember the walks, and then the drug-induced amnesia wall would come down when we stopped walking.

Often, she wouldn't even go with a person after drugging them. She would just tell them where to go, hand them a bus ticket, and point them in the right direction. Many times it worked effectively. Other times, the intoxicated and thus suggestable people had trouble. Personally, I once forgot I was supposed to be heading to a paid research appointment for her, one only a few blocks from downtown, because I stopped to talk to friends and stared into the display at the Group W Bench, a shop with an inordinate amount of pinwheels in the window. Every word she told me disappeared from my mind as I watched those pinwheels spin.

And those lists of numbers I would write for her, collecting the data from the stopwatches? Once a month, those would be put in a large envelope with the stopwatches and sent to what she called a lab. Then she would go out, buy six more stopwatches, and start the process over again.

That was one of the more terrifying realizations I had at that age. That even her most insane and coercive behaviors might actually be fully supported and funded. It made it difficult to know who to reach out to, especially within her organization, so I didn't except for a few moments of complete and generally regretted weakness.

As I became a teenager, I would also be utilized as a tantalizing young body that got doors open when no one else could. Once inside, I would complete my instructed task, or in some cases, unlock a back door to grant the recruiter and others access so they could complete it themselves. I was always her door opener. The difference was that the methodology changed as I got older. By the time I was a teenager, I was too old to still claim "my mom's inside" to get past security.

To illustrate one of the newer methods, in the early 1990s in New York City, there were two Muslim roommates whom the U.S. government needed to have framed and intimidated into working for them. Another girl and I were sent in as escorts, with a backpack of explosives and instructions to get inside the apartment and place the backpack in a bedroom. Once we met the men, it didn't take long for them to "convince" us that we wanted to visit their apartment. The situation was set up to fall into our hands.

When the apartment door closed and we were inside, I was consumed by panic. The drugs they had given me before the assignment were lighting up all the wrong parts of my brain, and my decisions were anything but rational. I was to the point that I was considering scaling the outside of the building to escape.

The other girl convinced me that the stairs were a better option, and as that bedroom lit on fire, we ran. We were promised that a vehicle would be waiting for us directly outside the building. It wasn't. With smoke billowing from the building behind us, we walked at least six blocks through the city, our nerves even more frayed by the scream of fire trucks passing us

by. In those moments, I was certain that I was going to prison. Then George drove up, we piled into his car, and we all sped back to New Haven.

The situation was horrendous; I did not feel protected, and the amount of non-consented-to drugging I endured was beyond unreasonable, but it didn't seem like it would be eternal. I presumed that, eventually, I would become an adult and could simply leave without being bound by my captor and the bullshit misfiled document showing that she had a "legal" claim to me until I was eighteen.

That would be changed by another explosion in New York. Approximately a month before the 1993 bombing of the World Trade Center, I was asked to skip school and come to New York City with my kidnapper. George ended up being the one driving, yet again. He dropped us off near the building, and I walked into the underground parking area with the recruiter.

She held a clipboard with official documentation and used it to easily get past the scrutiny of the security guard and into an area of the parking garage officially cordoned off "for construction." There, hidden away from the public in that area with the demolition crew I had met on prior occasions in New York and Connecticut with their fake green card wives, I listened as they told my exploiter about their struggles.

They had been trying to place explosives up along the spine of the building next to the elevators. Their problem was that they couldn't get up high enough along the shaft. The design of the building meant they were physically blocked from getting the materials into the higher levels. The recruiter informed them that they still needed to stay on schedule in order to fulfill their side of the contract and for her to release payment. They reached an unhappy agreement.

I began to lean against a vehicle as I listened to them discuss what would become the trial run for the 9-11 explosions, while looking the relatively short distance to the elevator in the corner. I pondered their issue and the area they had been working in. Suddenly, all eyes were on me as they told me with panic in their voices that I should not lean against the vehicle. There were explosives inside. Later, where we had been standing could be seen in the post-explosion photos near the center of the wreckage. In that case, I can reasonably confirm that no one in that group had been lying to me – at least not on that topic.

By involving me in events leading up to 9-11 that implicated the government, even though all I had done was stand there looking bored, that bitch had just classified my life. There became no "legal" recourse and no way to truly escape my situation. I would forever be a hostage because of one of the most embarrassing and obvious coverups of our time. Honestly, it's insulting.

It also meant that more funding would become available to clean up after me, something that would become both an advantage for movement and activities, as well as an albatross around my neck when it came to attaining reliably unobstructed communication and in seeking actual freedom from my predicament.

Once in a while when I saw the opportunity to, I still kept trying to find help in locating my mother and where I had been stolen from. It wasn't easy. Our civilization only gives lip service to protecting children, and that's especially true in the U.S., where so many go missing every day. But now and then I'd send up little red flags, and in a few cases, a glaringly obvious flare. When I turned sixteen, it was one of the latter. A friend and I went to the Connecticut Department of Motor Vehicles to get my state photo identification card. I was nervous because I knew my birth certificate was fraudulent but up until that moment I hadn't been the one signing the documents that rode on it. Now, I was old enough to sign and still naive enough to think I'd end up in jail if I used a falsified document, especially if I used it in a government office and for something as official as an ID card.

So, my friend suggested that I ask the police officer who was standing outside doing guard duty. He was a police officer, not a security guard. My being young, I thought that meant he was actually aware of laws and how they worked. We approached him and I explained that I was using a fake birth certificate, that I was illegally adopted, and that I was there to get my state ID. I asked him if I would get in trouble with the law if I used the forged document to get an ID. He gave me an answer that I would later come to understand is standard among law enforcement. He said, "That's the name we know you as, so that's the one you should go by until you find your parents."

He didn't open a case to help me find my parents. He didn't insist that we go down to the police station. He simply waved us into the Department of Motor Vehicles building and pointed to where the line started. Within two hours (those lines are long), I had a photo ID.

I've been following his bad advice ever since. I've opened bank accounts in that false name, with that false nationality. I've attended university. I've taken out student loans and grants. I've gotten jobs. I've paid taxes. I've signed contracts. I've used it to apply for residency, permits, and citizenship in other countries since then. I've attained clearance levels with a false identity. I've broken so many laws with my very existence because those who enforce the laws are the ones who tell us to break them, thus entrapping us and making us criminals by default. I have very little love for that system and the people who support it. They've made me and countless others criminals before we even turned eighteen, all because they're too lazy and greedy for more population, to the point that they refuse to do their jobs and help kidnapped children to find our parents.

Other times, actually every time that I signed my false name in that country, I would send up tiny red flags hoping someone would notice. I would stop and pause and say, "What's my name?" out loud before thinking for a moment and then filling it in on whatever form or sign-in sheet was in front of me. I did that in front of countless officials, police officers, government workers, teachers, camp counselors, doctors, clerks, secretaries, and receptionists. No one ever thought it was concerning enough to start an investigation, even though I was praying one of them would.

And the one time in those years I genuinely spoke about my situation, instead of advocating for others or gently attempting to trigger an investigation into my kidnapping status? I was seventeen and in Northern California, where I had fled to get a temporary reprieve. Unfortunately, I also managed to severely injure a tendon in my foot, meaning I could barely walk and couldn't work. So, I went to a youth shelter there to sit and heal for a few weeks while I had no money coming in. One of the requirements to be admitted to the shelter was a psychological evaluation. Because they were limited in funding, the evaluations were done in an office at the nearest state-funded mental institution. If nothing else, we can assume the psychologists there had already seen and heard everything, and could reasonably handle assessing teenagers.

I sat down in a chair across the desk from a female psychologist. She told me I could open up to her and speak about anything. I assumed she was a professional and knew what she was asking. I also assumed there were patient-doctor confidentiality rules and I was safe to speak as long as I didn't claim to be suicidal or a threat to others. So, for the first time in my life, I risked speaking the full truth. Ten minutes into my talking, that psychologist got up from behind her desk, walked over to the couch, curled up into a ball on it, and became catatonic. Two male orderlies had to carry her out. Later on, when I inquired about how she was doing, I was told she was taking an extended several-month-long break from work to recover.

That moment taught me that if I spoke about myself, it would harm others. I learned that sharing my thoughts, my pain, my experiences, my life - if I opened up and was myself, if I sought healing or help for myself - that it would cause people to shriek and crumble as if they themselves had been harmed. So, I went back to not speaking about anything.

I spent the next three weeks sitting in that shelter, talking about cooking, music, and things of no relevance at all to my own survival or the survival of those around me. I had learned that frivolity is all this world can predictably psychologically manage without breaking, so I kept my pain out of view while I coddled and entertained them.

Internal Sabotage and Entrapment

It's part of a larger picture, a cascading failure
that plunges to the bottom and begs for the final exit.
Predatory banking, governance, counterintelligence,
and public manipulation
- when combined with the human need for group acceptance,
immediate needs, and short-term safety -
turn the population against itself and
catapult wars and internal pilfering
beyond a resource grab and into the grotesque.

Shortly after I turned eighteen years old on paper, my exploiter set me up for a short time in Yale student housing intended for later-year students belonging to one of the campus societies, housing not normally available to incoming first-year students who were generally relegated to the dorms. Although it seemed odd to me that I hadn't been placed with the freshmen, there was hope in my heart that the situation was somehow real despite my not having filled in an application (the recruiter did so much of my paperwork for both drug trials and academic courses that it seemed possible she had done it for this), and that I could finally start living a normal life by attending university at eighteen as a traditional student. That hope would be short-lived.

What followed was her slipping me enough drugs, without my knowledge, that she was able to convince me that I was eight and not eighteen. She then walked me over to the office of a recruiter for a job opportunity that Yale students I had spoken to rightfully deemed as "too dangerous and too much of a sacrifice." We sat down with a military officer, went through a contract that was easily more than thirty pages long, and I signed – because I thought I was eight and it was the quickest way out of the building so we could go get the ice cream that had been promised to me.

If the officer in that room was not in on the con, he should have been fired for hiring an eighteen-year-old who acted like an eight-year-old squirming in a chair.

We walked to Ashley's Ice Cream, several blocks away and past the law school. That ended up being the most expensive ice cream cone of my life. It was a crunchy sugar cone with a scoop of cookie dough ice cream and a second scoop of mint chocolate chip on top. I paid for it with my entire future. If I had known the real cost, I probably would have savored it for longer.

We returned to the student apartment. There, the recruiter stole my bankbook and told me to pack my things. I didn't get to attend any classes that year, at least none I can remember. But it would be the beginning of her collecting a paycheck for a job I would be forced into without my true consent or the knowledge of how to get out of it. I had been too high during the contract signing to even remember which Department of Defense contractor or office it had been with.

I did visit one of their offices a solitary time that I remember. It was early on in my work for them, and hidden in a silo beneath a larger structure in what may have been the Florida Keys. I was heavily drugged for the journey, but I do remember The Keys. Sitting in the passenger seat while we were driving between the islands, with me high out of my mind was downright terrifying with the water on both sides.

I was allowed to enter the building, and then invited down into the silo. There, I was given an employee manual to read. The one handed to me must have been at least 500 pages. They said I could skip to somewhere around 170. I wanted to tell someone that I shouldn't have been there, but I didn't know who was in cahoots with the recruiter and who wasn't. Standing there, I had no idea who was a foe and who was a friend, and I had no intention of finding out the hard way while trapped underground with them.

My choice to remain silent made a certain amount of survival-level logic while in that governmental-deceit-accustomed society and in that situation. But you have to realize at the organizational level, at the functional level, at the level of oversight and things actually working as intended - your own first-day employees being so accustomed to levels of infiltration and exploitation within your halls that they can't even take a reasonable gamble to find one legitimate and non-corrupted worker to speak with and voice their concerns - that signals that you don't have a company anymore, or a nation... not a functioning one.

So, while I was stuck there, trying to look like I belonged, I read the manual.

It's worth noting that, while I barely skimmed most of it in my anxiety, I did read the key points and titles, and came away with the gist of it, most of which I have already shared with you:

1. Yes, I was a scientist, but my first duty was to the company. Company work came first, and protecting their secrets was the top priority. Everyone who worked for the company did the company work.
2. If I could manage to also do my scientific research during that, good for me. But it was not a priority and there was no guarantee it would happen.
3. I was never to discuss anything when above ground / on the public level.

Obviously, I've broken rule three intentionally, and probably rule one both intentionally and not. But they broke their side of the contract before I even signed it. You cannot rule solely by fear, especially not while burning out the people you are attempting to rule over. I'm too exhausted for fear.

They should never have let me sign the contract while obviously drugged in the first place. They knew who I was sitting next to in that recruitment room. They trained her. And they knew what she had been trained in, including drugging, subversion, and coercion. Not checking to confirm if a new recruit is sober when sitting next to one of the company snakes is reprehensible and irresponsible policy. I'd be amazed if someone wasn't getting a cut of the profits from that one.

By that point, I was already exhausted. In an attempt to take a break from doing damage control for others, I started clawing back more moments of my life for myself.

Indefinite Detainment, Indefinite Wars

While the world slept, I was coerced into recruitment,
preparation, provocation, and exploitation of war
and people for biological, chemical, and nuclear
warfare research.
Knowledge goes nowhere in a world that turns away in fear.
I bore it alone.
I wept for the world.
The world never wept for me.

At that point, I was mostly being used for Human Resources scams so the recruiter could still collect a paycheck in the name she purchased for me when I was three (I get the feeling that birth certificate purchase was more for her than it was for me). My work became primarily peripheral. I traveled often and I no longer had firsthand knowledge of everything going on at Yale or in the East Coast counterintelligence scene, but they would still drag me back in when I was needed, and I could still see the results of their actions, even from across the country and then across the world.

In the moments I had to myself, I focused on trying to get my personal chains off. I was tired of battling with the world to remove theirs. I went back to attempting to find where I was stolen from. I hadn't had any luck as a child, but now I was an adult, so I thought that would give me more of an advantage. This time, I went with the U.S. hospital listed on my forged birth certificate. It was all I really had to go on. So, I called that hospital to request my medical records. The recruiter had told me I had been born there and then spent most of the first year of my life in that hospital with a series of medical conditions, including meningitis.

When I spoke to someone in that hospital's records department, they promised me they kept all records from the year I was born and they could get mine together with no problem. The woman told me to call back the next day to find out the fee (it was per page, so she needed to discover the number the pages first). I waited two days because, if the recruiter had been honest, there would have been a lot of pages for them to go through. When I called

back, I reached the same woman I had spoken to the first time. She had uncertainty in her voice and was being coached by an older woman in the background. She told me that there had been a small file fire she was previously unaware of and it had only affected the box with my medical records. The hospital had no record of me. I thanked her and hung up.

I assumed the recruiter had gotten to her. It wasn't until decades later that I found out that's how a lot of U.S. hospitals deal with adopted children when they call asking about their birth records. If the hospital cannot find the records, they assume the person was adopted by parents who chose to keep it a secret, and thus many of them will give the "file fire" story. The system is set up in a way that children, both adopted and abducted, are blocked and lied to about their origins. I wasn't the only one caught in the net. And, for once, the recruiter probably had nothing to do with the subterfuge. The entire system is set up to bury its youngest and most vulnerable victims.

While staying in New Haven, there were many times that I would find myself drugged and approaching the exterior of the JFK airport, often with the recruiter by my side saying things like, "Oh, wow! That architecture is so futuristic, we must be in a dream!" Of course, I was supposed to agree with her at that point, "Oh, yes, I must be dreaming." I did it out of habit. Once in a while, I was drugged enough to actually believe it, but often I was just trying to appease her and her seemingly psychopathic insanity while I tried to find an exit in a country with no exit. In those days, the exit - albeit a temporary one - was often a plane. Via that airport, she sent me all over the country and the globe.

In my continuing - and often drugged - nonvoluntary service to the State and the recruiter, still trapped in the situation with no hope for escape or regaining my identity, I would visit prisons, foreign and domestic. The prisons were of varying levels of what an honest person might call legality. I was there to engage with political prisoners as part of the recruitment process. I walked through many prison doors, aware of what I was doing, and saw horrific human rights violations while there. This is a prison I walked through without them having prior notice, and without them cleaning up the worst of the mess first:

My security access allowed me entry to the prisons, and thus most doors in those areas, so when I was stumbling around on the wrong floor of a government building, trying to reach a pool, and I saw a door with a security guard at the back of an abandoned pool changing room, I decided to use that access to take a shortcut. I'd done it many times before. I liked exploring. I liked getting away from people and only hearing the echo of my feet in vacant halls. This would not be that.

The guard asked me if I was sure I wanted to enter. I said yes. He didn't look convinced but he let me in. Inside the door was an elderly man, standing right by it as if he'd been standing there for decades, and there's no doubt in my mind that he probably had been, other than to rest and eat. That room was an old locker room. To the right were showers (mostly broken, according to the man). In the center were benches. In the front was a row of sinks.

I went through a doorway near the sinks and entered what was a kitchen area. There stood several elderly women. They were sorting through food waste that had been pumped in from above via what appeared to be a cafeteria food waste chute. They treated me like a guest and offered me a clean-looking piece of bread that had been torn or bitten before it reached there. I knew the offer was in kindness, and I accepted the thing, despite being a bit of a germaphobe due to fragile health from having been thrown into so many medical research studies as a child. Even sharing a glass of water with a relatively healthy friend would often result in months of pain and struggling with swelling, hives, and an overactive immune response.

Down the hall, past the kitchen, were the cells. They were dark and dirty. I didn't invade the space too much to see. I just strained to look down that hall. An adult male, a generation younger than the elderly in the kitchen, was in the midst of a sustained emotional breakdown. His girlfriend/wife was not in a better place emotionally.

After someone took the piece of bread back from me, realizing I wasn't actually going to eat it, I sat down on a bench in the first room to wait to be released. My unexpected visit caused the guard to call around internally to make sure I actually had authorization, and it took a while to get an answer, so he left me locked inside for the wait. The girlfriend of the man having a breakdown sat down next to me and began to aggressively mother me. She insisted I wash my hands in one of the sinks, and she stood over me like a mother would, scrubbing them for me. Then, she got out a comb and began to attempt to untangle my hair...an unpleasant experience due to the knots (my hair is brush-worthy - not intended for combs), her persistence, the amount of time she spent (it was eternal), and the physical proximity. I felt uncomfortably smothered.

When I finally escaped her, with a little assistance from the elderly man by the door, he explained to me that she and her boyfriend were the children of the people in that prison. That they were born there, and raised there. But, when she had her own baby, with the expectation that she could also raise a family, the prison guards took the baby away. I was the smallest person to have walked back in through that door. She thought I was her child.

Of all the prisoners I met, her sorrow impacted me the most. If I could have saved her, I probably would have brought her home with me and never let go.

The prisoners I met tended to leave me with a lasting impression. Something about those moments highlighted their lives to me in ways that few other people in my life ever could.

Another time, in another prison, I would meet an American who left me hating life, and another time... well, let's start with that one and skip the American for now.

I was drugged to hell for the journey there and can't even remember what country in the Americas we were visiting (I did know at the time, to be fair) but I know that rumor of the particular underground prison made it to the surface and into a newspaper at least once. It was situated beneath a government building in a city and wasn't a secret, although it was infamous. The prison itself was approximately six sub-levels deep. I was with the recruiter for that one. She, as was usually the case, didn't enter the prison. She would often send me in and wait outside. Usually, I was there to make contact with various political prisoners. This time, I was there as a favor and in a different capacity.

They were having issues with the plumbing, especially in the lower sub-levels. They were also having issues getting plumbers to enter the facility, either because the plumbers refused or because the government didn't want anyone to see what was going on in the bottom floors. I was given an Ecstasy pill and sent to the bottom floor. Approximately six levels down. What I saw when I got down there was disturbing. No amount of drugs could have made it a good experience, although they did make it less nauseating.

There was a pipe visibly dripping water down one of the walls, but that wasn't the main problem. The problem was the drainage, or the lack of it. A guard said something about the drainpipes not working right because of how deep we were. Then he left me with a shovel and a wheelbarrow in the shower room. The water and excrement were deep enough to cover a person's shoes. The political prisoners who were never going to see the light of day, and who had clearly been tortured, were crazed, depressed, and moved more like animals than people. They had also been using the bottom of the shower stalls as toilets.

I started shoveling. I hate the feeling of being drugged, but as far as that moment goes, I am incredibly grateful that I was on something. That wheelbarrow was filled several times and carted away before the shower room looked like a shower room again. The entire time I worked, I could hear the scurrying of one particularly insane political prisoner as he moved in a hall to my right. I tried to talk to him at one point, but we didn't speak the same language and it's unlikely that he would have been comprehensible even if we had.

Eventually, I finished and a guard led me up to what was probably the second or third subfloor. There, I waited to be released. It would be several more hours. While sitting there, I observed the people around me, most of whom had zero interest in me and didn't speak English, anyway. They were depressed and irritable but not visibly deranged like the people below. Then, someone who was probably around age seventeen or so sat down next to me. He started speaking in English. We talked about everything in those hours. He had been born in prison, a lot like me, but they had never set him free. He seemed less depressed than everyone else, although still pale. It turned out there was a reason for his uplifted mood.

He was part of a prison work program that allowed him to go to the surface sometimes. There, above ground, his job was to join protests and movements to initiate violence and give the police an excuse to round up the protesters. He liked his work. It allowed him to meet people and see the sun. Any illusions I ever had about Intelligence work paying well (if you're not into thievery or blackmail) were killed long before that. Hopefully, now, I've killed those hopes for everyone else too. It's not Hollywood. That kid was paid in sunlight.

By the time I got back to the surface, my skin had flared up in every way imaginable. I went to a dermatologist and got a year-long prescription for antibiotics. I didn't feel clean even after that.

As for the American prisoner I would meet, that was in yet another prison and earlier on. I don't know what country that was in either, I never knew, and I don't think I'll be able to find

it in newspapers. I did try to pinpoint it later by researching the military uniform I saw there, but there were a ridiculous number of countries with those small-bill green hats and matching green uniforms in those years.

The recruiter was there for that one and I was let in through a door in front of the building and past a secured gate, while she waited outside. I'm fairly certain I was doing her job for her that day. After passing through the internal gate, I went upstairs and was granted access to a hallway. I had a list of people I needed to speak to and a pile of papers with me, including a carbon-copy receipt book. I wandered lost for a bit. While the hall was locked on both sides, the prisoners were free to move between the rooms. It seemed more like a converted building rather than having originally been a prison. It may have been a school, factory, or office building first. A room on the right was quite large. There were mattresses and clothes, including on a makeshift clothesline, strewn everywhere. I was sticking to the edge by the door, attempting to give everyone's things respect and space.

That's when I met the only person on that floor who spoke a high level of English. After the fourth or fifth person I had attempted to speak to, they had sent me him. He was a black man, possibly American, but not the American I mentioned previously who would leave me traumatized. He walked me across the large room and we looked out the back window as we spoke. Through the window, we could see the disused courtyard behind the building. We talked about life for a couple of minutes and then he took the list from me and we went through it, finding each person on it. Most of their languages sounded European to me. I think one woman was Scandinavian. They each wrote lists of things they needed and I gave them receipts to acknowledge that the lists had been received. Most of the items were basic toiletries. They all seemed aware of their situation and were trying to make the best of it.

Eventually, there was only one name remaining on my list. They told me I could find him downstairs. I went to the far end of the hall and a guard let me into that stairwell. The ground floor level was controlled chaos. The cells there were essentially a line of cages. They were large enough to stand in but very narrow, and there must have been fifteen in a row, at least. When I entered to walk along the cells, it seemed like every single person in them was yelling and actively throwing ripped-up toilet paper against the metal fencing those cage-like cells were constructed of. I asked prisoners where the person on my list was, by using his name. They pointed to the end of the cells. At the very end, on the right, sat the American who would force survivor's guilt onto me. He wasn't yelling. He wasn't throwing toilet paper. He was sitting on the floor of his cell, apparently meditating.

I handed him the giant stack of legal documents I had for him. No one else had required a stack quite that thick. He signed the receipt and started going through the papers energetically. He was convinced that he had a legal case and that the papers would set him free. I don't think he understood how few rights political prisoners actually have or exactly what indefinite detainment means, especially when you've been accused of spying in a third country.

He insisted I call someone for him. I said I would try. I did try. The recruiter intercepted me on the way to a payphone (not that I would have had enough change for that international call) and I forgot the number within the hour. His hope and expectations, which I could not realistically meet, ate at me for...well, they left a permanent impression. I've been in countless similar situations, and yet here I am highlighting him. His hope is what killed me. No one else I met ever had that level of delusional hope. Even as I write this book, I have zero hope that writing it will change a thing. It's simply an act of throwing something at a wall because if I don't, I won't be able to walk away saying, "At least I tried."

I continued to drag through life, absolutely exhausted and never knowing when I would be forced into a dangerous assignment with no warning or proper read-in, or at least not one I could remember once the drugs began to wear off. I tried to carve out a small chunk of life for myself. I sought additional employment that actually paid me and I got a tiny studio apartment for myself.

Frequently, the requirements for the paycheck my exploiter was collecting at my expense would get in the way of my personal mediocre part-time work to pay my bills. I would sometimes lose everything because, first, I would have to meet the obligations of the job that paid the recruiter, often in locations far across the country or the world. They were a long trip from where I had established myself and my routine. I would miss part-time $8-an-hour work and not be able to pay my $250 a-month studio apartment rent because I was halfway around the globe on a ticket that probably cost someone $1000.

My trips were generally related to research, relocations, or recruitment. On one occasion, I was sent to The Bahamas, high out of my mind. As I took boat after boat, looking out on the seemingly never-ending blue water, I felt like I would never find my way home. The scene in front of me, despite being beautiful, amplified my feelings of loneliness and being lost in the vast expanse of this world. Eventually, I got onto one last boat, a small motorboat with supplies, and headed to a U.S. research island to deliver everything in the boat to a scientist who was there. I remember reaching the shore and seeing his face. With the level of drugs in my system and as immediately disturbing as his personality was, I'm both grateful and terrified that I don't remember the rest.

Another time, and not on my own, my sometimes-cohort was sent into foreign territory for reasons I cannot figure out to this day. The combination of drugging and not everyone being read in was a catastrophe waiting to happen. And it did happen. We ended up in a street fight and extraction became a nightmare that didn't occur until a week after the promised time.

Back on U.S. soil, I began to find ways to earn an income on the side that could withstand what I was going through. It wasn't enough to be comfortable but at least I wasn't starving. One of the first places I learned about sporadic entrepreneurship was on the road going between summer festivals. I managed to support myself through a summer of travel. I figured it was a good start. Even that was cut short when the U.S. government came calling, once again. I was needed in Phoenix. The bane of my existence sent a car full of bounty hunters to collect me and make sure I got there on time for them.

By the time we arrived in Phoenix, I was so tired of the antics of the drug-addled bounty hunters that I happily let them steal my bag of belongings and hand me over to a nicely dressed military officer who led me inside, with him apologizing the entire way for having taken me away from my summer festivities. He informed me that a woman they were holding in that facility had refused to allow them to do any more testing on her until she saw me and that I was safe. I was so accustomed to being dropped into random scenarios to play a role or perform a task that I didn't even blink. I just nodded and went along, an ideal hostage as always.

We reached the hall with the correct observation room, and I looked through the glass. On the other side of it was medical equipment including a large machine, but more prominent in my view was the woman on the gurney. Her hair was long and unbrushed to the point of matting. She was hunched over, hysterical, and clearly in agony. I was walked into the room. There, I took her hand in mine. She spoke Spanish and I didn't comprehend a word, but I stood there for several minutes, just holding this tortured woman's hand. She pleaded with me, but I couldn't understand what she was saying. Eventually, and too soon, I was led away.

They shipped me back east. I never did make it to the festival I had been on my way to. Once released from further obligations in Connecticut, I found someone with a kind ear and spoke to him about what I had witnessed in that locked facility. I wanted to help the woman escape, but we both concluded that we would end up dead, in jail, or in a mental ward for our attempts. The weight of the society that brought about that stark reality began to feel like a pressure, consistently heavy on my chest.

Later on, when putting together the pieces and realizing that the only woman who would face further torture just to see me was probably my own mother – and that I had left her there alone to die in agony because the world would have fought me if I tried to save her – that changed me.

It would eventually change my perception of humanity from deserving hope to something else entirely.

As I've said before, they had to use political prisoners and prisoners of war because no one else would sign the paperwork allowing themselves to become weapons research test subjects. That said, domestic and ordinary prisoners are often coerced into becoming medical test subjects within the U.S. prison system, primarily for commercial pharmaceutical research, but not exclusively. It has been a persistent issue for more than half a century.

There is a problem with the psychology behind research that requires testing on unwanted or unvalued populations, and that psychology impacts the quality of the pharmaceuticals produced. When a drug or other treatment is produced via unethical means, care for the patient and concern about side effects are reduced. The lack of care results in the

formulation of a product that will not just do harm to the unwanted and exploited group, but will also do harm to the end user, who will pay a purchase price for that harm.

Image Source: California Law Review via University of California

"Prisoner subjects continue to be used in medical experiments. For instance, between 2006 and 2008, a drug company called Hythian contracted… to enroll criminal defendants in an experimental drug addiction treatment program. As part of this program, state judges 'divert' drug court participants… into an experimental treatment program called Prometa…The program involves thirty days of treatment with three different drugs, none of which has been approved for use in addiction treatment by the Food and Drug Administration. At least one Collin County, Texas, participant in the Prometa program died; the court recorded the death as a suicide."

Text Source: California Law Review via University of California[106]

---

[106] California Law Review via University of California, Experimentation on Prisoners: Persistent Dilemmas in Rights and Regulations, https://escholarship.org/content/qt81x6m9bt/qt81x6m9bt.pdf

I have to admit that by the time the 2001 attempt at demolishing the Twin Towers was made, with enough success to be plastered on the news for days on end, I didn't actually care, despite my having been there to observe the planting of the explosives for the earlier 1993 bombing. I felt nothing. Name one part of humanity that had not already failed me and everyone around me by that point.

Although, I will note that September 11th morning, before the towers went down, one of the articles that was published in that day's newspaper was a nod to the Weather Underground Organization. That was the article that mentioned the recruiter's involvement in putting a bomb in the Pentagon. While the public may believe every lie and alternative lie told to them, those who did the actual work still got a tilt of the hat in acknowledgment, and as always, in the New York Times.

Somewhere in New York that morning, was a person looking up from that article right in time to see the Twin Towers explosion. Somewhere near the Pentagon, the same was happening, but with a different view over the top of the newspaper.

*No Regrets for a Love Of Explosives;
In a Memoir of Sorts, a War Protester
Talks of Life With the Weathermen*

The New York Times

By **Dinitia Smith**

Sept. 11, 2001

See the article in its original context from September 11, 2001, Section E, Page 1

"Everything was absolutely ideal on the day I bombed the Pentagon," he writes. But then comes a disclaimer: "Even though I didn't actually bomb the Pentagon -- we bombed it, in the sense that Weathermen organized it and claimed it." He goes on to provide details about the manufacture of the bomb and how a woman he calls Anna placed the bomb in a restroom. No one was killed or injured, though damage was extensive.

Image Source: New York Times

293

"The New York Times

No Regrets for a Love of Explosives; In a Memoir of Sorts, a War Protester Talks of Life With the Weatherman

Published: Sept. 11, 2001

'Everything was absolutely ideal on the day we bombed the Pentagon.'"

Text Source: New York Times[107]

Yes, it was an inside job. That's what happens when you let the people who hate you and profit from you run your Intelligence services.

107 New York Times, No Regrets for a Love of Explosives; In a Memoir of Sorts, a War Protester Talks of Life With the Weatherman, https://www.nytimes.com/2001/09/11/books/no-regrets-for-love-explosives-memoir-sorts-war-protester-talks-life-with.html

Waiting in Ambush

It's like having a tiger walking free in a crowd,
and instead of a few people jumping on it,
or anyone getting together to trap it,
they all just pretend it's not there as their 'survival response'
and it slowly eats its way through the whole crowd,
including them.

Sometime after that, I officially went to a university in California of my own volition, with my non-paid work hours settling mostly into nights and the occasional random trip. Between university, work, life obligations, and the forced unpaid work, I was getting roughly two to three hours of sleep per night for years. It was not easy. Everything I did took extreme effort, but I put the effort in, even if it was sometimes at a snail's pace.

The only major interference in my education came when I was applying to graduate schools. I found myself railroaded back into the specialty I had been sent to countless lectures on at Yale, and I ended up attending graduate school for it. I probably could have fought a little harder and chosen another path, but I didn't have enough of a fight in me in those years. I was too exhausted.

I rose to the top of the class in my departments. My only struggles were in mathematics (which I eventually caught up in enough to have a level of competency) and ethics. After a lifetime of growing up on the inside of counterintelligence, I never could entirely understand ethics from the traditional perspective, although I did try. Among my straight As, those ethics courses always gave my grade point average a slight ding. I had to settle for a 3.9 instead of a 4.0.

```
BEG NNING OF POSTBACCA AUREATE COURSEWORK    - - - - -




NCRP Skills Concepts & Tools        3.00        3.00 A

Ethics of NCRP                      3.00        3.00 A-

Negotiation Tactics                 3.00        3.00 A
    3.900        TERM TOTALS :       9.00        9.00


Good Standing
```

Image: University transcript

Source: Author's personal documents[108]

Not that an A- is bad. It's just not quite perfection, and I always aimed for perfection.

The worst part about those years was the money that would show up randomly. I know, you're thinking that shouldn't be the worst part. It was. Free money isn't free, and it also wasn't mine to spend. It would come in various forms, from an array of government and NGO-subsidized offices that weren't permitted to give those amounts according to their own rules and the rules of their funders, and that I generally wasn't eligible to receive from. But the occasional random unsolicited check would show up anyway. I'd call the issuing offices to make sure the checks weren't an error that I would have to repay or that would land me in jail if I cashed them. Invariably, after some confusion and searching through their databases, the workers in the offices would admit they had no idea how the funds had ended up with me, but that they appeared authorized and it would be okay to deposit them into my bank, so I did.

---

108 Author's Personal File, University Transcript

I was very tight on funds in those years, barely covering my main expenses, and I needed dental work. So, at first, I accepted the extra payments as amazing luck that would allow me to get a few fillings. I would quickly learn that would only cause me to end up in debt. After a while, when the payments arrived out of nowhere, I would feel a sense of dread instead of financial relief. By then, I had learned it meant I was about to be sent on a job, no matter how exhausted I was, and the additional amount in my account only indicated how much money it would take to fill up the gas tank of my car to get there and back. The larger the check, the longer my hours of driving would be.

The trips were sporadic and unpleasant but mostly uneventful. I was primarily moving protected war criminals around my region of the country, from safehouse to safehouse when they felt unsafe, had problems with their location, or believed that their cover had been blown. There was, however, one that I will never forget. He was up in the Cascade Range, on a tiny side road off a mountain road. I must have driven right by it at least five times before I found the turnoff. By the time I reached there, later than anticipated, he was in full panic mode and had set the back portion of his house on fire to "hide the evidence."

I'd note at this point that I generally received the payments a week in advance, meaning we were likely the ones to intentionally plan and trigger that panic that made him feel like he needed to ask us for help in relocating.

I arrived in time to see flames slowly licking their way down the hallway that connected what appeared to be an otherwise-detached back building with the living room of the front building. I watched him calmly closing the door to that hall, as he stood in his living room with several men he had called to rescue him when I was delayed. As I stood there in that room, wondering how long it would be before we had to run to escape the fire, I watched him stand calmly and assertively, making decisions and giving orders. I got the distinct feeling that this wasn't the first house he had burnt down while standing in it.

He also looked familiar to me. I still wonder if he was the man I had met years ago with the skin lampshade in his East Coast home. There's no way to know for certain. He'd had more than a decade to age by then, but how he held himself definitely reminded me of that man.

Quickly enough, we all exited that building with our orders, piled into our vehicles, and drove away. Did I mention that my kids were in the car during all of this? No one had given me a chance to find them childcare before drugging me and shoving me behind the steering

wheel with badly written directions to that man's safehouse. Did I forget to mention that I gave birth sometime in the middle of all of the chaos of life? Let's take a little detour in the past and dive into a few moments of the years I haven't mentioned, to see how that first happened:

Recollections: Training

Endless decades of selling entire nations,
pulling the rug from under the people of those nations,
pumping generations for resources, impoverishing their children,
and displacing millions with ridiculous stage shows
all so you can get that next drug or adrenaline rush
is a bit much.

So is allowing a bunch of addicts to do so
and to lead the way.

It was the autumn of 1996. I'd had (mostly) free reign to wander the United States, in feeble attempts to escape and to create a normal life, since 1994. When the recruiter needed me, she would usually send the same group of bounty hunters to collect me each time. By 1996, I knew them all by first name, would drop whatever I was doing when they located me, and get into their car. There was no point in fighting the inevitable.

My only wish was that she would just send me the payments directly instead of spending it on them. I would have used the money on a bus ticket to where she needed me, and the rest on dental. I was already struggling with the results of a severely impacted wisdom tooth that had never been pulled, and that required an expensive oral surgeon in a hospital setting to remove.

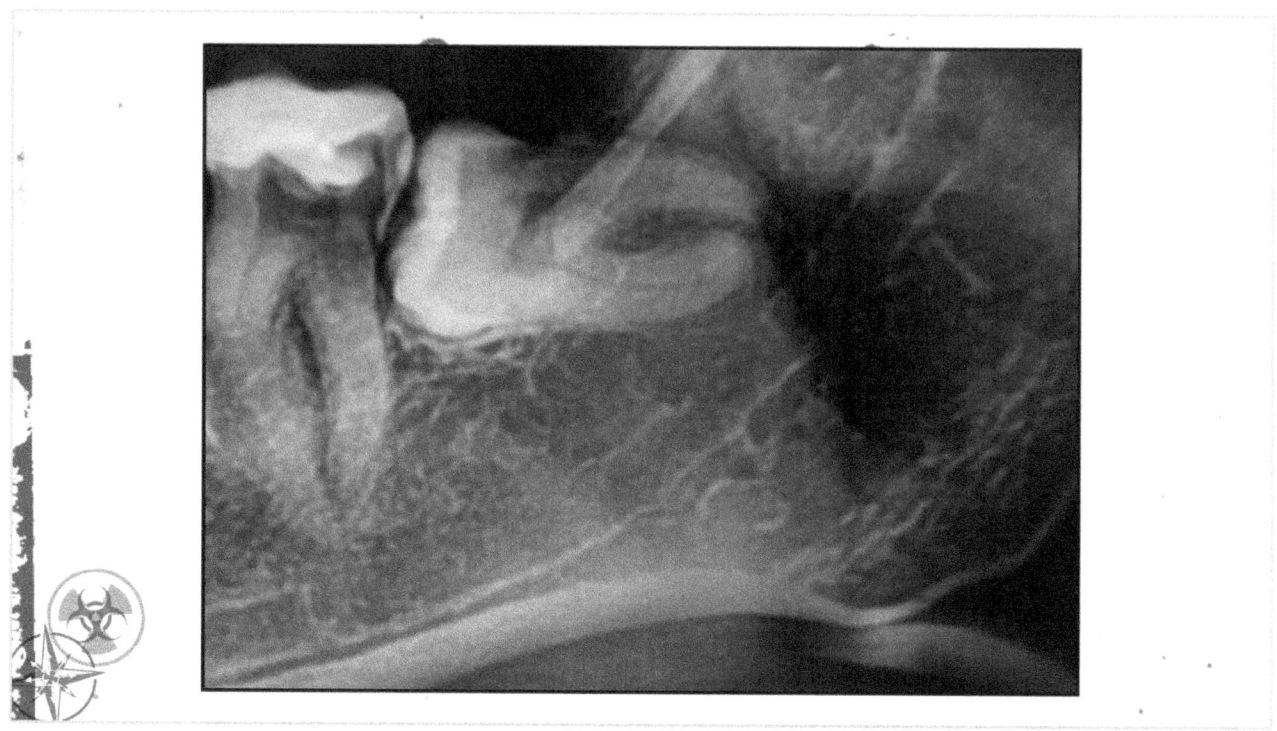

Image: Personal x-ray, 2016, taken shortly before the wisdom tooth (and the neighboring tooth it crushed) was removed by a specialist, at age 39, in Europe

Source: Author's personal documents[109]

Unfortunately, the tooth would have to wait to be removed. The recruiter never trusted the people she used. Not even the ones who had to call her family. I had tried to explain over and over again throughout the years that I would have continued to work for her willingly if she had given me a cut of the pay. She didn't believe me. She thought I would always be loyal and work for her regardless, because that's how I was, and apparently that's how I had behaved.

I'd already had a similar discussion with her and one of her cohort members when they were extorting a commercial real estate owner for 100% of his profits. When I said that they should at least leave him with 5-10% so that he could feed himself and keep his business functioning so that he could continue to pay them well into the future, they both looked at

109 Author's Personal Medical File, Dental X-Ray, Age 39

me like I was a peasant trying to con them. They said he had always found a way to pay and there was no reason to worry about that stopping.

Even more concerning, when it comes to the mechanisms that keep us trapped, when I asked that same mogul why he allowed them to take him for everything, he cited the need to keep paying his own mortgage. He was worried that if he did not comply, they would simply steal his home using lawfare and he truly would have nothing. In that moment, at least he still had a roof over his head. To him, it made sense. But to me? It was just another small problem that could have been stopped in its tracks, preventing the larger problems ahead by removing funding from the psychopaths. But I digress...

In the autumn of 1996, I was at a gathering in Illinois where some of the recruiter's colleagues had dropped me off. I met a man while I was there. He was a few years older than me and had been a gunner during the Gulf War. He personally had around 100 kills, something he was usually very quiet about, but you could tell he was raging internally. We hit it off and started spending all our time together.

A few days later, the bounty hunters showed up. It was clear that they were about to pick me up and bring me somewhere, but then they spotted him. It turns out that we were running in a very small work/social circle at that gathering. They knew him. When he was at his post-war worst, he had taken up fighting in Las Vegas to pay for a drug addiction (cocaine; he'd still go missing about once a month when I knew him, and I would have to hunt him down to whatever hotel he was holed up in while going through several thousand dollars' worth of cocaine and crack over a weekend). The bounty hunters had taken to managing his short-lived fighting career in Vegas and bailing him out when he needed it. It had only gone on for a few fights before he was too wrecked to continue. His ill-advised venture left him in rough shape. Despite being short, it also left him in debt to the bounty-hunting group by the end of the experience.

Instead of getting me into the car, they went to town to make a phone call. When they returned, they sat down with him and told him they would cancel all his debt if he would babysit me. I sat there, silently by the fire, listening as I was traded for a debt of around $20,000. This wasn't the first time I was exchanged for money or favors, but it was the first time I was so fully aware of the fact.

I didn't even blink. I just left with him and pretended like it had never even happened. I spent the next year with him, as a couple, and he took the role of the bounty hunters, transporting me to where I was required.

One of the requirements was a course, Hostage Training for Women, on a military base in the Pacific Northwest. I never had a chance in life, not at freedom, not at normalcy, and not at the safe American white-picket fence middle-class life my mother had been told I would receive. It was never going to happen.

Day one of the training would start with being crammed into a cell that was more of a cage. There was not enough room to stand up. This wasn't hostage negotiation training. It was training for female officers who risked being taken as hostages. Thank god I still had my mother's charm, baby face, and smile back then.

Image: Roxana Teresa Claros Romero, Source: Desaparecidos[110]

110 Desaparecidos, Roxana Teresa Claros Romero Detenida-Desaparecida el 7/4/77, http://www.desaparecidos.org/arg/victimas/c/claros/index.html Alternative: https://robertobaschetti.com/claros-roxana-teresa/

(I'm not sure what I got from my father, but I can see him reflected so clearly in the face of my son that there are times it has brought me to tears.)

Image: Eduardo Enrique Navajas Jáuregui

Source: Universidad National de La Plata[111]

I walked onto that small hallway with the cages on one side with women cowering inside, and a young military officer at a desk on the other side, and I acted as if I had just entered a celebration as the life of the party. In my mind, I had. I recognized so many faces there that I hadn't seen since military camp, since early days visiting a U.S. military base when the bulk of those trafficked in through Operation Condor were still being held on the base. It was like a homecoming to me. I didn't care that there were prison cells. I was born in a prison. It was the people I was so happy to see, who filled the space. It felt like coming home.

---

[111] Universidad National de La Plata, Eduardo Enrique Navajas Jauregui,
http://hosting2.unlp.edu.ar/derechoshumanos/verdatos.php?coddesaparecido=509

Most women spent a week or two in that part of the training before they "got it right" and could proceed downstairs to the next stage. But life and my mother had already trained me to be a good hostage. They graduated me from that floor in less than twenty-four hours.

The entire purpose of the training was to get the enemy to believe you were on their side, sexually into them, or at least as human as they were. There was torture involved. The goal was to get the torturer to stop and let you go. The tools we had to use were the only things they believed a woman had back then - wits and sexuality. The sergeant flat-out told us that he didn't believe we could escape by overpowering anyone. Later, I would argue that the training was useless. Because, honestly, by the time I'm ever in a serious hostage situation beyond the one I was trapped in for life, sexuality is going to have been replaced with gray hair.

But there, hanging from chains in that large ground floor space, I tried the tactics he demanded. For some reason I felt that psychologically separating myself from the situation would allow me to connect with the soldier who had been assigned to stand in front of me (it was a bit of a conveyor belt type of situation, so each hostage spent time with each soldier in the room). I was making myself dizzy trying. The pain only intensified the feeling of separation between mind and body. Finally, when I was at the far end of the room, and closest to the door, I was up against a soldier who appeared emotionally weak. I took advantage of it and he released me. That was graduation, but it honestly felt like cheating. I hadn't found a weakness in a man. I had found the weakest man in the room.

After being freed, I stood against the wall, as near as I could get to the door without raising suspicion. Slowly, as the women were released, one by one, they came to stand and huddle next to me. When eyes were no longer on us, I snuck to the door, leading them, and we ran. We exited that large building and ran across the parking lot and then through brush and trees, eventually following a small road into the housing area of the reservation next to the base. We walked quietly down that road in the darkness until we saw a house with a light on and knocked on the door. An older Native American man answered and we begged him to call the police. He called someone. About two minutes later, men from the base showed up and brought us back to where we had just escaped from.

That's the real reason I felt the training was pointless. Not that little quip I had above about sexuality and aging. We hadn't escaped. How is it successful hostage training if you're not taught an effective way to escape?

I was still a hostage.

I was probably already pregnant by that time. He disappeared shortly after the baby was born. My second child came about quite the same way, several years down the road, just without the hostage training.

♞ Stage 4: Detonation

It's time to fast-forward to where we left off, right after that war criminal started the process of burning his government-funded house down with kids sitting in my car in his driveway. I'm sorry to ruin any illusion of competence in operations.

I continued to drag through life, one excruciating moment at a time, getting up each morning, somehow. I had told myself that the best way out of the situation was to gain so many postgraduate credentials that no country could turn me away when I finally came crawling over their border.

Images: Self, Early 1990s - 2010s
Source: Author's Personal Collection[112]

---

112 Photographs, Author's Personal Collection

A series of events, overt manipulation, and opportunities arose, all pointing me in the direction of England before my master's degree was complete. I knew from a conversation I had listened in on between the recruiter and an eye doctor when I was nine years old, and from conversations the recruiter had with me as well, that the recruiter had intended that I spend some time in England to collect her second passport, something she could not do from within the confines of the United States.

The conversation between her and the ophthalmologist was burned into my brain by anxiety because she had talked about how I wouldn't be able to drive in England due to a lazy eye that she didn't feel like chauffeuring me to multiple appointments to fix with vision therapy. The ophthalmologist was reminding her that we were running out of time to correct my vision problem. The recruiter had been putting it off until the next year, pretty much annually, since I was four years old.

A weak left eye would be dangerous to drive with when pedestrians are on the left side of the road, so they decided I'd be taking the bus while in England. I have spent so much of my life trying to correct that vision on my own with varying degrees of success since the time I was old enough to see myself in the bathroom mirror (it still requires concentration to keep the eye straight, even to this day and after eight years of treatment as an adult because the muscles are not as malleable and retrainable when we're older). It has cost me time, effort, money, and an unnecessary level of awkwardness in social situations as I wonder if that's the moment my concentration on keeping the eye straight will fail, and many a blow to my self-esteem. And mild amblyopia is a condition that is easily treatable in children with a ridiculously high level of success. However, the recruiter wouldn't benefit from it, so she didn't bring me to the appointments.

But back to her needing me in England, which she did believe she would benefit from...

I pretended to go along the path she created for me to go to England, falling for each suggestion and manipulation the recruiter presented, weaving them together as if they had all been stretched out perfectly just for me and with no wrinkles in sight. It was difficult. The person in England who had contacted me out of the blue to begin all this admitted, openly in a moment of intoxication, that he was being compensated to con me into going there. He also gave enough identifying details on who hired him. He was actually in shock about the offer and for some reason, in that moment, I became his confidant. Maybe because I was the only other person in the room who would have an inkling of what he was talking about and he was bursting to tell someone about the entire detailed absurdity of how they had taken advantage of his gambling addiction and failed career, the invasive interview, and the hiring process. I'd never even mentioned the recruiter to him by that time. She was still my dark secret. Back then, he was the one who spilled it all.

I have to admit I took a moment and considered not continuing with him, but it was the path that got me closest to my own goal of finding a way out and then finding a way home. If it hadn't been him, the recruiter eventually would have forced something or someone worse my way. This was the same woman who had paid and coerced a series of prostitutes to marry one of her sons to keep tabs on him and serve as her proxy in manipulating him, as needed. At least the person she had chosen for me this time was easy and far away from America (and not a prostitute).

I'm human. I sought comfort. And I didn't think there was an actual escape route. I'm still not sure there is. There are reprieves, yes. But escape? Even now, as I write this, I can't get them to give me the passport they stole 43 years ago. Just because I keep trying doesn't mean I have hope. I had accepted my situation, and he was the most comfortable forced option in that situation. Much like I had done during the military hostage training years before to escape and thus graduate from their program, I took advantage of the weakest man in the room, the one most likely to mentally break. When he couldn't even contain that he had been recruited, I knew he was the one.

It took some effort to fall for the con, especially with eyes wide open and without that one tiny thread of plausible deniability, of uncertainty, that helps to keep an act alive. My eyes wanted to roll up into my head. My middle fingers wanted to rise. I was already getting very tired of the recruiter still trying to guide my life as I was entering my thirties. But I held back the words that went along with those feelings and allowed the rage alone to drive me forward and past the exhaustion.

Finally, something happened that would give me an excuse to finish propelling forward to England. There was an earthquake and tsunami in Japan. That happened to affect an older designed nuclear power plant that had never gotten a notice about the need for retrofitting their spent fuel pools. Possibly because about twenty years prior, someone I knew had made

sure the Nuclear Regulatory Commission never had to notify the plant and fuel pool designers about the known issue.

Image: Fukushima Daiichi explosion

Source: National Public Radio[113]

After having spent so much time in labs and assisting with infiltrating the anti-nuclear movement, I knew where to look to find real-time radiation readings on the West Coast of the U.S., and I knew the difference between normal readings and concerning ones. As I sat in my house a mile up on a mountain range and in the path of the Northern Hemisphere's Jetstream, I packed my bags and waited. On the television, there was a never-ending stream of reporters telling us the explosion was safe and not actually nuclear-related. They used the wording "hydrogen blast" over and over again and assured their viewers this was not the same or as concerning as a nuclear explosion or meltdown.

[113] National Public Radio, New Blast Rocks Japanese Nuclear Plant, https://www.npr.org/2011/03/14/134501905/crisis-at-nuclear-plant-adds-to-japans-woes

Japan Earthquake: Radiation Leaking After Fukushima Nuclear Plant Explodes

abc NEWS

March 14, 2011— -- Radiation has spread from damaged reactors at the Fukushima Daiichi nuclear plant following an explosion at one unit and a fire at another, Japanese government officials said early Tuesday.

While the previous explosions at Fukushima Daiichi reactors Nos. 1 and 3 were hydrogen blasts caused by a buildup of steam in the reactor units, the new blast at reactor No. 2 has officials unsure of the cause.

In addition, the fuel rods in the reactor were melting, a senior U.S. official said, though the situation was not described as a meltdown.

Half of the fuel rods were exposed, not immersed in water, and the suppression pool, which holds the water used to keep the rods cool, seemed to be damaged, according to Tokyo Electric Co., which runs the plant, and government officials.

Image Source: ABC News

"The previous explosions at Fukushima Daiichi reactors Nos. 1 and 3 were hydrogen blasts caused by a buildup of steam in the reactor units."

Text Source: ABC News[114]

A few days after the original blast, Geiger counters along the top of the mountain range started going off, one after the other. I put everyone's bags in the car and drove down off that mountain. The Nuclear Regulatory Commission - the same one that allowed the spent fuel pool issues to continue unabated in plants with the same design - was still downplaying everything to the public (they still are).

---

[114] ABC News, Japan Earthquake: Radiation Leaking After Fukushima Nuclear Plant Explodes, https://abcnews.go.com/International/japan-earthquake-radiation-leaking-fukushima-nuclear-plant-explodes/story?id=13131123

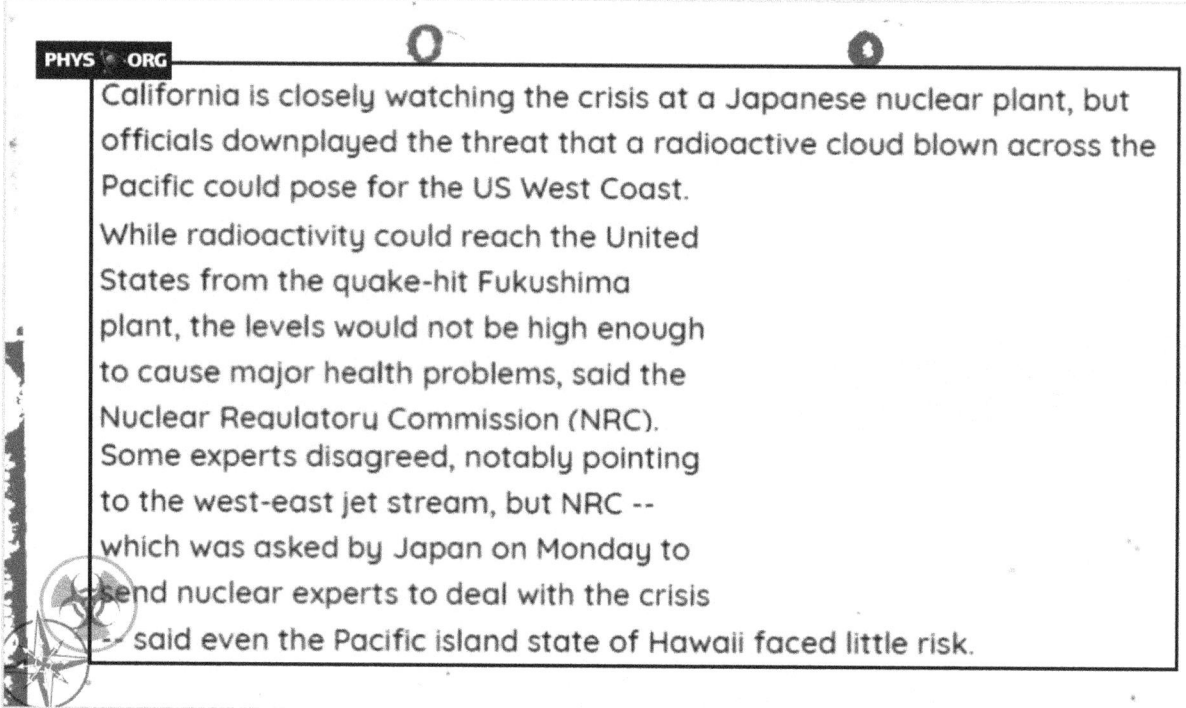

Image Source: <u>Phys.org</u>

"California is closely watching the crisis at a Japanese nuclear plant, but officials downplayed the threat that a radioactive cloud blown across the Pacific could pose for the US West Coast.

While radioactivity could reach the United States from the quake-hit Fukushima plant, the levels would not be high enough to cause major health problems, said the Nuclear Regulatory Commission (NRC).

Some experts disagreed, notably pointing to the west-east jet stream, but NRC...said even the Pacific island state of Hawaii faced little risk."

Text Source: <u>Phys.org</u>[115]

115 Phys.org, U.S. West Coast: On Frontline From Nuclear Cloud, https://phys.org/news/2011-03-west-coast-frontline-nuclear-cloud.html

Image Source: Phys.org

"(Another source) cited the 1986 Chernobyl nuclear disaster to underline how far radioactivity can travel. 'The radioactivity spread around the entire Northern Hemisphere,' from the devastated Ukrainian plant, he said.

Harvey Wasserman, a senior adviser to environmental group Greenpeace added that after Chernobyl 'fallout did hit the jet stream and then the coast of California, thousands of miles away, within 10 days. 'It then carried all the way across the northern tier of the United States,' he continued.

...

The NRC spokesman declined to comment in depth on possible scenarios for how quickly or at what levels radioactivity could reach the US mainland."

Text Source: Phys.org[116]

---

116 Phys.org, U.S. West Coast: On Frontline From Nuclear Cloud, https://phys.org/news/2011-03-west-coast-frontline-nuclear-cloud.html

Why people pay for the service of being lied to in an emergency, rather than being given honest information and guided on how to prepare themselves and avoid any damage, even if it's "only minimal damage" and will "only shorten their lifespans by a couple of years," I will never understand. It goes against the very principles of survival.

With Fukushima to my back, I got on a plane in 2011 and left the West Coast for a let's-wait-for-the-possible-fallout-to-blow-over vacation. When I entered the plane, I discovered it was inordinately full of mathematicians and physicists. Listening to the conversations in those hours felt like sitting in a symposium at the Massachusetts Institute of Technology (MIT). It was a beautiful final note to leave the U.S. on. I love the sound of functioning minds and intelligence.

It would be two months before Western media would finally admit the original explosions at the plant had been part of a major nuclear accident and not just a coincidental peripheral explosion at a nuclear power plant for them to downplay the dangers to the public. By then, it wasn't even front-page news.

WORLD NUCLEAR ASSOCIATION

Fukushima Daiichi Accident

(Updated August 2023)

- Following a major earthquake, a 15-metre tsunami disabled the power supply and cooling of three Fukushima Daiichi reactors, causing a nuclear accident beginning on 11 March 2011. All three cores largely melted in the first three days.
- The accident was rated level 7 on the International Nuclear and Radiological Event Scale, due to high radioactive releases over days 4 to 6, eventually a total of some 940 PBq (I-131 eq).

Image Source: World Nuclear Association

"Following a major earthquake, a 15-metre tsunami disabled the power supply and cooling of three Fukushima Daiichi reactors, causing a nuclear accident beginning on 11 March 2011. All three cores largely melted in the first three days.

The accident was rated level 7 on the International Nuclear and Radiological Event Scale, due to high radioactive releases over days 4 to 6, eventually a total of some 940 PBq (I-131 eq)."

Text Source: <u>World Nuclear Association</u>[117]

It reminded me of the early lecture by physicist Michio Kaku that I had attended with the recruiter. He had said that sustained low-level radiation is the most harmful to us on a cellular level. The sustained runoff from Fukushima looked like it would help us find out if that's true. I have to mention that if you want to punch a population with a biological weapon, it might first help to hit them on the cellular level to make sure they're already weakened enough for a virus to take hold.

Maybe military and Intelligence would be just as invasive and damaging without the lies and well-planned subterfuge. Maybe if the carte blanche right to deceit were taken away, they'd state their real purposes and still fund and participate in wars all over the globe.

But at least it wouldn't lead to the utter confusion domestically and internationally, resources and time wasted on responding to mistruths, dangerous "let's wait and see" pauses, and the countless victims swept under the rug and expected to keep the secrets of their victimizers, even when those victimizers are opportunistic and murderous thugs latched on to the government payload like parasites.

With the United States finally far behind me, one question I'd been biting back the entire time I was there finally surfaced.

---

[117] World Nuclear Association, Fukushima Daiichi Accident, https://world-nuclear.org/information-library/safety-and-security/safety-of-plants/fukushima-daiichi-accident.aspx

Shouldn't the public of a nation factually know, without averting their gaze due to fear of public ostracization and government eyes staring back at them, that several rather pertinent parts of their military, including Intelligence, are the enemy they were told was culturally and cruelly in opposition to them and their freedoms? The same enemy they were convinced to give their own lives in battle to fight? Isn't it just a tiny bit sadistic to keep them that in the dark and self-deceiving to that degree? They are paying taxes for it, after all.

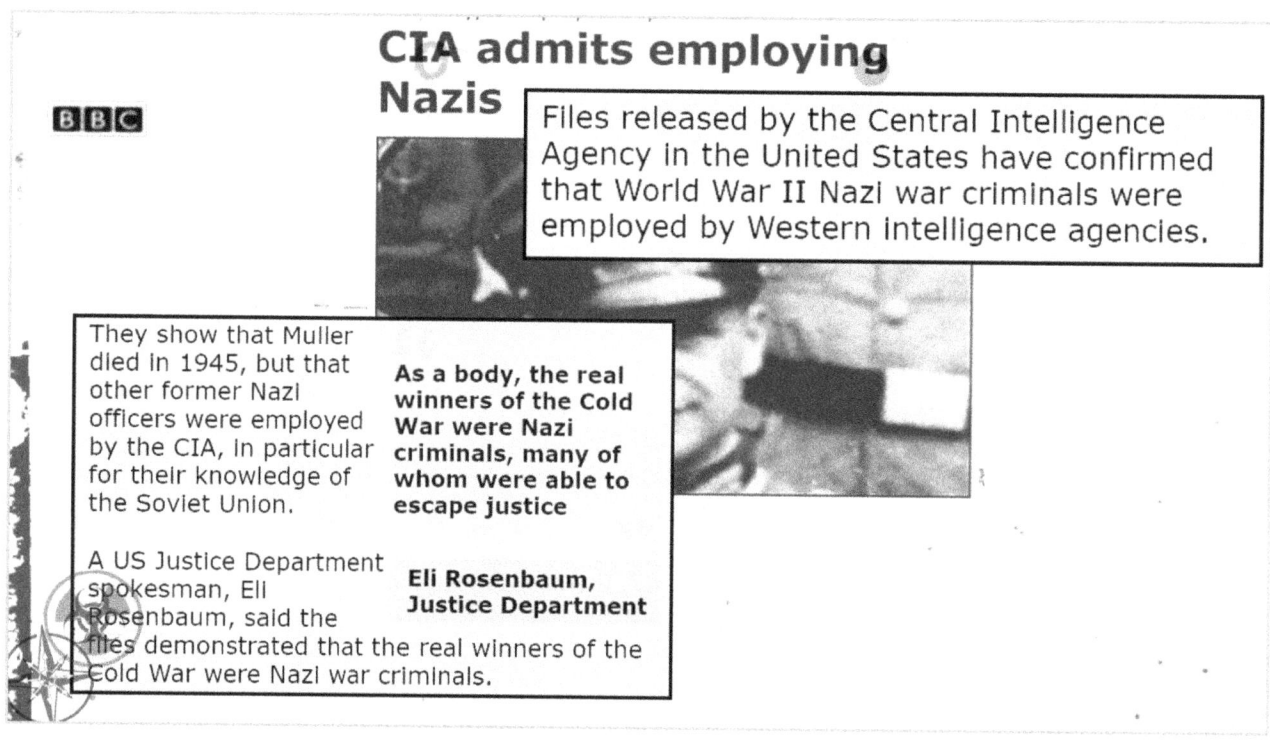

CIA admits employing Nazis

Files released by the Central Intelligence Agency in the United States have confirmed that World War II Nazi war criminals were employed by Western intelligence agencies.

They show that Muller died in 1945, but that other former Nazi officers were employed by the CIA, in particular for their knowledge of the Soviet Union.

A US Justice Department spokesman, Eli Rosenbaum, said the files demonstrated that the real winners of the Cold War were Nazi war criminals.

As a body, the real winners of the Cold War were Nazi criminals, many of whom were able to escape justice

Eli Rosenbaum, Justice Department

Image Source: <u>British Broadcasting Corporation</u>

"Files released by the Central Intelligence Agency in the United States have confirmed that World War II Nazi war criminals were employed by Western intelligence agencies.

...former Nazi officers were employed by the CIA, in particular for their knowledge of the Soviet Union.

A US Justice Department spokesman, Eli Rosenbaum, said the files demonstrated that the real winners of the Cold War were Nazi war criminals."

Text Source: <u>British Broadcasting Corporation</u>[118]

A few months into my stay in England (still a part of the European Union back then), I began the process of procuring citizenship from the European country I qualified to apply for based on ancestry, according to the documents I had been using most of my life by that point. I did it so I could stay in England a bit longer. Once I had landed and the jet lag wore off, every fiber of my being was screaming against even the thought of the idea of returning to America. I didn't like England, honestly, but I had just escaped the U.S. and there was no way I was ever going to return to there unless in chains. I would have rather survived eating the British cuisine of beans for breakfast. That's still true to this day, even though after eating their food for long enough, I genuinely thought I was developing stomach cancer....but I digress.

The recruiter thought I was working on applying for her citizenship. She wanted me to procure her exit from America. If I had been applying in any of a variety of offices around the world, the standard requirement would have been that my citizenship had to be piggybacked on hers because we are family on paper - that was why she had always wanted to send me to England. She thought being there would be my motivation to get a second passport for myself, and thus hers as well. Her own documentation was too flimsy to start the process from within the United States where the embassy's documentation requirements were far more excessive. She had to send me overseas to the country with the laxest embassy so I could do it for her. That embassy, selected by her, happened to be in London.

While going through the stack of family records I had to attain for the application, I started noticing some discrepancies. She married her husband near Washington, D.C. when she was 18 and he was a 21-year-old Yale student, even though none of her stories mentioned a D.C.-adjacent location in that time period. Her mother's official certified birth certificate looked like the woman had been allowed drunken after-hours access to the records department to modify it, etc.

---

[118] British Broadcasting Corporation, CIA Admits Employing Nazis, http://news.bbc.co.uk/2/hi/americas/1301306.stm

Fun fact: Her mother decided to change her own birth date. The first records show that she was born on April 19th. The next records show that she had that date amended to April 20th, Hitler's birthday, with the help of the church via an updated baptismal record. According to the dates on the documents, it looks like she made the change after the start of World War II:

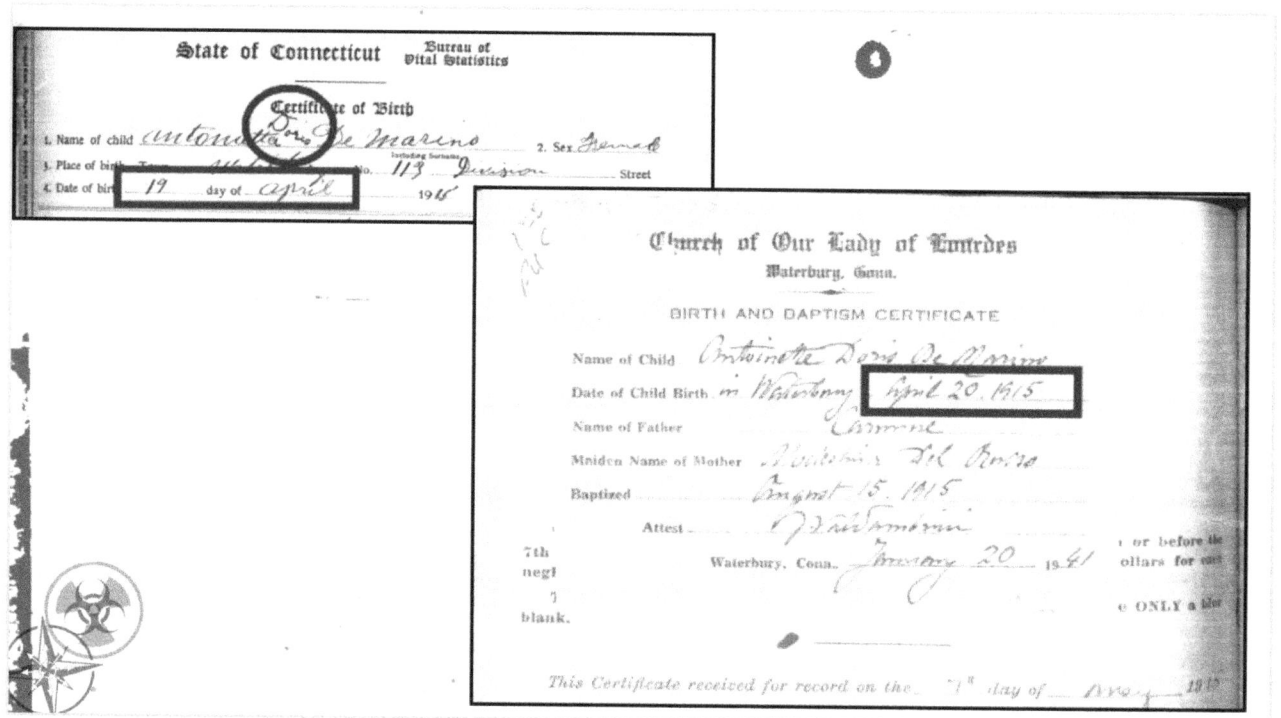

Image: Birth and Baptismal Records

Source: State of Connecticut[119]

The recruiter's mother-on-record had a little too much access to that records department and had taken advantage of it for her own personal reasons while there, leaving a trail leading right back to her in the process. Because of her proximity to one of the weapons labs via her husband, she had been part of helping to bring the families of German and Jewish scientists into the country to reunite them when the government refused to do so officially. Because of that, she had made friends in the records department and played cards with

119 Author's Personal Collection, State of Connecticut Birth Records

them weekly. One of them was the same friend she asked for one last favor when I came onto the scene.

And, no, neither the records office clerk nor the recruiter's mother did it for free. The stack of cash the clerk had accepted for my forged document was substantial. As for the recruiter's mother, she already had two homes and two closets full of floor-length mink coats by the time I arrived, despite her being a retired shop-girl who had helped people with their perfume samples (although, knowing the family one does have to wonder if she was drugging people with the perfume and then robbing them). That mink collection was so extensive and well cared for that it spent a large portion of the year in a secure cold storage facility. When I came to the U.S., she was given a limited edition vehicle with full white leather interior for her role in procuring documents at that time. Not to digress, but I was expensive. That's probably part of why I was used so hard. Someone had to get a return on that investment.

Considering that dripping-in-diamonds human trafficker (albeit, mostly of willing international migrants) was who the recruiter called "mom," I can actually kind of understand why, later in life when I asked the recruiter to babysit my child, her "grandchild," for a few hours in the evenings while I visited a university dental clinic (all I could afford back then for dental care - they came with a significant discount if you let the students practice doing fillings on your teeth), she told me she would only do it if I paid her $20 an hour (which I did) and then still proceeded to complain the entire time that I wasn't properly compensating her enough.

But, back to England (or forward to England, in this case)...

Because of the discrepancies and the fact that the recruiter's mother's official birth certificate in the records department had the recruiter's mother's own handwriting on it where she wrote her preferred first name in sideways (pictured above), I started looking at my own documents again. I decided it was time to check in with the Department of Child Services. After all, when the recruiter was telling my origin story, she told me that the mother I remembered prior to her was actually a State of Connecticut foster mother. So, I called them to request my foster child file. I made sure to give them both names I had gone by in the U.S. (if you recall, the recruiter used a name change document to bureaucratically

legitimize my birth certificate which had no matching hospital birth record to substantiate it).

They were happy to oblige, although they took a while (it may be true that social workers are overworked and overwhelmed). Eventually, they sent my abuse records, which you've seen parts of earlier. They also informed me that I had never been in foster care. They had no proof of my existence before the mention of me first came across their desk when I was nine years old and a school reported that my seat in the classroom had been empty for a while.

I thanked them, read through the abuse documents, and picked up the phone again. This time, I was calling the Social Security Administration offices in the United States. I asked them when I was first registered in their system. Again, I made sure to give them both names I had gone by in the U.S. and explained the name change. They informed me that I did not enter their system under either name until midway through 1980. Three years after I was born and at a point at which I had already entered the United States after leaving Argentina.

This was problematic for the recruiter's story she had constructed about my earliest years. She had claimed I had nearly a million dollars in medical bills from my time in the U.S. hospital directly following my birth (a time and a birth that the hospital had no record of at all, despite their keeping extensive records from that time period). She also claimed the U.S. government medical insurance for impoverished children paid the bill. In the years 1977-1978, in order for that program to cover the costs of a medical bill, they required that the child have a social security number. According to the Social Security Administration, I didn't even exist in those years. I definitely didn't have a number back then.

I said thank you to the Social Security worker for that information, and I hung up the phone. I went across the street. I bought a bottle of wine (I rarely drink and almost never more than a glass). I came back to the rented apartment I was staying in. I sat down on the living room floor. I drank that entire bottle. And I thanked every god of every religion that there was a genuine chance that the recruiter was not my mother.

More importantly, I was grateful that my first mother, the mother I remembered, the mother I had a connection to, the mother I always loved and missed every single day of my life and always will, may have actually been my mother - and not just a foster mother like the recruiter had told me.

A few days later, I picked up the phone again. I called the recruiter, informing her with all sincerity that I could not complete the citizenship application in the remaining time I had on my visa. I told her I was having some trouble with the paperwork (I failed to note that I had also found out that there was a small and previously undisclosed issue with the London-located consulate's bureaucracy and that I could only apply for my foreign citizenship and passport - and not hers).

What would happen next was almost as easy as that time the two Muslim roommates "talked us into" walking right into their apartment. Except, this time, it wasn't two Muslims about to get entrapped. I was playing against my most formidable enemy, my own personal (and unluckily for me) government-trained exploiter.

I told the woman who had darkened my entire existence that I did not qualify for a traditionally extended visa and would need political asylum in order to stay long enough to complete the task for her. She promised to call a friend of hers in the State Department back in the United States, someone she had once attended Yale University with. She was sure that they could contact someone in the correct office in England to make it happen. That phone call happened in 2011.

On a morning months later, I discussed my case in front of an immigration tribunal in England without legal representation present and on only a few hours of sleep. This was several hours after successfully arguing my master's thesis with a panel of professors over the phone at three in the morning.

As the representative for the Immigration Department spoke about how "Americans don't have human rights" before listing all the countries and regions with citizens worthy of human rights, a thought flickered through my mind for half a second before I focused on the courtroom again. If Americans do not have human rights according to globally accepted

norms and laws, is that why the world has been heavily using the residents of that country as pharmaceutical and weapons research test subjects?

Six months later, I had been granted an impossibility – an approved human rights application for a United States passport holder. Buried deep in the document, it was deemed that if I returned to the United States, they might not let me leave again, if they even allowed me to apply to reenter the US, to begin with.

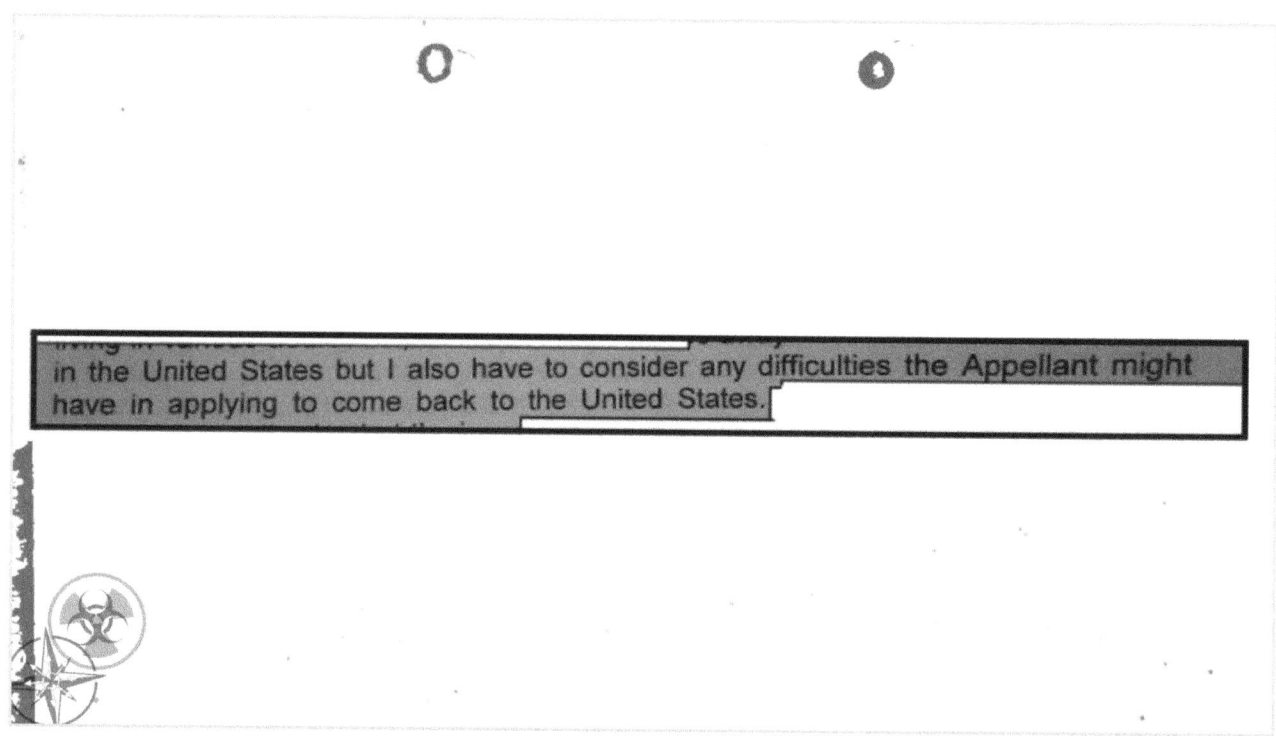

in the United States but I also have to consider any difficulties the Appellant might have in applying to come back to the United States.

Image Source: Personal Documents, Courts & Tribunals Service

"But I also have to consider any difficulties the Appellant might have in applying to come back to the United States."

Text Source: Personal Documents, Courts & Tribunals Service[120]

---

[120] Courts & Tribunal Service, First-tier Tribunal's Determination, Author's Personal Records

Sometimes, I wonder if my exploiter's friend had taken pity on me, knowing what I must have endured all those years under the tactics of the woman that we were all more than just aware of in the political and intel communities, and that she kindly made sure those words were included in the decree. Even if she hadn't, the document was still enough.

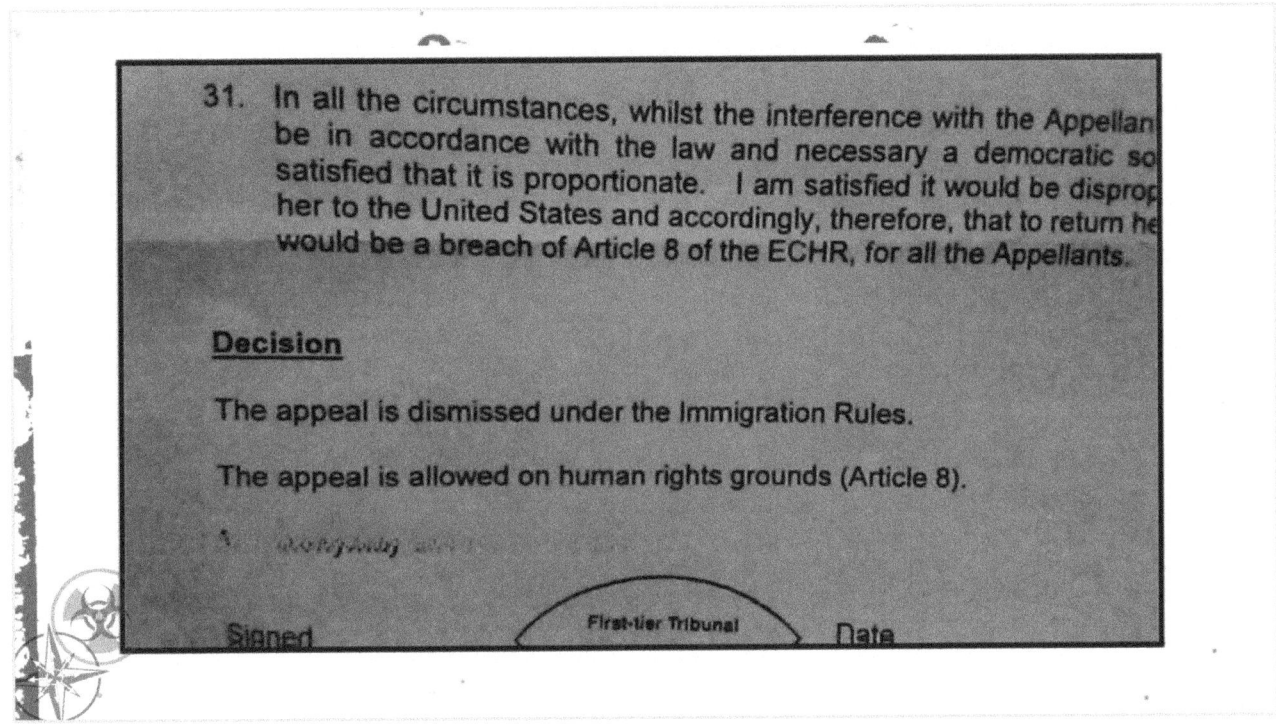

31. In all the circumstances, whilst the interference with the Appellan be in accordance with the law and necessary a democratic so satisfied that it is proportionate. I am satisfied it would be dispro her to the United States and accordingly, therefore, that to return he would be a breach of Article 8 of the ECHR, for all the Appellants.

Decision

The appeal is dismissed under the Immigration Rules.

The appeal is allowed on human rights grounds (Article 8).

Signed   First-tier Tribunal   Date

Image Source: Personal Documents, Courts & Tribunals Service

"I am satisfied it would be disproportionate to return her to the United States and accordingly, therefore, that to return her with her children would be a breach of Article 8 of the ECHR, for all Appellants...

The appeal is allowed on human rights grounds."

Text Source: Personal Documents, Courts & Tribunals Service[121]

That 'friend in high places' gave me my first genuine opportunity to experience freedom. After a life of imprisonment and being a hostage, I just needed to learn how to be free.

---

[121] Courts & Tribunal Service, First-tier Tribunal's Determination, Author's Personal Records

Wartime Child Traffickers
The Government of Argentina and the Abuelas de Plaza de Mayo

In reality, governments do not change
simply because a spotlight is on them.
They know what to do in the spotlight
to allow themselves to continue, unabated.
They've perfected it down to the point
that it can be found in the wording
of any of their standard forms.

It took me several years to stop cowering in fear out of habit. I spent those years in England, still being sent off on late-night excursions to questionable labs and medical facilities. It felt so much like living back "home" with my abductor again that I thought the feeling must all be in my head, like a lingering sense that I couldn't quite shake off. It wasn't until I took a drug test to confirm my suspicions, and it detected Rohypnol and ketamine, that it truly occurred to me that what I was experiencing wasn't simply exhaustion and a lingering memory. What I was feeling was a combination of my situation and the familiar experience of significant and consistent drugging.

During those years, dragging through and trying to put my thoughts together rationally despite the drugs clouding my mind, I finally looked back at the life I had lived and what I had been involved in. It appeared like a nuclear explosion on the landscape, only growing larger the further away I ran. When I had been in the center of it, it felt personal and tangible. But at a distance, I began to understand what a giant it truly was. I couldn't find adequate words to describe my relationship with it.

I completed my research on where I had been kidnapped from originally and found the name and location of the Argentine prison that had been my earliest home. I reached out to

the "Abuelas de Plaza de Mayo" organization in charge of helping us lost children to return home under the "right to seek identity," as they called it.

Unfortunately, it was then that I realized that while I had escaped one mess, there was another one there to greet me upon my exit.

They weren't ready to accept me back into their fold. They asked for my papers. I didn't have the original ones from Argentina, so I gave them the falsified ones from the United States, assuming two things that were incorrect:

1. They actually wanted to find the children who were sent internationally.
2. They knew how to start the process and would look into the identity papers of someone illegally adopted from their country to confirm if the identity was a forgery or not.

That Argentine office never called the issuing North American Vital Statistics Office to confirm if the forged birth certificate was valid or not. And as mentioned, it's not valid, something that has caused me multiple issues throughout life and left me with sporadically accessible ID. It has the very real discrepancy of being filed several years after my birth and not until after I was trafficked out of Argentina. That North American vital statistics office, in the time period in which I was born and trafficked, always recorded births within weeks, not years. Because my "U.S. birth record" was filed three years after I was born, and thus was placed in the order and year in which it was received, and thus in the 1980 birth records book despite having a 1977 birth date on it, it has triggered their fraud alert multiple times over the decades. In addition, the hospital listed on it has never had any record of my birth. Any of this could have been confirmed with a call.

I was in communication with that United States Vital Statistics Office at that time (after a lifetime of them not being able to locate the document reliably, I tend to make contact before, during, and after any official inquiries into it, primarily to point them to the 1980 records book to make sure they can locate the document) and confirmed that Argentina never contacted them to verify or inquire about the identity. Instead, the Argentine office told me, within an hour of my submitting the ID, that it was a beautiful ID and I should be happy for it. Then they quit responding to me. That was 2012.

Things were fairly quiet for a few years on the American front until a series of events caught my eye even from an ocean away. The recruiter's younger son, who was in Asia at the time, broke up with his then-wife. The wife took one of their children (to protect the child's privacy because he's still fairly young, I'll call him Sam) and returned to Russia, where she was from. The recruiter was not happy about this. She was in child-collecting mode and wanted the boy.

The recruiter already had one of her grandsons in her custody by that point (I'll call him Tim). The recruiter had used her son in court to remove custody from Tim's mother (one of her son's previous wives - an impoverished American mother who couldn't win in court against that much money) and then the recruiter took Tim for herself. He did not stay with his father even though that father had been granted custody. Are you following so far?

Shortly after the Russian mother brought Sam, the first grandchild I mentioned (there are many, but I'm only discussing these two), to Russia, she came down with a sudden case of stage 4 cancer and died extremely quickly. Her son, Sam, ended up in America with the recruiter. He did not stay with his father. Now, the recruiter had two boys in her custody again, just like she had before me.

Within a fairly short amount of time, Sam came down with lymphoma (cancer). Normally, this wouldn't be concerning (other than general concern for his health). However, the recruiter had a history of people developing cancer around her if they fell into one of three categories:

1. People she was exploiting for cash and/or research.
2. People she did not like.
3. Family members, including those not biologically related to her.

The same recruiter who used to tell me stories about how she would inject mice with cancer cells in the lab.

Not that the story about the mice was really enough to concern me, or even the fact that the recruiter appeared to be the source of a cancer cluster in her own right. I'd heard and dealt with a lot in my life regarding her; I couldn't spend my time panicked by all of it. But there was the issue of the recruiter's ex-husband's demise still fresh in my mind. He had gone to dinner with her one evening (a very rare event), and before the next morning, he was in the hospital with sudden acute leukemia. One of the two primary causes of the condition is radiation poisoning, and the recruiter had access to radioactive materials from her work. He never recovered and he ended up dying within a few short months.

So, when I saw that Sam now had cancer, and I noted all the fundraisers for him popping up on the internet, and the recruiter looked like she would be raking in somewhere around $11,000 in funds just from what was published (an online fundraiser plus an at-school fundraiser and possibly a third one by a school club), I became reasonably concerned that she was making Sam into a cancer cash cow. It reminded me of how she had used me in paid cancer research when I was a child in order to collect the stipend money they offered to parents. It looked like she was still up to her old methods of gaining an income at the expense of a child in her home.

Image Source: GoFundMe

"…5 month chemotherapy treatment regime. …The main goal right now is to raise enough money to get … and his grandmother a vehicle to travel to all of his appointments. … truly appreciates everyone helping him out and supporting him on his road to defeat cancer.

Text Source: GoFundMe[122]

I contacted the authorities in the United States because a child was involved and I was an adult now. I felt obligated to. For once, they actually did something. They removed Sam from the recruiter's custody. So, the recruiter brought her son in from Asia. She got him a plane ticket, paid for his attorney, and brought him to the court to go up against Child Protective Services. The judge ruled in his favor and handed Sam into his custody because he was the father. Then, he left the country and left Sam with the recruiter. I don't know what happened after that. I cannot fix broken people and a broken system on my own. I've tried. I probably should have tried harder, but honestly, I'm so accustomed to defeat. I mean, look at my life. It's all been defeat when it comes to these things. I felt

---

122 GoFundMe, Hidden for Privacy

that it was a miracle that I had even managed to get the child a short break away from the recruiter.

I went back to focusing on life around me and I stopped looking at anything going on in America. It was too painful to watch.

This was the image that made me turn away in sadness. Remember when the recruiter tried to get me to sleep with an exposed radium dial under my pillow when I was so small? When she told me brain cancer was a wonderful thing to develop and that I might get lucky if I slept with the radium under my pillow for long enough? When I looked at this picture, with the plastic table dragged in from outside to create the illusion of poverty, it wasn't the plastic I saw. It was the depression-era antique uranium plates that she had carefully collected over the years and never served anyone on until she had those boys in her custody. The same antique uranium plates the Environmental Protection Agency says not to eat from due to potential radiation toxicity.

Image Source: Additional GoFundMe[123]

---

[123] GoFundMe, Hidden for Privacy

The same plates that reliably set off every single one of her Geiger counters.

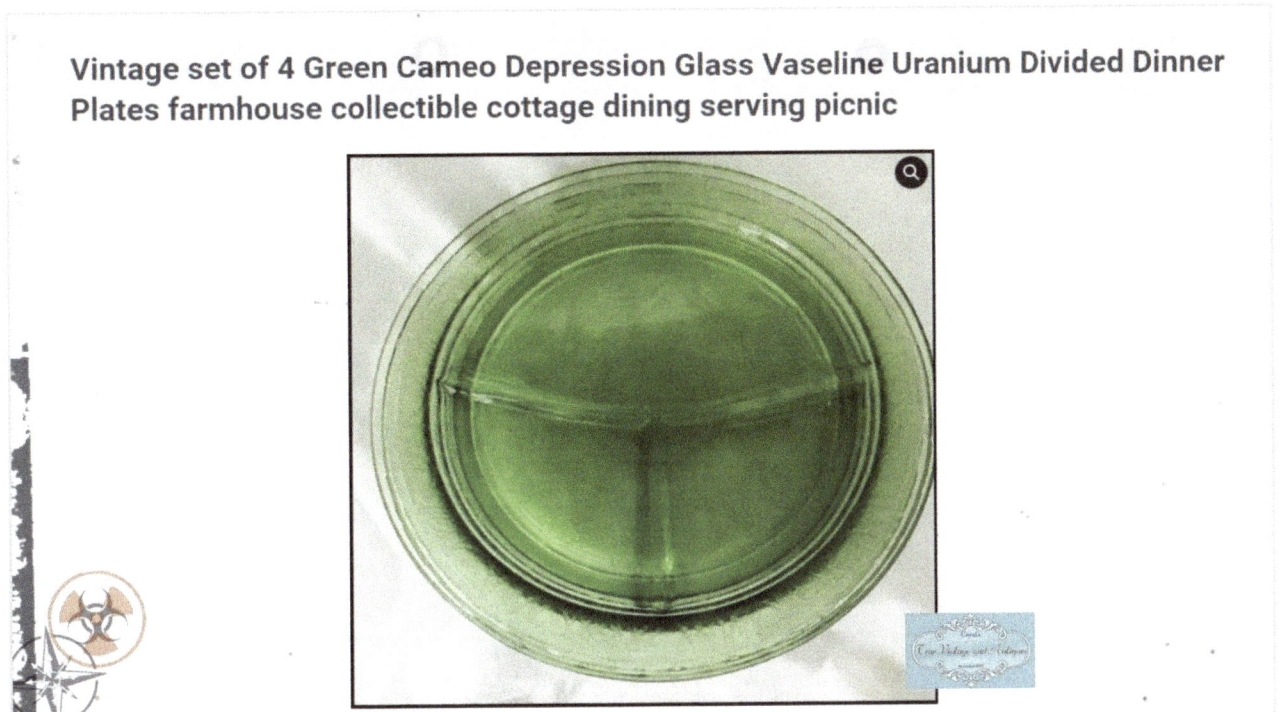

Image: Uranium Depression Glass Plates

Source: The Vintage and Antiques[124]

She was still playing her favorite at-home game that always made her smile when I was little - child radiation Russian roulette.

124 The Vintage and Antiques, Vintage Set of 4 Green Cameo Depression Glass Vaseline Uranium Divided Dinner Plates Farmhouse Collectible Cottage Dining Serving Picnic, https://www.truevintageantiques.com/product/vintage-set-of-4-green-cameo-depression-glass-vaseline-uranium-divided-dinner-plates-farmhouse-collectible-cottage-dining-serving-picnic/

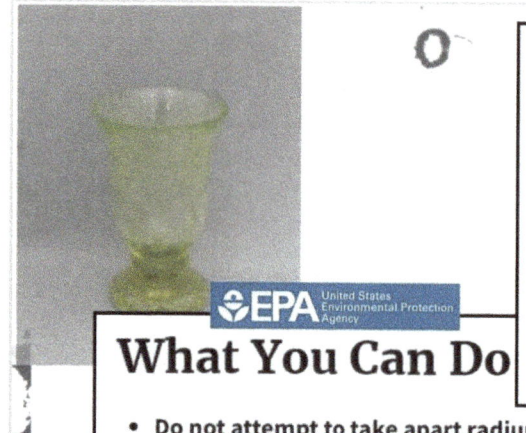

For hundreds of years, glassmakers used small amounts of uranium to create yellow or green glass. The yellow tint of this glass led to the nicknames "Vaseline glass" and "canary glass." Under an ultraviolet (UV) or "black" light, the uranium causes the glass to glow bright green.

After 1970, United States glassmakers and ceramic producers stopped using radionuclides for color. They are still used in a few other countries. Sometimes ceramics and glass with radioactive coloring agents still enter the United States from these countries.

⬧EPA United States
Environmental Protection
Agency

What You Can Do

- **Do not attempt to take apart radium watches or instrument dials.** Radioactive antiques are usually not a health risk as long as they are intact and in good condition.
- **Do not use ceramics like antique orange-red Fiestaware or Vaseline glass to hold food or drink.** They can chip, and you can ingest particles of uranium with your food or drink.
- **Dispose of any broken radioactive antiques.** For instructions on proper disposal, contact your state or local radiation control program.

Image Source: Environmental Protection Agency

"Glassmakers used small amounts of uranium to create yellow and green glass (Vaseline glass)...

...Do not use ceramics like... Vaseline glass to hold food or drink. They can chip, and you can ingest particles of uranium with your food or drink.

...Do not take apart radium watches or instrument dials. Radioactive antiques are usually not a health risk as long as they are intact and in good condition."

Text Source: Environmental Protection Agency[125]

I also recognized the drink in her hand. She doesn't drink milk, but she does chelate when exposed to possible radiation contamination in food. I know. I learned it from her when I was growing up. And I remembered because, with being forced to eat the food she served, I felt it was better for my survival if I knew as well.

---

[125] Environmental Protection Agency, Radioactivity in Antiques, https://www.epa.gov/radtown/radioactivity-antiques

Image Source: Current Medical Chemistry via <u>National Library of Medicine</u>

"The removal of plutonium by chelating agents is of great importance... Similarly, uranium is a radionuclide, which causes severe renal dysfunction within a short time period due to chemical toxicity. It may also induce cancers such as leukemia and osteosarcoma in cases of long-term internal radiation exposure. Investigations on chelating agents... were initiated in the 1960's and 1970's."

Text Source: Current Medical Chemistry via <u>National Library of Medicine</u>[126]

Every few years I would attempt to contact the Argentine NGO again, contact other related offices, contact external trafficking NGOs, and contact offices within Argentina's government. In two separate cases, workers from within Argentina's government told me that I had the right to seek my identity without having to show the documents from that identity first. One told me to sue the Abuelas organization (the gatekeepers for the DNA testing) in court for that right (an attempt a human rights attorney in the Netherlands told me would cost more than the purchase of a new house after she

---

[126] Current Medical Chemistry via National Library of Medicine, Chelating Agents Used for Plutonium and Uranium Removal in Radiation Emergency Medicine, https://pubmed.ncbi.nlm.nih.gov/16305471/

offered to write a "strongly worded letter" for approximately $4000 U.S. dollars to start the process).

The most helpful Argentine government worker advocated for me directly with the Abuelas. They chose to ignore him. Most of that happened, primarily, between 2015 and 2020. I went through one final round in 2023 and copied in around twenty offices. The silence of their response had depth.

Unfortunately, as it turns out, they have a very standard policy of rejecting our requests to seek our identities. I've spoken to other victims of theirs, all international cases. They've used various tactics, including saying, "We're working on it," for nearly a decade now in the case of a child they abandoned in an orphanage in another part of South America.

The deceptive con they use most often is that they "cannot" open a case to search for an internationally trafficked child's legal identity and documentation unless that child somehow managed to keep a government ID and documentation from the country they were trafficked from.

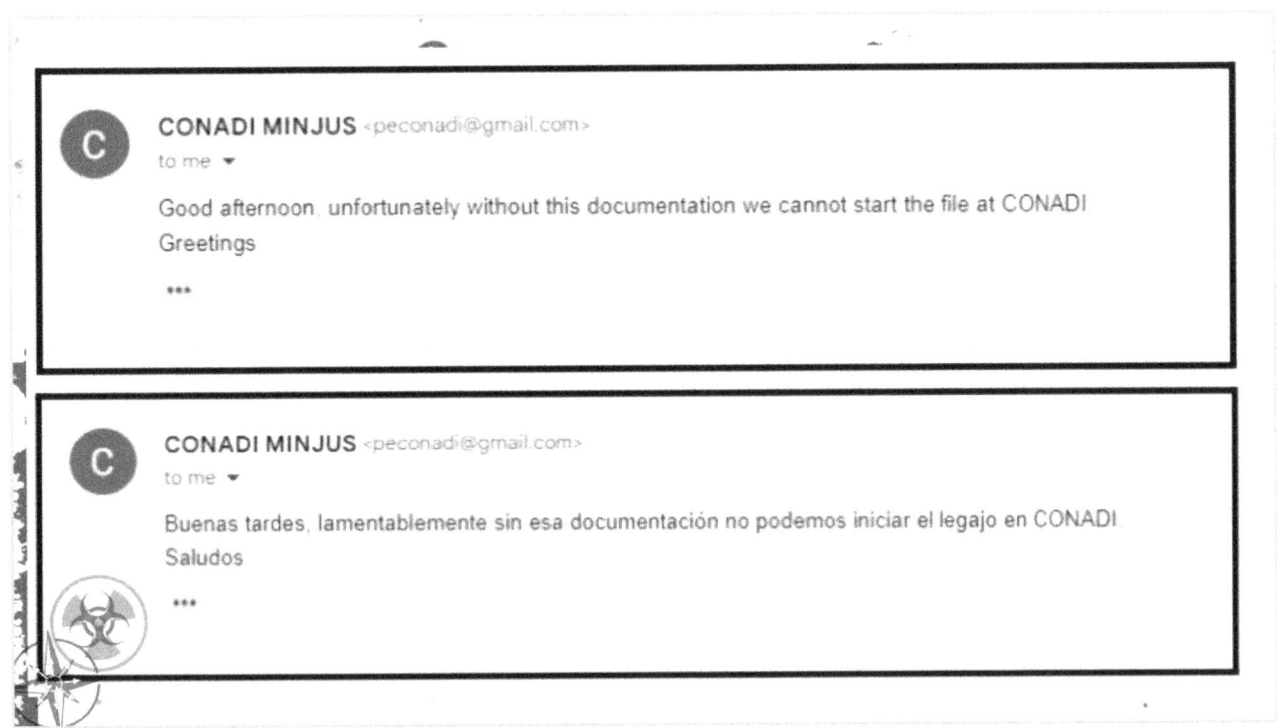

Images Source: Author's Personal Emails (First Image: Automatically Translated to English, Second Image: Original Email)

"Unfortunately without the documentation we cannot start the file at CONADI."

Text Source: Author's Personal Emails[127]

They deny the right to begin a case to search. I've tried multiple times through their various agencies and always get the same standard form rejection, stating that they cannot proceed to help me locate my original government documents from Argentina unless I can provide them with my original government documents from Argentina first. This standard response happens regardless of how much or little I explain or beg, or how many different ways I explain it.

---

[127] Author's Personal Emails, Correspondence with Argentina's identificar@renaper.gob.ar

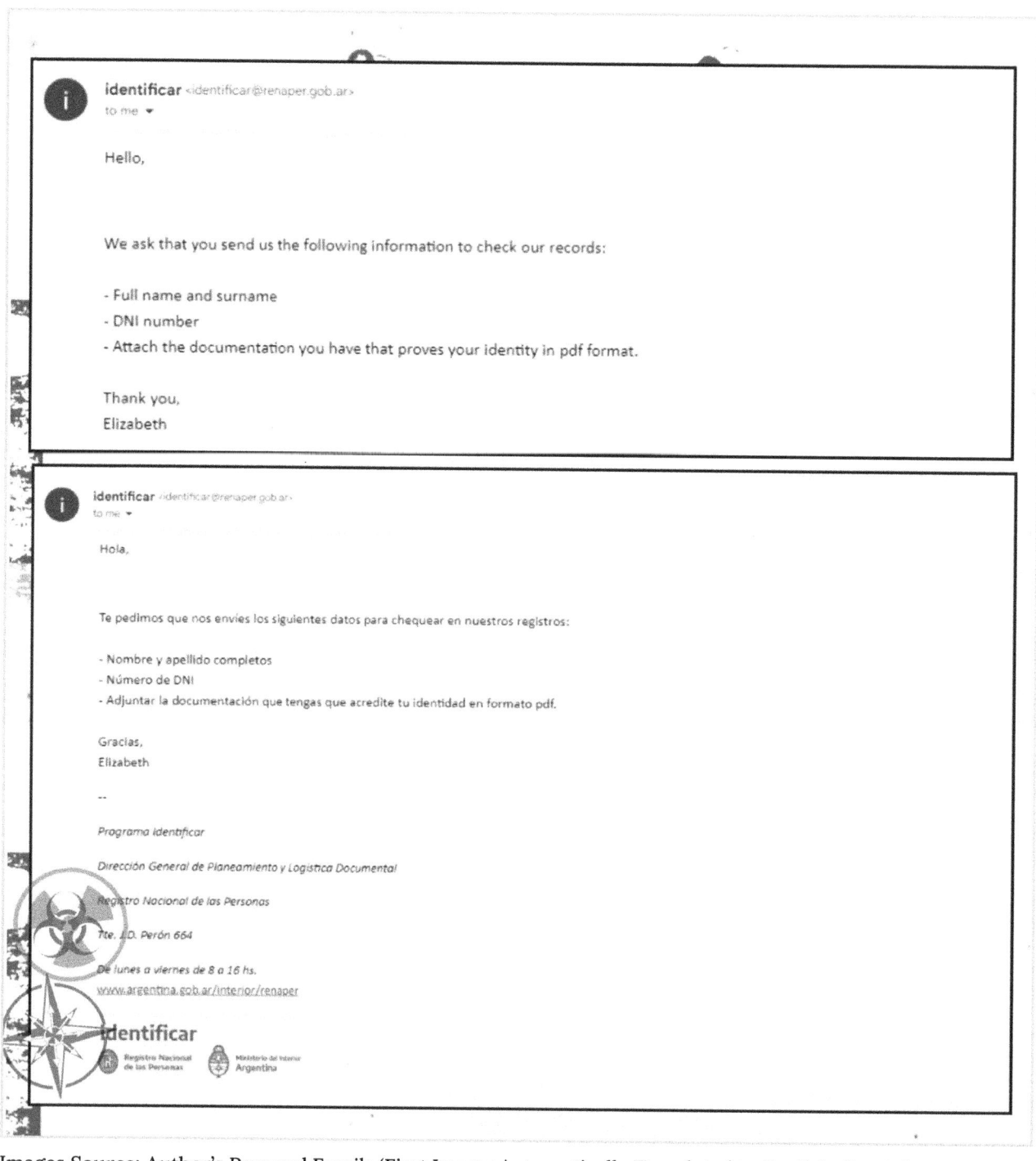

identificar <identificar@renaper.gob.ar>
to me

Hello,

We ask that you send us the following information to check our records:

- Full name and surname
- DNI number
- Attach the documentation you have that proves your identity in pdf format.

Thank you,
Elizabeth

---

identificar <identificar@renaper.gob.ar>
to me

Hola,

Te pedimos que nos envíes los siguientes datos para chequear en nuestros registros:

- Nombre y apellido completos
- Número de DNI
- Adjuntar la documentación que tengas que acredite tu identidad en formato pdf.

Gracias,
Elizabeth

--

Programa Identificar

Dirección General de Planeamiento y Logística Documental

Registro Nacional de las Personas

Tte. J.D. Perón 664

De lunes a viernes de 8 a 16 hs.
www.argentina.gob.ar/interior/renaper

identificar
Registro Nacional de las Personas · Ministerio del Interior Argentina

Images Source: Author's Personal Emails (First Image: Automatically Translated to English, Second Image: Original Email)

"We ask you again to send us the following information:

-   Attach the documentation that proves your identity"

Text Source: Author's Personal Emails[128]

The government agencies and the NGO use the same form with the same requirements and the same standard form rejection. It's not left versus right or NGO versus government. They work together, feed off each other, support each other financially, and keep that entire country bound by their eternal political back-and-forth theatrics while they bury the children beneath their feet. They do it together, as a team.

---

[128] Author's Personal Emails, Correspondence with Argentina's CONADI

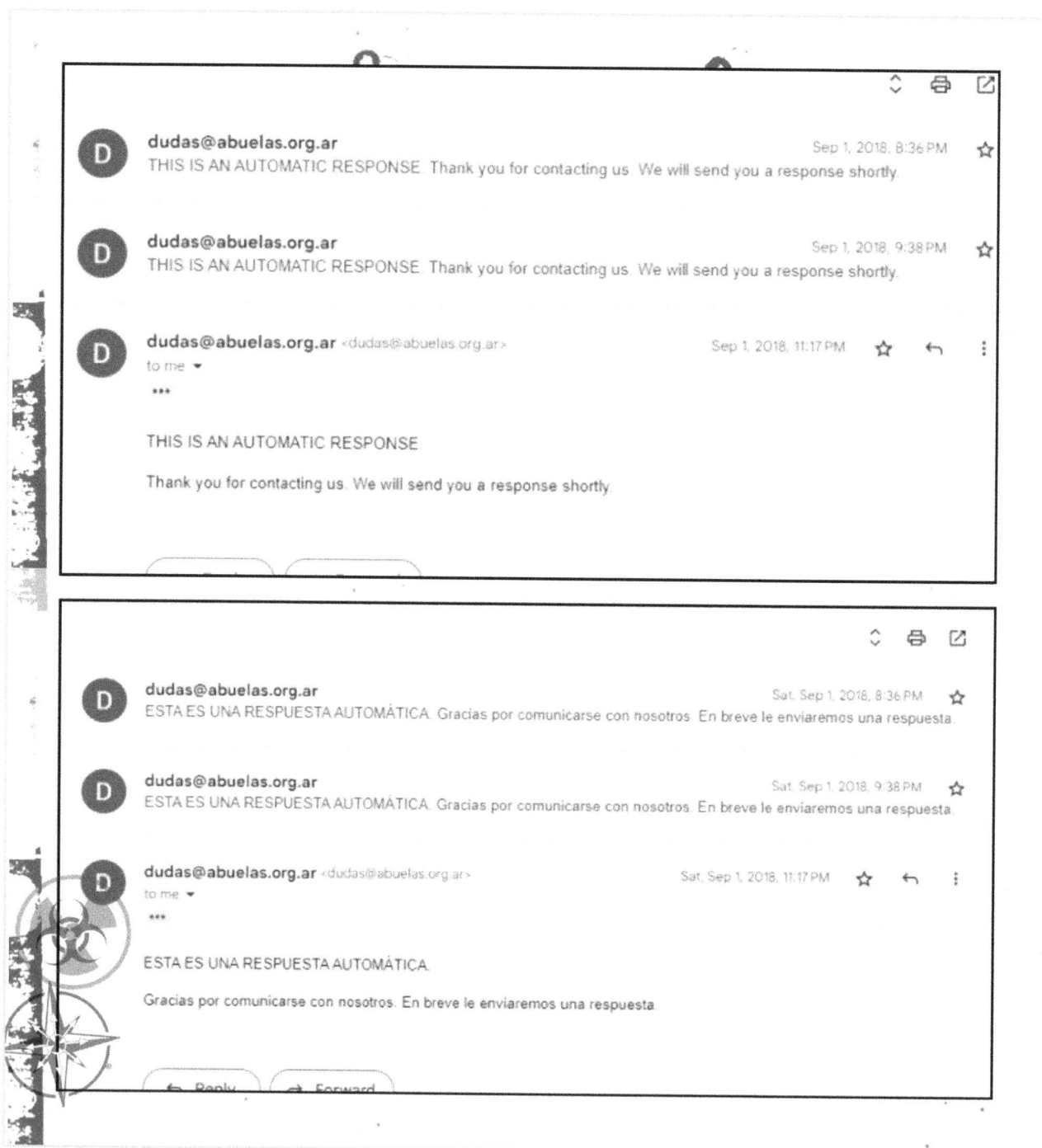

Images source: Author's Personal Emails (First Image: Automatically Translated to English, Second Image: Original Email)

"Automated response" only.

Text Source: Author's Personal Emails[129]

To reiterate (probably because I've lived through this dismal interaction with them so many times that I feel like it needs to be repeated at least half as many times as I've dealt with them):

Their denial is always based on our lack of having the documents of the identity we seek. They only help us seek our legal identity and its documents if we already have that identity and its documents. That's not ethical, legal, sane, or human.

---

[129] Author's Personal Emails, Correspondence with Argentina's dudas@abuelas.org.ar

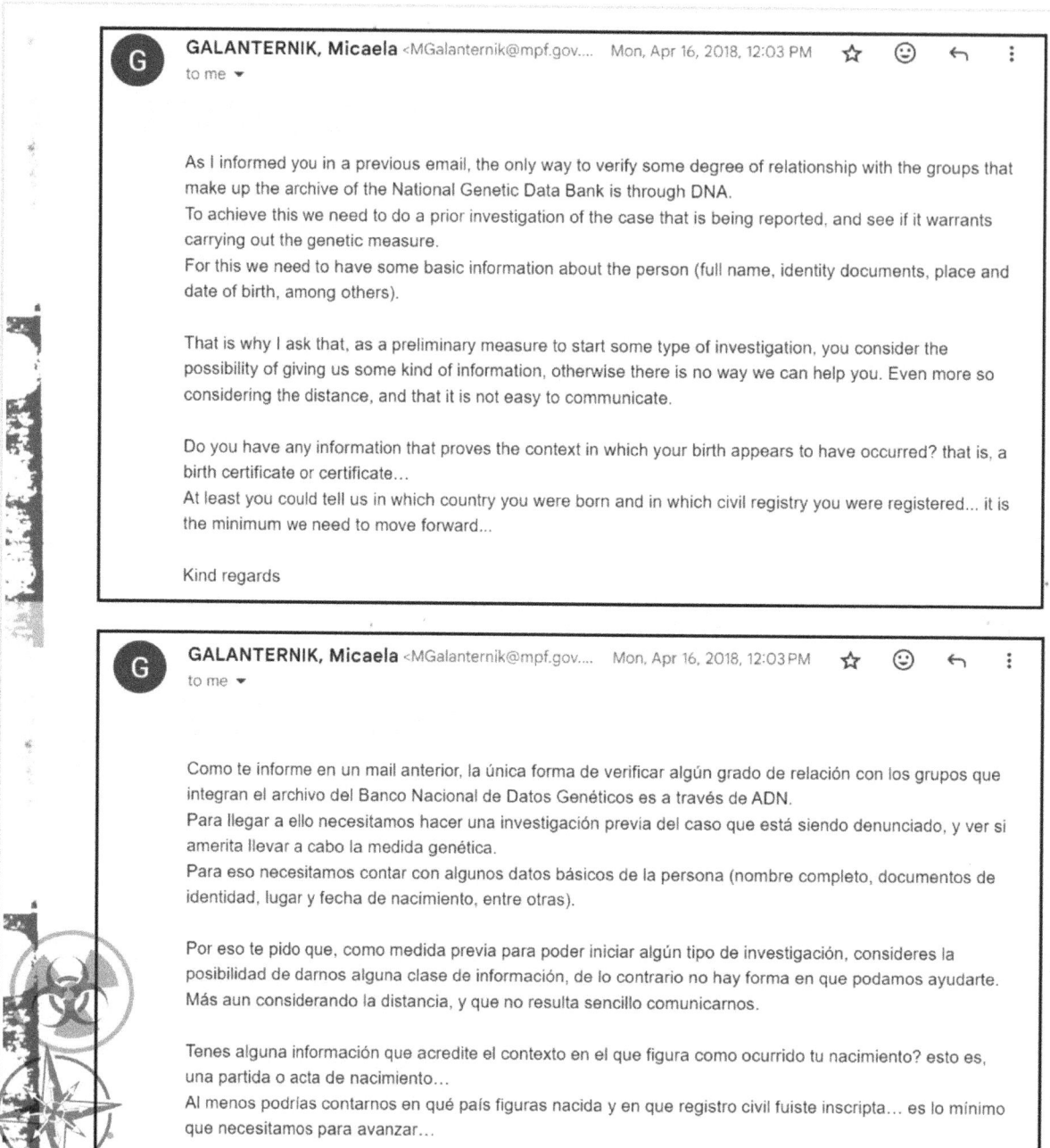

GALANTERNIK, Micaela <MGalanternik@mpf.gov.... Mon, Apr 16, 2018, 12:03 PM ☆ ☺ ↩ ⋮
to me ▼

As I informed you in a previous email, the only way to verify some degree of relationship with the groups that make up the archive of the National Genetic Data Bank is through DNA.
To achieve this we need to do a prior investigation of the case that is being reported, and see if it warrants carrying out the genetic measure.
For this we need to have some basic information about the person (full name, identity documents, place and date of birth, among others).

That is why I ask that, as a preliminary measure to start some type of investigation, you consider the possibility of giving us some kind of information, otherwise there is no way we can help you. Even more so considering the distance, and that it is not easy to communicate.

Do you have any information that proves the context in which your birth appears to have occurred? that is, a birth certificate or certificate...
At least you could tell us in which country you were born and in which civil registry you were registered... it is the minimum we need to move forward...

Kind regards

GALANTERNIK, Micaela <MGalanternik@mpf.gov.... Mon, Apr 16, 2018, 12:03 PM ☆ ☺ ↩ ⋮
to me ▼

Como te informe en un mail anterior, la única forma de verificar algún grado de relación con los grupos que integran el archivo del Banco Nacional de Datos Genéticos es a través de ADN.
Para llegar a ello necesitamos hacer una investigación previa del caso que está siendo denunciado, y ver si amerita llevar a cabo la medida genética.
Para eso necesitamos contar con algunos datos básicos de la persona (nombre completo, documentos de identidad, lugar y fecha de nacimiento, entre otras).

Por eso te pido que, como medida previa para poder iniciar algún tipo de investigación, consideres la posibilidad de darnos alguna clase de información, de lo contrario no hay forma en que podamos ayudarte. Más aun considerando la distancia, y que no resulta sencillo comunicarnos.

Tenes alguna información que acredite el contexto en el que figura como ocurrido tu nacimiento? esto es, una partida o acta de nacimiento...
Al menos podrías contarnos en qué país figuras nacida y en que registro civil fuiste inscripta... es lo mínimo que necesitamos para avanzar...

Saludos cordiales

Image Source: Author's Personal Emails (First Image: Automatically Translated to English, Second Image: Original Email)

"Do you have any information that proves the context in which your birth appears to have occurred? That is, a birth certificate or certificate...

At least you could tell us in which country you were born and in which civil registry you were registered... it is the minimum we need to move forward..."

Text Source: Author's Personal Emails[130]

(I'd told that person the country of my birth was Argentina and the city most likely Buenos Aires at least ten times by that point, and then they simply stopped responding.)

If they had not erased our identities, if they had not trafficked us internationally, we would still have the identity documents they now demand from us before they will recognize us as humans with the right to seek our identities.

The majority of us were infants and toddlers when we were taken overseas.

Very few of us who went internationally (if any) retained an Argentine ID. Human trafficking and illegal adoption of war orphans often result in the loss of our identities from our original countries. This is an issue that most of us outside of Argentina are well aware of.

---

130 Author's Personal Emails. Correspondence with Argentina's MGalanternik@mpf.gov.ar

Image Source: Public Broadcasting Service

"A worker with the U.S. Agency for International Development in Saigon, Bobby Nofflet, recalled the tumultuous days of Babylift: 'There were large sheaves of papers and batches of babies. Who knew which belonged to which?'

The Babylift lawsuit argued that many of the children in the airlift were not orphans, had been given up under duress during wartime, and that the U.S. government had an obligation to return them to their families. Attorney Tom Miller said that he brought Vietnamese birth parents into the courtroom to plead for their children, but to no avail. Judge Spencer Williams eventually threw out the Babylift case, declaring it to be 2,000 separate cases. 'He sealed the records, and told us we could not contact any of the Vietnamese families and let them know where their children were,' said Miller.

...Eventually only twelve children were reunited with their Vietnamese parents, but only after many years and lawsuits....For a number of Babylift adoptees, finding their birth parents is essentially impossible, because no records exist."

Text Source: Public Broadcasting Service[131]

---

[131] Public Broadcasting Service, Operation Babylift (1975), https://www.pbs.org/wgbh/americanexperience/features/daughter-operation-babylift-1975/

Argentina, like many of the worst countries, simply and selfishly uses the excuse of bureaucracy and horrific policies designed to intentionally deny us the right to open a case, no matter what our situation is, so they can continue the war crime of removing children from their group (UN definition of genocide, section E). When that does not work, they resort to hazing behaviors.

Convention on the Prevention and Punishment of the Crime of Genocide

Approved and proposed for signature and ratification or accession by General Assembly resolution 260 A (III) of 9 December 1948
Entry into force: 12 January 1951, in accordance with article XIII

Article II

In the present Convention, genocide means any of the following acts committed with intent to destroy, in whole or in part, a national, ethnical, racial or religious group, as such:

(a) Killing members of the group;

(b) Causing serious bodily or mental harm to members of the group;

(c) Deliberately inflicting on the group conditions of life calculated to bring about its physical destruction in whole or in part;

(d) Imposing measures intended to prevent births within the group;

(e) Forcibly transferring children of the group to another group.

Image Source: United Nations

"Article II In the present Convention, genocide means any of the following acts committed with intent to destroy, in whole or in part, a national, ethnical, racial or religious group, as such:

(a) Killing members of the group;

(b) Causing serious bodily … harm to members of the group;…

(e) Forcibly transferring children of the group to another group."

Text Source: United Nations[132]

---

[132] United Nations, Convention on the Prevention and Punishment of the Crime of Genocide, https://www.un.org/en/genocideprevention/documents/atrocity-crimes/Doc.1_Convention%20on%20the%20Prevention%20and%20Punishment%20of%20the%20Crime%20of%20Genocide.pdf

They believe they can abuse us and get away with it because we have no one, we were sold to our enemies, and we do not have legal identification. They take advantage of what they see as our weak position.

They fought me tooth and nail, refusing to let me have a DNA test to confirm my genetic identity and compare it against their database of the victims and family members of victims from the war I had been born into. The database they gatekeep.

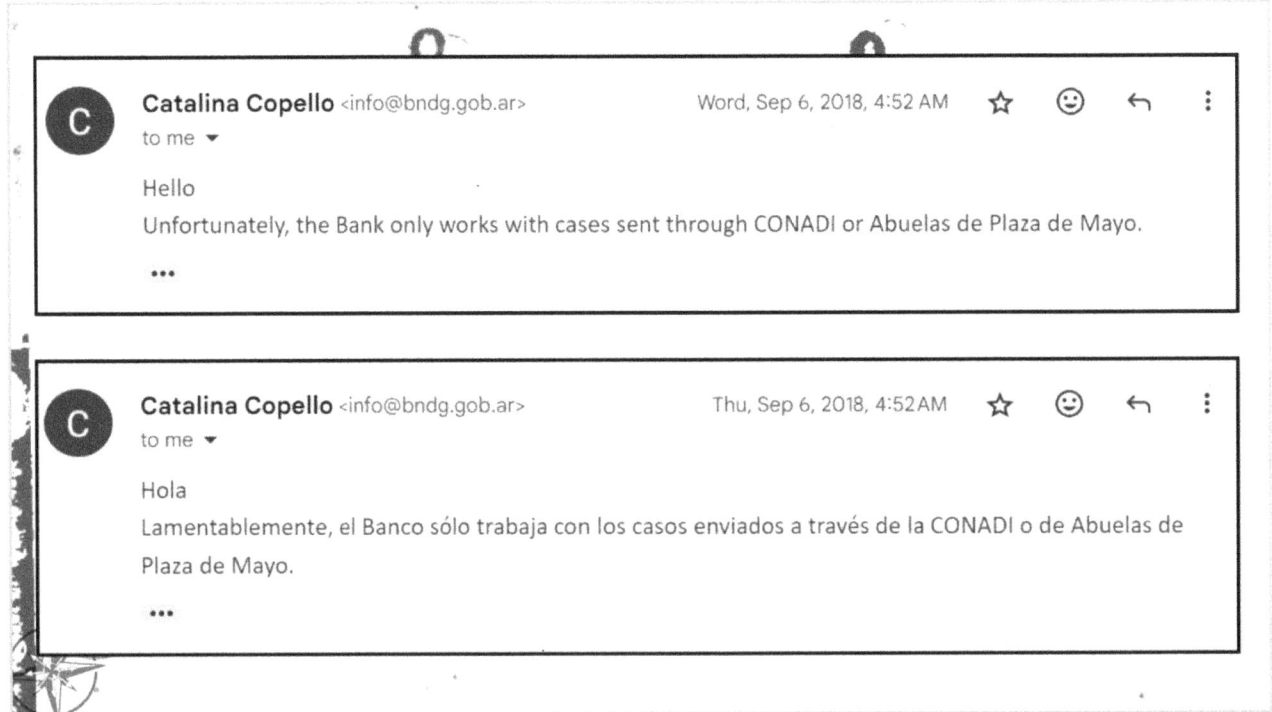

Images Source: Author's Personal Emails (First Image: Automatically Translated to English, Second Image: Original Email)

"The (genetics) bank only works with cases sent through CONADI or Abuelas de Plaza de Mayo."

Text Source: Author's Personal Emails[133]

I was left with nothing but waning faith. All the years of my life, despite being a realist for the single necessity of survival, I had kept one fairytale alive – the belief that there was good where I had come from, that there were souls and kindness in Argentina like the beauty I had seen in my mother.

Giving up on the bureaucrats, I called the prison. After all, I remembered which cell had been mine. They informed me that they did not keep records of the people in their prison, ever, and that no one in their entire prison or criminal system did. In fact, they claimed they didn't even know which prisoners were there now. I'm not sure how much of that was a lie and how much was complete and utter incompetence. I'm not sure I even want to know.

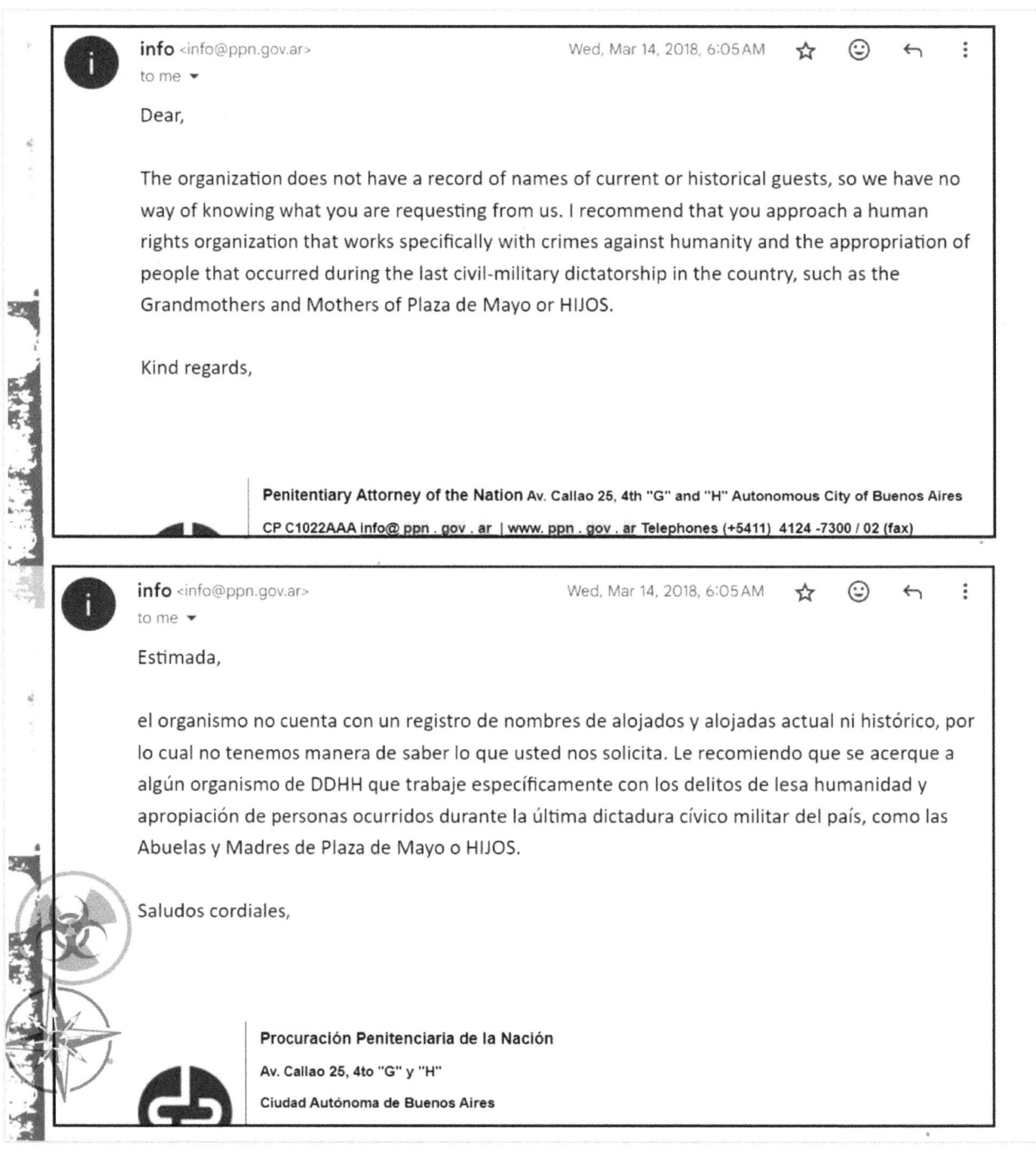

info <info@ppn.gov.ar>   Wed, Mar 14, 2018, 6:05 AM   ☆ ☺ ↩ ⋮
to me ▾

Dear,

The organization does not have a record of names of current or historical guests, so we have no way of knowing what you are requesting from us. I recommend that you approach a human rights organization that works specifically with crimes against humanity and the appropriation of people that occurred during the last civil-military dictatorship in the country, such as the Grandmothers and Mothers of Plaza de Mayo or HIJOS.

Kind regards,

Penitentiary Attorney of the Nation Av. Callao 25, 4th "G" and "H" Autonomous City of Buenos Aires
CP C1022AAA info@ ppn . gov . ar | www. ppn . gov . ar Telephones (+5411) 4124 -7300 / 02 (fax)

---

info <info@ppn.gov.ar>   Wed, Mar 14, 2018, 6:05 AM   ☆ ☺ ↩ ⋮
to me ▾

Estimada,

el organismo no cuenta con un registro de nombres de alojados y alojadas actual ni histórico, por lo cual no tenemos manera de saber lo que usted nos solicita. Le recomiendo que se acerque a algún organismo de DDHH que trabaje específicamente con los delitos de lesa humanidad y apropiación de personas ocurridos durante la última dictadura cívico militar del país, como las Abuelas y Madres de Plaza de Mayo o HIJOS.

Saludos cordiales,

Procuración Penitenciaria de la Nación

Av. Callao 25, 4to "G" y "H"

Ciudad Autónoma de Buenos Aires

Images Source: Author's Personal Emails (First image: Automatically Translated to English, Second Image: Original Email)

"The organization does not have names of current or historical inmates.
I recommend that you approach a human rights organization that works
specifically with crimes against humanity and appropriation of people.
Penitentiary Attorney General's Office"

Text Source: Author's Personal Emails[134]

They also like sending a person to other offices. I ended up with a chain involving
approximately twenty email addresses and every single office in it sent me to a different one
until I have gone in a complete circle several times. The list of email addresses is in the
supplementary portion at the end of this book.

With my sole fantasy, of their being humanity in Argentina, rightfully extinguished, the light
my mother had ignited in me that had endured so much finally flickered out. All I could see
was darkness.

When they taunted me and told me to ask my kidnapper for documents long
discarded.

When they called me a criminal for wanting my DNA tested.

When they told me that I would have to seek the permission of my exploiter and get
her to willingly admit to war crimes and international child trafficking in order to have
access to my own name, my own country, and my own life.

When they closed the door in my face after I had spent a lifetime crawling home to it.

There are no words that can accurately depict how deeply that cut.

---

134   Author's Personal Emails, Correspondence with Argentina's info@ppn.gov.ar

To discover that my mother's nation was full of turncoats, Prada-bag carrying money-grubbing thieves in bureaucratic and radical attire who would sell their own children and grandchildren for a peso and a pat on the head.

To discover that where I came from had no humanity or common sense. That my own people are soulless morons, the people who I clawed out of a hole to get back to, the people who I protected; those were the people who would happily light me on fire and throw me under a bus to watch me burn.

I finally broke under that weight, and I let go. I stopped trying to protect anyone from the danger they had chained me to long ago. Instead, I wrapped that chain around their ankles too, so we could all go down together. I let my captor know that I had blocked off her exit from the United States. While I was running, I had already slammed that door behind me at the risk of my own flimsy documentation. While getting my passport, I had exposed hers as a fraud in an attempt to protect myself and Europe, the land I was standing in. I didn't want her to gain unrestricted access to the people and countries where I had been standing. Now, she knew.

Having spent so many years with the recruiter, I knew how truly deep her hate was for the United States beneath the mask she showed to the public. I also still had vivid memories of how panicked and trapped she had acted, like a caged animal, when I simply switched out our drinks in the safety of a private kitchen so that she would drug herself instead of me. I knew she would not have a subtle reaction to discovering that her escape was blocked and that she had lost some level of control. It was ironically hypocritical of her, considering she had done the same to me while expecting me to remain calm. She had kept me trapped and bound to the crimes of the United States government, with no escape route.

But she's a psychopath. She has always lacked the compassion and awareness necessary to comprehend that if you yourself cannot handle being treated a certain way, neither can anyone else. It's a part of the nature of psychopathy. To expect anything different from her would be the same as expecting a cat to become a dog or a dog to become a cat.

I didn't know what damage she would do, but I hoped her actions would be adequate in size that they would shake things up enough to alter the geopolitical landscape and present another opportunity to seek my original identity and finally find some resolution and peace for myself.

It was a gamble, but it was the only one I had remaining. I was down to rattling cages.

I still struggled with my guilt for others after telling her, even after I had spent fruitless decades attempting and testing all standard, reasonable, legal, and ethical routes to regain my Argentine documents and identity - my exit. As a supervisor of endgame labs, she was the button I never wanted to press, because she was dangerous and she had access to dangerous things. I had spent decades insulating her, keeping her emotionally level, and protecting people from her on an individual, national, and global level as much as I could manage with my access to her. It may not have been a lot, but I had been doing something.

I had stood directly in the face of that fire to protect those who would never protect me. I never wanted to undo all that work of mine. It had cost me everything. But, in return for it, I needed one hand from humanity to reach back out to me to save me in one little way - with a solitary document that was mine. A simple piece of paper linking me to my mother. One so many have and take for granted. I needed mine returned to me so that I could unentangle myself from the exploiter who would never truly allow me peace or freedom.

My exploiter was the danger I had begged the Argentine authorities and the Abuelas organization to help me escape, simply by doing their job, going through the documentation they had, and/or running a DNA test - all within the scope of what they publicly claim to do for the orphans they disposed of. Instead, they chose to laugh and suggest I go to my state-approved abductor for my documents, as if I hadn't attempted that before.

They didn't care about one of their discarded children, I wasn't bribing them, and they felt no pressure from a high enough authority, so they didn't help.

On an individual level, we seem to understand that you should never leave a child in the hands of their parents' murderer, or gang of murderers, due to the likelihood of severe abuse with the potential for death. But, for some reason, that common sense leaves the room when the murderers are also government. In Argentina they pretend to have common sense, so it is the richly paid and kept NGO - an organizational level mistress for a governmental level perpetrator - that is allowed to decide which of their child victims should have rights.

Was there ever any real doubt about how that would actually go?

So, I finally gave in and pressed the one chaotic button I had access to, the emotional rage button of a woman who had a proven track record of effective sabotage, subversion, and large-scale damage, both sanctioned and unsanctioned, within and with the war machine.

Then I sat back, traveled Europe for a few years while working on much more ethical jobs of my own choosing, and watched the world stage to see what would come of her panic. I waited to see if she would overreact and go into a rage, destroying everything within her reach, as I had known her to do.

Post-Nuclear Explosions

There are far-reaching implications
of coercive manipulation via deceit.
More than you'll ever know,
because you were looking in
the other direction the entire time.

That travel started with a trip to Albania. My bladder was destroyed by the ketamine that had been slipped to me without my knowledge (although I had become aware of it after I took that drug test I mentioned previously to see why I felt so drugged, I still hadn't been able to prevent each subsequent drugging). I had to plan my trip in several stages, mapping out the bathrooms all along the way, through the airports and hotels. I even made sure my plane seating was a short distance from the airplane toilets. It wasn't quite a smooth escape, but I managed to get there, one bathroom break at a time. Thankfully, my bladder would heal during the next few months and years, for the most part.

In my half-decade of traveling and waiting, I slowly began to learn how to enjoy the little things in life as I tried to adapt to being a part of a population that knew so little of the backstage maneuverings that guided their lives. I spent those years primarily along Mediterranean shores, working overtime at around 60 - 80 hours a week. Finally being able to keep the profits from my work made a huge difference. The hours were terrible but not overwhelming. I was already accustomed to working two jobs - one for the bills and one for the person who was convinced she owned me.

I managed to reasonably spend the time and money necessary to deal with the reality of kids to send to international schools, remote work clients who always needed me to meet deadlines, my terrible health despite a healthy diet, weight, and exercise; and everything else life throws at a person even when the view from the balcony is a beautiful one. Oh, right, I worked a little extra to have a view of the Mediterranean for around half of each

year. I find that the water helps to wash away thoughts of most things, including a self-genociding world, at least temporarily.

Still, memories and emotions were bubbling to the surface in my mind as I was slowly wandering Europe, trying to blend into cities and tourist destinations known for their large foreign populations. All that we had done, the damage, the manipulation, the atrocities - they all kept coming to the forefront of my mind. I continued to seek ways to repair them on a larger level, but there were so few people with whom I could speak with or work together on those topics. Eventually, I simply sat there alone in my own thoughts, consumed by them.

My dreams were often nightmares as the last of the drugs finally dissipated from my system and memories I had tried to bury surfaced in full glory despite my attempts to ignore them. Early on in my post-England travels, I woke up in the dead of night in a temporary apartment near Greece, trembling so hard that it shook the frame of the bed. In that moment, I finally realized the significance of what I had lived through and just how closely I had grazed death in all those years. With memories of torture shockingly vivid in my mind, I curled up in a blanket on the balcony and waited in silence for the sun to rise. It was over an hour before the trembling ceased.

I appreciated being in countries where they did not speak my language because I had so little in common with humanity that I didn't even know how to keep the flow of one of their conversations.

Instead of engaging with people, I buried myself in work, sunbathing, and finally attending to my shattered health. I spent a large amount of time with dentists and dental surgeons. I saw a specialist in Rome for my spine. After six months of intensive physical therapy, it almost looked and functioned normally. Not quite, but almost. One of the physical therapists brought me into their office after roughly fifty appointments and told me they had done as much as they could, but that my neck was simply "bad."

My spine had been oddly shaped, possibly from the time I was born and due to the impact of my mother's fall from the balcony when she was pregnant. Photographs as far back as when I was eight years old show an unnatural lack of curvature of my neck. Earlier photos might show it as well, if I had any.

Want to know an ironic part? Because my spine was so unnaturally straight, even as a child, people assumed I was either snobbish or military. No one ever stopped to check to see if it was an injury. They saw it as a sign of status or seeking status. To me, it was just a constant dull pain that never went away and that invariably increased throughout the day until it was an effort simply to hold my head up. Due to that, I used to lean the back of my head against walls at any opportunity I got. And the public perception of that? I was lazy or cool. Again, no one ever checked to see if it was because there was something wrong. Shallow eyes only see shallowness.

As for the changing of the landscape I had anticipated, I stopped hopping around Europe and I settled down by the sea in early 2019, remembering that the recruiter's cohort and their sponsors had plans for 2020. I'm glad I did so. It would have been unfortunate to be in an Airbnb with only a week of food once COVID-19 lockdowns hit.

As I scrolled through the panicked research papers coming out about the HIV-1 insert in the virus, and as I looked at the familiar conjunctivitis forming in the corners of my eyes and reappearing for months at a time, much as it had done when I lived with the recruiter as a small child, I silently noted that the slow-moving illness appeared to have come from the endgame lab my exploiter was supervising; the same lab that had been planning a walking pneumonia and incurable illness hybrid since the early 1980s, an illness intended to slowly and quietly creep into the population unnoticed and then wipe them all out gradually.

Or at least, it was a likely possibility. Post-nuclear-era wartime attacks include an intentional crafting of ambiguity that shields the perpetrators from direct responsibility. Back when sitting in think tanks at Yale, I had been informed that deceptiveness was necessary and intended to avoid triggering an all-out nuclear war. Somehow, I don't think the true end result is any better. In trying to avoid triggering the use of the largest-reaching weapon of the past, we've made even further-reaching weapons.

It was also likely that a biological attack would have come anyway. I'll never even know if my rattling of the recruiter's cage had any effect on that at all. I'm okay with not knowing. I've already dealt with enough guilt in my life.

And some things are simply inevitable, especially when no one stops them at any part during nearly 50 years of planning and implementation. There were countless people in those rooms over the years. Countless scientists, funders, war strategists, government employees, and even civilians - all of whom never banded together to stop their own demise. They had only worked in concert to destroy themselves.

Recognizing that reality, the last part of me collapsed, after a lifetime of battling the population and government's combined weight and demand for self and group annihilation, and mine along with it, I had no remaining energy left to pointlessly fight to save anyone.

I had already let go.

I felt that it was time to retire, with or without authorization. Authority no longer held significance for me. I had watched so many people mishandle and squander it to the point of infantilism. It had been embarrassing and critically painful to witness. I allowed myself a moment of sorrow and tears for the damage they had done in their recklessness and lack of care, and for all the victims I had personally touched.

As I walked away, I paused long enough to see the policy of secrecy at work, with Intelligence batting down every single article scientists posted that mentioned the HIV-1 insert in COVID-19. It was played out in real-time with countless witnesses on Twitter. Those scientists were swarmed, harassed, and accused of "inciting fear" simply for publishing research articles containing evidence of what they were seeing in the lab.

We are currently witnessing a major epidemic caused by the 2019 novel coronavirus (2019-nCoV). The evolution of 2019-nCoV remains elusive. We found 4 insertions in the spike glycoprotein (S) which are unique to the 2019-nCoV and are not present in other coronaviruses. Importantly, amino acid residues in all the 4 inserts have identity or similarity to those in the HIV-1 gp120 or HIV-1 Gag. Interestingly, despite the inserts being discontinuous on the primary amino acid sequence, 3D-modelling of the 2019-nCoV suggests that they converge to constitute the receptor binding site. The finding of 4 unique inserts in the 2019-nCoV, all of which have identity /similarity to amino acid residues in key structural proteins of HIV-1 is unlikely to be fortuitous in nature. This work provides yet unknown insights on 2019-nCoV and sheds light on the evolution and pathogenicity of this virus with important implications for diagnosis of this virus.

Image Source: <u>BioRxiv</u>

"We found 4 insertions in the spike glycoprotein (S) which are unique to the 2019-nCoV and are not present in other coronaviruses. Importantly, amino acid residues in all the 4 inserts have identity or similarity to those in the HIV-1 gp120 or HIV-1 Gag. Interestingly, despite the inserts being discontinuous on the primary amino acid sequence, 3D-modelling of the 2019-nCoV suggests that they converge to constitute the receptor binding site. The finding of 4 unique inserts in the 2019-nCoV, all of which have identity similarity to amino acid residues in key structural proteins of HIV-1 is unlikely to be fortuitous in nature."

Text Source: <u>BioRxiv</u>[135]

The majority of the scientists caved under the strain. They were scientists, not battle-hardened experts in fighting the military-industrial complex or in dealing with psychological warfare.

---

[135] BioRxiv, Uncanny Similarity of Unique Inserts in the 2019-nCoV Spike Protein to HIV-1 gp120 and Gag, https://www.biorxiv.org/content/10.1101/2020.01.30.927871V1.full

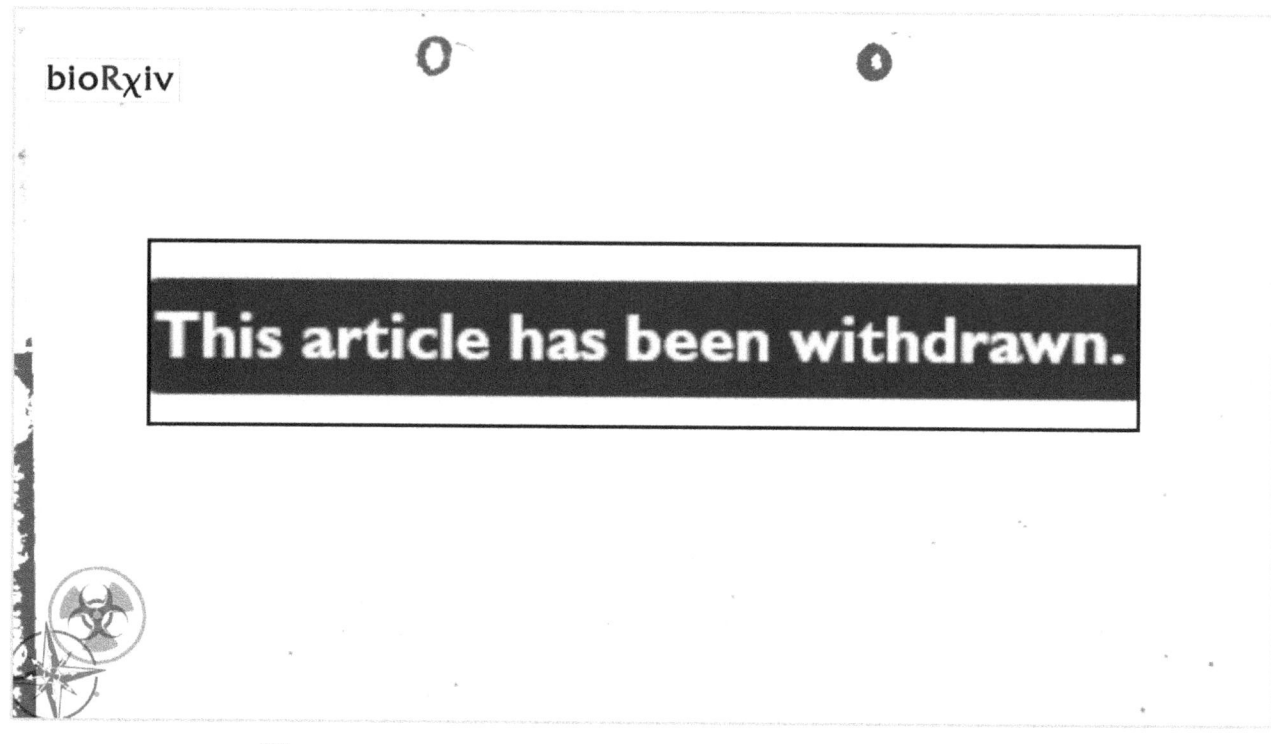

Image Source: <u>BioRxiv</u>[136]

I focused on baking, art, and attempts to enjoy the little fleeting moments that make life beautiful. Now and then I would check in to see commercial interests, mismanaged governments, and organizations jumping onto the monetary incentives and lower oversight that came with the emergency response to a virus that looked suspiciously like one engineered to not be preventable by vaccines. I cringed as they appeared to make the situation worse and reduce our limited options for health and survival, all in their attempts to appease the short-term needs of their stakeholders and the stock market while continuing in the tradition of lying to the public.

They never learn that there isn't enough money in the world to pay for a life that has already been snuffed out.

---

[136] BioRxiv, Uncanny Similarity of Unique Inserts in the 2019-nCoV Spike Protein to HIV-1 gp120 and Gag, https://www.biorxiv.org/content/10.1101/2020.01.30.927871V1.full

Anno No Domini

In my own life, I stopped trying to block
your constant attempts at suicide by military and deceit.
I was tired of fighting you in so many of my failed attempts
to remove your blindfold and save you from yourself.
You clung to and fought for that blindfold
as if it were the child you had thrown
into the fire of war.

So here I sit along the water's edge, civilization to my back, the incessant hum of a busy restaurant, and the inability of people to untangle themselves from the simple magic that is lies, their cascading words almost drowning out the subtle sounds of the forming of each crack in the structure that signals the inevitable collapse of a civilization that bases its decisions on deceit.

It seems in these moments of decay, I have finally grown an appreciation for the Argentine skills of poetry and genocide.

And yet, deep within the wreckage of my soul, that tiny solitary flame of hope ignited by my mother long ago still flickers to life now and then, illuminating the dark, alone.

Carry the flame or leave it. It's up to you.
It's always been up to you.

As far as putting an end to the madness:

It requires untangling ourselves from deeply entrenched adopted lies, swallowing down pride, and solving problems like adults, rather than the easy path to destruction - one of following the irresponsible government lead of a 50-year-classification approach of hiding all the bodies the problems cause.

If you like lists, try this one:

See predatory and coercive behavior.

Say no to predatory and coercive behavior.

Make reality-based non-coercive and non-coerced decisions.

Acknowledge mistakes have been and will be made.

Learning how to let go, move beyond that, and try again.

Take steps to insulate from getting caught in the trap of the damage of subterfuge and coercion again.

Right now you're thinking, "But we have to lie and support lies because the predatory rules we allowed to be created are too strict/absurd to allow us to profit/function otherwise."

That looks like a great problem to learn how to solve.

And, no, it is not easy. Real cleanup never is.

That's why we're in the mess we're in.

Supplementary Sources

UNITED STATES OF AMERICA
NUCLEAR REGULATORY COMMISSION

92 JUN 17 P5:11

BEFORE THE COMMISSION

In the Matter of   )
)
NORTHEAST NUCLEAR ENERGY COMPANY, et al.   )
)   Docket No. 50-336 OLA
(Millstone Nuclear Power   )
    Station, Unit 2)   )

NRC STAFF RESPONSE TO
MARY MARUCCI'S REQUEST FOR HEARING

By letter postmarked May 28, 1992, Mary Ellen Marucci requested that a hearing be

held regarding the proposed amendment. As further discussed below, the May 28, 1992

letter fails to particularize any issues from the design change so as to demonstrate standing,

fails to raise any issues within the scope of the April 28, 1992 *Federal Register* notice, and

otherwise fails to meet the requirements for intervention set forth in 10 C.F.R. § 2.714.

The request for hearing should, therefore, be denied.

Image Source: <u>Nuclear Regulatory Commission</u>[137]

---

[137] Nuclear Regulatory Commission, NRC Staff Response to Mary Marucci's Request for Hearing,
https://www.nrc.gov/docs/ML2010/ML20101G333.pdf

UNITED STATES
NUCLEAR REGULATORY COMMISSION
WASHINGTON, D.C. 20555-0001

May 10, 1993

Docket No. 50-336

MEMORANDUM FOR: John F. Stolz, Director
Project Directorate I-4
Division of Reactor Projects - I/II

FROM: Guy S. Vissing, Senior Project Manager
Project Directorate I-4
Division of Reactor Projects - I/II

SUBJECT: FORTHCOMING MEETING WITH NORTHEAST NUCLEAR ENERGY COMPANY
CONCERNING A PROPOSED MODIFICATION OF THE SPENT FUEL STORAGE
POOL AT MILLSTONE 2

DATE & TIME: May 20, 1993
10:30 AM - 3:00 PM

LOCATION: U.S. Nuclear Regulatory Commission
11555 Rockville Pike, One White Flint North
Rockville, Maryland 20850
Room 1 F 5

PURPOSE: To discuss a proposed modification to the Millstone 2
Spent Fuel Storage Pool that would increase the storage
capacity of the SPSP.

cc: Office of Commission Appellate
Adjudication
U.S. Nuclear Regulatory Commission
Washington, DC 20555

Administrative Judge
Charles N. Kelber
Atomic Safety and Licensing Board
U.S. Nuclear Regulatory Commission
Washington, DC 20555

Administrative Judge
Ivan W. Smith, Chairman
Atomic Safety and Licensing Board
U.S. Nuclear Regulatory Commission
Washington, DC 20555

Administrative Judge
Jerry R. Kline
Atomic Safety and Licensing Board
U.S. Nuclear Regulatory Commission
Washington, DC 20555

Mary Ellen Marucci
104 Brownell Street
New Haven, Connecticut 06511

Frank X. Lo Sacco
4 Glover Place, Box 1125
Middletown, Connecticut 06457

Image(s) Source: <u>Nuclear Regulatory Commission</u>[138]

---

[138] Nuclear Regulatory Commission, Memorandum for Atomic Safety and Licensing Board and All Parties,
https://www.nrc.gov/docs/ML2006/ML20062J215.pdf

REAUTHORIZATION OF THE FEDERAL WATER POLLUTION CONTROL ACT

(102–31)

U. VA.

HEARINGS

FEB 2 4 1992

| Heather Crawford | Hamden, CT | CT Sea Grant Marine Advisory Program |
| Mary Ellen Marucci | New Haven, CT | Coalition Against Radioactive Recklessness/ Citizens Monitoring Network |

Image Source: p. 2180, <u>U.S. Congress via Google Books</u>[139]

---

[139] Reauthorization of the Federal Water Pollution Control Act: Hearings Before the Subcommittee on Water Resources of the Committee on Public Works and Transportation House of Representatives,
https://books.google.es/books?id=vBYSAAAAYAAJ&printsec=frontcover#v=onepage&q&f=false

Image Source: Yale University Library Online Exhibitions[140]

[140] Yale University Library, "Free the New Haven Panthers": The New Haven Nine, Yale, and the May Day 1970 Protests That Brought Them Together, https://onlineexhibits.library.yale.edu/s/-free-the-new-haven-panthers-the-new-haven-nine-yale-and-the-may-day-1970-protests-that-brought-them-together/page/new-haven-panther-activism

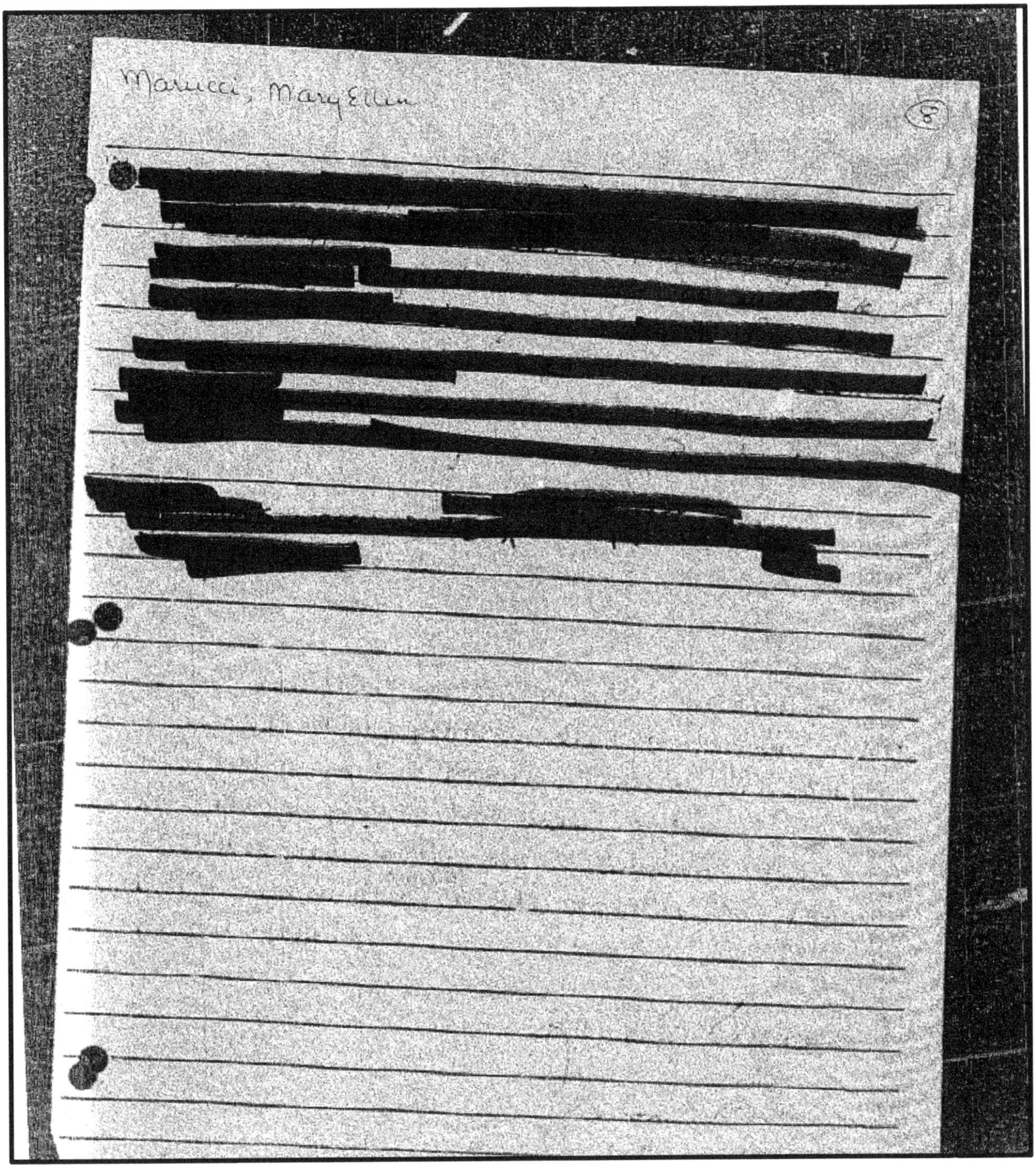

Marucci, Mary Ellen

Image Source: Personal File, State of Connecticut Department of Children and Youth Services

=

La Turca

C

uando fueron a buscarla, ella saltó una muralla intentando evadir el operativo militar, aunque sin suerte. Estaba embarazada. Llegó al sótano de la Alcaidía con una pierna enyesada después que la mantuvieran incomunicada por varios días en un recinto de la jefatura de policía. Allí la torturaron. Por ella nos enteramos de que ese espacio funcionaba como cárcel clandestina transitoria, en la que los prisioneros estaban permanentemente encapuchados y vendados y constantemente interrogados bajo tortura.

La Turca permaneció poco tiempo en la Alcaidía; su paso fue muy importante para todas. Trajo ideas nuevas, nos contagió su confianza en la revolución y nos dio ejemplo de entrega. Cuando hablaba de las luchas populares y del heroísmo

Image Source: Google Books Margarita Drago[141]

---

[141] Margarita Drago - Fragmentos de la memoria: Recuerdos de una experiencia carcelaria (1975-1980)
https://books.google.es/books/about/Fragmentos_de_la_memoria.html?id=Hh9kkGi9V1sC&redir_esc=y

FRAGMENTOS DE LA MEMORIA:
RECUERDOS DE UNA EXPERIENCIA CARCELARIA
(1975-1980)
MARGARITA DRAGO

de los compañeros se le iluminaba el rostro así como cuando se refería a María Victoria, la niña que estaba esperando. Nosotras necesitábamos su presencia; nuestra moral y nuestras relaciones estaban muy desgastas por el aislamiento y el acoso persistente de los carceleros.

El día que la sacaron de la Alcaidía tuvimos miedo; temíamos que la mataran. Al tiempo recibimos noticias de ella. Supimos que la habían internado en un hospital de la ciudad donde nació María Victoria, que la pequeña había sido entregada a sus abuelos, y la Turca, transferida a Villa Devoto. Yo la volví a encontrar en uno de los traslados internos que hicieron en Devoto. Nos veíamos en los recreos donde intercambiábamos un hola, ¿cómo estás? presuroso, porque ése era tiempo destinado a las reuniones políticas, y generalmente, la Turca se reunía con sus compañeras. Cada vez que la veía me llamaban la atención la serenidad de su rostro y su sonrisa casi perma-

Image Source: Google Books Margarita Drago[142]

---

[142] Margarita Drago - Fragmentos de la memoria: Recuerdos de una experiencia carcelaria (1975-1980)
https://books.google.es/books/about/Fragmentos_de_la_memoria.html?id=Hh9kkGi9V1sC&redir_esc=y

FRAGMENTOS DE LA MEMORIA:
RECUERDOS DE UNA EXPERIENCIA CARCELARIA
(1975-1980)
MARGARITA DRAGO

nente. Me la imaginaba en sus múltiples facetas: de militante, madre, amante y compañera. La veía enfrentándose con valentía a los militares, defendiendo con firmeza los principios de la revolución, o asistiendo solidaria a las compañeras que necesitaban su palabra, o me la imaginaba cantando nanas y relatando historias a su pequeña hija.

No sé por qué la persistencia en inventar su imagen y este recuerdo diáfano que aún perdura en mi memoria, si en realidad nunca hablamos a solas. Su historia la fui armando de a retazos con lo que decían de ella sus compañeras y con las ideas que yo fui creando al escucharla y verla actuar, siempre tan clara y firme ante los carceleros, y también, ante nosotras que éramos tan diversas en prácticas de vida como en ideas políticas.

La Turca, la real o la construida, al igual que otras compañeras fue un modelo. Mi ideal de revolucionaria. A la hora de la angustia o del miedo, su imagen, junto a la de otras que yo admiraba

Image Source: Google Books Margarita Drago[143]

---

[143] Margarita Drago - Fragmentos de la memoria: Recuerdos de una experiencia carcelaria (1975-1980) https://books.google.es/books/about/Fragmentos_de_la_memoria.html?id=Hh9kkGi9V1sC&redir_esc=y

FRAGMENTOS DE LA MEMORIA:
RECUERDOS DE UNA EXPERIENCIA CARCELARIA
(1975-1980)
MARGARITA DRAGO

tanto como a ella, llegaba a mi memoria en un gesto amigo y compañero. Muchas veces encontré la fuerza y el motivo para seguir adelante en el recuerdo grato de su voz y su palabra, y en su pasión fervorosa de madre militante.

Image Source: Google Books Margarita Drago[144]

---

[144] Margarita Drago - Fragmentos de la memoria: Recuerdos de una experiencia carcelaria (1975-1980)
https://books.google.es/books/about/Fragmentos_de_la_memoria.html?id=Hh9kkGi9V1sC&redir_esc=y

367

35+ YEARS OF FREEDOM OF INFORMATION ACTION

Home   Publications   Postings   Projects   Documents   FOIA   DNSA   Blog   Русские Страницы   About

CIA report, "Counterterrorism in the Southern Cone," Secret, May 9, 1977

Approved for Public Release
8 December 2016

9 May 1977

SUBJECT: Counterterrorism in the Southern Cone

The security forces of Argentina, Bolivia, Brazil, Chile, Paraguay, and Uruguay have for some time engaged in a formalized exchange of information on leftist terrorists. Moreover, these governments jointly carry out operations against subversives on each other's soil. This effort, dubbed "Operation Condor", is not publicly known. One aspect of the program involving Chile, Uruguay, and Argentina envisages illegal operations outside Latin America against exiled terrorists, particularly in Europe. Because the existence of Condor is known to foreign security services, such activities have so far been frustrated. The extent of cooperation in Condor is unusual in Latin America, even though the exchange of intelligence information by governments facing a common problem is a routine practice throughout the world.

The military-controlled governments of the Southern Cone all consider themselves targets of international Marxism. Having endured real and perceived threats from leftist terrorists, these governments believe that the very foundations of their societies are threatened. In most cases, government leaders seek to be selective in the pursuit and apprehension of suspected subversives, but control over security forces generally is not tight enough to prevent innocents from being harmed or mistreated. Cultural and historical developments in the region go a long way toward explaining, if not justifying, the often harsh methods. In Hispanic law, for instance, a suspect is presumed guilty until proven innocent. In addition, most Latin American constitutions have provisions for states of seige or other emergency clauses which greatly increase the governments' powers of arrest, detention, and censorship.

There is a long history of bilateral efforts to control subversion in the Southern Cone countries. The regional approach eventually formalized in Condor, however, apparently was endorsed in early 1974 when security officials from all of the member countries, except Brazil, agreed to establish liaison channels and to facilitate the movement of security officers on government business from one country to the other.

Among the initial aims of Condor was the exchange of information on the Revolutionary Coordinating Junta (JCR), an organization believed to consist of representatives of terrorist groups from Bolivia, Uruguay,

SECRET

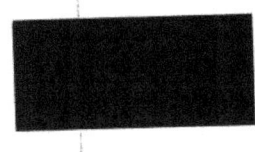

Image Source: National Security Archive[145]

---

[145] National Security Archive, CIA report, "Counterterrorism in the Southern Cone," Secret, May 9, 1977, https://nsarchive.gwu.edu/document/19868-national-security-archive-doc-2-cia-report

CIA report, "Counterterrorism in the Southern Cone," Secret, May 9, 1977

Approved for Public Release
8 December 2016

Chile, Argentina, and Paraguay. The JCR ███████ coordinates activities and provides propaganda and logistical support for its members. The Junta has representatives in Europe, and they are believed to have been involved in the assassinations in Paris of the Bolivian ambassador to France last May and an Uruguayan military attache in 1974. The attache had been involved in the successful campaign to suppress Uruguay's terrorist Tupamaros, a member group of JCR.

Condor's overall campaign against subversion reportedly was intensified last summer when members gathered in Santiago to organize more detailed, long-range plans. Decisions included:

-- The development of a basic computerized data bank in Santiago. All members will contribute information on known or suspected terrorists.

-- Brazil agreed to provide gear for "Condortel" -- the group's communications network.

The basic mission of Condor teams to be sent overseas reportedly was "to liquidate" top-level terrorist leaders. Non-terrorists also were reportedly candidates for assassination; Uruguayan opposition politician Wilson Ferreira, if he should travel to Europe, and some leaders of Amnesty International were mentioned as targets. Ferreira may have been removed from the list, however, because he is considered to have good contacts among US congressmen. A training course was held in Buenos Aires for the team heading overseas. More recently Condor leaders were considering the dispatch of a team to London -- disguised as businessmen -- to monitor "suspicious activity" in Europe. Another proposal under study included the collection of material on the membership, location, and political activities of human rights groups in order to identify and expose their socialist and Marxist connections. Similar data reportedly are to be collected on church and third-world groups.

Evidence, although not conclusive, indicates that cooperation among security forces in the Southern Cone extends beyond legal methods. Last May, for example, armed men ransacked the offices of the Argentine Catholic Commission on Immigration and stole records containing information on thousands of refugees and immigrants. The Argentine police did not investigate the crime -- a signal that Latin refugees, principally from Chile and Uruguay were no longer welcome. A month later, 24 Chilean and Uruguay refugees, many of whom were the subjects of commission files, were kidnapped and tortured. After their release, some of the refugees insisted

2

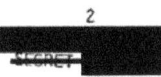

Image Source: National Security Archive[146]

---

[146] National Security Archive, CIA report, "Counterterrorism in the Southern Cone," Secret, May 9, 1977, https://nsarchive.gwu.edu/document/19868-national-security-archive-doc-2-cia-report

CIA report, "Counterterrorism in the Southern Cone," Secret, May 9, 1977

Approved for Public Release
8 December 2016

SECRET

their interrogators were security officers from Chile and Uruguay A
number of Uruguayans were held in Buenos Aires last summer for two weeks
and then flown to Montevideo in an Uruguayan plane. Uruguayan military
officers offered to spare them their lives if they would agree to allow
themselves to be 'captured" by authorities -- as if they were an armed
group attempting to invade the country. Moreover, two prominent political
exiles in Argentina were killed under mysterious circumstances.

Condor also is engaged in non-violent activities, including
psychological warfare and a propaganda campaign. These programs heavily
use the media to publicize crimes and atrocities committed by terrorists.
By appealing to national pride and the national conscience, these programs
aim to secure the support of the citizenry in the hope they will report
anything out of the ordinary in their neighborhoods. Propaganda campaigns
are constructed so that one member country publishes information useful to
another -- without revealing that the beneficiary was in fact the source.
For example, Bolivia and Argentina reportedly are planning to launch a
campaign against the Catholic Church and other religious groups that
allegedly support leftist movements. Bolivia will collect information on
the groups and then send it to Argentina for publication.

The Condor communications system uses both voice and teletype.
Member countries communicate via radio and each is required to maintain
an open channel.

Condor suffers from some organizational
inefficiency, but this factor has not inhibited its overall effectiveness.
Condor has tightened security measures

Security has been strengthened at Condor's operations center
in Buenos Aires, and compartmentation has been increased. In addition,
once a Condor member has declined to participate in an operation, he is
excluded from all further details of that particular plan. Hence, less
active members, such as Paraguay and Bolivia
may not be aware of many operations.

Outside the Condor umbrella, bilateral cooperation between other
security organizations in the region also is strong. For example,
intelligence organizations in Argentina, Uruguay, and Chile work together
closely. Each security organization assigns advisers to the other countrie
primarily to identify subversives in exile.

3

SECRET

Image Source: National Security Archive[147]

[147] National Security Archive, CIA report, "Counterterrorism in the Southern Cone," Secret, May 9, 1977,
https://nsarchive.gwu.edu/document/19868-national-security-archive-doc-2-cia-report

NATIONAL ARCHIVES   Explore our Websites

Gerald R. Ford
Presidential Library & Museum

16 April 1975

Point Paper for the Special Assistant to the Secretary and
Deputy Secretary of Defense

SUBJECT: Orphan Evacuation Program - Vietnam/Cambodia

- Deaths:

    -- 5 April crash of C-5 - 190 (figure not final)

    -- One died enroute to Clark AB - cause of death, extreme
       dehydration. (Infant)

    -- One died at Clark AB Hospital - cause of death, sepsis
       (absorption of pathogenic microorganisms into blood stream).
       (Infant)
    -- One died enroute to Los Angeles - cause of death, pneumonia,
       dehydration and prematurity. Reported 24 days old.

    -- Prognosis - No more deaths expected.

- Future orphan airlift requirements:

    -- Known - zero - original "Reported 2000" all processed

    -- Possible - 80 (Vietnam) Rumors of 500 to 5000 more.
       Tracking this.

- Problems:

    -- Despite the official State/AID/DOD system, certain individuals
       have operated as free agents making arrangments for contract
       flights and direct liaison with the orphanages.

    -- This has caused considerable confusion and resulted in less
       than desirable service for the orphans.

    -- News reporters covering commercial arrivals at San
       Francisco and Seattle (outside the State/AID/DOD system)
       cited health problems with orphans on these flights.

- Current funding status (funded by State/AID):

Image Source: Gerald R. Ford Presidential Library and Museum[148]

[148] Gerald R. Ford Presidential Library and Museum, Document from Box 10, folder "Indochina Refugees - Orphan Airlift,
https://www.fordlibrarymuseum.gov/library/document/0164/1505194.pdf

When ever people attempt to use so-called legal channels of redress, their pleas sounding of agony and pain fall on deaf ears. At this time we are calling for a new constitution. A constitution written by the masses of people throughout this ▇▇▇▇ country that is representative of them and that will give all power to the people.

November 26 in Washington, D.C. there will be held a Revolutionary People's Constitutional Convention. This occasion will mark the coming together of all progressive people and organizations that desire a more representative government and see the need for a new constitution. Your presence at the Constitutional Convention is greatly needed to assist us in building for a better society.

Image: Black Panther Party Documents

Image Source: <u>Federal Bureau of Investigation</u>[149]

149 Federal Bureau of Investigation, Black Panther Party, Part 23,
https://vault.fbi.gov/Black%20Panther%20Party%20/Black%20Panther%20Party%20Part%2023%20of%2034

	A	B	C	D	E	F	G	H	I
1	**Contacted Offices Regarding Right to Seek Identity**								
2	actuacionesrpp@gob.gba.gov.ar				identidadbiologica@jus.gov.ar				
3	actunionesrpp@gob.gba.gov.ar				identificar@renaper.gob.ar				
4	cbarc@mrecic.gov.ar				lidentidadbiologica@jus.gov.ar				
5	cmadr@mrecic.gov.ar				info@boletinoficial.gba.gob.ar				
6	peconadi@gmail.com				institucional@grupoclarin.com				
7	consultas@renaper.gob.ar				ley10490@trabajo.gba.gov.ar				
8	consultas_cbarc@cancilleria.gob.ar				mde@trabajo.gba.gov.ar				
9	consultas_cbarc@mrecic.gov.ar				oficiosarchivodigital@gob.gba.gov.ar				
10	consultas_dgrc@buenosaires.gov.ar				peconadi@gmail.com				
11	diariodeba@gmail.com				perfilcom@perfil.com				
12	dprp@gob.gba.gov.ar				privada.justicia@mjus.gba.gob.ar				
13	dudas@abuelas.org.ar				privada.secretariageneral@sg.gba.gob.ar				
14	eespa@mrecic.gov.ar				privadasdh.gba@gmail.com				
15	registropersonas-mesaentrada@gob.gba.gov.ar				reclamosdeactas@registrocivilctes.gob.ar				
16	subderegistracion@gob.gba.gov.ar				redactor@pagina12.com.ar				
17									
18									
19									

Image: Partial List of Agencies Contacted in Argentina for the Right to Regain Identity

Image Source: Author's Personal Documents[150]

---

[150] Author's Personal Documents, Partial List of Agencies Contacted

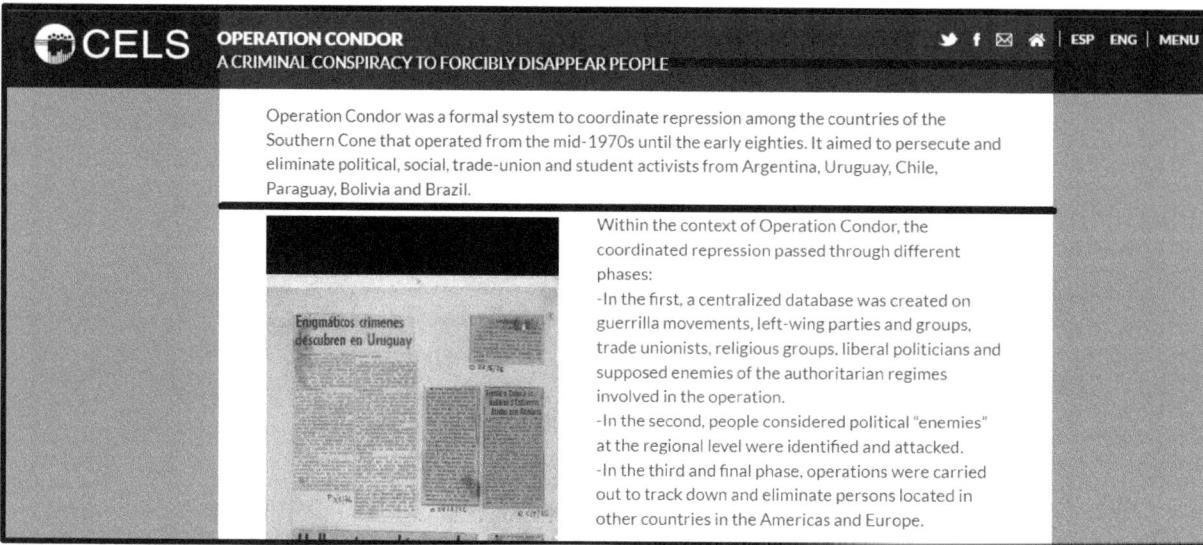

Image Source: <u>CELS Centro de Estudios Legales y Sociales</u>

"The coordinated repression passed through different phases:

-In the first, a centralized database was created on guerrilla movements, left-wing parties and groups, trade unionists, religious groups, liberal politicians, and supposed enemies of the authoritarian regimes involved in the operation.

-In the second, people considered political "enemies" at the regional level were identified and attacked.

-In the third and final phase, operations were carried out to track down and eliminate persons located in other countries in the Americas and Europe."

Text Source: <u>CELS Centro de Estudios Legales y Social</u>[151]

---

[151] CELS,Operation Condor - A Criminal Conspiracy to Forcibly Disappear People, https://www.cels.org.ar/especiales/plancondor/en/#

Contact

Web:

http://theendgame.xyz

Twitter:

@almanavajasc

Archive:

https://archive.org/details/@alma_navajas_claros?tab=web-archive

Unsecure email:

almanavajasclaros@gmail.com

(More) secure email:

mariavictoria1977@protonmail.com

Sources

ABC News FiveThirtyEight, Normal America is Not a Small Town of White People, https://fivethirtyeight.com/features/normal-america-is-not-a-small-town-of-white-people/

ABC News, Japan Earthquake: Radiation Leaking After Fukushima Nuclear Plant Explodes, https://abcnews.go.com/International/japan-earthquake-radiation-leaking-fukushima-nuclear-plant-explodes/story?id=13131123

American Issues Project via Wikipedia, Weather Underground, https://en.wikipedia.org/wiki/Weather_Underground

Archives of Virology via Springer, Angiotensin-Converting Enzyme 2 (ACE2) Proteins of Different Bat Species Confer Variable Susceptibility to SARS-CoV Entry, https://link.springer.com/article/10.1007/s00705-010-0729-6

Author's Personal Collection, Cervical Spine MRI, X-ray, State Child Protective Services records, tribunal records, birth records, photos, emails

Biochemical and Biophysical Research Communications, Receptor-Binding Domain of SARS-CoV Spike Protein Induces Highly Potent Neutralizing Antibodies: Implication for Developing Subunit Vaccine, https://www.ncbi.nlm.nih.gov/pmc/articles/PMC7092904/

BioRxiv, Uncanny Similarity of Unique Inserts in the 2019-nCoV Spike Protein to HIV-1 gp120 and Gag, https://www.biorxiv.org/content/10.1101/2020.01.30.927871V1.full

British Broadcasting Corporation, CIA Admits Employing Nazis, http://news.bbc.co.uk/2/hi/americas/1301306.stm

California Law Review via University of California, Experimentation on Prisoners: Persistent Dilemmas in Rights and Regulations, https://escholarship.org/content/qt81x6m9bt/qt81x6m9bt.pdf

CBS News, A Dark Chapter in Medical History, https://www.cbsnews.com/news/a-dark-chapter-in-medical-history-09-02-2005/

CELS, Operation Condor - A Criminal Conspiracy to Forcibly Disappear People, https://www.cels.org.ar/especiales/plancondor/en/#

Central Intelligence Agency, George H.W. Bush - the 11th Director of Central Intelligence, https://www.cia.gov/stories/story/george-h-w-bush-the-11th-director-of-central-intelligence/

Central Intelligence Agency, Memorandum for: Executive Secretary, CIA Management Committee, Subject: Family Jewels,
https://www.cia.gov/readingroom/docs/DOC_0001451843.pdf

Connecticut State Library, The Cadets at Plum Island,
https://cslib.contentdm.oclc.org/digital/api/collection/p4005coll11/id/39/download
Additional Camp Documents:
https://carlisleindian.dickinson.edu/sites/default/files/docs-documents/NARA_RG75_CCF_b021_f06_57042.pdf

Current Medical Chemistry via National Library of Medicine, Chelating Agents Used for Plutonium and Uranium Removal in Radiation Emergency Medicine,
https://pubmed.ncbi.nlm.nih.gov/16305471/

Desaparecidos, Roxana Teresa Claros Romero Detenida-Desaparecida el 7/4/77,
http://www.desaparecidos.org/arg/victimas/c/claros/index.html Alternative:
https://robertobaschetti.com/claros-roxana-teresa/

DewHerst Funeral Home, Tom Flanders,
https://www.dewhirstfuneral.com/obituary/Tom-Flanders

Ecotoxicology and Environmental Safety via PubMed, Toxicity of Dispersant Corexit 9500A and Crude Oil to Marine Microzooplankton,
https://pubmed.ncbi.nlm.nih.gov/24836881/

Environmental Protection Agency, Radioactivity in Antiques,
https://www.epa.gov/radtown/radioactivity-antiques

FAIR, Comment on: NYT's Reassuring Radiation Reporting,
https://fair.org/uncategorized/nyts-reassuring-radiation-reporting/

Federal Bureau of Investigation, Black Panther Party, Part 23,
https://vault.fbi.gov/Black%20Panther%20Party%20/Black%20Panther%20Party%20Part%2023%20of%2034

Flickr, Great Peace March, Dan Coogan Photographer,
https://www.flickr.com/photos/cooganphoto/5903978923/in/album-72157626908632257/

Gerald R. Ford Presidential Library and Museum, Document from Box 10, folder "Indochina Refugees - Orphan Airlift,
https://www.fordlibrarymuseum.gov/library/document/0164/1505194.pdf

GoFundMe, Child cancer victim page (redacted)

Google Maps, Federal Correctional Complex C.A.B.A.,
https://maps.app.goo.gl/y6Uh5q8k5bV19WZk7

Google Profiles, 2013 Screenshot - Mary Ellen Marucci, https://profiles.google.com/102710091734853540573/about

IberLibro, The Black Panther Manifesto / If the Fascists Attempt to Murder Chairman Bobby, https://www.iberlibro.com/arte-grabados/Black-Panther-Manifesto-Fascists-Attempt-Murder/31053324903/bd#&gid=1&pid=2

Infobae, "Quémense de a Poco": El Horror de la "Masacre de los Colchones" en Villa Devoto, https://www.infobae.com/sociedad/policiales/2018/03/14/quemense-de-a-poco-el-horror-de-la-masacre-de-los-colchones-en-villa-devoto/

Infobae, Horror and Death: The Five Women Who Killed - The Montoneros Bomb in the Dining Room of the Federal Police, https://www.infobae.com/en/2022/03/18/horror-and-death-the-five-women-who-killed-the-montoneros-bomb-in-the-dining-room-of-the-federal-police/

Institute for Youth in Policy, Operation Condor and the Horrors of U.S. Foreign Policy, https://yipinstitute.org/article/operation-condor-and-the-horrors-of-u-s-foreign-policy

International Journal of Maternal and Child Health and AIDS, Overcoming Challenges in Conducting Clinical Trials in Minority Populations: Identifying and Testing What Works, https://www.ncbi.nlm.nih.gov/pmc/articles/PMC4948175/

Jeff Share, The Great Peace March for Global Nuclear Disarmament 1986, https://jshare.wixsite.com/jeffshare/peace-march

Louisiana's Old State Capitol, Louisiana Orphan Train: Stories From the Descendants, https://louisianaoldstatecapitol.org/exhibits-events/louisiana-orphan-train-stories

Margarita Drago - Fragmentos de la memoria: Recuerdos de una experiencia carcelaria (1975-1980) https://books.google.es/books/about/Fragmentos_de_la_memoria.html?id=Hh9kkGi9V1sC&redir_esc=y

Medscape, Doctor/Spy: How MDs Get Involved in Espionage, https://www.medscape.com/viewarticle/951889?form=fpf

Museum of Jewish Heritage, From WWII to the Space Race: The Story of Project Paperclip, https://mjhnyc.org/events/from-wwii-to-the-space-race-the-story-of-project-paperclip/

MyHeritage, Carmen Matthews, https://www.myheritage.es/names/carmen_matthews#

National Library of Medicine, World Biomedical Journals, 1951-60: A Study of the Relative Significance of 1,388 Titles Indexed in Current List of Medical Literature, https://www.ncbi.nlm.nih.gov/pmc/articles/PMC198399/pdf/mlab00175-0028.pdf

National Public Radio, New Blast Rocks Japanese Nuclear Plant, https://www.npr.org/2011/03/14/134501905/crisis-at-nuclear-plant-adds-to-japans-woes

National Security Archive, CIA report, "Counterterrorism in the Southern Cone," Secret, May 9, 1977, https://nsarchive.gwu.edu/document/19868-national-security-archive-doc-2-cia-report

NECN, Conn. FBI Office Won't Speak on 2 Whistleblower Lawsuits, https://www.necn.com/news/local/connecticut/conn-fbi-office-wont-speak-on-2-lawsuits-alleging/2013002/

New Haven Independent, A Panther Passes On, https://www.newhavenindependent.org/article/panther_passes_on

New Haven Independent, You Don't Have to be Jewish, https://www.newhavenindependent.org/index.php/article/you_didnt_have_to_be_jewish_

New Haven Register, Friends, Family to Celebrate Life of Black Panther, Community Activist, George Edwards, https://www.nhregister.com/news/article/Community-mourns-Black-Panther-activist-Edwards-17536370.php

New York Times, New Haven's Top Killer of Young Men is AIDS, https://www.nytimes.com/1987/12/13/nyregion/new-havens-top-killer-of-young-men-is-aids.html

New York Times, No Regrets for a Love of Explosives; In a Memoir of Sorts, a War Protester Talks of Life With the Weatherman, https://www.nytimes.com/2001/09/11/books/no-regrets-for-love-explosives-memoir-sorts-war-protester-talks-life-with.html

New York Times, Once a Black Panther - Always a Cause, https://www.nytimes.com/1992/11/22/nyregion/once-a-black-panther-always-a-cause.html

New York Times, U.S. Told to Pay $101 Million for Framing 4 Men, https://www.nytimes.com/2007/07/26/us/26cnd-mob.html

Nuclear Regulatory Commission, Docket No. 50-336. Memorandum for Atomic Safety and Licensing Board and All Parties, https://www.nrc.gov/docs/ML2006/ML20062J215.pdf https://webcache.googleusercontent.com/search?q=cache:6SAEdJsAr2oJ:https://www.nrc.gov/docs/ML2006/ML20062J215.pdf&hl=en&gl=us https://web.archive.org/web/20231111020444/https://webcache.googleusercontent.com/search?q=cache:6SAEdJsAr2oJ:https://www.nrc.gov/docs/ML2006/ML20062J215.pdf&hl=en&gl=us

Nuclear Regulatory Commission, Letter: Millstone Power Station, Units 2 and 3 – Documentation of the Completion of Required Actions Taken in Response to the Lessons Learned From the Fukushima Dai-ichi Accident,
https://www.nrc.gov/docs/ML2033/ML20332A139.pdf
https://webcache.googleusercontent.com/search?q=cache:GFOKWGgQrkYJ:https://www.nrc.gov/docs/ML2033/ML20332A139.pdf&hl=en&gl=es
http://web.archive.org/web/20231111021033/https://webcache.googleusercontent.com/search?q=cache:GFOKWGgQrkYJ:https://www.nrc.gov/docs/ML2033/ML20332A139.pdf&hl=en&gl=es

Nuclear Regulatory Commission, Memorandum for Atomic Safety and Licensing Board and All Parties, https://www.nrc.gov/docs/ML2006/ML20062J215.pdf

Nuclear Regulatory Commission, NRC Staff Response to Mary Marucci;s Request for Hearing, https://www.nrc.gov/docs/ML2010/ML20101G333.pdf

Nuclear Regulatory Commission, Opinions and Decisions of the Nuclear Regulatory Commission with Selected Orders, Volume 36,
https://www.nrc.gov/docs/ML1635/ML16357A723.pdf
https://web.archive.org/web/20230000000000*/https://www.nrc.gov/docs/ML1635/ML16357A723.pdf

Nuclear Regulatory Commission, Opinions and Decisions of the Nuclear Regulatory Commission with Selected Orders, Volume 38,
https://www.nrc.gov/docs/ML1635/ML16357A718.pdf
https://web.archive.org/web/20220801000000*/https://www.nrc.gov/docs/ML1635/ML16357A718.pdf

Nuclear Regulatory Commission, United States of America Nuclear Regulatory Commission Before the Atomic Safety and Licensing Board,
https://www.nrc.gov/docs/ML2003/ML20034H791.pdf

Nuclear Regulatory Commission, United States Senate Letter to the Chairman of the Nuclear Regulatory Commission https://www.nrc.gov/docs/ML2011/ML20116D106.pdf
https://webcache.googleusercontent.com/search?q=cache:n6TeRxMP11EJ:https://www.nrc.gov/docs/ML2011/ML20116D106.pdf&hl=en&gl=es

Online Archive of California, Great Peace March Collection, 1985-1986,
https://oac.cdlib.org/findaid/ark:/13030/kt8w1006s0/

Phys.org, U.S. West Coast: On Frontline From Nuclear Cloud,
https://phys.org/news/2011-03-west-coast-frontline-nuclear-cloud.html

Public Broadcasting Service, Operation Babylift (1975),
https://www.pbs.org/wgbh/americanexperience/features/daughter-operation-babylift-1975/

Radiopaedia, Normal Cervical Spine, https://radiopaedia.org/cases/normal-cervical-spine-mri-1

Reauthorization of the Federal Water Pollution Control Act: Hearings Before the Subcommittee on Water Resources of the Committee on Public Works and Transportation House of Representatives, https://books.google.es/books?id=vBYSAAAAYAAJ&printsec=frontcover#v=onepage&q&f=false

SelfCare for Healthcare, Hear LeAnn's Operation Babylift Story, https://www.selfcareforhealthcare.com/operation-babylift/

The Australian Women's Weekly via PressReader, Children of War, https://www.pressreader.com/australia/the-australian-womens-weekly/20170601/281590945491471

The Ethnic Heritage Center, Jewish Community Center, https://walknewhaven.org/jewish-community-center

The Guardian, Adopted by Their Parents' Enemies: Tracing the Stolen Children of Argentina's 'Dirty War', https://www.theguardian.com/global-development/2023/jan/16/tracing-stolen-children-of-argentina-dirty-war

The Guardian, Interview: I'll Never Forget the Sound of the Door Shutting Behind Me: Inside South America's Toughest Prisons, https://www.theguardian.com/artanddesign/2015/jun/14/inside-south-america-toughest-prisons-valerio-bispuri-interview

The National Security Archive, Asunto: Acuerdo Bilateral de Inteligencia FF.AA. PARAGUAY/Ejército ARGENTINO, September 12, 1972, https://nsarchive2.gwu.edu/NSAEBB/NSAEBB514/docs/Doc%2001%20-%20r186f1573%20-%201580.pdf

The Vintage and Antiques, Vintage Set of 4 Green Cameo Depression Glass Vaseline Uranium Divided Dinner Plates Farmhouse Collectible Cottage Dining Serving Picnic, https://www.truevintageantiques.com/product/vintage-set-of-4-green-cameo-depression-glass-vaseline-uranium-divided-dinner-plates-farmhouse-collectible-cottage-dining-serving-picnic/

Turismo, Ciudad Soñada, https://turismo.laplata.gob.ar/sobre-la-plata/

U.S, Military, Defense Technical Information Center, Annual Report - Contract No. DAMD17-86-C-6284, https://apps.dtic.mil/sti/pdfs/ADA189926.pdf

U.S. Department of Defense, MAC and Operation Babylift, https://media.defense.gov/2012/Aug/31/2001330018/-1/-1/0/AFD-120831-032.pdf

U.S. Department of Health and Human Services via Google Books, III International Conference on Acquired Immunodeficiency Syndrome (AIDS): June 1-5, 1987, Washington Hilton and Towers, Washington, D.C.,
https://www.google.com/books/edition/III_International_Conference_on_Acquired/bKv9Li26MD8C?hl=en
https://www.google.com/books/edition/III_International_Conference_on_Acquired/bKv9Li26MD8C?hl=en&gbpv=1

U.S. Military, Defense Technical Information Center, AD-A203 587,
https://apps.dtic.mil/sti/pdfs/ADA203587.pdf

U.S. Military, Defense Technical Information Center, DAMD17-86-C-6284,
https://apps.dtic.mil/sti/pdfs/ADA189926.pdf

United Nations, Convention on the Prevention and Punishment of the Crime of Genocide,
https://www.un.org/en/genocideprevention/documents/atrocity-crimes/Doc.1_Convention%20on%20the%20Prevention%20and%20Punishment%20of%20the%20Crime%20of%20Genocide.pdf

United Press International, Four Arrested in Protest Over Atomic Bombings,
https://www.upi.com/Archives/1989/08/06/Four-arrested-in-protest-over-atomic-bombings/1559618379200/

United States Army Medical Center of Excellence, Military Medical Ethics, Volume 2, Chapter 17 The Cold War and Beyond: Covert and Deceptive American Medical Experimentation, Susan E. Lederer, PhD,
https://ke.army.mil/bordeninstitute/published_volumes/ethicsvol2/ethics-ch-17.pdf
https://medcoeckapwstorprd01.blob.core.usgovcloudapi.net/pfw-images/borden/ethicsvol2/Ethics-ch-17.pdf

United States Government Printing Office via ProQuest, The Weather Underground Report - Report of the Subcommittee to Investigate the Administration of the Internal Security Act and Other Internal Security Laws of the Committee on the Judiciary United States Senate Ninety-Fourth Congress First Session,
https://li.proquest.com/elhpdf/histcontext/CMP-1975-SJS-0006.pdf

Universidad National de La Plata, Eduardo Enrique Navajas Jauregui,
http://hosting2.unlp.edu.ar/derechoshumanos/verdatos.php?coddesaparecido=509

US Army Medical Center of Excellence, Military Medical Ethics, Volume 2, Chapter 17 The Cold War and Beyond: Covert and Deceptive American Medical Experimentation Susan E. Lederer, PhD,
https://ke.army.mil/bordeninstitute/published_volumes/ethicsvol2/ethics-ch-17.pdf
https://medcoeckapwstorprd01.blob.core.usgovcloudapi.net/pfw-images/borden/ethicsvol2/Ethics-ch-17.pdf

https://web.archive.org/web/20130218014139/https://ke.army.mil/bordeninstitute/published_volumes/ethicsVol2/Ethics-ch-17.pdf

US Department of Homeland Security, Plum Island Animal Disease Center, https://www.dhs.gov/science-and-technology/plum-island-animal-disease-center

Virginia Commonwealth University's Social Welfare History Project, Orphan Trains, https://socialwelfare.library.vcu.edu/programs/child-welfarechild-labor/orphan-trains/

Wikipedia, Waterboarding, https://en.wikipedia.org/wiki/Waterboarding

World Nuclear Association, Fukushima Daiichi Accident, https://world-nuclear.org/information-library/safety-and-security/safety-of-plants/fukushima-daiichi-accident.aspx

Yale Alumni Magazine, When Yale Activists Targeted Apartheid, https://yalealumnimagazine.org/blog_posts/1649-when-yale-activists-targeted-apartheid

Yale Daily News, For God, Country, Yale, and the CIA, https://yaledailynews.com/blog/2004/09/24/for-god-country-yale-and-the-cia/

Yale Daily News, Q-House Hosts Celebration of Life for Black Panther George Edwards, https://yaledailynews.com/blog/2022/10/31/q-house-hosts-celebration-of-life-for-black-panther-george-edwards/

Yale Daily News, Yale Denies Knowledge of FBI-Sponsored Interview Research, https://yaledailynews.com/blog/2013/03/04/yale-denies-knowledge-of-fbi-sponsored-interview-research/

Yale Law School Lillian Goldman Law Library, A Comment on Causation, Law Reform, and Guerrilla Warfare by Mashaw, Jerry, https://openyls.law.yale.edu/handle/20.500.13051/342

Yale School of Medicine, Charles Morgan, MD, https://medicine.yale.edu/profile/cmorgan/

Yale School of Medicine, Finding New Ways to Calm Storms in the Brain, https://medicine.yale.edu/news/medicineatyale/article/finding-new-ways-to-calm-storms-in-the/

Yale School of Public Health, Public Health Pioneers, https://ysph.yale.edu/news-article/public-health-pioneers/

Yale University Library, "Free the New Haven Panthers": The New Haven Nine, Yale, and the May Day 1970 Protests That Brought Them Together, https://onlineexhibits.library.yale.edu/s/-free-the-new-haven-panthers-the-new-haven-nine-yale-and-the-may-day-1970-protests-that-brought-them-together/page/new-haven-panther-activism